The Journals of

ANDRÉ GIDE

ANDRÉ GIDE

Richard Heyd

The Journals of

ANDRÉ GIDE

TRANSLATED FROM THE FRENCH,

WITH AN INTRODUCTION AND NOTES, BY

Justin O'Brien

VOLUME IV: 1939–1949

1 9 5 1

Alfred A. Knopf : *New York*

FIRST AMERICAN EDITION

INTRODUCTION

BY

JUSTIN O'BRIEN

I heartily scorn," André Gide wrote at the age of sixty-one in his *Journal* for January 1931, "that sort of wisdom which is attained only through cooling off or lassitude." We must not then expect to find him, even twenty years later, soothing himself or his reader with the maxims of senility. In this, the fourth volume of his *Journals*, written between his seventieth year and his eightieth, his mind has lost neither its incisive vigor nor its vital warmth. We find here the same disciplined intelligence freely expressing itself, equally removed from facility and dryness, in a constantly maturing thought as far from smugness as from feverish restlessness. Ever in contact with life, that intelligence has maintained a perpetual ardor — the hard, gemlike *ferveur* that his *Fruits of the Earth* extolled over fifty years ago. This is doubtless the secret of Gide's perennial youth and of his undiminished favor with the young.

Rich with the lessons of experience, a man in his eighth decade must of necessity take many a backward glance. The second World War naturally suggests parallels with the first one; voluntary exile from France and loved ones recalls the past and even the dead. Problems encountered in writing and fresh attacks launched by his enemies cause him to review his judgments of earlier works: in 1942, for instance, and again in 1946 he reconsiders the significance, effectiveness, and artistic achievement of his *Corydon* and again returns to that book through an interviewer's indiscreet question at the time of the Nobel Prize. Several times he turns back to the period of his flirtation with Communism, the better to define the misunderstanding that led to his position of the early thirties. And the postwar emphasis, largely among the existentialists, on the necessity of committing oneself and writing a *"littérature engagée"* leads him to re-examine his past commitments and eventually to issue, in 1950, under the ironic title of *Littérature engagée* a collection of his tendentious and polemical writings, all of which he considers as extra-literary. Indeed, he had already noted here in mid-1940:

"The social question! . . . If I had encountered that great trap at the beginning of my career, I should never have written anything worth while."

But, like his own Theseus venturing into the unknown while unwinding, in the form of Ariadne's thread, his tie with the past and tra-

dition, André Gide finds it more natural to look forward. Even in the
early stages of the war he foresees with remarkable clarity the postwar
plight of France; elsewhere he reflects on the literature and art of the
future. Despite his extensive travels and those he undertakes the moment Tunis is liberated, he deplores the fact that the map is still
studded with territories unknown to him. Finally, but without dread
or false solemnity, he frequently meditates on death and the possibility of an afterlife. Some of the finest pages of this last *Journal,* in
fact, reflect a serene contemplation of his own — of everyman's — future.

Nothing is perhaps more characteristic of André Gide than this
consistently healthy forward-looking attitude. Not altogether lightly,
he early identified himself with Prometheus, who revolted against the
gods and communicated to man "the devouring belief in progress."
That active belief has never left him. Recognizing his inaptitude for
contemplative stagnation, he can state at seventy-three that "Real old
age would be giving up hope of progress." Thus it is that, smiling at
his impulse to improve himself so late in life, he continues the study of
German, exercises his memory by learning hundreds of lines of French
verse by heart, and, rediscovering Virgil, devotes three or four hours
a day to the arduous and delightful deciphering of Latin. His mind always open and alert, he rereads the French classics and Shakespeare
and Goethe and Euripides, often revising his impressions with star-
tling results. And, leaving the main highway, he explores such diverse
writers as Cyril Tourneur, Eichendorff, Grimmelshausen, James Hogg,
Dashiell Hammett, Pearl Buck, Jorge Amado, and Ernst Jünger. In his
eightieth year we find him discussing the latest volume by Sartre,
catching up on the contemporary dramatists, disputing with Koestler
and James Burnham. Simultaneously he can become captivated, as in
the past, by a new treatise on radioactivity, a study of the metamorphoses of sea animals, a history of Moslem customs, or a revolutionary
approach to surgery. A lively curiosity has always been one of his
dominant characteristics.

Because these last ten years cover the period of the second World
War, the reader might justly expect that conflict and the occupation of
France to play a large part in André Gide's reflections from day to day.
In the beginning, however, he deliberately planned to omit events,
noting that thought was most valid when it could not be modified by
circumstances. In September 1940 he reflected that "The number of
stupidities an intelligent person can say in a day is not believable. And
I should probably say just as many as others if I were not more often
silent." In contrast to the invasion of the timely, to the anguish resulting from current events, there is always the timeless, to be found in
the classics of art and literature. In an article dated 1936, he had writ-

ten: "I have a great need to maintain in myself the feeling of permanence; I mean a need of feeling that there are human products invulnerable to insults and degradation, works on which temporal changes have no influence." But viewed without perspective the timeless often appears to be merely the untimely; to some it may seem shocking that only a month after the French defeat of 1940 Gide could momentarily forget his country's tribulation by reading Goethe in the original. Throughout the *Journals,* to be sure, from 1889 to 1949, thoughts out of season abound: *Unzeitgemässe Betrachtungen,* to borrow from Nietzsche a title that Gide obviously likes. Almost equally frequent are statements to the effect that the artist is "out of harmony with his time" and that this constitutes his *raison d'être:* "He counteracts; he initiates. And this is partly why he is so often understood at first by but a few" (6 July 1937).

Yet, whether in the south of France for the first two and a half years of the war or in North Africa for the duration, Gide is unable to maintain here such an ideal aloofness. Never do his *Journals* come so close to journalism — "I call 'journalism' everything that will be less interesting tomorrow than today," he wrote in 1921 — as during the long siege of Tunis in 1942–3. There we have a marginal history of events recorded by an eyewitness whose vision was necessarily limited, a sort of *Journal of the Plague Year* with all the dispassionate, flat reportage of Defoe's document. There is, indeed, for us who were on the outside, a fascination in sharing the intimate feelings of a particularly sensitive person on the inside of the vast concentration camp set up by Hitler. Despite Gide's effort to heighten and enliven that account by a running description of little Victor, a portable microcosm of all that was distasteful in the world around him, none the less this is the part of the *Journals* that will doubtless age least well. Several times in recent years André Gide has expressed the desire for simultaneous publication of those pages in French and English, in the naïve hope, unshared by his French publisher, that such a delicate attention would somewhat mitigate the sting of his remarks about the American forces in Tunisia. But Americans are hardly so susceptible as not to appreciate such frankness; the men who took part in the North African campaign should be interested in the way they looked to those they were about to liberate, especially as that view changed so drastically upon contact.

During the decade from 1939 to 1949 André Gide's creative activity did not slacken, for he wrote (in addition to this *Journal*) the *Imaginary Interviews,* a play entitled *Robert ou l'intérêt général,* a book on *Paul Valéry,* his *Autumn Leaves,* and *Theseus,* which should soon come to be considered as one of his major works. Meanwhile he finished his inspired translation of *Hamlet,* compiled an *Anthology of French Poetry,* wrote several prefaces, including that for the collected edition of Goethe's drama, and with Jean-Louis Barrault adapted to the stage Kafka's *The Trial* — besides working on still unrealized film-scenarios of his novels *Isabelle* and *Les Caves du Vatican*. One of the last entries in this volume (4 June 1949) states: "Some days it seems to me that if I had at hand a good pen, good ink, and good paper, I should without difficulty write a masterpiece."

An index of Gide's continuing vitality can be found as readily in the attacks directed against him as in his own production. Throughout his long career he has been the object of frequent, often savage assaults. If they are remembered at all in literary history, some of his accusers, such as Henri Béraud, Jean de Gourmont, René Johannet, Camille Mauclair, Eugène Montfort, and Victor Poucel, will receive mention only for the crude shafts they aimed at Gide. Others, like Francis Jammes and Henri Massis, have sullied their reputations by contributing to the picturesque and fanciful Gide legend. But, despite the intention of such critics, they did not bury their enemy very deep. During and after the recent war the weight of his years did not keep him from serving frequently as whipping-boy. As early as July 1940 an anonymous journalist in *Le Temps* accused him of exerting a baneful influence on youth and contributing to form a "deliquescent generation." A year later, in California, Fernand Baldensperger blamed such demoralizers as Gide and Proust for the French defeat. In January 1942 René Gillouin echoed in Geneva an unfounded accusation of Gide's having led a susceptible young reader to suicide. Hardly had Paris been liberated when Louis Aragon, the literary spokesman of the French Communist Party, which cannot forget Gide's return from Moscow, repeated the charge of antipatriotism and defeatism made in the Provisional Consultative Assembly in Algiers by a certain Giovoni (see Appendix II). Soon thereafter Julien Benda and Edmond Buchet separately accused Gide of anti-intellectualism and Alexandrianism, somewhat as Arthur Koestler was to do in English. Probably the most categoric crushing of Gide was found in an interview with the Catholic poet Paul Claudel, a contemporary and early friend, published in March 1947. "From the artistic point of view, from the intellectual point of view, Gide is worthless," said Claudel.

Gide himself is more equitable toward his former friend, for in February 1943 he noted in the *Journals*:

"There is and always will be in France (except under the urgent threat of a common danger) division and parties; in other words, dialogue. Thanks to that, the fine equilibrium of our culture: equilibrium in diversity. Always a Montaigne opposite a Pascal; and, in our time, opposite a Claudel, a Valéry. At times one of the two voices prevails in strength and magnificence. But woe to the times when the other is reduced to silence! The free mind has the superiority of not wanting to be alone in enjoying the right to speak."

If there could have been any doubt before, it must now be recognized, since the publication last year of the correspondence between Claudel and Gide, that to the world at large the name of Paul Valéry is less appropriate in the foregoing passage than would be that of André Gide.

Another important Catholic writer, François Mauriac, who has never ceased to admire and to acknowledge his debt to Gide, seems to have recognized this when, writing in the *Figaro* about certain pages detached from the latest *Journal,* he finds Gide's thought "serenely aggressive as on his finest days" and regrets that "this elderly Faust, who is so dear to us, should fix himself permanently in the definitive affirmation that man must be put in the place of God."

Coming from the pen of Mauriac, the expression "serenely aggressive" is most appropriate. In his eighth decade André Gide *has* achieved a measure of serenity, manifest in his *Theseus* and *Autumn Leaves* as well as in this *Journal.* One thinks of the Olympian serenity of Goethe, Gide's lifelong companion, and notes with pleasure that during the ten years covered by this volume Gide reread both the *Conversations with Eckermann* and Boswell's *Life of Samuel Johnson,* as if recognizing the company in which he belongs. In fact, the complete *Journals,* representing sixty years of a varied life, form one prolonged intimate conversation, a single, often interrupted dialogue of the author with himself. Such a document precludes the necessity of any other interlocutor; after all, Montaigne had neither Boswell nor Eckermann. The serenity to which Gide has attained is that of a dynamic equilibrium between opposing tendencies within him, the classic balance toward which he has tended since youth. Yet, even today, there is nothing static about this condition; as the author notes in this *Journal:* "The sole art that suits me is that which, rising from unrest, tends toward serenity."

On the last page of this installment of his *Journals,* André Gide has scribbled a note implying that he has forever ceased to keep a journal. If this is the end of his long and rich self-scrutiny, the final distillation of his reflections on man and the universe, what definitive revelation or ultimate message does it contain for his readers? Those who have followed him this far know him better than to expect such a thing or be surprised by his note of 15 December 1948:

"*Last words . . .* I do not see why one should try to pronounce them louder than the others. At least I do not feel the need of doing so."

I should like to take this occasion to thank those who have contributed valuable information to the notes and the Glossary of Persons of all four volumes, and notably to André Gide himself, always most gra-

cious and most helpful, to Jean Amrouche, Yvonne Davet, Julien
Green, Richard Heyd, Dr. F. Jonas, Jean Malaquais, Roger Martin du
Gard, Adrienne Monnier, Jules Mouquet, Arnold Naville, Maurice
Saillet, Roland Saucier, Jacques Schiffrin, and Herbert Weinstock. To
such colleagues at Columbia University as Jean-Albert Bédé, Otis
Fellows, André von Gronicka, James Gutmann, Henry Hatfield, Gilbert
Highet, Jean Hytier, Edwin B. Matzke, Kurt Pinthus, Norman L. Tor-
rey, and Mark Van Doren, and to my former pupils Renée Lang and
William S. Rogers, I express the same warm gratitude.

Canterbury, Connecticut, September 1950

CONTENTS

CONTENTS

The Journals of

ANDRÉ GIDE

VOLUME IV: 1939–1949

1939

Yes, all that might well disappear, that cultural effort which seemed to us wonderful (and I am not speaking merely of the French effort). At the rate at which we are going, there will soon not be many to feel the need of it, to understand it; not many left to notice that it is no longer understood.

One strives and strains one's ingenuity to shelter those treasures from destruction; no shelter is safe. A bomb can do away with a museum. There is no acropolis that the flood of barbarianism cannot reach, no ark that it cannot eventually sink.

One clings to wreckage.

11 September

My body is not so worn out that life with it has ceased to be bearable. But as for giving a reason, an aim to one's life . . . Everything is suspended in uncertainty.

War is here. In order to escape its obsession, I am going over and learning long passages of *Phèdre* and of *Athalie*. I am reading *The Atheist's Tragedy* of Cyril Tourneur and Eichendorff's *Taugenichts*.[1] But the oil lamp throws a poor light; I must close the book and my mind returns to its anguish, to its interrogation: Is this the twilight or the dawn?

19 September

I doubt if I have ever enjoyed more propitious conditions. But my mind is open only to anguish. I do not even try to escape the preoccupations besieging us. In this dreadful struggle now beginning, everything for which we live is at stake, and the sacrifice of those dearest to us may not be able to save those values. One would like to put them in safekeeping, like the stained-glass windows of the churches; but those very precautions isolate and detach them from life; they are beginning to become like objects in museums, which will perhaps survive the catastrophe, to be found later on with amazement.

I have forsaken Racine, these last few days, for La Fontaine and learned by heart again some ten of the fables. La Fontaine's perfection

---

[1] *The Atheist's Tragedy* first appeared in 1611. *Aus dem Leben eines Taugenichts* (*The Happy-Go-Lucky, or Leaves from the Life of a Good-for-Nothing*) by the German romantic poet Joseph von Eichendorff dates from 1826.

is more subtle but no less exigent than Racine's; it fills less space with
an apparently more negligent art; but one has only to give it sufficient
attention: the touch is so discreet that it might go unnoticed. Nothing
is farther from the romantic insistence. It goes on at once, and if you
have not understood, that's just too bad. It is impossible to imagine a
more discreet, apparently less intentional art. To such a degree that
one wonders if one is not sometimes adding to it, if La Fontaine is
really conscious himself, in certain lines or expressions, of all the emotion they contain; one is also aware of an element of cunning and that
one must enter into the spirit of the game at the risk of not altogether
understanding him; for he takes nothing seriously. Oh, how far we are
from the war with him!

I wondered, in *Andromaque*, at how little Racine was bothered by
the repetition of the same words:

Percé de tant de coups, comment t'es-tu sauvé?
Tiens! Tiens! Voilà le coup que je t'ai réservé.

And three lines later:

Elle vient l'arracher au coup qui le menace.

Or again:

Venez-vous m'enlever dans l'éternelle nuit?
Venez . . .

I could quote many other examples.

And at first I told myself: yes, this is true of *Andromaque*. Later on,
Racine was more difficult. But no, I find these same repetitions likewise in *Phèdre*.

Œnone, prends pitié de ma jalouse rage . . .

and four lines later:

Dans mes jaloux transports. . . .

Yet the examples become much rarer; and I am not even finding
any for the moment. Moreover, I do not see that by avoiding them
Racine's perfection would have been much increased; I even like the
fact that it is a fundamental rather than a mere surface perfection. The
only thing I can manage to regret, in *Phèdre* particularly, is the somewhat too frequent use of the epithets "just" or "unjust," which fill up
the gaps with ease: "an unjust stepmother," "a just terror," "unjust re-
proaches," all in the same group of lines (or should one see here an indication in Phædra's character, inherited from Minos, of the obsession
for justice?). But is not the most admirable thing in Racine's style precisely that apparent ease and the fact that not a single word appears to
have been *sought after*?

Everything in his behavior seemed to say: since he has ceased to
love me, nothing matters to me. But I still loved him and, indeed, I had

never loved him so much; but it was no longer possible for me to prove
it to him. That was by far the worst of it.

30 October

No, decidedly, I shall not speak on the radio. I shall not contribute
to pumping oxygen into the public. The newspapers already contain
enough patriotic yappings. The more French I feel, the more loath I
am to let my mind be warped. If it regimented itself, it would lose all
value.

I doubt that it is very fair to write, as Lucien Jacques did in 1914
or 1915, about certain particularly ridiculous utterances: "Is it so hard
to keep silent?" and am aware how painful silence is when one's heart
is overflowing; but I do not want to have to blush tomorrow for what
I should write today. Yet if I keep silent, this is not because of pride;
I am almost inclined to say that it is because of modesty and even more
of uncertainty. I may be, and I often am, in agreement with the majority; but the approval of the majority cannot become in my eyes a
proof of truth. My thought does not have to follow the fashion, and if
I do not think it more valuable from the mere fact that it is different and
isolated and separate, at least it is when it differs that it seems to me
most useful to express it. Not that I take pleasure in that difference,
having otherwise great trouble in doing without agreement, and not
that the thoughts seem to me less important when widely shared; but
it is less important then to express them.

It is by insisting upon the value of the particular, it is by its force
of individualization, that France can best and must oppose the forced
unification of Hitlerism. Today, however, it is essential to meet one
united front with another, and, consequently, to enter the ranks and
be a part of the unit. Temporarily, it is said. . . . Let us hope so.
Moreover, isolated voices can no longer make themselves heard today.
My unseasonable thoughts, until better times, I will store up in this
notebook.

Are my thoughts, then, so very different — and so often so today —
from those of others? Perhaps not. But in that case why should I express in an undertone what others excel in shouting? As soon as I do
not differ, I keep silent. It is partly because I am definitely aware only
of my differences, whereas I am no longer sure of anything as soon
as I am in agreement.

31 October

Through great fear that my memory may weaken, I have greatly
exercised it of late, and it now seems to me that it has never been
better, nor even, by far, so good. Large sections of poems come, as if

at will, to take their place in it; groups of lines from La Fontaine, Racine, Hugo, Baudelaire, which I repeat tirelessly while walking.

1 November

Reading the newspapers shocks me. The war warps all minds. Everyone blows in the direction of the wind. And Maurras still complains that the censorship does not allow patriots to speak frankly! . . . In short, everything urges me to frank silence.

13 November

No desire to write anything in this notebook. Better to work on my play, of which I am completely doing over the third and fourth acts.[2]

I received the day before yesterday a letter from M. Nicolas, who deplores not seeing reproduced in the Pléiade edition of my *Journal* the letter of rectification he wrote me last year and which the *N.R.F.* published in July.[3] I have just reread that letter; it again seems to me most remarkable and I too deplore that omission, though very understandable, since nothing called this text to attention. That letter establishes in most competent fashion the fact that Nietzsche's attitude, or rather the position he took in regard to Christ and Christianity, is quite analogous to mine. There will be occasion to bring out that text later on.[4]

---

[2] *Robert ou L'Intérêt général* (*Robert or The Common Weal*), first published in Algiers in 1944–5.

[3] The letter from M. P. Nicolas to André Gide was published in the July 1938 issue of *La Nouvelle Revue Française*, the monthly literary review founded by Gide and his friends in 1909. The letter refers to a passage published in the same review in May 1938, which may be found in *The Journals of André Gide*, Vol. III, pp. 370–1. The Pléiade edition of the *Journal*, the first complete publication covering the years 1889–1939, did not appear until the summer of 1939.

[4] This is perhaps the occasion. The letter, followed by footnote references to each quotation from Nietzsche, appeared in the *N.R.F.* with a note by André Gide to the effect that "it contributes a very useful rectification, which even seems to me indispensable, to certain imprudent affirmations of my *Recovered Pages*," as follows:

"You write, in *La Nouvelle Revue Française* of the first of May: 'I cannot set up against Christ that proud and jealous resistance of Nietzsche. When he speaks of Christ, his marvelous perspicacity seems to me to fail him; yes indeed, he seems to me to accept an already second-hand and distorted image of Christ, and, in order to oppose him the better, to hold Christ responsible for all the clouds and all the shadows projected on this earth by the sorry misinterpretation of his words.'

"Is this quite fair? — To be sure, Christianity *and* Christ are the butt of Nietzsche's criticism, but what care he takes (and what insistence he

20 December

Been to see Hélène Martin du Gard. Spoke to her of that extraordinary evening at the rue du Cherche-Midi when Roger had so greatly
frightened us.

---

puts upon it) to distinguish between the two, to judge them separately! Far
from accepting a second-hand and deformed image of Christ, he rises up,
more than anyone, against that deformation. 'Absolutely arbitrary interpretation,' he writes, underlining the word 'arbitrary.' He clearly notes: 'Christianity has become something fundamentally different from what its founder
did and wished,' and again: 'The life of the Christian ends up by becoming
altogether the life that Christ taught us we had to *give up*.' He adds that
Christianity according to Christ remains intact, unapplied but always possible; that he 'is not bound to any of the unwise dogmas that have taken
his name.' And often he examines in detail the falsifications that revolt him,
and often returns to this idea: 'What is Christian, in the Church's sense, is
what precisely is anti-Christian.'

"You also say: 'I feel in Christ's teaching as much emancipatory power
as in Nietzsche's'; but did not Nietzsche himself recognize the tremendous
emancipatory power of Christ's teaching — its eminently 'revolutionary' character? Does he not say somewhere of Jesus: 'Wherever there was judging,
he took sides against those who judged. He wanted to be a *destroyer of
ethical rules*'? Indeed, he goes farther. Consult, I beg you, *The Twilight of
the Gods*: 'That holy anarchist,' it says of Christ, 'who called upon the
lowest of the people, the outcasts and the sinners, the chandala of Judaism,
to resist the established order — in words which, even today, would lead
to Siberia; if the Gospels can be believed, that anarchist was a political
criminal.'

"As for Christ's opposition to the notion of State, Nietzsche recognizes it
as you do and emphasizes it on many an occasion. He reproaches St. Paul
for having got away from it: 'The tragic humor of the matter is that St. Paul
re-established and gave tremendous importance to what Christ had precisely
canceled by his life. When the building of the Church was finished, it
sanctioned even the existence of the State.' But he never imputes such a mistake to the original Church. He praises it, on the contrary, for having represented 'the suppression of the State' and he professes that even today whoever would reject its authority, whoever would say: 'I will not be a soldier,'
'I am not concerned with the tribunals,' 'I do not claim the help of the
police,' would, in a way, be returning to orthodoxy.

"The same agreement with you in regard to the *joy* contained in the true
preaching of Jesus. Nietzsche felt it and expressed it. You wrote some time
ago in the *Nouvelles Nourritures*: 'It required the abominable interpretation of men to found on the Gospels a cult, a sanctification, of sorrow and
suffering,' and Nietzsche wrote in *The Antichrist*: 'In all the psychology of
the Gospel there is no idea of guilt and punishment, nor any idea of reward.
Sin, or any relationship of distance between God and man, is suppressed.
This is just the "happy message." '

"I am well aware that he says elsewhere: 'Hatred of the senses, of joy

"It was, I believe, at the time of *La Sorellina*;⁵ after a very pleasant dinner we three had talked at length in the apartment beneath Roger's studio and I was about to withdraw when, suddenly, Roger told us that he did not feel well and thought he was about to die. Since he almost never goes off on a crazy tangent, Hélène and I were very frightened. Where was the trouble? His heart? His stomach? . . . He was unable to say. Did he have a pain somewhere? . . . No. Merely the very keen sensation that he was dying. We made him stretch out on the big bed, where he remained for some time, utterly motionless, his eyes open but with a vacant stare; I ought rather to say: with a fixed stare; and as I recommended sleeping a bit: 'If I close my eyes, I am lost. I am clinging to life solely by my stare. . . .' A few minutes later he asked me to go in haste and fetch Duhamel. It was about eleven o'clock. I rushed down the stairs, dashed to a taxi, and was driven to rue Vauquelin, on the other side of the Latin Quarter. At Duhamel's a maid told me that the master had gone out with his flute to indulge in some music at the house of friends, whose address was given me. The auto was waiting at the door, and since, in order to get Duhamel, I had to go by the rue du Cherche-Midi again, I wanted first to see if Roger felt better or worse. I found him already reassured.

---

of the senses, of joy in general, is Christian.' But it is so clear that the word 'Christian' has two meanings with him — which stand in opposition to each other. This opposition becomes abundantly evident when he writes of *altered* Christianity: 'It is the upsurge of pessimism (— *whereas Jesus wanted to bring the peace and happiness of lambs*).'

"If he did not resuscitate, as you would have wished, a true Christ, Nietzsche at least showed with what vigor the theologians and the world had massacred him. And in the ruins of his own massacre (for it is quite true that Christ himself does not wholly escape) could be found the elements necessary to reconstruct a Nazarean very close, I fancy, to the real one.

"This profound remark by you has been reported to me: 'Nietzsche was jealous of Christ.' It struck me. It is beyond doubt that this Legislator envied the other one, who 'succeeded' so well. He envied and respected him. He 'loved' his person and his very ideal, treating him with such regards as this: 'I have declared war on the anemic ideal of Christianity (as on what is close to it), not with the intention of destroying it, but simply in order to put an end to its *tyranny* and clear the ground for a new ideal.'

"How these mitigated regards justify you! How clearly one feels the 'jealousy'! — But the emulation also, and despite everything, beneath the verbal hostility, the interest that Nietzsche, as creator of new values, bears toward the earlier creator whose place it is essential to take.

"Sincerely, etc. . . .

M. P. Nicolas."

⁵ *La Sorellina,* which appeared in 1928, is Part V of *Les Thibault* (*The World of the Thibaults*) by Roger Martin du Gard.

"'False alarm,' he said. 'You may get rid of your taxi.' Then he made many excuses for having so stupidly alarmed us; but really he had thought it 'was the end.' . . ."

Amazing evening.

But, no less amazing: Hélène had *no recollection* of it.

1940

Chapters lxii and lxiii of *Roderick Random* (story of Melopoyn, the dramatist who cannot get his plays acted) — which form an integral unit — might, if well translated, be published in the *N.R.F.*

It is now more than twenty years that I had been promising myself to reread one of Smollett's novels. In the good parts (the life on the sea), far superior to *Gil Blas*,[1] and far inferior in the others, more numerous, alas!

13 January

Amused to discover in Hugo (*Légende des siècles*, Book VI, 1: *Le Pont*) a hemistich of Mallarmé (*Brise marine*).

> *Il ressemblait au lys* que sa blancheur défend
> *Ni le vide papier* que la blancheur défend [2]

Coincidence, doubtless, rather than a borrowing or recollection on the part of Mallarmé. Moreover, Mallarmé's half-line is much better motivated than Hugo's.

> *Of all these streets, tell us why*
> *You chose the darkest of all?*
> *And why you always try*
> *To stay in the shade of the wall?* [3]

7 February

One must expect that after the war, and even though victors, we shall plunge into such a mess that nothing but a determined dictatorship will be able to get us out of it. One can see the soundest minds gradually progressing in that direction (if I am to judge from myself, as the fellow says), and many insignificant facts, one little decision after another, which taken singly seem absolutely wise and altogether unavoidable, are progressively accustoming us to that idea.

---

[1] *The Adventures of Roderick Random* was modeled upon Lesage's picaresque novel *Gil Blas*.

[2] Mallarmé's *Sea Breeze*, with the line:
> *Nor the empty paper protected by its whiteness*
is better known than Hugo's *The Bridge* (from *The Legend of the Centuries*) with the similar line:
> *He resembled the lily protected by its whiteness.*

[3] *Dis ce qui, de toutes ces rues,*
> *T'aura fait choisir la plus sombre?*
> *Pourquoi toujours tu t'évertues*
> *A rester du côté de l'ombre?*

. . . So that one could guess their opinions merely by knowing to what they are insensitive. It is easy to remain a conservative when one is well taken care of oneself and but little touched by the misfortune of others.

Their mind moves in a dry world, boiled down like a problem. At first I tried to believe that they were urged to Communism by a tormenting love for our brothers; I was not able to mislead myself for long. Then I tried to believe that those dry, insensitive, abstract creatures were bad Communists, that they were doing a disservice to a noble cause, and I refused to judge the cause according to them. But no, I was mistaken altogether, from top to bottom. The real Communists, as I was told, as it was proved to me, were they. They were following the line exactly; and it was I who was wrong by introducing the heart, with which they had no concern, and grounds of judgment they claimed to do without. And first of all when I claimed to preserve through Communism my individuality, my individualism. There could and must be no question but of equality, of justice. The rest (and it was that remainder that especially mattered to me) belonged to Christianity. And slowly I came to the conviction that when I thought myself a Communist, I was a Christian, if it may be that one can be a Christian without "believing," if Catholicism as well as Protestantism did not put above everything else and as a condition *sine qua non:* Faith. So that, with either one side or the other, I could not and would not come to terms. It's a pity: were it not for that damned question of belief which unfailingly makes my reason bristle, I should get along well enough with the latter, at least as to the virtues they advocate, but which very often they convince themselves that Faith allows them to do without.

Anything I buy at the expense of others I cannot enioy.

In increasing that of others lies my greatest joy.

15 February

"Truth is perhaps sad" (I should like to be sure of quoting this little remark of Renan exactly, but I haven't his *Dialogues philosophiques* at hand). This remark, which sends people into rapture, bothers me. Truth can be neither sad nor gay. But awakening from a falsehood, believing oneself forsaken by God because of having originally believed in Providence — yes, that may well distress one at first. The only person who can be saddened by the fact that two and two are but four is the one who had originally fancied that they "were" more.

I should have been quite capable of being "converted" at the last moment — I mean at the hour of death, in order not to cause her too much suffering.

And this is what made me long rather to die at a distance, in some accident or other, of a sudden death, far from my family, as Montaigne likewise wished to do, without any witnesses ready to attach to those last moments an importance that I refused to grant them. Yes, without any other witnesses but chance and anonymous ones.

25 April

Twenty-third day in bed and on a diet. Better informed, I might have forestalled this attack of nephritis, which leaves me as if with a wound in the side.

Never before have I approached so close to nonexistence.

I am reading and rereading with the keenest admiration the articles that Benda has collected under the title *Précision*. Encouraged by them, I pick up again *Les Sentiments de Critias*; [4] so much less good (not yet ripe, 1917) that one can understand why, subsequently, Benda does not list this book among the "works by the same author."

Mansfield Park with an almost constant rapture.

Trying to discover still more that is new in Baudelaire, and over-looking the disappointing clumsiness and insufficiencies of his poems in prose,[5] I am very much amused to find in *Le Joueur généreux*: ". . . The cleverest of the devil's deceits is to convince you that he does not exist." [6]

Moreover, this whole poem seems to me especially noteworthy, and particularly its paradoxical conclusion. The following poem likewise contains great beauties, particularly in the last lines.

. . . A slope that it is in no wise certain I shall climb back up.

1 May

I have again missed the early spring. More than twenty days in bed. When, at last, I can get up and go out, the wisterias have already half lost their blossoms. The strict diet has left me very weakened, but

---

[4] *Clarification*, a collection of essays on method, Communism, national-ism, and pacifism, etc., which appeared between 1930 and 1937, came out in book form in 1937. *The Sentiments of Critias*, Benda's philosophic essays written in wartime, appeared in 1917.

[5] Upon rereading them again, I find many fewer examples of clumsiness than there had first seemed to me to be. [Note supplied by Gide in the French edition. Such notes will hereafter be indicated by an A. in brackets.]

[6] *The Generous Gambler* is one of Baudelaire's *Poems in Prose*. For Gide's expression of the same thought, see *The Journals of André Gide*, Vol. II, pp. 189–90.

all the more sensitive. I have made the acquaintance of morphine. Somewhat disappointed. It effectively silenced pain when the attack of nephritis became excessively bothersome, but without bringing in addition any of the paradisiacal quality I had anticipated. (Rouveyre explains to me that it is always this way with morphine when you ask it to perform a service, when you call on its activity to cancel a pain, that it really does its best only when idle.) If I do not let myself be caught by the craze to smoke, if I am able to take advantage of the impetus coming from an obligatory abstention from tobacco in order to rid myself of that absurd vice, which has gradually become an imperative need, I shall not have paid too dearly for my liberation.

Another subjection I should like to shake off: the "unpunished vice" of reading [7] — or at least that habit I have got of reading constantly and everywhere, of never letting my thought wander aimlessly without a guide or companion.

What do I still expect from a book today? What ultimate enrichment? A lesson that is henceforth rather useless, for, at my age, "the die is cast." . . . Amusement? Not so much so, probably, as mere distraction. Yes, by reading I seek to distract myself from myself; and whereas it would be essential to commune with myself, it seems that, almost without choice, I welcome everything that may help me to forget myself. And that vague dispersion of my thought which takes me away from any real work flatters and encourages a certain smug laziness. For if I fear leaving my mind unoccupied and constantly bring it some new nourishment from the outside, this is partly because I know that it produces nothing good without effort. But it would be still better to give it a total holiday than constantly to interpose a screen between it and God. I must learn to know solitude all over again. What I must take walking with me henceforth is not a book, but this notebook, and prefer not to think at all rather than not to think on my own.

I never wrote anything good save in joy; and at moments I wonder if my heart still contains a single spark of it.

Of what might I be able to speak with real competence? On any subject whatever, what I feel first and foremost is my inadequacy.

4 May

Not able to keep faith. Yesterday I already broke over twice: smoked a cigarette (the first in a full month) with Mme Théo, come

---

[7] Valery Larbaud brought out in 1925 a provocative essay entitled *Ce Vice impuni, la lecture* (*That Unpunished Vice, Reading*), in which he described the pleasures and dangers of an addiction to reading.

from Cabris; and in the afternoon took a book on my walk. *La Conquête des pôles* by Bidou had interested me so powerfully that I got myself the account of his travels in Brazil: *Neuf Cents Lieues sur l'Amazone* [8] — which I take along again this morning in that bit of exploration to Beaulieu. The hotel that Bussy recommended to me is closed, as are all the vacation hotels. There are moments, periods, when one would be inclined to think it impossible to stay fixed anywhere. Less frequent periods, most happily, than those in which one would be glad to drop anchor anywhere whatever, so readily does happiness seem to await you almost everywhere, so little would it take to make one happy!

5 May

Reserved a seat in the Paris express for Wednesday. Made this decision suddenly yesterday evening on my return from a visit to Vence, where I had gone to make sure of two rooms at the "Domaine de la Conque" for Mme Théo and me. But, having calculated everything carefully, I cannot allow myself that expense; and, anyway, I see nothing but a fatiguing complication in that plan. Regret does not come easy to me and I am readily able to convince myself that what I am led to do, whether freely or under duress, is what was preferable. Strange and quite instinctive mechanism of my mind, with a view to protecting its equilibrium and its happiness.

6 May

And yet, as if to keep me here, the countryside yesterday clothed itself with a thousand graces "as on the finest days." [9] The air was soft, the sky ineffably pure. A warmth, more exquisite for having been longer awaited, seemed to invite the whole being to blossom forth in joy. Why use the imperfect tense? This morning it is the same splendor; enough to make one wonder whether one has not imagined that atrocious shadow which the war casts over our thoughts.

I considered it indecent to leave the region without first going to say farewell to those at Cabris, and particularly to see Catherine [10] again. I accepted Loup's offer to spend the night at La Messuguière in that same room I occupied so pleasantly six months ago. That long time has gone by for me so evenly, despite the monstrous events that give that time a place in history, that it seems to me I could join May directly to October, so readily do these six months of calm felicity

---

[8] *The Conquest of the Poles* and *Nine Hundred Leagues on the Amazon.*

[9] "The water was transparent as on the finest days" is the fourth line of La Fontaine's fable of *The Heron* (Book VII, 4).

[10] The author's daughter, Catherine Gide. Loup is Mme Mayrisch de Saint-Hubert.

among perfect friends form a complete whole sheltered from the torment.

What am I going to Paris for? Nothing imperative calls me there. Still not completely recovered from that attack of nephritis, weakened by this prolonged semi-fast, I feel as if I had but little endurance. Yesterday that half-hour walk in the mountains on which Élisabeth and Catherine took me (the little cat accompanied us) wore me out, and last night, my nerves overtaut despite the sedative against spasms, I was barely able to rest completely for a few hours. Unbearable anguish, which forced me, as it were, to get dressed and to stretch out on the bed fully clothed. In short, a miniature hell, if I may say so.

Vence, 7 May

Again in this charming "Domaine de la Conque" where I had already stayed in '37 or '36. Mme Théo is with me. My fatigue makes me congratulate myself on having postponed my return to town. Incapable of writing anything this evening.

8 May

A pity that so often in this war our spirit of fairness can look like stupidity.

People seem to discover one by one coarse truths that it is dangerous to overlook. When they shout: "There is not a minute to waste," this is a sign that weeks have been wasted and that they are getting ready to waste hours and days more. "Not an inch of ground" or "until our last drop of blood" . . . empty formulas in which vanity takes refuge and which evoke the shadow of the great ghost of defeat. It is not known to whom they are addressed nor whom they have a mission to convince. It seems that they take the place of action, and I find it hard to imagine a case in which it is proper to use them.

9 May

"The more one thinks about it . . . the more one is convinced of this obvious truth: it doesn't make sense" (Antoine Thibault [11]). But what kind of sense did you expect it to make?

"Man is a miracle without interest" (Jean Rostand). But what in the world would it take for this miracle to assume importance in your eyes, for you to consider it worthy of interest?

As for me, the more I think about it, the less I manage to understand you. It is enough to make one wonder at times whether you do not miss "the good Lord." Then it would be much more likely — from

[11] Spoken by the dying brother, Dr. Antoine Thibault, in *Epilogue,* the last part of Roger Martin du Gard's long novel, *The World of the Thibaults.*

noting the inadequacy of His goodness, the failure of His justice, or His helplessness (if I believed in Providence) — that my cry of despair would burst forth. It never occurs to me to regret not "believing"; but it often occurs to me to say to myself: "Fortunately I do not *believe!*"

10 May

There is a certain . . . romanticism in grieving that things are not otherwise than what they are; that is to say, than what they can be. It is on the real that we must build our wisdom, and not on the imaginary. Even death must be admitted by us and we must rise to the point of understanding it; to the point of understanding that the wondrous beauty of this world comes, it so happens, from the fact that nothing in it lasts and that constantly this must make way and matter to permit that which has not yet been to come forth; the same, but renewed, rejuvenated; the same and yet imperceptibly closer to that perfection toward which it tends without knowing it and from which is gradually formed the very visage of God. Ever in a state of formation and never finished, from the unthinkable abyss of the past to the unthinkable "consummation of the centuries."

Nothing more irritating, more absurd, than the: *What is everything that is not eternal?* when it is said without irony.[12] That would be gay, wouldn't it, always to be faced with the immutable! Rigid yourself, to what season of the year would you limit yourself? The season of buds? or of flowers? or of fruits? At what moment (even in your own life) would you dare to say: This is it! Don't move!

11 May

I should have reached Paris yesterday (my seat was already reserved); I should have been just in time to learn the shocking news.[13] Shocking but not surprising, alas! The radio yesterday evening managed to talk a great deal without exactly telling us anything. They protest, they express indignation, in a noble and formal tone of voice, with outbursts based on history; enough to make Hitler chuckle if he didn't have something better to do than listen to our announcers.

13 May

Whatever I am doing, that anxiety consists in interrupting me by suddenly telling me that first I have something better to do, something I have not yet done though I should have done it. Thus I am distracted from the most fascinating reading in order to file my nails, for instance, or to change my shoelaces. My mind never, or almost never, succeeds

---

[12] See *The Journals of André Gide*, Vol. III, p. 31.
[13] Of the German invasion of the Low Countries.

in relaxing; it remains on the alert and constantly in contact with the whole outer world. So that, playing on the word, I can say that it takes hardly anything at all to distract me, or that, according to the current meaning, I can never distract myself.

14 May

Distressing insignificance of these notes. I force myself, however, to this little daily effort with the sole purpose of not letting my pen get rusty.

Though the days are so short, oh, how this insipid prolongation of my life seems to drag out!

17 May

After all, no! The events are too serious; I have no further attention but for them. Less saddened by them than by the state of mind the commentaries reveal; and not *solely* that of the French, but *especially* that of the French. The great inspiring sentiments are played up to such an extent that it seems as if *they* were getting a thrashing under the circumstances and dragging us along to our downfall; that it seems likewise as if the genius of evil were winning out, since it is just this that people enjoy discerning in the enemy's every action rather than the order and discipline accompanying it and always ensuring its triumph. Yet it would be good to recognize that the very shortcomings of the German people are among those that favor victories, whereas our very virtues stand in our way.

I had set out to write much longer on this subject. Interrupted by the visit of Janie Bussy. Yesterday I had gone to Nice to pack in a trunk the few things I had left with my friends. The tension of the situation with regard to Italy urges them to leave Nice. They come to settle for a time at Vence, to which I returned that same evening in their company. Mme Théo, to whom we telephoned, found them a very pleasant lodging into which they moved at once.

Since I have been at Vence I have been reading every morning a few pages of Eckermann. These *Conversations with Goethe* are an inexhaustible resource. One rarely encounters sublime, unexpected flashes; but it is a continuous flow of smiling wisdom, rather similar, altogether, to Montaigne's, and almost always profitable; which is less likely to elevate the soul than to temper it, without ever subduing it.

What would he have thought of Jean Rostand's little book? [14]

---

[14] Impossible to know whether Gide was thinking of *Pensées d'un biologiste* (*Thoughts of a Biologist*), *La Vie et ses problèmes* (*Life and its Problems*), or *Science et génération* (*Science and Generation*) — all of them short books appearing in 1939 or early 1940.

The image of man that Goethe leaves us is exemplary; I mean that
it is according to that model that one would like to live and think.

18 May

Admirable night. Everything swoons and seems to be enraptured
in the light of an almost full moon. The roses and acacias mingle their
scents. The undergrowth sparkles with fireflies. I think of all those for
whom this so beautiful night is the last and I should like to be able to
pray for them. But I have ceased even to understand very well what
the words "pray for someone" mean; or rather, I know that they can
no longer mean anything for me. They are words that I have carefully
emptied of all meaning. But my heart is filled with love.

Through a sense of decency I am concerned in this notebook only
with what has nothing to do with the war; and this is why I go for so
many days without writing anything in it. Those are the days on which
I have not been able to rid myself of the anguish, not been able to
think of anything but *that*.

Sunday

Unbearable itchings kept me awake until dawn. This morning, not
a cloud in the sky, not a mist. A glorious and calm felicity pours down
on earth. Everything invites man to happiness.

Deadly vulgarity of Bromfield's book (*The Rains Came*). I give up
after the first two parts — already surprised at having been able to endure it for three hundred pages. It is true that I was reading with ever
less and less attention. The beginning had misled me.

21 May

How hard I find it to tell myself that there are things I am no
longer of an age to do and that I should do better not to try!
   Or at least I tell this to myself all right, but without convincing myself. So that, after all, I do those things none the less; but afterward I
am almost done in.
   I am writing this seated on the edge of a road above Vence, on my
way back from a dangerous climb, tiring because there was no path,
through undergrowth that became thicker and thicker as I approach
the summit, which is constantly withdrawing and which, eventually,
I give up reaching.
   Great effort without any reward other than the satisfaction of my
vanity (for the landscape from the top was much less beautiful than
I had a right to expect from my trouble) and the joy I take in new
plants: a small spurge forming a cluster close to the ground, which I

believe I had never seen before; a geranium with very broad purplish-red flowers; a little member of the lily family similar to asphodels. . . . A bit lower down, the poppy-red cistus dotted the moor, and occasionally, rising from among the rocks, robust valerians. Not a butterfly.

O incurably frivolous people of France! You are going to pay dearly today for your lack of application, your heedlessness, your smug reclining among so many charming virtues!

25 May

Long study of the garlic plants growing abundantly in the hotel garden. I cannot explain the formation of the cloves at the base of the stems of certain florets, similar to those that spring from the axilla of the leaves of certain lilies. Substitutes for seeds, equally good for reproduction? . . . Oh, would that Strohl were with me!

That systematic disindividualization toward which Hitlerism strove prepared Germany wonderfully for war. And that is especially the point, it seems to me, on which Hitlerism is opposed to Christianity, that incomparable school of individualization, in which each is more precious than all. Negate individual value so that each one, fused into the mass and adding to the number, is indefinitely replaceable; so that, if Friedrich or Wolfgang gets killed, Hermann or Ludwig will do just as well, and that there is no occasion to be greatly grieved at the loss of this or that one.

Letters from young men at the front, letters from Belgian refugees; enough to fill one's heart with tears and horror. May tomorrow not bring still worse.

A telegram from Marc,[15] which at first I do not very well understand, urgently advises me, in the name of an imaginary Dr. Dubois who has been consulted, to begin at once my treatment in the Pyrenees. This is obviously because he judges that there is peril in remaining — or, if not peril, immediate danger; and this after talking with the Ministry of the Interior. Who knows even if D. did not especially beg him or commission him to warn me?

But I haven't the heart to go and leave behind me the Bussys and all those at Cabris. The danger is no greater for me than for them. The Bussys, to whom I transmit the telegram, tell me they have made up their mind to stay, whatever happens — unless, of course, a general command is given to evacuate Vence; most improbable . . . !

[15] Marc Allégret.

Marcel,[16] likewise, writes me of the decision arrived at with Jeanne not to leave Cuverville; after they have sent the children to the other side of the Seine, I don't know just where; will they be able to?

30 May

Certain days, or rather certain hours of every day (I am speaking of the most recent past), I feel as far from my books as if they were the work of someone else; or, if my thought can still inhabit them, at least I should be incapable today of rewriting them. There was necessary also, in order to achieve them, a fixity of mind I no longer have.

The social question! . . . If I had encountered that great trap at the beginning of my career, I should never have written anything worth while.

I assume the profound and almost prophetic tone (in conversation) solely when I am not at all sure of what I am saying.

31 May

Not a day, not an hour when I do not tell myself my age. I did not say: when I do not feel it.

Wonderful automobile ride on which the charming Mme Bourdet takes the three Bussys and me. We leave the Coursegoule road a moment to get to the very small village of Saint-Barnabé. A tiny chapel where in front of the altar burns a coarse candle in place of a taper, stirring evidence of a very humble piety. Admirable mountain landscape all about.

La Tourette, 5 June

The young Belgian who brought us here in his auto had just come from Belgium. He told us how he had been detained a whole night at the frontier, close to Dunkerque, of which he saw the bombardment. Innumerable autos, like his, were waiting to be allowed to enter France. At 8 a.m. the frontier was finally opened and the flood rushed forward like a torrent of autos and pedestrians without any check of any kind, without any identity papers being examined. All those who wanted to pass were allowed to pass without distinction, and thus a vast number of Germans were able to enter France and spread out over the country without even having to use planes or parachutes. It will do no good later on to chase after them and to increase zeal. Three quarters of our efforts in France are only with a view to making up for negligences.

---

[16] Marcel Drouin.

We reached Saint-Genès-la-Tourette in twenty-two hours, with a single stop of two hours at Le Puy, where we lunched (but stopped twenty times during the night for verification of our identity papers). The young Belgian and Dr. Cailleux took turns at the wheel. Having left Vence at about 7 p.m., fear of a sudden withdrawal of driving-permits and of a requisition of autos made us drive fast. That very morning Menton had been evacuated. The doctor who had just learned this had come in haste from Nice to take me away and to allow me to take advantage of the unhoped-for chance he was offering me.

On the way through Valence I looked in vain for Mlle Charras's dwelling. I should have been happy to say hello to her. Despite the moonless night, crossing the mountains was splendid, then the day-break in an utterly clear sky. But the first news we got was that of the bombardment of Paris.

Vichy, 8 June

At the general delivery window I find a telegram that finally quiets my fears about Domi,[17] of whom we had had no news since the 10th of May. Caught in the "glorious" Dunkerque retreat, he is in England, saved!

All communications with invaded Belgium have been cut off, and the unfortunate refugees can get no news of the members of their family who stayed there.

The roads are cluttered by wandering families fleeing at random and without knowing where. Children have got lost, whom the wretched parents are seeking. Last night, through the open window of my room giving onto the end of the park, I thrice heard a heart-rending cry: "Pierre! Pierre!" and almost went down to find the poor demented man who was uttering that call, desperately, in the night. And for a long time I could not go to sleep, ceaselessly imagining that distress. . . .

This morning I speak of it to Naville. He too heard the cry all right; but, he tells me, it was the night watchman, who shouts: *"Lumière! Lumière!"* [18] when he sees a lighted window, like mine.

Vichy, 11 June

In *Le Temps* an article by J. L., in which I read: "A man of letters, quoted by M. Géraldy, boasted of being sensitive and proclaimed: 'There is no truth but in the nuance.' Was it not one of those colorless writers who get lost looking for the right shade when it is impossible

---

[17] Dominique Drouin.
[18] "Lights! Lights!"

for them to reflect light?" What an absurdity! I believe that "man of letters" was Renan, and the remark by him that is quoted is profoundly misinterpreted here.

Those few intellectuals who today beat their breast and accuse themselves of having "loved literature too much," will they never understand how prejudicial it is to culture to forsake and negate certain graces of the mind? Are we, by a "strategic withdrawal," to turn our back on everything subtle, finely shaded, and delicate that French art has produced? Shall we be enjoined to prefer *La Madelon* [19] to the works of Debussy and Ravel? Neuville and Détaille to Corot? Béranger to Baudelaire, Déroulède to Verlaine . . . (to cite only the dead), through great fear of what might enervate and weaken us?

Today our literature is incriminated; it is reproached for its refinement and for having striven to weaken rather than to electrify our energies; some go so far as to wish that we had never had any poets but the Borniers and the Déroulèdes. . . . Would it not be wiser to recognize that any advanced literature, whatever it may be, tends to exhaust what produces it? That flower of civilization develops and blossoms at the expense of the plant, which gives and sacrifices itself to this end. With more tendency to blossom, Germany would have been less strong. It is to protect the delicate that force is brought out. It is essential to maintain everything.

I recall that in 1914, seized with a great zeal, if I had been listened to, there would have been nothing but vegetables in the Cuverville garden. How much wiser my wife was not to accept the suppression of the flowers!

This evening Naville learns that the Paris tiains are not running. . . .
Atrocious anguish for those at Cuverville.

14 June

I have read with a pleasure at moments very keen Istrati's *Kyra Kyralina,* of such a special flavor that it makes one think of certain tales of *The Arabian Nights* or of some picaresque novel, but reflecting a much more iridescent sensitivity than Lesage or Smollett.

14 June

That "important announcement" that Reynaud is holding in store for us, Naville thinks that . . .
Yes, that is it. And one ceases to understand where that "soul" or

---

[19] *La Madelon* is the well-known song sung by the soldiers of World War I.

that "genius" of France may still be that they are claiming to save in spite of everything. Its very support is going to be taken away from it. From now on (and this was clear even the day before yesterday), the struggle is useless; our soldiers are getting killed in vain. We are at the mercy of Germany, which will strangle us as best she can. Despite everything, we shall shout very loud: "Honor is saved!" resembling that lackey in Marivaux who says: "I don't like people to show disrespect for me" while receiving a kick in the rear.

Doubtless there is no shame in being conquered when the enemy forces are so far superior, and I cannot feel any; but it is with an indescribable sorrow that I hear these phrases that exhibit all the shortcomings that have brought us to our ruin: vague and stupid idealism, ignorance of reality, improvidence, heedlessness, and absurd belief in the value of token remarks that have ceased to have credit save in the imagination of simpletons.

How can one deny that Hitler played the game in masterful fashion, not letting himself be bound by any scruple, by any rule of a game that, after all, has none; taking advantage of all our weaknesses, which he had long and skillfully favored. In the tragic light of events there suddenly appeared the deep decay of France, which Hitler knew only too well. Everywhere incoherence, lack of discipline, invoking of fanciful rights, repudiation of all duties.

What will the well-intentioned young men who yesterday were concerned with remaking France do with the miserable ruins that will remain? I am thinking of Warsaw, of Prague. . . . Will it be the same with Paris? Will the Germans let the best of our energies breathe and recover themselves? They will not limit their attention solely to our material ruin. Today we cannot yet envisage the frightful consequences of the defeat.

We should not have won the other war. That false victory deceived us. We were not able to endure it. The relaxing that followed it brought us to our ruin. (On this subject Nietzsche spoke words of wisdom. *Thoughts out of Season.*) Yes, we were ruined by victory. But shall we let ourselves be taught by defeat? The evil goes so deep that one cannot say whether or not it is curable.

Pétain's speech is simply admirable: "Since the victory, the spirit of enjoyment has won out over the spirit of sacrifice. People claimed more than they served. They wanted to save effort; today they are meeting misfortune." It cannot be better expressed, and these words console us for all the *flatus vocis* of the radio.

23 June

The armistice was signed yesterday evening. And now what is going to happen?

24 June

Yesterday evening we heard with amazement Pétain's new speech on the radio. Can it be? Did Pétain himself deliver it? Freely? One suspects some infamous deceit. How can one speak of France as "intact" after handing over to the enemy more than half of the country? How to make these words fit those noble words he pronounced three days ago? How can one fail to approve Churchill? Not subscribe most heartily to General de Gaulle's declaration? Is it not enough for France to be conquered? Must she also be dishonored? This breaking of her word, this denunciation of the pact binding her to England, is indeed the cruelest of defeats, and this triumph of Germany the most complete, by getting France, as she hands herself over, to debase herself.

24 June

Nothing but the *Conversations with Goethe* succeed in distracting my mind somewhat from the anguish. At any other time I should note many reservations; some of them are important. Today I reach, under the date of 12 February 1792, the passage in which Goethe opposed the first line of a recent poem:

Kein Wesen kann zu nichts zerfallen

to the opening of a poem that he now declares absurd and that he is annoyed to have seen engraved in golden letters above the entrance of a natural-history gallery by his Berlin friends:

Denn alles muss zu nichts zerfallen
Wenn es im Sein beharren will,

the lesson of which seems to me much more profound and almost to join that of the Gospel.[20] But Goethe, as he approached death, got farther and farther away from the shadow, instead of trying to pass through it to reach the supreme light. Likewise he rejected any metaphysical preoccupation; and his desire-need for *"mehr Licht"* [21] became more and more urgent. And this did not fail to be accompanied by a

---

[20] The text of Eckermann's volume reads: "Goethe read me the thoroughly noble poem *Kein Wesen kann zu nichts zerfallen* ('No being can dissolve to nothing'), which he had lately written.

"'I wrote this poem,' said he, 'in contradiction to my lines:
Denn alles muss zu nichts zerfallen
Wenn es im Seyn beharren will,' etc.
(For all must melt to nothing
Would it continue still to be)
— which are stupid; and which my Berlin friends, at the late assembly of scientists, set up in golden letters, to my annoyance.'"

[21] Goethe is reported to have called on his deathbed for "more light."

certain narrowing of his thought. I should like to talk of this with Marcel.[22] But when shall I see him again?

And so many ruinous illusions! We see the cost of it today. We shall have to pay for all the absurdities of the intangible Versailles Treaty, the humiliations of those who were then the defeated, the useless vexations, which used to enrage me in 1919 but against which it was useless to protest; the shameful abuse of victory. Now it is their turn to abuse.

What a lack of psychology we revealed then, when infatuated with our triumph! As if the wisest thing would not have been to hold out one's hand to the defeated, help him get up instead of striving to crush him even more, absurdly and without being aware that this merely fed his rancor and stiffened his will. But how can you persuade anyone, when it is a matter of politics, that generosity is not always and exclusively reserved for dupes? Probably it would have been fantastic to count on "gratitude," but the best way of preventing Hitler was not to provide him a justification.

Moreover, great historic events are invested with a character of such inevitable fatality that the great man who directs things seems to me much more created *by* events than *for* them. My sentence is not very clear; but neither is my thought. I mean that in the formation of any great statesman one must consider as tremendous the role of *circumstances*. Nothing differs more from poetic genius. And yet the perfect blossoming of a masterpiece corresponds, likewise, to some participation of the seasonable,[23] to the preliminary mood of the public, to its unconscious anticipation.

I have just reread, with an often very keen satisfaction, *La Fortune des Rougon*.[24] Certain chapters are worthy of Balzac at his best.

25 June

Hostilities ended last night. One hardly dares rejoice. thinking of what lies in store for us.

26 June

Frightful idleness of expectation. The radio is henceforth mute. Could we hear, at least in the evening, the English communiqués? I ought to take a cure at Ginoles; but shall I be able to stay some time

---

[22] André Gide's brother-in-law, Marcel Drouin.
[23] This word appears in English in the French text.
[24] *The Fortune of the Rougons* is a novel by Zola.

away from Cabris and Vence until it will perhaps be possible for me to return to Paris, to Cuverville?

Is there still someone with whom I take real pleasure in talking? I can no longer assert anything without my imagination's seeming at once to force my thought somewhat. None of my convictions is now sufficiently solid for the slightest objection not to upset it immediately; even though others' assertions most often strike me as empty and, they too, ill assured. More and more I fear that an idea may seem to me right merely because it is well expressed.

As for the present situation . . . the time has not yet come when one will have to "declare oneself." The real questions have not yet arisen. For the moment I feel nothing in me but expectation; and hope . . . but I do not yet know of what.

After having long nourished myself on the *Second Faust*, I take up again the first part, which it happened that I knew less well, though having read it many times. What beauty I still discover in it! What abundance! Everything in it is saturated with life. Thought is never presented in it in an abstract form, just as sentiment is never separated from thought, so that the most individual is still heavy with meanings and, so to speak, exemplary. Goethe enters the sublime regions in such a natural way that with him one always feels on an even footing.

However tempered, however reasonable he is and strives to be, it is in the unexplained, the unexplainable, and what he would call the demoniacal that he seems to me greatest. I like the fact that, conversing with Eckermann and urged by him to comment on the role of the "Mothers" in the *Second Faust*, to define the significance he grants them, Goethe sidesteps and shelters from too logical and too reasoned an investigation that "cone of shadow" on which his wisdom rests, from which his poetry springs, and without which he would occasionally belong in a class with Béranger. If *"das Schaudern"* is the best part of man,[25] it is likewise the best part of Goethe.

This morning finished Zola's *La Débâcle*, which I had not yet read.[26] To be sure, it is not the novel I most like of his, though he occasionally achieves in it a special grandeur. But in it Zola is constantly tied, bound by a thousand bonds to historical events, and one is ex-

---

[25] In *Faust*, Part II, Act I, line 6272, Goethe makes Faust say: *"Das Schaudern is der Menschheit bestes Teil."* Gide has frequently referred to that "tremor of awe."

[26] In August 1914, likewise, Gide proposed to read Zola's *The Collapse* and Margueritte's *Le Désastre* (*The Disaster*), both fictional accounts of the defeat of 1870. See *The Journals of André Gide*, Vol. II, p. 68.

cessively aware that the book is made up of a patient series of slight documentations. It could not be otherwise, but a simple and honest history of the war of 1870 and the Commune would then interest me more. Whence the fact that *Germinal, La Terre,* or *Pot Bouille* [27] is superior to it.

Ginoles, 3 July

Under the window of my room, a huge plane tree, which is indeed one of the handsomest trees I have ever seen. I remain at length in admiration of its huge trunk, its powerful ramification, and that equilibrium depending on the weight of its largest branches. The contemplation of a century-old tree has just as calming an effect as that of the big pachyderms that Butler so strongly recommended.

Here the broom, later in development, is still in flower; and, besides, since the wilted flowers loosen from the stem and fall, each branch preserves the appearance of complete freshness. That rapid falling of the flowers also results in a very small number of them reaching the seed stage. [28]

4 July

Belgian soldiers people the region. Most of them still very young, some even have charming faces not yet marked by life, with smiling lips and eyes, much more inclined to joy than the faces of our French soldiers. They can be seen wandering in the streets of Alet in little groups, but more often seated in a row against the houses, back to the wall, frightfully idle, not one of them thinking up any form of distraction, waiting for something or other in the dull flight of time. In the evening they go to the cabaret, whence they come out drunk to the point of not being able to walk, rolling, pitching, and sometimes vomiting, full of wrath and changed into brutes with swollen, pasty faces. How useful the obligation to work is for those who do not yet know how to fill their leisure time pleasantly or profitably! But in this complete uprooting, in the uncertainty of the morrow, not knowing how much longer their exile will last, how can they undertake anything and even try to distract themselves? This imposed inaction of men as soon as they are far from combat is indeed one of the worst results of war; and it was of boredom, of fierce boredom, that those who were mo-

---

[27] *Germinal, The Earth* and *Piping Hot* are other novels by Zola.

[28] I examine the broom again and notice on certain plants a great many pods; on others, more frequent to be sure, none at all. It seems, moreover, that the last flowers fruit more often than the first ones nearer the center — justifying, it might be said, what I have always maintained about the desirable spreading of the progeny. [A.]

bilized before May especially complained, a boredom that made them
long for combat. And now this waiting for demobilization . . . for
those who are still alive.

6 July

I am advancing more and more easily in the *Gesprächungen mit
Goethe* [29] and am making undeniable progress in the understanding of
German. This is partly because I never let a word go by until I understand it completely. Had I shown the same zeal for learning in my
childhood, where would I not be today! But it always seems to me
that I am merely beginning really to know how to learn, to take advantage. What joy I find in diligence! — and a semiforgetfulness of the
present anguish.

Goethe recovers in the *Second Faust* all his greatness, which he
somewhat lost in the common run of the *Conversations*. At times one
hears him utter almost embarrassingly heavy sententious remarks. The
only thing that saves them is the tone of smiling guilelessness present
throughout.

7 July

And we shall still continue to accuse Germany of "being short on
psychology"! . . .

The thing seems to me to have been prepared with consummate
cleverness: France and England are like two puppets in the hands of
Hitler, who now amuses himself, after having conquered France, by
aligning against her her ally of yesterday. I can see nothing but an invitation to England to hurl herself, through great fear, on our fleet, in
that clause of the armistice which did not ask (at least at first) that it
be handed over, but left it "intact," bound simply by a mutual promise
(which allowed Pétain to say that at least our "honor" was untouched).

Was it not obvious that England should come to fear that that entire
fleet might eventually be turned against her, and that Germany, if only
the luck began to turn, would not hesitate to throw that decisive
weight into the scale? It was better not to run that dangerous risk.

I doubt that this sudden turn surprised Hitler much. He was counting on it, I would swear; perfidious, cynical if you wish, but here again
he acted with a sort of genius. And what I wonder at the most is perhaps the variety of his resources. Since the beginning of the war (and,
indeed, since long before) everything has taken place exactly as he
had foreseen it, wanted it; even with no delay; on the appointed day,
for which he can wait, letting the engines that he has wound up and
that must not explode beforehand act stealthily. No historic game is

---

[29] Eckermann's *Conversations with Goethe*.

known or can be imagined that is more skillfully engineered, that involves so little chance. . . . Soon the very people he is crushing will be obliged, while cursing him, to admire him. He does not seem to have been mistaken in any of his reckonings; he correctly evaluated the power of resistance of each country, the value of individuals, their reactions, the advantage that could be drawn from this, with everything involved. Oh, how our shocked bewilderment, our honorable indignation in face of the English attack at Mers-el-Kebir must have amused him, and the sudden souring of our relations with England! [30] To have got the French aviation, already half decommissioned, to return to the field and, as a reprisal, to bombard the English ships is wonderful! And, furthermore, we shall have to be grateful to Germany and Italy for canceling their prohibition at once in order to allow us to strike out likewise against what becomes "the common enemy" and thus to give us — indeed! — full permission to help the Axis. We have been prettily maneuvered, without even being aware of it, by Hitler, the sole master of the circus ring, whose sly and hidden smartness surpasses that of the great captains.

One awaits with breathless curiosity the next chapter of this great drama he had so minutely and patiently elaborated.

I should like to be told which of his insults that made us call him a monster, which of his contempts has not been found, and proved in practice, to be motivated. His great cynical strength consisted in not deigning to take account of any token values, but only of realities; of acting according to the prompting of an unhampered mind. He has never taken any but others in with fine words. One may well hate him, but he most decidedly has to be taken into account.

8 July

A few yards from the bench where I sit reading, I hear a dialogue going on. A voice full of assurance, but somewhat tremulous and broken by age, asserts:

"Yes, sir, it's the infantry that wins battles, the infantry alone; it has been proved and generally recognized that the infantry alone . . ."

I pretend to be absorbed in my reading for fear of being taken to task by the very respectable old man (over eighty-two), the head of the establishment and of the hotel, who goes on:

"Aviation! Your aviation makes me laugh. Oh, I am well aware that . . ."

He walks away with his indulgent interlocutor, and for a few mo-

---

[30] On 4 July 1940, after the French Admiral Gensoul had refused the British terms offered by Vice-Admiral Somerville, the English fleet bombarded French units off Mers-el-Kebir, near Oran.

ments I cease to hear him. But when the group comes back again, I
hear once more:

"On the battlefield it's classic: the great and only victor is the foot-
soldier. Your airplanes are all nonsense."

Alas! It is just because we clung, perhaps not particularly to that
idea, but to similar ones, that we lost those battles. Since the methods
of attack and defense change, the best ideas in strategy can in time
become mere stupidities; and the officers who refuse to relinquish them
can become generals. Faced with an inventive enemy who manages
to renew his methods and means of attack, nothing is worse than leaders who stick to routine. It is even better to have men without any experience but ready to welcome and take advantage of it rather than
those who stubbornly persist in their memory of an earlier war with
hardly any resemblance to the present one, ready to conclude that the
victory is wrong when it inclines toward the new.

9 July

Splendid morning; radiant sky. The mountain, opposite, is dripping
with luminous azure. The countryside with its golden wheat is saturated with peace, with joy, and every bird, intoxicated with the sun-
light, relates it. Amid so much serenity I cannot manage to feel very
sad; besides, I do not try to, and believe that even in grief it is bad
to force oneself. Effort must be carried into action; in sensations or
emotions it distorts everything. The speeches I heard yesterday on the
radio are a proof of this.

It is not given to so many Frenchmen to be constantly aware of the
nation's great affliction. One is much more likely to experience individual sufferings; for most people, this means the inconvenience of
the restrictions, the discomfort of exile, the fear of tomorrow's famine.
If the German domination were to assure us abundance, nine Frenchmen out of ten would accept it, and three or four of those with a smile.
And there is no occasion to be shocked by this, any more than by
what I am saying of it. Those who are capable of being genuinely
moved for intellectual reasons are very rare; [31] capable of suffering
from nonmaterial deficiencies. And perhaps it is better that it is so.
Hitler's great achievement consists in having made the youth of his
country want something other than comfort. But the spirit of conquest
and domination is still a relatively easy thing to inspire.

---

[31] This 13th of July I receive a letter from Mauriac reassuring me about
his son Claude. It is dated the 9th. In it I read: "For public misfortunes our
sensitivity is more limited than we dare to admit." [A.]

10 July

In the eyes of obstinate partisans they will seem shamefully and contemptibly to be "opportunists" who, not granting much importance altogether to the regime or the social state, above all loathe disorder and claim little else than the right to think and choose freely. If it were but granted me, I should rather gladly put up with constraints, it seems to me, and should accept a dictatorship, which is the only thing, I fear, that might save us from decomposition. Let me hasten to add that I am speaking here only of a *French dictatorship.*

13 July

It requires considerable imagination, and of the rarest type: imagination within the reasoning faculty, to visualize the remote consequences of a defeat and the way in which each may suffer from it. Solidarity among all the citizens of a nation is not very firmly established, at least in France, and but little *felt;* it remains an abstract thing; and, moreover, for many has very little existence in reality. It would have been appropriate, not exactly to create it, but to inculcate this feeling among the masses and the school-children. To tell the truth, it is through the privations it involves, and only thereby, or almost, that the great majority will feel the defeat.[32] Less sugar in one's coffee, and less coffee in one's cup — that is what they will feel. But since they will be told that it is the same in Germany, these privations will seem to them due not so much to the defeat as simply to the war; and they will not be altogether wrong.

The whole education of children ought to tend to raise their minds above material interests. But try to talk to the farmer of France's "intellectual patrimony," of which he will be very little inclined to recognize himself as an heir. Is there one among them who would not willingly accept Descartes's or Watteau's being a German, or never having existed, if that could make him sell his wheat for a few cents more? I fear that we shall be obliged to witness a retrogression, an obliteration of noble values, or at least their volatilization into the realm of mysticism; and this will be at one and the same time the most serious and the most imperceptible of the items on the "bill."

My heart is quite restored and reinvigorated by Mozart's wonderful Concerto in D Major admirably played by Wanda Landowska, of which I have just heard the recording over the radio. Strength and kindness, grace, wit, and tenderness — none of these is absent from that work (which I recognize note by note) any more than from the perfect

---

[32] See Appendix I. [A.]

playing of the artist; one of my regrets will be not having heard her more often.

14 July

The patriotic feeling is, moreover, no more constant than our other loves, which some days, if one were utterly sincere, would be limited to very little; but one rarely dares to admit to oneself the small place they occupy in our hearts at such times. "And the resurrection of the flesh," says the Church, which knows the great need the soul has of the body to become attached, and that, if the Word had not "become flesh," it would have few adorers.[33] Can one imagine them bowed down before a triangle? We are irremediably sunk in matter, and even our most mystical loves cannot do without material images. The contemplation of the image excites and sustains the ecstasy which, without some concrete sign to cling to, would subside. We need symbols, monuments, statues, flags, something for sentiment to cling to; perches to allow what flies up from our hearts, but could not long sustain its flight, to alight.[34] One can no more do without them than language can do without metaphors. In order to express itself the pious feeling invents the gesture, or adopts it, then slips away from under the gesture, and soon the gesture substitutes for it; this allows the deficiencies and absences of our sensitivity not to be too apparent.

Today the national holiday; a day of mourning. The general grief can only be made up of the accumulation of all the individual griefs. As for the lost provinces, I fear that the peasant of the Midi doesn't give them a thought; the battlefields were too far away from him. Yet the mass of refugees came from there to warn him, to upset his happy torpor. To be sure, he is not incapable of sympathy and most often has shown himself to be most obliging; but all the same the shops in the tiniest villages have never been so well stocked, and this enters into consideration, although it is not readily admitted.

I am writing in this notebook (forbidding myself, for the moment, to reread anything), letting my mind wander at will, notably in what precedes, without any feeling, indeed, of disparagement or of blasphemy. But, not much inclined to observe anniversaries, I must admit that I do not feel particularly moved to emotion on this day. My pro-

---

[33] In this regard the Moslem reveals himself to be much more really mystical than the Catholic and for this reason has rather great contempt for him, as for all our Christian religion. This is what I feel and must note upon rereading these pages at Fez in December 1943. [A.]

[34] What I said applies, it seems to me, only to us Occidentals. The state of mind (or, as people say today, the mentality) of Orientals and Arabs remains, on this very important point, extremely different from ours. [A.]

found sadness over the loss of my native land is constant, but remains latent, and I should be unable to express it.

I am assiduously pursuing my reading of the *Second Faust* and discover in the *Gespräche mit Eckermann* many charming little touches of naïveté and bits of nonsense. Under the date of 20 March 1831, this for instance: "It would be impossible to imagine in our day a great painter of flowers; too much knowledge of natural history would be expected of him. The botanist counting stamens is insensitive to the charm of colors and will fail to appreciate in the painting of a bouquet the lighting and the picturesque grouping of the flowers." (I am translating freely.)

The only Frenchman in the hotel, I listen to today's communiqué in the company of four Belgians and three Austrians.

15 July

Outside of my constant anxiety about those at Cuverville, I am most particularly worried about Saillet and Thomas, among so many others from whom I have not yet been able to get news. Is it a presentiment? Or merely the trial of my affection for them? It is partly because I was counting on them and basing so much hope on them! Where are they? Wounded or prisoners perhaps? With every mail I expect a word from them. They have probably written me and their letters are following me; they are amazed to get nothing from me, cannot believe in my indifference or forgetfulness. Oh, how I should like to see them again!

16 July

From Vichy, where he had to return, Arnold Naville, that most faithful friend, sends me an article from *Le Temps* of 9 July on "The Youth of France." (I am generally a very regular reader of *Le Temps,* but cannot get it here.) That article, which makes him angry, takes me to task and denounces, among others and specifically, my influence over youth as a public danger, probably on the basis of the titles it quotes of two of my books, *Le Traité du Narcisse* and *L'Immoraliste.*[35] It is "against that considerable, but baneful, influence that there must be a reaction today," it says, for I have presumably "founded a lamentable school, forming a vain and deliquescent generation." But did not people take pleasure in pointing out that the men of that generation had fought rather valiantly in 1914? Yes, to be sure, it would say,

---

[35] *The Treatise of the Narcissus* and *The Immoralist* were first published, respectively, in 1891 and 1902.

but only those, it so happens, who managed to escape my fatal domination. What a strange idea that anonymous author of the article has of the kind of influence my works exerted! If only he could know the letters I receive from the young. Protest, as Naville would like me to do? As both judge and accused, I cannot. Besides, what is the use? In addition, that old accusation of *"corrumpere juventutem"* is more likely than praises to assure fame; this is generally known anyway, and how ill founded it usually is. But in this sorry period it might get my writings banned. It is not up to me, it is up to youth itself to defend me; up to those who have read me to prove that I have not perverted them. Doubtless the education of youth is today the most important task. The article in question implies that people are inclined, as in the past, to take youth, and themselves, in with empty phrases. The tendency toward grandiloquence is a shortcoming that I fear we shall not get rid of so soon. It is especially important to teach to children (and for this purpose to possess it first oneself) what bears the beautiful name of *clairvoyance*. This is also what we most lacked before and during the war and what we most lack today, if I can judge from this article. To develop the critical sense in the child ought to be the first and most constant effort of the teacher. There is nothing better against "nazism."

The people of this district seem to those of the north almost indifferent and insensitive to the catastrophe that is mutilating France. It requires very rare qualities of heart and mind in order to be sincerely moved by what does not touch us personally. But here, as everywhere else, let us take care not to judge too quickly: one can be deceived by very different ways of expressing and showing an emotion.

17 July

A most interesting letter from Dr. Cailleux, who took care of me so devotedly during my recent kidney inflammation and who has just volunteered in the navy (which allowed him to treat and save some of those who returned from Mers-el-Kebir), which was given me by Dorothy Bussy, and another from Roger Martin du Gard, whom the storm has just tossed across invaded France, lead me to regret not having been more directly tried by the war. After all, I shall have known nothing of it save at second hand, shall have suffered from it only through sympathy. The "intellectual" who aims first and foremost to take shelter loses a rare opportunity to learn something. The imagination is powerless to substitute for real contact and experience that cannot be invented. On this score at least, the real "profiteers" of the war will be those who have directly suffered from it. I am angry with myself, just now, for having stayed on the outside and for having "profited" so little.

Read much German of late. I am learning lists of words, patiently copied into a little notebook that I carry on my walks. It is probably a little ridiculous at my age to still try to learn, and all this effort is quite useless; but the moment I am not stretching toward something, I become mortally bored and cease to enjoy life. And yet I tell myself that it is the state of pure and simple contemplation that it would be appropriate to achieve and in which it would be good to go to sleep. My mind is not yet sufficiently at peace for that; still too curious, too greedy.

19 July

The last few days, an avalanche of letters, long held up, which eventually come to me from Vence, by way of Vichy, whence great delays.

Yesterday one from Thomas, at last, who says he has often written me. . . . But still nothing from those at Cuverville.

It seems that the Germans, until now at least, have respected private property, certainly by command. It is obvious that they are dealing gently with us; the French are too much inclined to think that that is quite natural, and yet it might well not last. Isn't it to dissociate us the more from England, now become the "common enemy," that they are momentarily granting us special treatment; and also to hold something in reserve, possibilities of pressure when the moment comes to sign the peace treaty? As for me, who, methodically and temperamentally, always expect the worst, thus protecting my optimism and making happiness of anything this side of the worst, I once more admire Hitler's consummate cleverness and the habitual stupidity of the French, our illusory confidence in rights which, once conquered and disavowed by our only ally, we have no means left of getting him to respect; our incompetence. It is on all this that he is speculating. People talk of "remaking France," as if we were still free to remake it according to our wishes; as if we were not at his mercy. Doubtless it is good, it is indispensable, to get back to work at once; but of whatever that work produces we shall have only what he is willing to leave us; and it will not be we who remake France, but he.

Radiant midsummer days; on which I constantly repeat to myself that it would only depend on man for this sorry earth on which we are devouring one another to be so beautiful!

The incompetence of our military leaders comes partly from the fact that, outside of war and so long as it is not taking place, their knowledge remains theoretical and ceases to correspond to the technical progress that the adversary takes great care to let them overlook. They cannot practically keep in training. What skill would one have a right to expect of a carpenter, even though he knew his plane thoroughly, if he had never been allowed to use it previously on some boards and thus to acquire experience of his trade? Those across the way had been able to keep their hand in. Hitler had educated them in a series of easy victories. They came upon us already tried in combat.

In addition, what about the superiority of their arms, of their number, of their discipline, of their impetus, of their confidence in their leaders, of their unanimous faith in the Führer? What did we have to set up against them but disorder, incompetence, negligence, internal divisions, decay? But what is the good of going back over all that? In the present state of France she was no longer in a position to hope for victory. I am almost inclined to say that she did not deserve it. So that it soon appeared that she had hurled herself into the adventure, or rather that she had let herself be dragged into it, with dangerous improvidence. So that one can think today that it would have been much better for her had she been conquered in 1918 rather than to win that deceptive victory which put the finishing touches on her blindness and put her to sleep in decadence.

Cabris, 22 July

Thanks to the exquisite kindness of Mme Roumens, I was able to reach Carcassonne in her auto. The buses from Quillan had become impossible, loaded even on the roof with Belgians who were beginning to be demobilized. Having left Ginoles at nine in the morning, I was able to see Alibert and Bousquet at Carcassonne. I expected to take the 2 p.m. train for Marseille, but, having met Germaine Paulhan in the street, I most willingly let myself be taken to Villalier to see the survivors of the *N.R.F.*,[36] with whom I lunched. The Gaston Gallimards are still without news of their son, and Gaston seems quite aged by anxiety. Paulhan is working and *Les Fleurs de Tarbes*,[37] he says, is almost finished. Charming cordiality of them all.

---

[36] *N.R.F.* stands for the *Nouvelle Revue Française*, to which a publishing house under the same name was added soon after its founding in 1909. Gaston Gallimard was the business manager of the review and head of the publishing house, and Jean Paulhan had been the editor in chief since 1925.

[37] *The Flowers of Tarbes or The Reign of Terror in Literature,* a series of subtle essays on style, was first published in book form in 1941, though several fragments had appeared in periodicals between 1925 and 1939.

I return to Carcassonne to see Alibert and Bousquet again. Dined most pleasantly with Benda.

Alibert accompanies me to the station where I am to take the train at 12.50 a.m.; but new orders prevent him from entering the station. Fortunately I had gone in the morning to check my luggage and to get my ticket; otherwise I believe I should not have been able to get in either. The train arrives so filled with Belgian soldiers that I give up taking it. But it is announced that a second one will follow half an hour later (*id est:* at 2 a.m.), in which I manage with great difficulty to lodge my bag and suitcase. On the other hand, the train from Marseille to Cannes is almost empty. From Cannes to Grasse a bus. But since the bus from Grasse to Cabris does not leave until 7 p.m., I hire a private car, which drops me at La Messugière at teatime. Happy to find still here the Simon Bussys, who are preparing to return to Nice the following morning. The pleasure of finding my Cabris friends again makes up for a sleepless night.

25 July

I made a point of writing in this notebook yesterday; but these few days' interruption and my moves have broken the thread. It required the stagnation and idleness of Ginoles to permit an attempt at focusing my thought. Again I feel nothing in me but confusion and disorder.

Read and reread much Goethe of late: some poems, the beautiful introduction to *Farbenlehre,* and, urged on by Eckermann's admiration, the *Novelle,* which really is unbelievably silly (*blissful*).[38] Goethe could not have written it at present. It is doubtless impossible to speak of progress in the realm of art, but he would have seen that nothing but the specific individuality of the notations can sustain the interest of such a tale, in which everything is invented, constructed "at will"; and to prove what? That kindness achieves more than violence? . . . That the wildest forces of nature, when tamed, can be of use? . . . That poetry and music overcome the most savage instincts? . . . That the trusting simplicity of a child wins out when brutality fails? . . . Obviously; but what wins out here is artifice. A work of art cannot be achieved by the mere application of good rules; and moreover those that Goethe has applied in this brief tale are most debatable. Likewise, Goethe would blush today at many of his reflections on painting, which Eckermann has handed down to us. The arts have evolved in a manner that he could not foresee, and certain great painters have appeared all of whose work rises up against his theories. It is amusing to note

---

[38] The *Novelle* was translated by Thomas Carlyle as *Goethe's Novel* and by others as *A Tale;* the *Farbenlehre* is known in English as *Goethe's Theory of Colors.*

that in many other fields likewise the most advantageous path has been cut in a direction in which he foresaw nothing but a dead end. And, furthermore, this which is very serious: his whole intelligence, however spontaneously inquisitive it was, did not keep him from thinking that he had to direct his curiosity away from what he judged human intelligence to be incapable of ever achieving (Lord! how complicated my sentence is! — but no more so than my thought) and in regard to which inquiry seemed to him useless: astronomy or prehistory, and any problem concerning origins, initial formations. . . . Some of the lofty problems he refused to envisage, through fear and dislike of disappointment, are the very ones in which the mind, subsequently, has risked its boldest excursions and with the most amazing advantage.

Will it be said that France had ceased to be the great nation whose role she continued to play? Just the same, I see no other nation on earth that can assume that role today in her place, and it is essential to convince her, to convince oneself, of this.

If tomorrow, as it is to be feared, freedom of thought, or at least of the expression of that thought, is refused us, I shall try to convince myself that art, that thought itself, will lose less thereby than in excessive freedom.

We are entering a period in which liberalism is going to become the most suspect and least practicable of virtues.

27 July

Dr. Cailleux (who treated me with such utter devotion during my recent attack of kidney inflammation and who has just joined the navy, thus getting an opportunity to save some of the survivors of Mers-el-Kebir) lends me a *Revue de Paris* in which I enjoy reading an excellent article by Thérive on Zola, which I would gladly endorse, and a study on Germany, signed XXX, which does not satisfy me at all. Would it not be appropriate, instead of outlining the shortcomings that led the German people to victory, to point out the eminent qualities that brought the French people their defeat (a defeat that will perhaps prevent those qualities from continuing to exist)? I am speaking ironically, for one cannot make our qualities or our virtues responsible for our defeat; but rather the ruinous shortcomings that were in a way their counterpart, and which we do not yet seem to be making any effort to get rid of.

It is true that the Frenchman is moved by a need for perfection probably more often than any other modern people; that the sense of perfection is inseparable from the idea of measure and, consequently, of limitation; so that that very perfection necessarily involves, in art, a certain contraction – indeed, even narrowing (much more apparent than really profound, moreover) – of the theater and field of thought. And it was likewise the invitation to a rapid sclerosis, against which the extraordinary outbursts of romanticism and of so many powerful individuals, in painting as well as in literature, protested.

It is likewise true that the German, less a draftsman than a musician (the reflections I noted on this subject more than twenty years ago still seem to me quite correct today), delights in the vagueness of the disproportionate. And that this need of restless expansion, of evasion into the unformulated and the unformed, readily slips toward a desire for conquest, we have seen at our expense. It remains for us to see, however, whether or not that sudden leaping of boundaries, that excessive expansion, are reconcilable with the equilibrium of an organism.

I am rereading excellent pages of Suarès in *Présences*,[39] concerning Dostoyevsky, Musset, Loti, etc. There are few men with whom I should have more enjoyed conversing, if only his vanity had not set up so many and such absurd obstacles to that.

28 July

Indulgence. Indulgences. . . . That sort of puritan rigor by which the Protestants, those spoilsports, often made themselves so hateful, those scruples of conscience, that uncompromising integrity, that unshakable punctuality, these are the things we have most lacked. Softness, surrender, relaxation in grace and ease, so many charming qualities that were to lead us, blindfolded, to defeat.

And, most often, mere ignoble absence of constraint, listlessness.

Les Ronds de cuir, which I have just tried to reread, has plunged me into a fit of indescribable blues.[40] "It's Daumier," I am told. Not at all! Daumier was satire; Daumier stigmatized what Courteline seems to put up with. He delights in abjection, sides with the trickster, the malingerer. What can one expect from such second-rate humanity, the portrait of which is only too exact, alas! Kindly, indulgent portrait in which so many Frenchmen recognize themselves; or at least one recognizes so many Frenchmen!

Sorry reign of indulgence, of indulgences. . . .

---

[39] *Présences*, first published in 1925 and enlarged the following year, is a collection of essays on Musset, Molière, d'Annunzio, and others.

[40] Georges Courteline's novel in tableau form, *The Stick-in-the-Mud Pen-Pushers* (or, as we might say today, *The Chair-Borne Infantry*), depicts French bureaucrats. Though first published in 1893 and a favorite with the French, it has never been translated into English.

Ah yes, I laugh with Courteline, at times irresistibly; but the laughter over, nothing remains but despair.

12 August

The *N.R.F.*

"The only ones in whom they recognized real ability were their friends," it used to be said. Would it not have been fairer to say: "The only ones they recognized as friends were those who had real ability"? The group that was formed here, contrary to all the surrounding groups, deigned to take into account only the quality of writings and not their color. Nothing was harder to get accepted, even by some of our contributors.

As for me, I maintain that there is no country in Europe that has more to lose from a unification of opinion, of thought, and that is more impatient of it, than France. Yet that is what we tend toward today.

20 August

A long time, again, without writing anything but letters. Charming stay at Cap d'Antibes, in the company of Marc Allégret, the René Lefèvres, the Marcel Achards; then at Vence, at Hugues's, whose welcome is most cordial.

La Messuguière again houses me, and in its calm I try to resume my thoughts. I feel more *ad libitum* than ever and cannot succeed in forming a lasting opinion on events, or even in "taking a stand" resolutely from day to day. There is no protest in me against the ineluctable; but I cannot push my *amor fati* to the point of accepting the disaster. That implies too great a surrender of what is dearest to my heart. Meanwhile I go about persuading myself, or trying to persuade myself that what constitutes my reason for living cannot be touched by the defeat. I am not entirely convinced of it. . . .

21 August

Two years ago, reading Marie Delcourt's remarkable *Euripide*,[41] I had been sadly surprised by the little attention she seems to give to *The Bacchantes*. That tragedy seemed to me, not perhaps more admirable than others, but more disturbing, more revelatory, and it had been more decisive for me when I first read it; yet Marie Delcourt speaks of it only in passing. Having the great good fortune to be at Cabris with her, both of us guests, together with Jean Schlumberger and Curvers, of our friend Loup, I tell her of my astonishment. They unanimously admit laughingly that in regard to *The Bacchantes* they feel "the same boredom as in regard to Shakespeare's *Tempest*." All

---

[41] *The Life of Euripides* by the Belgian scholar first appeared in 1930.

this said lightly, humorously, and quite candidly. Giving great credit to their judgment, I reread the play, question myself. . . .

Doubtless the profound impression made by my first reading owed a great deal to its timeliness. I encountered *The Bacchantes* at the time when I was still struggling against the stifling effect of a puritanical moral code. Pentheus' resistance was mine to the suggestions of a secret Dionysus. On the path I glimpsed then I feared to find but disorder and disharmony. "I say there is no good in these orgies," Pentheus protests until the moment when the messenger comes to warn him: no, those women dominated by the god, the Bacchantes, were not indulging in shameful debauch, "drunk with wine and the sound of flutes and pursuing Cypris in the solitary woods"; but, crowned with smilax and ivy, they were sleeping under the foliage of firs and oaks, "their heads modestly resting on the ground," or "were dancing in harmonious figures." The crude rock, struck by their thyrsus, ran abundantly with honey, wine, and milk. It was only when threatened and forced that they became furious.

That admirable play took its place in my mind beside Ibsen's *Ghosts* or *Emperor and Galilean* and Goethe's *Roman Elegies*. It is very closely linked to *Hippolytus with the Crown,* which shows a similar refusal and in which the god likewise takes revenge for the rejection.

Moreover, Euripides takes sides no more than does Ibsen, it seems to me. It is enough for him to throw light on and set forth the conflict between natural forces and the soul that intends to elude their domination. Pride is involved and similarly exposed. Pentheus praises himself excessively for his resistance; then Agave, under an illusion like Ajax, likewise congratulates himself for having accomplished a superhuman deed.

And, from an entirely different angle, I recognized in the scene of Pentheus' disguise the disguise, so tragic, of Lorenzaccio [42] agreeing, the better to approach the one he wants to kill, to put on his livery for a while. Each of them is caught in his own game, trapped by his own device.

Rereading that play today, "I recognize the scars of the prejudices it took from me when first I read it." (Stendhal uses this image in regard to Buffon. See his *Journal,* 29 Pluviôse 1803.)

I should like to transcribe as an epigraph for *The Bacchantes* the two sentences from Goethe that I set down here the day before yesterday:

> *Sie freut sich an der Illusion.*
> *Wer diese in sich und andern zerstört, den*

---

[42] In Musset's comedy of *Lorenzaccio.*

Sträft sie als der strengste Tyrann. Wer
Ihr zutraulich folgt, den drückt sie
Wie ein Kind an ihr Herz.

(Goethe: *Die Natur*) [43]

I should like to write, if only out of gratitude, in praise of the works that taught me to know myself, that formed me. The great defect of *Si le grain ne meurt* . . . is that I do not tell in it who were my initiators. There would be substance in this for another book, on a quite different plane. But it is fifteen years ago that I should have written it.

I shall continue to cover the pages of this notebook *as if nothing were happening.* By nature little inclined toward complaints, even less toward sulkiness, I attribute small value to certain superficial liberties in which art has everything to lose and the mind very little to gain.

26 August

How at one and the same time can the days seem to me so tragically short and I be unable to fill them? Is not that perhaps the chief evidence that I am aging? If only I could harness myself to some long task! . . . I have tried to get back to the preface for the *Anthologie*; [44] but I have such trouble formulating the least thought that it seems to me I have forgotten how to write. Everything I experience at present is too remote from words; I am marking time in the moving sands of the inexpressible.

28 August

I am rereading Kafka's *The Trial* with an even greater admiration, if that is possible, than when I discovered that amazing book.

However skillful Groethuysen's preface may be, it does not wholly satisfy me; it tells us far too little about Kafka himself. His book eludes all rational explanation; the realism of his descriptions is constantly encroaching upon the imaginary, and I could not say what I admire the more: the "naturalistic" notation of a fantastic universe, but which the detailed exactitude of the depiction makes real in our eyes, or the unerring audacity of the lurches into the strange. There is much to be learned from it.

---

[43] "She [Nature] takes delight in illusion. He who shatters it in himself and in other men, him she chastises as the harshest tyrant. He who follows her trustingly, him she gathers to her heart like a babe." (Translation of the ode in prose entitled *Nature* made by Agnes Arber in *Goethe's Botany*.)

[44] Doubtless his *Anthology of French Poetry*, which was not published until 1949.

The anguish this book gives off is, at moments, almost unbearable, for how can one fail to repeat to oneself constantly: that hunted creature is I.

30 August

X., the only one from the U.S.S.R. with whom I have been able to feel "comfortable," told me of a conversation he had with Lunacharsky. The latter was consulting him about the means of protecting culture, which he felt to be in great danger. "Why try to protect it?" X asked him. "Let those who are working to destroy it go ahead. And even help them." His voice was trembling, and with a touching stammer he added: "That is the only way that there will be some chance, later on, of finding some remains of it in the catacombs."

Culture, too, like the seed in the Gospel, needs to sink into the tomb in order to burst forth again.

31 August

I did not know these *Études critiques* of Gobineau,[45] which I find in Loup's library. I read in the first of these studies:

"Whatever may be said against our century" (written in 1844), "the best literature can boast of such names as Béranger, Lamennais, George Sand, Hugo, Lamartine; with such lights an epoch might go astray, but it could not be justly said that it has lost its feeling in matters of art."

Such a judgment, on the contrary, simply shows to what a degree that "feeling" was lost; for Gobineau is merely repeating here the opinions of his epoch. He is not revealing his own taste here: the first three names he cites may well surprise us today, but they then enjoyed, and particularly the first one, universal approval. Goethe frequently speaks of Béranger in dithyrambic terms,[46] which lead us to wonder if we are not unjust and if nothing really remains of a work that then seemed so worthy of admiration. I have recently skimmed through again the collection of Béranger's *Chansons* [47] without finding a thing in them that does not seem to me vulgar, flat, and tedious. Does this amount to saying that our epoch has better taste? Or merely a different taste? I often stop to wonder if, among the writers we praise and the artists we prefer, there are not some from whom the following

---

[45] *Critical Studies* (1844–8), not published until 1927, is a collection of Gobineau's neglected journalistic criticism of Balzac, Musset, Gautier, Heine, Jules Janin, and Sainte-Beuve.

[46] See quotation from Lamartine. [A.]

[47] Various collections of Béranger's *Songs*, expressing perfectly the spirit of the average man, appeared from 1815 to 1833.

generation will turn away. On the other hand, the men of the future
will be amazed that we failed to recognize at once as important some
to whom we have failed to give what will be thought their due, which
will be subsequently showered upon them, as was done for Baudelaire
and Rimbaud.

In Renan's time the tendency was to consider the most serious literature as the most lasting; and this was very stupid. But are we any
wiser today in our preferences, and will they not likewise amaze the
men of the future?

2 September

I have written, and am ready to write again, this, which strikes me
as a self-evident truth: "It is with fine sentiments that bad literature
is made." [48] I never said, nor thought, that good literature was made
only with bad sentiments. I might just as well have written that the
best intentions often make the worst works of art and that the artist
runs the risk of debasing his art by wanting it to be edifying. I take
care not to add: always; the example of Péguy keeps me from that;
but, aside from the fact that I consider very ordinary (to speak with
moderation) the lines so often quoted from his *Eve*, [49] I claim that those
who admire them leave the realm of art and take a very different point
of view; that of the priest or the major-general can coincide with that
of the poet only most accidentally. It is none the less true that a literature may be more or less virile and virilizing and that ours, in the main,

---

[48] In his *Dostoïevsky* (1923) he had added to Blake's *Proverbs of Hell*
two others of his own invention: "It is with fine sentiments that bad literature is made"; and "There is no work of art without collaboration of the
demon."

[49] Doubtless the lines beginning:

> *Heureux ceux qui sont morts pour la terre charnelle,*
> *Mais pourvu que ce fût dans une juste guerre.*
> *Heureux ceux qui sont morts pour quatre coins de terre.*
> *Heureux ceux qui sont morts d'une mort solennelle.*

These lines are translated by Anne and Julian Green in *Basic Verities,* by
Charles Péguy (New York: Pantheon Books; 1943), pp. 275–7, as follows:

> Blessed are those who died for carnal earth
> Provided it was in a just war.
> Blessed are those who died for a plot of ground.
> Blessed are those who died a solemn death. . . .

In translation the poem ends:

> Blessed are those who died, for they have returned
> Into primeval clay and primeval earth.
> Blessed are those who died in a just war.
> Blessed is the wheat that is ripe and the wheat that is gathered in
> sheaves.

was not. It had other virtues, which it runs the risk of losing if, on order or through need, it seeks to acquire artificially those that are not natural to it.

That, for a time, the art of Clodion or of Carpeaux should be less appreciated than that of Rude or of Barye, it may be; but it amounts to distorting judgment to rate art according to its moral efficiency.

5 September

To come to terms with one's enemy of yesterday is not cowardice; it is wisdom, and accepting the inevitable. *"Untersuchen was ist, und nicht was behagt,"* [50] Goethe says excellently. Whoever balks at fate is caught in the trap. What is the use of bruising oneself against the bars of one's cage? In order to suffer less from the narrowness of the jail, there is nothing like remaining squarely in the middle.

I feel limitless possibilities of acceptance in me; they in no wise commit my innermost self. The much greater risk for the mind is letting itself be dominated by hatred. As for restricting my comfort and pleasures, I am quite ready. To tell the truth, my aging body cares little. It would probably not be the same if I were twenty, and I consider that the young are more to be pitied today than the old. In order not to have to distort one's thought, it will perhaps be necessary to keep silent; those who will have to suffer most from this are those who have not yet spoken.

9 September

I have been braver in my writings than in my life, respecting many things that were probably not so respectable and giving much too much importance to the opinion of others. Oh, what a good Mentor I should now be for the man I was in my youth! How effectively I should be able to drive myself to extremities! If I had listened to my own advice (I mean: the man I once was, listening to the one I am today), I should have gone around the world four times . . . and I should never have married. As I write these words, I shudder as at an act of impiety. This is because I have remained nevertheless very much in love with what most held me in check and that I cannot affirm that that very check did not get the best out of me.

I believe that it is harder still to be just toward oneself than toward others.

In my *Vie de Thésée,*[51] Minos and Rhadamanthus, those two brothers and future judges in the underworld, will never be of the same

---

[50] "To investigate what is and not what pleases."

[51] When this work finally appeared in 1946, it was entitled, not *Life of Theseus,* but simply *Theseus.* No such scene as this figures in it.

opinion about anyone. Æacus and Rhadamanthus, when it comes time to judge Pasiphaë, will out of delicacy agree to take advantage of an "absence" of Minos and to pardon her.

I am writing this between three and four in the morning, unable to sleep. During a similar insomnia yesterday, I read Marguerite Yourcenar's amazing article on the amazing poet Kavafis — and his poems translated by her and by Constantin Dimaras, whom I remember having met in Athens in 1938. I recall that I had liked him very much. He read us (we were gathered together with Robert Levesque and a few others) some poems, not by him, but by Kavafis I believe.

12 September

Upon reading the notebook that Thomas lent me, I enjoy it even more, and more profoundly, than I had hoped. If he had died at the front, these pages, when published, would have instilled new confidence, hope, and vigor in many. The writing is excellent, already rich in substance, harmonious and beautifully ordered: "In uncertain dreams are already sketched out vaguely the great figures of eternity."

Picked up Hölderlin again, whom I certainly understand much better. To convince myself of the uselessness of any progress at my age would be the worst gloom of old age. Repose in contemplation does not suit me and I scarcely can be satisfied with it. I like myself only when active and straining. . . . Straining toward what, great God? Oh, for the moment, merely toward self-development.

> *Zu wild, zu bang ist's ringsum, und es*
> *Trummert und wankt ja, wohin ich blicke!* [52]

But in my inner sky the same constellations sparkle; otherwise I should find it hard to understand, having to navigate in uncertainty and under this European sky now stripped of stars, why I do not feel more gloomy.

13 September

The number of stupidities that an intelligent person can say in a day is not believable. And I should probably say just as many as others if I were not more often silent.

14 September

Before giving them to Thomas to read, I have just reread, for the first time, the pages of this notebook. The only ones that seem to me

---

[52] "It is too wild and too frightening round about and indeed
   Things fall apart and reel wherever I look!"
are lines 3–4 of Hölderlin's *Der Zeitgeist*, written between 1798 and 1800.

to deserve attention and for which I still have regard are those without any direct relation to events, which I should have written just as well, it seems to me, at any other time. It is only in its timeless elements that thought can remain valid, in the qualities that circumstances, however adverse they may be, are and will be unable to modify.

20 September

Read much German these last few days; Goethe's *Roman Elegies* charm me perhaps less than when I understood them less well and when the sensual paradise they offered seemed to me less easy to attain.

Tomlinson's *All Hands* (in translation) disappointed me; I did not find in it the delight I took in reading *The Sea and the Jungle*. It is true that I read the latter in the original.

Many poems of Hebbel. Marie Delcourt's *Eschyle* [53] with great interest and profit.

22 September

Even Carco (*Figaro* of 21 September) sings the return to the soil. This is what Barrès would have called the "withdrawal to *one's minima.*" It may be that this "return" is expedient; but failing to see that it is a withdrawal, and that this withdrawal plays into Hitler's hands, is what seems to me lamentable. To reduce France's productivity to the domain of agriculture, while keeping industrial, commercial, and intellectual power for himself, is his plan; and to keep for himself unlimited possibilities of levy on our subjugated agricultural production, what could be more clever?

This does not mean that I look upon this "return to the soil" as bad; but I am frightened by the blindness of those who fancy that such a return will allow France to rise again; of those who see in this withdrawal a promise of rebirth. I see in it nothing but retreat and resignation.

Doubtless it is good, it is wise to be resigned when one cannot do otherwise; and as for me, I am in no wise inclined toward revolt. But it is bad not to see clearly, not to understand, what this "return to the soil" means.

24 September

All my love for France could not keep me from being aware of our country's state of decay. To my constant awareness of that decay it merely added a great melancholy. It was obvious that that was leading us to the abyss. The shock of the war merely hastened the ruin of a

---

[53] *Æschylus* appeared in 1935, five years after the same scholar's *Life of Euripides.*

state already quite undermined. Then came the sudden and utter collapse of an edifice hollowed out by termites. What remains of France
after that disaster? Still many virtues, the rarest and most beautiful in
many domains; but disjointed and unemployed as they were before the
war, and unable today to catch hold of themselves and unite among
the ruins. We are living in the expectation of further blows that will
strike us even lower. Is it wise to try to rebuild before the foundation
has been strengthened? I am making a virtue of patience.

It strikes me today that I have not always been utterly sincere and
that I have sometimes shown, for the sake of others, more confidence
and hope and joy than I really had in me.

27 September

In Dubious Battle by John Steinbeck. Impeccable translation of a
most remarkable book. If I were less tired, I should enjoy praising it.
But I could do so only at too great length. It is the best (psychological)
portrayal that I know of Communism, and perfectly lighted. If it leaves
the capitalist and bourgeois counterpart in the shadow, at least it very
cleverly gives one a glimpse of this in the dialogues, and that is
enough. The main character is the crowd; but from that amorphous
and vague mass there stand out various individuals in whom the varie-
gated aspects of the problem are set forth without the discussion's ever
cluttering and interrupting the action. And likewise there stand out
against the vast general movement, in harmony or opposition with the
great wave of common interests, the passions or individual interests of
the leaders or minor characters; and all this presented so fairly that
one cannot take sides for or against the flood of demands any more
than the author has done. The legitimacy of those demands, like the
outcome of the struggle itself, remains "dubious." Especially dubious
the legitimacy of using treacherous means to bring about the triumph
of even the most legitimate cause. But Steinbeck reveals admirably
(yet without *demonstrating* anything) how those who are refused all
other means of fighting are led and forced to treachery, injustice, de-
liberate cruelty; and how the noblest and most generous characters are
distorted thereby. Whence the great distress inherent throughout this
beautiful and painful book.

When a certain stage of history is reached, everything appears in
the guise of a problem. And man's responsibility increases as that of
the gods decreases.

It devolves upon man alone, in the final reckoning, to solve all these
problems which he alone has presumably raised.

28 September

If tomorrow, as I fear, all freedom of thought or at least of expression of that thought is denied us, I shall try to convince myself that art, that thought itself, will lose less thereby than through excessive freedom. Oppression cannot debase the best; and as for the others, it matters little. Hurrah for thought held in check! The world can be saved solely by a few. It is in non-liberal epochs that the free mind achieves the highest virtue.

29 September

Roger Martin du Gard has kindly gone to the trouble of copying out for me a judgment in dialogue form (why in dialogue form since the two interlocutors bray in the same key?) by Claudel on Goethe — extracted from *Figures et paraboles* [54] — which I did not know. These pages are hilariously silly and unjust. Seeing in *Faust* "an atmosphere of despair, of calamities and frenzy, an environment suggestive of the cemetery and the madhouse," amounts to revealing too clearly what one would like to find in it.

"Everything ends with the grave-digging lemurs." . . . This is what Massis [55] would call a "judgment."

"Calm yourself! You are frothing at the mouth," the other interlocutor interrupts.

No; keep on, rather. This is all most edifying; I am wrong to greet it with laughter: it is less laughable than revolting. Such denials of justice can engender nothing but hatred. I rest my heart and mind by reading in the *Gespräche mit Goethe: "Dumont (?) erwiderte Goethe, ist eben ein gemäszigter Liberaler wie es alle vernünftigen Leute sind und sein sollen, und wie ich selber es bin und in welchem Sinne zu wirken ich während eines langen Lebens mich bemüht habe."* [56] (3 February 1830.)

We are entering a period in which liberalism will become the most suspect and least practicable of virtues.

Nietzsche's reflections, which open the first of his *Unzeitgemässe Betrachtungen*,[57] on the danger of victory (after 1870) are excellent, and of great profit when reread today. It would be a great mistake to

---

[54] Claudel brought out in 1936 a collection of essays entitled *Figures and Parables.*

[55] Henri Massis, a Catholic critic, wrote two volumes of essays entitled *Jugements*, in the second of which he disposed of André Gide.

[56] "The point is," Goethe replied, "that Dumont is a moderate liberal as all reasonable people are and ought to be, and as I am myself; and this has been the intention of my work during a long life."

[57] *Thoughts out of Season.*

think, he says in substance, that the victory of our armies implies likewise the triumph of German culture and that there is any occasion to
weave garlands for that culture. "That error," he continues, "would be
most dangerous, not just because it is an error — for there are productive errors — but because it might turn our victory into a defeat, yes:
defeat (subjection) of the German mind for the greater advantage of
the German Empire."

And Nietzsche goes on to note that the cultures of the two countries were in no wise involved in the war of 1870 and by no means met
in opposition. Discipline, severity, stubbornness in combat, prestige of
the leaders, sheeplike submission of the soldiers . . . all elements that
have no connection with any culture whatever, permitted victory over
an adversary who lacked the most effective of these elements.

The last three nights have been better. If I did not know my age
"by heart" and constantly remind myself of it, I should hardly be aware
of it and even then should not suffer from it. Only I am less venture-
some, and the inner urge is less keen.

Nietzsche's fine reflections on the advantages of forgetting, which
I was reading yesterday at the beginning of the second of his *Thoughts
out of Season,* lead me to believe that it is to that above all that I owe
my extraordinary disposition and propensity toward happiness, to that
antihistoricity of my mind, which on the other hand may offer serious
disadvantages.

9 October

Of late I have yielded again and more than ever to the pleasure of
reading. Loup's library, however broken up it may be from moving, is
still so well provided that I could spend three years here without exhausting its resources.

Read especially in German. In French, some Saint-Évremond with
delight; picked up the *Mémoires d'outre-tombe* [58] once more, only to
find the same reasons for admiring the amazing artist and being exasperated by the actor constantly setting himself off to advantage, never
stumbling or finding himself at a loss. Since he is constantly concerned
with the effect he is aiming to produce, his deeds and words have no
other import than that very effect. He would take away my enjoyment
of life if life were to be but such a vain show with the ever present
foretaste of death. Religion, it goes without saying, has no trouble setting itself up on that dreadful emptiness and *tædium vitæ;* the cross
can rise up without difficulty when it is the *Spes unica.* Finally, that
love of tombs, that perpetual commemoration, those recalls of a dead

---

[58] Chateaubriand's *Memoirs from beyond the Grave.*

past, that poetic ennui yawning and stretching through everything, cause me to applaud more vigorously the praise of historical forgetfulness sung so wonderfully by Nietzsche, which I was reading the day before yesterday in the second of his *Thoughts out of Season*.

12 October

Art inhabits temperate regions. And doubtless the greatest harm this war is doing to culture is to create a profusion of extreme passions which, by a sort of inflation, brings about a devaluation of all moderate sentiments. The dying anguish of Roland or the distress of a Lear stripped of power moves us by its exceptional quality but loses its special eloquence when reproduced simultaneously in several thousand copies. Isolated, it is a summit of suffering; in a collection, it becomes a plateau. I sympathize with the individual; in the multitude I become bewildered. The exquisite becomes banal, common. The artist does not know which way to turn, intellectually or emotionally. Solicited on all sides and unable to answer all appeals, he gives up, at a loss. He has no recourse but to seek refuge in himself or to find refuge in God. This is why war provides religion with easy conquests.

14 October

The very long (but not *too* long) dialogue of Riemer with Charlotte in Thomas Mann's *Lotte in Weimar*, which I am reading with great application at first and then rereading immediately afterward with rapture, strikes me as extremely intelligent; a marvel of literary and psychological penetration throwing light on the character of Goethe and on the functioning of his genius. Furthermore, wonderfully situated in the book, in relation to the plot and the characters even more cleverly than the too long conversations (it seems to me) of *Der Zauberberg*.[59] This reveals an accomplished art and it increases the stature of Thomas Mann in my eyes.

Certainly I am making progress in German. And yet it does not seem to me that I am reading *Lotte in Weimar* today much more easily than I did *Der Zauberberg* a few years ago.

Oh, why did I not put forth such an effort in my early youth! But at that time it seemed to me much more important to taste life directly, to push away the screen of books and everything education interposed that might hamper the sincerity and innocence of my vision. Was I wrong? I cannot get myself to believe so. And even if I thought so, what could I do about it? Nothing more useless than regrets.

---

[59] *Der Zauberberg* (*The Magic Mountain*) appeared in German in 1924, and *Lotte in Weimar* (*The Beloved Returns*) in 1939.

There are always certain regards in which the most intelligent of women, in her reasoning, remains below the least intelligent of men. A sort of conventional agreement takes place, involving considerable regard for the sex "to which we owe our mother," for many a lame argument that we should not accept if it came from a man. I am well aware that, nevertheless, their counsel may be excellent, but on condition that we constantly rectify it and expurgate from it that element of passion and emotivity which almost always, in a woman, sentimentalizes thought.

To love the truth is to refuse to let oneself be saddened by it.

There can be seen cropping out already and vying with one another the vices that led to our downfall, for we are not and never shall be cured of them: taking words for realities and deceiving ourselves with empty phrases. Hitler's great strength comes from the fact that he never tried to take in anyone but others with fine words. He knows what suits the French, alas, and that when they are told very forcefully and very often that their honor is intact, they eventually almost believe it. "Loyal collaboration," "neither victors nor vanquished" — so many checks without funds, and one doesn't know whether he who issues them or he who accepts them is the bigger dupe. Yet it seems to me that the wise man, today, would be the one who did not show too clearly that he knows he is a dupe and who consequently would cease to be one though acting as if he were. It is a dangerous game, to be sure; but probably less so than a desperate resistance or, even worse, a revolt, which at very least would be premature and would run the risk of involving in horrible sanctions even those who had not taken part in it.

9 November

My thought remains so irresolute and uncertain, or rather so divided, that it could properly express itself, I feel, only in dialogues like those of Renan, or rather like those of my *Enfant prodigue*. It is toward this that I ought to work.

I am taking much more pleasure and interest than I expected in Renan's *Dialogues philosophiques*. Much better, it seems to me, than his *Drames* and written in a less negligent or neglected manner, though too flaccid for my taste. There is a great moral satisfaction in correcting an injustice; certainly I used to underestimate Renan.

12 November

I drop *Microbe Hunters* by Paul de Kruif in the last third of the volume. Too much wit and not of the best; underrating of the reader and fear of not holding his attention by the straightforward account of research that is none the less captivating; need of constantly tickling it by intervening indiscreetly.

23 November

I finish rereading *Werther* not without irritation. I had forgotten that he took so long to die. It is drawn out and one would eventually like to take him by the shoulders and push him. On four or five occasions what one hoped to be his last sigh is followed by another even more ultimate. . . . Frayed departures exasperate me.

Then, to rest my mind and reward me (for I read German only with effort and difficulty), I turn from German to English. Each time I plunge again into English literature I do so with delight. What diversity! What abundance! It is the literature whose disappearance would most impoverish humanity.

The sole art that suits me is that which, rising from unrest, tends toward serenity.

25 November

Looking for the moments of life that one would most enjoy reliving, I begin to wonder if they are not those of pure physical pleasure; I mean of purely sensual pleasure, in which no element of sentiment or thought was involved. But I do not say that those are the moments I should be most willing to relive, for however great may be the nervous agitation they cause us, our inmost self is not greatly enriched by them.

But what is the use of writing down these risky ratiocinations instead of enjoying simply and immensely the divine spectacle unfolding before my eyes. The last, still warm rays of a sun about to disappear behind the last shoulder of the mountains are flooding the rolling landscape at my feet, giving the village houses, there on the left, a caressing farewell kiss and bathing with a golden tranquillity the bench where I have sat down to write. From each valley bluish columns of smoke arise and spread out broadly as a shroud would spread over the world on the point of going to sleep. . . .

I ought at least to have dated these *Feuillets* taken from my *Journal*, which I have just reread with displeasure in the issue of the resuscitated *N.R.F.*[60] I am no longer in the same state of mind that made me

---

[60] Temporarily suspended after the issue of June 1940 by the French defeat, the *Nouvelle Revue Française* resumed publication in December 1940 with a new editor, Pierre Drieu La Rochelle, who favored collaboration with the enemy. This explains how Gide's *Detached Pages* appeared in

write them, a mind still filled with the defeat. Furthermore, my reflections on the lapses and intermittences of the patriotic sentiment no
longer seem to me quite fair. There is nothing like oppression to give
that sentiment new vigor. I feel it reawakening everywhere in France,
and especially in the occupied zone. It assures and affirms itself in
resistance like any thwarted love. And that struggle of the spirit
against force, of the spirit that force cannot dominate, bids fair to become admirable. Could it be that our defeat has at last reawakened
our virtues? Many an example justifies such a hope, and France shows
herself to have fallen less low than I at first feared.

December

I find it hard not to be convinced that we should be much better
off if we had had the sense to recognize loyally our debts toward
America. The great effort our country would have had to impose on
itself in order to acquit them, the rule of discipline, the discomfort,
would have been salutary to her, while preserving her sentiment of
national honor, which, alas, she learned to value too cheaply as a result of the violence done it on that occasion. I think that our French
leaders underestimated the French people at that time, when it was
not difficult to convince them that their dignity, that the right to hold
up their heads and hearts, were worth the few vexatious restrictions
they would have had to accept, which, perhaps, by the recovery that
one could legitimately expect from them would have spared us today's
trials, much harsher and more mortifying.

19 December

All human acts involve more chance than decision.

Jean S. points out to me that if I claim God to be the product of
man, I ought likewise to admit this for the Holy Virgin, and indeed a
product that it is much easier to achieve much more readily.

A novelist's imagination or anything that ordinarily constitutes a
creator is not generally attributed to me. On the other hand, the critical mind is granted me; according to them, that is my strong point; it
is esteemed and many of my judgments of still unclassified works were
premonitory, it is recalled. . . . None the less, if, on the subject of this
or that new book, I happen not to share the opinion of Peter or Paul,
I am the one who rereads the book and wonders whether I am right,
not Peter or Paul.

an apparently familiar review newly dominated by a different spirit. Those
pages were made up of extracts from the *Journal* for late 1939 and 1940,
closing with the entry of 12 September.

1941

. . .A shift of which it is already impossible to be completely aware. My contributing to the review, the *Feuillets* I gave to it, the very plan of resuming publication — all that goes back to the period of dejection immediately following the defeat. Not only was resistance not yet organized, but I did not even think it possible. To fight against the inescapable seemed to me useless, so that all my efforts at first tried to find wisdom in submission and, within my distress, to right at least my thought.

12 January

My torment is even deeper; it comes likewise from the fact that I cannot decide with assurance that right is on this side and wrong on the other. It is not with impunity that, throughout a whole lifetime, my mind has made a practice of understanding *the other person.* I succeed in this so well today that the "point of view" it is most difficult to keep uppermost is my own.

In this vacillating state of mine what decides, too easily, is sympathy.

Oh, I should like to be left alone, to be forgotten! Free to think in my own way without its costing anyone anything and to express without constraint or fear of censure the oscillation of my thought. It would develop in a dialogue as at the time of my *Enfant prodigue* and would simultaneously put forth branches in opposite directions. This is the only way that I might more or less satisfy myself.[1]

---

[1] "Neither victors nor vanquished!" I do not much like that slogan. It implies on both sides a pretense so flattering for our self-esteem that I am suspicious. A "collaboration" such as is proposed to us today could not be "loyal" when it is thus based on a lie. It is doubtless fine and noble and reassuring after a boxing match to see the opponents shake hands, but there is no question of denying that one has beaten the other. We are defeated. As soon as we showed any inclination to doubt this, our opponent would be able to remind us of the fact; let there be no doubt about it. And if he helps us to get to our feet today, this is only to allow us an effort from which he plans to reap the profit. He supposes quite rightly that our labor and the production we can supply will be better (or, to speak more clearly, that our output will be greater) if we are not reduced to slavery and if we keep the illusion of working freely and for ourselves."

"Is it therefore your opinion that we should refuse to play this game?"

"Perhaps be a party to it at first, and, if possible, without too much bitterness, but also without illusions, in order to avoid, subsequently, too bitter a disappointment. Shall I tell you just what I think? I believe it is good for

I doubt if I would use that freedom of expression which is denied us today especially for the purpose of protesting against despotism. Yes, I wonder if this constraint does not hamper me even more in the other direction, for it takes away any value from everything I might think just now or say that might seem to be in agreement with *them.* Any advantage one may derive from it taints thought with self-interest.

⁓⁓⁓⁓⁓⁓⁓

France to bend for a time under the yoke of an enforced discipline. Just as she was not capable, in the depths of moral laxity and decay into which she had fallen, of winning a real victory over an enemy much better equipped than she, a united, resolute, tenacious, and pugnacious enemy skillfully led by a man with his mind made up to override all the scruples that weaken us, all the considerations that stand in our way; just so I do not believe France capable today of rising to her feet again all alone and solely by her own efforts. I say 'today' but as early as 1914 I wrote: 'We have everything to learn from Germany; she has everything to take from us.' I abide by that formula." [See *The Journals of André Gide*, Vol. II, p. 220.]

"Do you not feel something mortifying, insulting, and intolerable in what you are saying?"

"The most elementary wisdom consists in taking things, people, and events as they are and not as one would like, or would have liked, them to be. A wisdom we have often lacked, for we have a great tendency to take words for things that exist and we are satisfied with a bit of eloquence. One has to play with the cards one has."

"We hold excellent trumps."

"But they are scattered and we don't know how to use them properly. This is what keeps me from being too upset if the conqueror, with his fine method, assumes responsibility for our hand, temporarily."

"Those trumps will not endure giving up their freedom of self-determination."

"Too much liberty led to our downfall."

"And then you are leaving out the fact that the conqueror will not tolerate our revealing ourselves, in any domain whatever, as superior to him. He will manage in such a way as to subjugate our virtues and talents and to discredit those that will not submit; our virtues and talents, our men of virtue and talent."

"That may be, but what can we do about it? Besides, it occurs to me as we are talking that the only virtues and talents I really value are uncooperative."

"The uncooperative will be brought to heel. Yes, I recall that remark of yours that you quote. But I also recall another remark I have read in your *Journal.* It too comes from the period of the other war. 'I sometimes think,' you wrote, 'I think with horror' (and, to be sure, it was justified!) 'that the victory we are longing for is that of the past over the future.' [See *The Journals of André Gide*, Vol. II, p. 232.] Well, you must be satisfied: this time the forces of the future have triumphed."

"And, indeed, nothing saddens me more than seeing France at present

Consequently, forgetting (or forcing myself to forget) that constraint for a time, if I let the voice of hell speak out, I hear it whisper in my brain:

"But after all, why and against what are you protesting? Have you not said yourself: 'The family and religion are the two greatest enemies of progress'?[2] Were you not wont to look upon humanity as it still is — prostrate and sprawling — as abject? Were you not wont to scorn heartily the paltry interests that keep man from rising above himself? Did you not even write, at the time when your mind was bold: 'I do not love man; I love what devours him'?[3] A paradox doubtless, but not altogether. You meant, if I understood you correctly, that nothing great or beautiful is achieved but by sacrifice, and that the loftiest representatives of this miserable humanity are those in whom the sacrifice is voluntary. Have you not constantly denounced as the worst obstacle the cult of false gods? Are you not to be grateful to me for paying no attention to what you were accustomed to call so properly 'fiduciary values' — that is, the ones that have no other reality than what we grant them? Did you not discover, when you used to indulge in gardening, that the only way of preserving, protecting, safeguarding the exquisite and the best was to suppress the less good? You are well aware that this cannot be done without apparent cruelty, but that such cruelty is prudence. . . ."

Immediately the other voice speaks up, heard perhaps less by my brain than my heart: "Why are you speaking of the *best*? The work undertaken by him who aims to be the great gardener of Europe is not so much superhuman as inhuman. Probably, if he were to complete it, there would remain on earth neither a voice to moan nor an ear willing to hear it; and no one left to know or to wonder whether what his force is suppressing is not of infinitely greater value than his force itself and what it claims to bring us. Your dream is great, Hitler; but for it to succeed costs too dear. And if it fails (for it is too superhuman to succeed), what will remain on earth, after all, but death and devastation? Until the present moment this is the most obvious result of your undertaking, and everything suggests that it will be the only one."

expecting her salvation to come only from an attachment to everything about her that is oldest and most worn out. Their fine 'National Revolution' gives me a pain in the neck. If our country is to be reborn (and I firmly believe that it will be), it will be in spite of that and against that. I expect our salvation to come from what is getting ready in the shadows and cannot emerge into the light of day until tomorrow." [A.]

[2] See *The Journals of André Gide*, Vol. III, p. 180.

[3] Spoken by Prometheus, the hero of *Le Prométhée mal enchaîné* (1899).

15 January

Often I am tempted, in the course of my daily reading, to draw up a sort of anthology, the seed that I harvest here and there.

In support of what I wrote yesterday, I find in Jean Schlumberger's brief commentary on Thucydides a reflection that had not struck me sufficiently during my earlier readings. Today it seems to me singularly pertinent.

"It is not through hatred of the Athenian demagogy," he says, "that Thucydides *listens to* the arguments of Sparta. *It is through an inclination of the mind far rarer and more suspect, which compromises him to the very roots of his will.* Thucydides wants to know 'the affairs of both sides,' not in order to penetrate the enemy's secrets, point out the reasons for his successes, and bring out his weak points. Does such a desire rise to his heart in moments of impatience and fatigue? We do not know. Nowhere do we surprise such a weakness of his thought and such a contraction of his emotion. One must admit in him, *even in regard to Sparta,* that impulse of sympathy and curiosity without which there is no impartiality."

I should like to know if Jean Schlumberger would still have written these reflections, which he wrote in 1913, after the summer of 1914, and if he thinks they are still pertinent in today's situation. However that may be, I recognize myself in them. I make them mine. I should like not to take pleasure in doing so.

As a counterpart, I should like to set down also in this notebook these lines from *L'Année terrible,* so gaily caustic and so painfully applicable to our policy of surrendering our principles:

> *Why be heady? Jesus forgets the golden mean*
> *When rejecting Satan's offer sight unseen;*
> *I don't say he should have accepted; but it's odd*
> *When so fair a devil meets an impolite God.*[4]

16 January

What they are seeking and hoping for is a return to the past, and that past, however pleasant it was for some, did not seem very respectable to me. It may even be said that people took pleasure in a rather shameful state of affairs. Humanity seemed to me rather to deserve slavery; and if only the slavery that threatened us, and still threatens

---

[4] *A quoi sert d'être à pic? Jésus passe le but*
En n'examinant point l'offre de Belzébut;
Je ne dis pas qu'il dût accepter; mais c'est bête
Que Dieu soit impoli quand le diable est honnête.

These lines are from Victor Hugo's *The Dreadful Year* (1872), inspired by the Prussian siege of Paris.

us, had been a submission to nobler values, I am not sure that I might not have gone so far as to welcome it. Liberty seems to me deserved solely by the man who could utilize it for an end other than himself or who would demand of himself some exemplary development. The stagnation of the greatest possible number of representatives of a second-rate humanity in a second-rate everyday happiness is not an "ideal" to which I can lose my heart. We can and must aim toward something better.

24 January

He (Hitler) discovers then to his own disadvantage that things are not so simple as he liked to think, that certain values he despised were not altogether negligible, and that through constraint he runs the risk of giving renewed consciousness and vigor to what he intended to subjugate or suppress. Indeed, persecutions act like plant-pruning, which precipitates into the remaining buds all the sap that was previously insufficient to nourish the whole shrub. "Allow to die without trying to kill." Hitler was familiar with this maxim; but he was too inclined to fancy that in certain countries he would encounter nothing but dead wood.

9 February

At last I finish Grimmelshausen's *Simplicissimus* (1670); that patient reading of the three volumes (that is, roughly a thousand pages) took me about six weeks. I should like to translate from this work, which is so little known (in France at least) and so remarkable, one of the initial chapters (the hermit's death and burial) and Chapters xix, xx, and xxi of the sixth and last book under this title: "The First and Last Adventures of Simplicius Simplicissimus." [5]

Very curious to know whether Defoe knew that last adventure when he wrote his *Robinson Crusoe*.

Finished yesterday Arthur Koestler's *Spanish Testament*, very well translated from the English by Denise Van Moppès (1939). Wonderful book; invaluable document.

11 February

A racy style that is almost excessively so. . . . Oh, how I like Colette's way of writing! What unerring boldness in the choice of words! What a nice feeling for the nuance! And all without seeming to pay attention — the exquisite result of a painstaking elaboration.

"I sat down rather glum before a piece of work undertaken with-

---

[5] Whether or not André Gide made such a translation, it has not been published.

out appetite and forsaken without decision." This "forsaken without decision" is a marvel of the intentional, discreet to the point of going unnoticed by the average reader, most likely, which delights me.

After *Bella-Vista,* which is quite recent, I take up *La Maison de Claudine,*[6] which I did not yet know. I enjoy reading in it: "Neither my brothers' enthusiasm nor my parents' disapproving amazement got me to take an interest in *The Three Musketeers.*" Yes, I am glad not to be the only one who failed to lose his heart to Dumas *père* when my companion in boredom is Colette. Quite recently again, during the three weeks when I was kept in bed by an attack of nephritis, Mme Théo brought me *Monte-Cristo* at my request, but it soon fell from my hands without awakening the slightest curiosity for the complicated tribulations of its puppets.

To declare that one looks upon oneself as the most perfect representative of classicism at the present time — what could be more immodest! I did so, Massis, only after having written that I held modesty to be the first virtue of the classics, and thus I snatched away with one hand the gift I was making with the other. But it pleases you to recall from my sally only the presumptuousness without deigning to see that the affected presumptuousness was itself but a joke. I even added, as I recall, for greater humorous effect: "The best representative of classicism, with Gonzague Truc and Julien Benda,"[7] in order to be quite sure of not being taken seriously. But Massis never uses anything from a writing but what can serve his thesis. He is one of the most dishonest minds I know, for whom everything is fuel when he wants to burn someone else.

23 February

Another "Proverb of Hell,"[8] a fine one, that I invent for Jean Schlumberger, who tells me he no longer attaches any importance to, or at least no longer feels bound by, the remarks on Thucydides that he wrote in 1913, which, after copying them in this notebook, I reread to him the other day. He has developed; his point of view of today seems to him superior to the one he shared with Thucydides . . . in short:

> *The promise of the caterpillar*
> *Binds not the butterfly.*

---

[6] *Bella-Vista* appeared in 1937 and *Claudine's House* in 1922.

[7] The passage is found in the *Billets à Angèle* (*Notes for Angèle*) in the *N.R.F.* of 1921, reprinted in *Incidences.*

[8] A recollection of the "Proverbs of Hell" in William Blake's *Marriage of Heaven and Hell,* which Gide translated. See *The Journals of André Gide,* Vol. III, pp. 277, 322.

I am reading, in another connection, a most amazing book by Joubin on the *Métamorphoses des animaux marins.*[9] It contains many subjects for dramas. But I imagine the dialogue between two intimate friends (or husband and wife), one of whom had passed from one condition to another — through progress, he would say — whereas for the other it would seem treason not to remain faithful to his original rule of conduct.

28 February

I am rereading *Cinna* once again with extreme rapture and admiration. Once more it strikes me as the play of Corneille that I prefer; it lacks the bombast of certain others and it rises quite naturally to the most sublime regions. Did he ever write lines heavier with meaning, more beautifully sonorous, bolder in syntax? To tell the truth, Cinna's love for Émilie, as well as Émilie's for Cinna, seems an intellectual love, less affectionate than Cinna's friendship for Auguste; but this too is in keeping with the drama and maintains a tension that never relaxes. In Racine's tragedies love effeminates the heroes rather than exalts them; here it fuses with esteem and draws forth the noblest and best of which each is capable.

In Act IV, scene iv, one set of characters takes the place of another; there is no logical sequence, so that it may be said (and doubtless it has been already) that the play is in six acts, since the fourth is made up of two.[10]

I am much inclined to include in my anthology the sixteen lines of the dialogue between Auguste and Livie, beginning with

Cease yearning, Rome, for your freedom. . . .[11]

They remain, as it were, buried in the play, and when standing alone take on an incomparable brilliance.

6 March

My soul has remained young to such a degree that I constantly feel as if the septuagenarian I indubitably am is a role I am playing; and the infirmities and failings that remind me of my age come along like a prompter to call it to my mind when I might be inclined to for-

---

[9] *The Metamorphoses of Aquatic Animals* by Louis Joubin (1926).

[10] Indeed, the Emperor Auguste and his wife Livie leave the stage to make way for Émilie, the instigator of the plotters. This sudden change in viewpoint reflects the audience's change of sympathy from China to his intended victim, Auguste.

[11] Gide's *Anthologie de la poésie française,* which appeared in 1949, contains neither these lines, beginning:

Cesse de soupirer, Rome, pour ta franchise . . .

nor any others by Corneille.

get it. Then, like the good actor I want to be, I slip back into character and pride myself on playing the part well.

But it would be much more natural for me to surrender to the coming spring; I am merely aware that I no longer have the proper costume for that.

On Malraux's recommendation I am reading (after several tales by Chekhov translated into English) *The Devil*, by Tolstoy, without managing to see what he finds particularly wonderful in it. But I note this revelatory sentence that might be quoted as occasion arises:

"The idea of baring his secret to his uncle, whom he did not esteem, the thought that he was about to reveal himself to his uncle in the ugliest light and humiliate himself before his uncle, was pleasing to him" (p. 364).

30 March

I am reading with amazement and dismay Chardonne's book that I have just received.[12] Present circumstances give it a rather considerable importance. And in the same mail I receive a letter from Drieu La Rochelle trying to persuade me that it would be good for me to put in an appearance in Paris. . . . He is himself in Lyon temporarily, but does not give me his address; I notice that omission just as I want to send him this telegram:

"APPRECIATE YOUR CORDIAL LETTER AND REGRET comma AFTER READING LAST PAGES OF CHARDONNE'S BOOK CLARIFYING YOUR POSITIONS comma HAVING TO ASK YOU REMOVE MY NAME FROM COVER AND ADVERTISEMENTS OUR REVIEW."

That sort of facile superiority which colors Chardonne's book from one end to the other comes closer to revolting than to enchanting me. Speaking of the "historical events" we are witnessing, he says: "*People* consider them very obscure and in general dreadful." The word "people" obviously does not include Chardonne, who adds immediately: "Much later they will be explained" (those events); "they will seem natural" (well and good) "and *almost always favorable.*" Favorable to whom? To what? Little does he care, apparently, for he does not even raise the question. In that extra-sensory and suprareasonable region in which he asphyxiates us, nothing is any longer, no longer is anything, everything is equivalent and interchangeable and the word "favorable" has ceased to have any but an infinite value.

"The political figures brought before the Riom court," he says on page 102, "charged with laxity are innocent," and here is something

---

[12] *Chronique privée de l'an 1940* (*Personal Chronicle of the Year 1940*), by Jacques Chardonne.

that seems clear, but he takes care to add at once: "like all criminals," with a sort of thoughtlessness or innocence, which becomes criminal in the present situation.

Yet I am grateful to Chardonne for having written this book, which leaves everything in doubt except himself and the position he has taken, in consultation (or at least in company) with A. de Chateaubriant and Drieu La Rochelle. This book provokes a reaction in me, for as I read it I feel clearly that this position is at the opposite pole from the one I must and will take; and it is important for me to declare it at once. My mind is only too inclined by nature toward acceptance; but as soon as acceptance becomes advantageous or profitable, I am suspicious. An instinct warns me that I cannot accept being with them on "the right side"; I am on the other.

6 April

I have just sent off to *Le Figaro* an article on Chardonne's *Chronique*,[13] which would have been better if I had had complete freedom of expression; such as it is, it barely satisfies me. At least it will serve to reassure a few friends.

Would that I might have quoted the excellent passages from the preceding *Chronique*, which give some measure of the depth of his fall and make us regret it all the more! I want to transcribe some of them here:

"The words *justice, right, ethics,* have served as a cover for so much laxity and deceit that eventually one finds a clear and pure ring to the word *force;* with use it is likely to lose this fine ring" (p. 131).

"It is a waste of time to define these 'totalitarian' regimes and to seek to know the mind of their leaders, whether they are conquerors or high priests of a religion, whether they ever had a doctrine or merely a sense of opportunity. They are revolutionaries, that's all. They fomented a very popular economic revolution, which cannot tolerate that state of well-being we call civilization or any of the things that for us make up human worth" (pp. 149–50).

"The various forms of collectivism under state domination, all the types of tyranny triumphing just now, called Communism or dictatorship, are already excluded from the future. But the way in which they will disappear may alarm" (p. 175).

"The Frenchman is a liberal as he is a Christian at heart though he may not frequent churches much! He is instinctively a liberal even when he thinks he is smitten with a party of the extreme right or left.

---

[13] The article, which appeared in *Le Figaro* on 12 April 1941 and seems outspoken in view of the circumstances, is included in *Interviews imaginaires* (*Imaginary Interviews*), of 1943.

He is so fundamentally liberal that he is not even aware of his originality and hardly suspects how isolated the likes of him are today on a
narrow fringe of Europe" (p. 236).

"Despotism with its program of human retrogression, its bestial rule
of conduct, its horrible religion, just as it rose out of the Asiatic hordes
and Mongol Germany, cannot be reconciled with the liberal spirit, its
lofty reason and respect for mankind. This question is by no means
suitable for today. An indisputable and urgent and perhaps limited
task is on hand for the tranquillity of our country. It requires that the
liberal spirit be momentarily checked in order to survive at least in its
native countries" (pp. 237–8).

Excellent remarks also on relations between authors and publishers,
pp. 101, 179, 180, 183, and 184.

8 April

Too often, through negligence or laziness, I have omitted to set
down in this notebook the mark of an evolution in my thought; and
thereby my *Journal* betrays me, preserving a passing trace of a feeling
and no reflection of that feeling after I have modified it, often defin-
itively. Thus it is that some were able to think that I did not like
Rome because I had originally said that I was bored there and then
left without mention the delightful and studious days I subsequently
lived there.[14]

10 April

Seeking examples for Catherine and inventing diction exercises to
teach her to distinguish and differentiate the pronunciation of our
vowels, I discover that Racine's line from *Phèdre*:

N' était *qu'un faible* essai *des tourments que j'endure*

contains in its first seven syllables six repetitions of the open *e* sound,
almost the same, but which it is nevertheless essential to distinguish
subtly. The charm of French classic poetry is made up of the play of
such imponderables.

Nice, 12 April

. . . At that time my speech was akin to song, my gait to dance. A
rhythm carried my thought along, ordered my existence. I was young.

---

[14] Gide is thinking of *The Journals of André Gide,* Vol. I, p. 51, but
doubtless forgetting Vol. III, p. 291.

La Croix, 15 April [15]

Yesterday evening, going to the shore alone, I saw the beach covered near the water-line by the washed-up remains of an odd little animal I had never seen before. Its flat body looks like an oval disk varying from three to five inches long, quite translucent in the center, but with edges that darken to a most intense purplish blue. Above the oval rises like a comb a sort of transversal sail, colorless and almost transparent, to catch the wind. And I saw that the near-by waves were covered with hundreds or thousands of these frail skiffs, which the breeze was slowly bringing in to run aground on the beach. Observing the nearest ones, I saw that the inner surface of each disk was covered with delicate tentacles like those of starfish. I wondered if they were not one stage of a zoophyte, but believe rather that it was an adult animal, the name and description of which I shall try to find in the Brehm at Les Audides.[16] I was filled with wonder and more deeply moved than I could have been by the most beautiful landscape.

17 April

"Sade and La Mettrie, the only two real atheists of the eighteenth century," Jean Strohl used to say. I almost thought so too, not being able to consider as such Voltaire, d'Holbach, Grimm, Montesquieu, and even less Rousseau. As for Diderot, his article on Spinoza remained confounding to me.[17] Oh, to be sure, none of them believed in miracles, in Providence, in some God accidentally bringing about his particular wishes. But it is not so easy as that to be an atheist. I can understand Hume's saying to d'Holbach that he had never had the luck to meet a single one; and when the Baron replied (in 1764); "This evening you will have the pleasure of dining with seventeen of them," he was using the word rather freely; when forced into a corner, those guests would have revealed more vague skepticism than a very definite and very decisive negative affirmation. The anecdote (*Vie de Romilly* by Diderot) is related by Buckle (Vol. II, p. 228), whose *History of Civilization* I am reading with the keenest interest.[18]

---

[15] The date "*1ᵉʳ avril*" in the Paris edition marks a hasty correction of a misprint in the page-proof.

[16] Gide is referring to the *Illustrated Life of Animals* by the German naturalist Alfred Edmund Brehm.

[17] See *The Journals of André Gide*, Vol. III, pp. 36, 46.

[18] Diderot never wrote a *Life of Romilly*. After repeating the anecdote, Buckle gives a footnote beginning: "This was related to Romilly by Diderot. *Life of Romilly*, vol. i, pp. 131, 132. . . ." The story is indeed told on those pages of *The Life of Sir Samuel Romilly Written by Himself* in recording a conversation with Diderot that took place in 1781.

That Péguy is a great figure, and particularly noble and representative, goes without saying; I consider admirable his very life and many a page of his *Jeanne d'Arc,* as well as numerous others scattered throughout his *Cahiers*.[19] But those lines from *Éve* which are quoted everywhere today and over which everyone goes into raptures belong among the worst I have read and the worst that were ever dashed off in any language.

Honor, integrity, good faith — merely to pride oneself on them amounts to relinquishing them somewhat.

6 May

"France . . . France alone," they say. Alas, I doubt if she has the power to climb back up the fatal slope! In her youth, perhaps, but she is too divided. Our present state of decay, which our defeat so sadly revealed, concerns me even more than the defeat itself. Yes, I doubt that, alone, we shall be capable of getting back on our feet when England gives back to us that "beloved liberty" which we shall simply turn into license. I even go so far as to think subjection to Germany preferable for a time, with its painful humiliations, less harmful for us, less degrading, than the discipline that Vichy offers us today. There can be no shame in being conquered by an adversary that is more robust and prepared so long in advance for the struggle; but shame indeed in returning to normal (or trying to) in the position to which one has so miserably been forced back. Collaboration with Germany would strike me as acceptable, even desirable, if I were sure it were fair. But it is best, probably, not to seem to doubt the fairness of the contracting party. I have always believed and said that our two peoples were much less opposites than complements, and the weakness of the Versailles Treaty lies in not having already grasped this. It is true that at that time there was no question of Hitlerism; but this is just why we should have taken advantage of it. Instead of forestalling Hitlerism we acted in such a way as to make it necessary for the recovery of Germany, which we made a point of humiliating, of mortifying. We can reproach Hitler with the means of recovery he is using, feel indignant about his summary, cruel, iniquitous methods. . . . But without them would he have achieved the amazing results that give him mastery of the situation today? We are now at the mercy of a power that knows no mercy. And nothing seems to me more useless than an impotent revolt.

The "Crush me, or I shall never bow" of *Quaïn*[20] is not for me. I

----

[19] Most of Péguy's writings appeared in his own periodical *Cahiers de la quinzaine.*

[20] *"Ecrase-moi, sinon jamais je ne ploierai,"* is line 360 of Leconte de Lisle's poem "Quaïn" in the *Poèmes barbares.*

hold that in such cases it is better to obey without a word. I should doubtless not talk like this if I did not believe all the values that are dear to me utterly inalienable, if I did not know force to be powerless against them. And probably the regime I prefer is the one that will most honor them (indeed, I am not saying: that will bestow the most honors on them), but I hold that it would be debasing them to put them at the service of any regime whatever. I also hold that there is no regime in which the cult of these values can fail to restore to man his dignity, nor any cause so beautiful that it is worth man's subjugating to it his freedom of thought (and dignity is the same thing).[21]

8 May

As for everything I wrote above, I should prefer that there were danger in thinking it. An opinion begins to bother me as soon as I can find an advantage in it. Judgment finds its freedom much more seriously compromised when circumstances favor it than when they thwart it, and one suspects one's impartiality much less in resistance than in assent.

10 May

If the English succeed in driving the Germans out of France, a party will form in our country to balk at that deliverance, to discover that the recent domination had something to be said for it, since it at least imposed order, and to prefer it to the disorder of freedom. A freedom for which we are not yet ready and which we do not deserve. Freedom is beautiful only because it permits the exercise of virtues that it is first essential to acquire. How much time will be left me to suffer from this period of turbulence? Shall I live long enough to see the dawn breaking beyond the confusion and not to die in despair?

11 May

Yet no! Despair is not at all typical of me. But more than ever I depend on the weather, the currents, the surroundings, the circumstances. When I was young, it seemed to me that my spirit could escape from the environment more easily. I had not yet discovered to what an extent each of us, whether or not we wish it or know it, be-

---

[21] "A good policy consists not in opposing what is inevitable but in being of use to it and in making use of it." (Renan, *Réforme intellectuelle et morale*, p. 143.)

". . . a fatal circle in which common sense is called cowardice, sometimes treason" (p. 152).

"How many questions, in the affairs of this poor human race, must be settled without being resolved. After a few years one is quite surprised that the question has ceased to exist" (p. 176). [A.]

longs to the whole, is involved, remains, even without knowing it, dependent. But today it is impossible not to know it, for events have assumed such an importance! One can no longer detach one's thoughts
from them. One is bound up in them to the very heart, and suffering
with those who suffer. Descartes's stove has gone out. One can get
warm only by exercising. Bad for pure thought! What remains pure
today? Everything compromises itself on *use*. Thought enters the service. And how can it avoid joining up? I have ceased to count on any
but the deserters.

16 May

"Why do you French always have (and nothing but) half-tones,
nuances, and reticence in matters of color?" I was not aware of this and
hardly understood Rosenberg when he said: "In Russia we like fresh
and bold colors, daring tones, gay oppositions. In France everything
seems monotone and dull, whether clothing, draperies, or stage sets
and those of life itself. Nothing but whispers, refined subtleties, discreet allusions; in contrast to them, with our violent tastes we seem to
ourselves good-humored savages."

Shortly after that conversation there came to Paris the Russian
Ballet bringing its well-known dash and new life.

6 June

"Unselfconsciousness"; yes, this is indeed the proper word, and
Montherlant uses it wonderfully. He excels in passing off as a virtue
(and what is more, as a rare virtue) and "freedom of mind" what, I
fear, is but an egotistic lack of interest in public affairs. He indulgently quotes a remark by Gourmont and it can be felt that the war
"does not bother" him either. Many people are well enough off not to
have to suffer much from the restrictions, and they look upon the present situation as better than merely tolerable. They would be hypocritical not to admit this simply and to assume a contrite appearance,
for the poverty of others touches them but little and sympathy does
not bother them; but there is nothing to boast about in that. The remarks of the "rat who has withdrawn from society," whether he is an
artist or a philosopher, always smack somewhat of his cheese.

14 June

Le Figaro has opened a column entitled "Anti-Littré," in which to
point out the grammatical mistakes that can be found even in the best
writers. It is enough to keep one from writing. Some of these mistakes
are trumped-up quarrels, such as the *de suite* that already annoyed
Baudelaire when George Sand confused it with *tout de suite*. Is there
really any reason for getting alarmed about that? On the other hand

(yes, I am well aware that the improper use of *par contre* is also pointed out), I do not recall ever having seen criticized the use, which is beginning to come in, of *autrement* followed by *plus*, which strikes me as "*autrement plus*" deplorable. I read, for example, in the *Journal de Genève* for 13 June over the signature of Captain Eddy Bauer: "It would have been, it seems, *autrement plus utile*." *Autrement* was enough, or else *bien plus utile*.

I like being a "victim" of the Legion. I do not like the fact that it should be for so small a reason.[22]

I was kept from speaking not so much by the threatening letter of M. de Tissot as by the insignificance of my lecture. Brave that threat in order to say so little! Not worth it. . . .

At first I congratulated myself on the hundred and eighty (soon after there were two hundred and forty) members of the Legion who handed in their insignia "*de suite*" by way of protest.

But of that little adventure nothing remains, as far as "public opinion" goes, but this: that they prevented me from speaking and that I was silent "recognizing that I was wrong and giving in to their reasons," as the papers said. Any article that might have clarified the matter would have been stopped by censorship.

12 June

The shortest night of the year.

The last four days have been more beautiful than one can say; more beautiful than I could endure. A sort of call to happiness in which all nature conspired in a miraculous swoon, reaching a summit of love and joy in which the human being has nothing further to wish for but death. On such a night one would like to kiss the flowers, caress the tree trunks, embrace any young and ardent body whatever, or prowl in search of it till dawn. Going off to bed alone, as I have nevertheless to decide to do, seems impious.

26 June

After several bad nights I made up my mind last night to take gardenal. Dreamed even more than I slept.

I dreamed, once more, that I was losing my wife. I do not mean that she was dying, but indeed that I was losing her as one loses an

---

[22] On 21 May 1941 Gide was to give a lecture in Nice on the poet Henri Michaux, but this was made impossible by the newly formed SOL or fascist-inspired Legion in the service of the Vichy government. The lecture was published in July by Gallimard under the title *Découvrons Henri Michaux* (*Let Us Discover Henri Michaux*).

object and I was seeking her everywhere, filled with an increasing anxiety, especially at the thought of the anxiety she must have felt at being lost. We had arrived, I don't know why or how, at Loèche-les-Bains. And to begin with she had had a most painful impression of the appearance of the place. The baths were sordid: each tub, a sort of hole in which one had to stand up. There were about a dozen like that and in so little space that, up against one another, they formed a sort of honeycomb. The hotel was as miserable as possible; and in fact there was no inn at all, in the true sense of the word, but simply a group of old stone houses, and we did not know in which of them we should be able to find lodging. They were like the houses in the Cévennes, and this made me say to my wife (she was still with me): "This reminds me of Lamalou," in as playful a tone as possible, though there was no connection. But I felt her anxiety and wanted to reassure her. Not far away, however, was a sort of casino, which we entered. Many people were eating their meal at small tables. In vain we looked for an unoccupied one, wandering from room to room, for there were many in a row. And going off ahead, I said: "Wait for me here. I am going to see if I can find one farther on." And, naturally, my wife was not there when I returned a little later to the room where I had left her. Moreover, I did not recognize that room at all. Hence I set out to look for my wife, ever more anxious. Perhaps she had gone out (the atmosphere in the rooms was stifling). I began to scour the country-side and even hired a carriage, which I soon left after it had taken me to a sort of "natural bridge," the marvel of the region, which I recognized from having seen on postcards. Famous spot, surrounded by steep rocks, and I had just time to think: "She will never be able to endure this country." Then I went back into the casino. There was a crowd. A great many people, particularly young servant-girls in Swiss or Tyrolean costumes and wearing aprons; all of them knew that I was looking for my wife. Whereupon one of them, approaching me, told me that she knew where to find her and was ready to tell me: "But first one would like to know what you think of Russia?" As she asked me this question, she winked at two strapping fellows whom I felt, rather than saw, beside me. I grasped that they were ready to seize me if my reply was not satisfactory. My only concern was to say exactly the right thing, and consequently I made a great effort to see what might be suitable. I thought: "Come, come, we are in Switzerland . . . is Switzerland 'for' or 'against' just now?" not knowing in what direction the country inclined. Fortunately I recalled (this was a sudden invention of my dream) the ship captain with his telescope trained on the open sea who was asked: "What are you trying to see?" and who replied, shrugging his shoulders as if it were self-evident: "How can you ask?" This device seemed to me excellent and I adopted it. "How can you ask?" I exclaimed spiritedly, even adding for greater assurance: "And in Switzerland?" The young servant, easily reassured, at once retorted, laughing: "That is the best reply I have ever got." And thereupon I woke up.

1 July

Of all Molière's plays, it is decidedly *Le Malade imaginaire* that I prefer. It is the one that strikes me as the most novel, the boldest, the most beautiful — and by far. If that play were a painting, how people would wax enthusiastic over its *substance*. When Molière writes in verse, he succeeds by dint of expedients; he knows many a little device to satisfy the requirements of measure and rhyme. But, despite his great dexterity, the alexandrine rather distorts his tone of voice. That tone is utterly natural in *Le Malade* (and in *Le Bourgeois Gentilhomme*). I know no more beautiful prose. It does not obey any definite law, but each sentence is such that not a single word could be changed without spoiling it. It constantly achieves a wonderful plenitude, muscular like Puget's athletes or Michelangelo's slaves and as if swelling, without bombast, with a sort of lyricism made up of life, good humor, and health. I never tire of rereading it and shall not cease praising it.

2 July

I reread, immediately after, *Le Bourgeois Gentilhomme*. However fine and wise certain scenes may be, an intentional drawing-out of the dialogues allows me, by comparison, to admire even more the tight texture of *Le Malade imaginaire*, so solid, so thick, so sturdy. And what solemnity, what a *"schaudern"* each scene receives from the secret contact with death. It is with death that everything sports; it is made a sport of; it is made to enter the dance; it is invited thrice, whether by little Louison or by Argan himself with his wife and later with his daughter; death is felt prowling about; it is seen reconnoitering; it is braved and flouted; even to the death of Molière himself, which comes at the end to round out atrociously this tragic farce. And all that, in the bourgeois key, achieves a grandeur that the theater has never surpassed.

4 July

Considerable guile has been marshaled on the subject of the mute *e* and of alliteration. In general I don't like people who think they are smart, even if they are poets, who try to keep the profane at a distance. As for the moats with which they surround themselves, I claim to ford them.

The position of the mute *e* in the line of poetry is, you say, of prime

importance; likewise you have noticed that the repetition of the same
sound within a line, as by echo, can delight you. This is true; but the
charm is broken if one feels the intention and the artifice as in:

De la bombarde grave à la morne cromorne,[23]

A typical verse of the early symbolist period; or even in this over-
exquisite line by Mallarmé:

De blancs sanglots glissant sur l'azur des corolles,[24]

It is rather artificial and I much prefer certain preceding or subsequent
lines from the same poem of his early period.

C'etait le jour béni de ton premier baiser,

for example, or

La féel . . .

Qui jadis sur mes grands sommeils d'enfant gâté,

in which there is no alliteration at all.

That sort of syncopation (to use a musical term) provoked by the
mute *e* would not have so surprising an effect if it did not strike us as
natural and apparently unintentional.

I propose this reform in which I see no disadvantage. Without completely suppressing dictation, which can first accustom children to relate writing to sound, *proofreading* might occasionally be substituted
for it with a view to teaching them spelling. The teacher's task would
be vastly simplified and the child would take great interest in this. It
would not be difficult to draw up the text of a galley involving a certain number of mistakes that the teacher would know. A copy would
be given to each pupil. There would be — let us say twelve misprints to
correct. Grading would be easy and the emulation more definite, the
most deserving pupil being the one who had corrected all twelve. This
method would have the further advantage of teaching the pupils the
technique of proofreading, which might later on be a help to some of

[23] Gide is doubtless quoting from memory an early sonnet by André
Fontainas in which occur the lines:

Peureux un airain rouge étouffe en la viorne
Le sombre sanglot d'ombre d'où l'Unique écoute
Monter un deuil d'angoisse au roc noir de la route
D'une bombarde grave ou d'un morne cromorne.

Mais du grave cromorne à la bombarde morne
L'ouragan n'aura bu que le sang de mon doute;
Es-tu debout, la Mort que le doigt à la voûte
Suscite pour ma peur un vol de l'Unicorne?

The sonnet is number iv in *Les Estuaires d'ombre* (1895).

[24] From the short poem *Apparition*, which, though first published in
1883, had been composed some twenty years earlier.

them; but, above all, it would put them on their guard against the authority of the printed word, which too often inspires awe.

5 July

Proud of being French. . . . Alas, for months, for years now, France has hardly given us any reasons to be proud. At moments France seems so little like herself that it is enough to make one wonder if one had not originally been wrong about her. She seems to have deliberately set out to disown her good qualities, her noblest and rarest virtues, one after another, or to cast them off like unutilizable luxury articles or possessions that, in time of need, are too costly to maintain. The France of today [25] has ceased to be France. Where are those qualities, those virtues, which made me love my country? If the figure she cuts in the world today is her true countenance, I disown her.

Alas, may one not think that those who best represented our France are just those who died in the other war? By that sacrifice of the best we are today most atrociously impoverished. If those valiant men of yesterday were alive, they would not allow France to be driven back, trampled underfoot, and depreciated; and there would be less talk of *honor*, since it would not have been lost.

7 July

Midsummer. I like being too hot. A sort of heavy splendor spreads over the plain, and the mountains roundabout seem like floating blocks of azure. How beautiful the earth would be none the less! . . . Is not man the artisan of almost all his misfortunes?

Suddenly and frequently fatigued as if I had just risen from a sickbed. Oh, how readily I feel at the end of my strength! And this too keeps me from undertaking anything: doubt of being able to realize a project. I no longer achieve anything but rough drafts.

9 July

That letter from Malaquais, dated 18 June, still lies on my table. If I knew where to write him, I should have done so long ago. I can hear him accuse me, accuse Pierre: we are forsaking him, we are tired of him; besides, he had foreseen this long ago; and his bitterness does not stop with us, but overflows onto the whole human race. . . . He finds all sorts of reasons for our silence except the real one: that he neglected to give his address.

---

[25] I am speaking, of course, of the France of Vichy. [A.]

14 July

. . . I was obliged to recognize my error and that it was Christian virtues I hoped to find in Communism.

15 July

I finally make up my mind to read *La Thébaïde*.[26] It is obviously not a good play, yet it contains some very fine scenes and many lines already worthy of Racine, particularly in the dialogue between Créon and Étéocle in Act IV:

> *I want his hate in order that I may hate him.*[27]

I should have noted them all.

Créon's declaration is very curious, if not very good:

> *. . . I am not moved by remorse this time;*
> *My heart no longer fears committing crime.*
> *Initial misdeeds always cost most dear,*
> *But second crimes do leave the conscience clear.*[28]

What would Racine have been as an Englishman in the time of Elizabeth? One cannot imagine Racine any less enamored of perfection, but rather of a different perfection. To what a degree the perfection he desires and achieves was dictated to him, marked out for him, by his associates and his epoch! It could not be more so. But his knowledge of the human heart, his cruel sensibility, his formal beauty, his nobility — all belong properly to him. What works would he not have produced if his genius had been able to have free rein and recognize no other laws but self-imposed ones? Useless question. And it is possible to wonder just as well and just as uselessly: what would Shakespeare have been under constraint? It is better to think that constraint suited Racine's genius whereas Shakespeare's would not have gained in perfection what it would have lost in ease.

17 July

I receive four books by Valéry: the poems of Father Cyprien, a *Descartes*, *Mélange*, and *Tel Quel*.[29]

---

[26] *The Thebaid* (1664) was Jean Racine's first tragedy.

[27] *Je veux qu'il me déteste afin de le haïr.*

[28] *. . . Le remords n'est pas ce qui me touche,*
  Et je n'ai plus un cœur que le crime effarouche:
  Tous les premiers forfaits coûtent quelques efforts;
  Mais, Attale, on commet les seconds sans remords.

[29] Valéry prefaced the poems of the unknown Father Cyprien de la Nativité de la Vierge (1605–80). The *Descartes* is doubtless the selections from the philosopher chosen and prefaced by Valéry: *Pages immortelles de Descartes, choisies et expliquées par Paul Valéry* (1941). *Mélange de prose et de poésie* (*Mixture of Prose and Poetry*) of 1939 and *Tel Quel* (*As Is*)of 1941 are collections of Valéry's poetic and aphoristic writings.

In reading Valéry one acquires that wisdom which consists in feeling a bit more stupid than before.

"Lasst ihn machen, er ist doch ein dummer Kerl," [30] remark made by Blücher about Napoleon, quoted by Treitschke in his *History of Germany*, Vol. I, p. 505, and given me by Viénot.

I greatly enjoy that use of the word *divaguer* that I encounter in Simenon (*Pietr le Letton*, p. 104): *"Il divaguait dans les coulisses de l'hôtel."* [31]

18 July

Racine's *Alexandre* [32] would, I believe, be impossible to stage to-day. What allusions people would see in Porus' resistance and in the acquiescence of Taxile, who nevertheless had protested at the beginning of the play that he would not yield:

> . . . *Could I betray those chiefs*
> *Now banded together to liberate our fiefs?*
> *Is there among them even one commander*
> *Who is crushed and disarmed by the name Alexander*
> *And, granting him world mastery gained,*
> *Begs in advance to be a slave enchained?*
> *Far from being frightened to see him so renowned,*
> *They will attack him though with victory crowned;*
> *And you wish, sister, to see me, as if afraid,*
> *On the point of fighting him, now beg his aid?* [33]

Moreover, I don't know why I am quoting these few lines especially; the opening scene of the tragedy, that dialogue between Taxile and his sister Cléofile, would deserve transcribing almost in its en-

---

[30] "Let him go ahead, he is but a stupid fellow, after all."

[31] "He was divagating behind the scenes in the hotel."

[32] In Racine's second play, *Alexander the Great* (1665), the Indian King Porus fights to preserve his lands from the conqueror while King Taxile yields to Alexander without battle.

[33]
> . . . *Trahirais-je ces princes*
> *Que rassemble le soin d'affranchir nos provinces?*
> *En voyez-vous un seul qui, sans rien entreprendre,*
> *Se laisse terrasser au seul nom d'Alexandre,*
> *Et, le croyant déjà maître de l'univers,*
> *Aille, esclave empressé, lui demander des fers?*
> *Loin de s'épouvanter à l'aspect de sa gloire,*
> *Ils l'attaqueront même au sein de la victoire;*
> *Et vous voulez, ma sœur, que Taxile aujourd'hui*
> *Tout prêt à le combattre implore son appui?*

tirety; at least all the beginning. And, in the following scene, this reply
of Porus:

> But what price do you think Alexander demands
> For the shameful peace betraying us to his hands?
> Inquire, my lord, of a hundred different races
> Whom that deceitful peace in chains disgraces.
> Be not misled: his kindness serves his ends
> By ever enslaving those he calls his friends.
> Uselessly might one plan half-fealty to bestow:
> One must be his slave or else his bitter foe.[34]

And the following lines. I am even struck here by the need Taxile
feels to speak of honor, in order to cover up, even in his own eyes, his
cowardice!

> Like you, my lord, I too hear honor's voice;
> But to save my empire is my proper choice.[35]

19 July

Indeed, those *Cahiers* of Montesquieu deserved to be brought to our
attention.[36] The first pages above all, that self-portrait with which the
publication opens, are masterful, and I know but few that are more ex-
alting in all our literature. But we already knew them; and it required
all Grasset's skill, so consummate in the art of publicity, to present
them as new, as "eagerly awaited for two centuries." I am especially
delighted by their calm and radiant optimism, which moves me more
than the most entrancing lamentations. Doubtless Montesquieu, greatly
aided by circumstances, did not have to go to great effort to achieve
that state of joy. The difficult thing was rather to maintain it. It required an acquiescence, an agreement of his whole being, a sort of
physiological permission; but even with perfect health, that state of
superior joy is most rare and implies an equilibrium of all the faculties

---

[34] *Mais encore à quel prix croyez-vous qu'Alexandre*
Mette l'indigne paix dont il veut nous surprendre?
Demandez-le, Seigneur, à cent peuples divers
Que cette paix trompeuse a jetés dans les fers.
Non, ne nous flattons point: sa douceur nous outrage;
Toujours son amitié traîne un long esclavage.
En vain on prétendrait n'obéier qu'à demi:
Si l'on n'est son esclave on est son ennemi.

[35] *J'écoute comme vous ce que l'honneur m'inspire,*
Seigneur; mais il m'engage à sauver mon empire.

[36] In 1941 the publisher Bernard Grasset edited under the title of
Cahiers (1716–1755) a selection from the three manuscript volumes of
Pensées, the contents of which had already been published in 1899–1901 in
an edition by Baron Gaston de Montesquieu, R. Céleste, H. Barckhausen,
and R. Dezeimeris.

rarely attained, and even more rarely without self-indulgence or egotistic limitation.

One must confess that the rest of the book is rather disappointing.
Often this is but the rejects and left-overs from his principal books,
and I doubt if, left to himself, he would have put them into the hands
of the public. Yet certain reflections on history still strike me as among
the best.

Of all of these, there is one that we may reread and meditate upon
today with very great satisfaction:

"One of the things to be noted in France is the great ease with
which she has always recovered from her losses, from her epidemics,
from her decreases in population, and with what resourcefulness she
has always borne or even overcome the inherent vices of her different
governments. Perhaps she owes the cause of this to that very diversity
which has kept any evil from becoming sufficiently rooted to deprive
her completely of the fruit of her natural advantages" (p. 143).

There is indeed great comfort in thinking that, but not without a
shadow of fear that one may come to rely upon it.

The whole thing in an ever virile style, not so much alert as assured,
often rather similar to that of the Cardinal de Retz; and I do not believe there is any I prefer to it; tighter, more muscular than Stendhal's;
beside it all Chateaubriands seem adipose, sticky, and overdressed.
Yes, sentences like this might be by Retz: "That devotion sufficed to
divest him of the little genius Nature had given him." He is speaking
of Louis XIV, but of how many others this could be said!

And, speaking of Mme de Maintenon: "It is true that the King had
a greater soul than hers, so that she was constantly abasing the King's,"
could be said of how many women!

Returning to this subject, he says also: "Louis XIV had a soul
greater than his mind. Mme de Maintenon constantly abased that soul
to bring it to her level." But perhaps it would be fairer to say that
Louis XIV descended to her level "in his last attachment, pitiably
weak."

Moreover, the same distinction could be made here as for Tartuffe,
between true and false religion, for we read farther on: "He loved fame
and religion and was prevented all his life from knowing either one."
And in conclusion: "He would have had hardly one of all these shortcomings if he had been better brought up or had had a better mind."

> But their scant love of life
> Is often prejudicial to them,[37]

---

[37] *Mais leur peu d'amour de la vie*
Leur nuit en mainte occasion,
from La Fontaine's fable of "The English Fox" (XII, 23).

La Fontaine said of the English (*Le Renard anglais*). Compare with Montesquieu's reflections: "There is no nation that needs religion more than the English: those who are not afraid of hanging themselves must be afraid of being damned," and again: "The English kill themselves without any other reason than their sorrow," or "The English kill themselves at the slightest setback." . . . Curious to know if this is still true today? And even in La Fontaine's time, and again in Montesquieu's, how many examples would have proved their statements?

It is true that, personally, I have but very little to suffer from the present condition (this is partly because my life, my reason for living, takes refuge in a domain that setbacks cannot touch), and I even have to make a slight effort to imagine the effects of our disaster. But I cannot open a newspaper without painfully seeing in it the moral and spiritual decadence, at once cause and effect of our defeat.

I no longer write an affirmative sentence without being tempted to add: "perhaps."

X. talks of himself with great modesty, but constantly.

I also read in Montesquieu:
"Wonderful maxim; not to talk of things any more after they are done."
Excellent remark to quote to those who ask me for explanations of my books.

20 July

A new issue of *Poésie 41* brings me some surprising poems by Aragon.[38] This is the best I have read in poetry for some time and the most authentically new. I feel the need of writing this here, for I had not at all enjoyed his most recent books and feared he might henceforth be almost lost to us.

26 July

I come away delighted from Catherine's dancing class, which I have just attended. No doubt but that daily training of this type gives the body that undergoes it slimness, grace, and decision. Spiritualization of desire. But it is desire none the less. Desire for something or other. And if the body is ugly, nothing can be done about it.

---

[38] Four poems entitled *"Les Nuits"* ("Nights") appeared first in the fourth issue of *Poésie 41* (May–June 1941), a small and excellent poetry review published by Pierre Seghers at Villeneuve-lès-Avignon in the Gard. These poems, entitled individually "May Night," "Dunkerque Night," "Night of Exile," and "Night in the Deep South," were reprinted in *Les Yeux d'Elsa* (*Elsa's Eyes*) the following year.

Were I a ballet-master, I should go and recruit on the beach some of those little Italians (perhaps French boys) with tanned bodies whom I was watching yesterday on the beach and whose elegant and rhythmical way of swimming I was admiring. Trained in dancing, they would seem so provocative that, out of regard for public morals, no one would dare to "produce" them.

29 July

The last part of life. . . . Rather listless last act; recalls of the past; repetitions. One would like some unexpected rebound and one doesn't know what to think up.

The first of the tales in Steinbeck's *Long Valley*, remarkable for its complete adroitness, seems like a short story by Chekhov; one of the best by Chekhov.

La Croix-Valmer, 2 August

I left at Cabris the other notebook, almost filled up, which I was too much afraid of losing. Not that the pages I wrote in it seem to me indispensable; but, however ordinary they may be, they represent the only harvest of these last months. I can measure the depth of my original dejection by the efforts I had to put forth in order to pull myself together.

There is much talk, in the newspapers, of the recovery of France. This notebook relates but a personal recovery, which does not always follow the direction proposed by Vichy's commands. But the young, to whom those directives are addressed, naturally did not experience the spiritual upset of their elders, and yet it is not good that there should be a break between them and us. There is no culture but in a continuation, and I deem to be disastrous certain repudiations of our past. I have gardened too much myself not to be aware of the risk, when pruning, of amputating branches still full of sap, and I fear the impoverishment following upon too summary a simplification.

8 August

I wrote all the ridiculous preceding page in order to try to prime this notebook. But it didn't work. I no longer feel so unhappy to spend days and days without writing.

Read the short stories of Steinbeck's *Long Valley*, some of them with the greatest of pleasure, which I am now rereading aloud to the Little Lady and Élisabeth. ("The Red Pony" and "The Flight.")

Aloud (to Catherine too) *Bajazet* and, now, *Mithridate*.[39]

---

[39] *Bajazet* (1672) and *Mithridates* (1673) are both tragedies by Racine.

Between times I am rereading Duvernois's *Edgar*. With amazement. Can this really be the book that charmed me some fifteen years ago? And on my approval of which Grasset built up his publicity for *Les Sœurs Hortensias?* . . .[40] I note that I had retained no memory of it. Enough to make me doubt ever having read it or that, perhaps, the other edition contained a totally different version; certain chapters in dialogue form are really delightfully turned out; but how profane such a literature seems to me, and of so little weight! After which one hears ring out the dreadful *Mene, Mene, Tekel, Upharsin* of the Scriptures.[41]

9 August

I had never before seen lizard's eggs. Six were brought me. Rather like the snake's eggs I used to dig up as a child in the old sawdust by the Val Richer sawmill. Big enough so that I thought they must be those very large green lizards which used to amaze me, and which, I am told, are rather common in this region. They were ready to hatch and from one of them that we broke open there emerged a small fully formed lizard, but still having its unresorbed nutritive sac on its side. It wiggled for a few minutes. We buried the other five in a pot full of dirt, and examining the pot four days later, we noticed that nothing remained of three of them but empty shells. The little ones, having hatched, had got away. I hastened the hatching of one of the two remaining eggs, cutting the soft shell with a razor blade. The little lizard came out slowly then, having gauged the weather, trotted off with astonishing agility, with as complete assurance in his movements as an adult and as if in no wise surprised by the sudden discovery of the outer world.

12 August

When I recall the role of Pauline,[42] it seems to me that I know no finer one. But I am rereading *Polyeucte* with a discomfort that at times becomes unbearable. Protest wins out over admiration, beginning with the initial situation of the play; I cannot play the game, for it is too arbitrary a constraint. What! Pauline would have accepted from her father a husband she "hated"! What is this duty which is indistinguishable from idiotic obedience? Corneille, moreover, was so well aware of this that he did all he could to attenuate the absurdity of that filial submission: very real virtue of Polyeucte, supposed death of Sévère.

[40] Duvernois's *Edgar* was first published in 1919, and his *Hortensia Sisters* in 1931. For the story of how the publisher Grasset exploited Gide's enthusiasm, see *The Journals of André Gide*, Vol. III, pp. 152–3.

[41] Daniel v.

[42] The heroine of Corneille's tragedy *Polyeucte*.

. . . None the less, what gives preference to Polyeucte is that this choice seems more advantageous:

But what good is merit where fortune is lacking? . . .

> . . . *Too rarely over so great an impediment*
> *Does a virtuous suitor win a father's consent.*[43]

And it is to this that his daughter submits! The dialogue between Sévère and Pauline upon meeting again is, to be sure, most nobly beautiful, almost succeeding in being completely natural and as little strained as possible. But one's discomfort returns immediately afterward when Polyeucte declares to Néarque his untimely ardor as a neophyte. And he has the nerve to ask Pauline to go with him to the temple though he is plotting against the gods she venerates his brutal and stupid plan! His faith may lead him to martyrdom, but did not call for the scandal of upsetting the pagan ceremony with a schoolboy's scoffing or even less by noisy destruction of the idols. Polyeucte does all that is required here to make himself hateful, and one can approve him only in the name of a religion of which he brings out here only the awkward side. He behaves as a revolutionary rather than as a Christian, and one can be a very good Christian without at all approving his deed: he rises up against Décie much more than against Jupiter, against that

> *Tiger athirst for blood, Decius the pitiless.*[44]

The effort Corneille puts forth in order to lift us to this sublime level stretches his style, and his verse shows the result most unfortunately; but, the level once attained, his style again assumes a wonderful amplitude, and the dialogue between Polyeucte and Pauline (Act IV, scene iii) is of the loftiest beauty, a worthy match for that other, utterly human one between Pauline and Sévère in Act II.

13 August

After *Bajazet,* reread aloud *Mithridate* with the greatest success with my little audience (Mme Théo, Élisabeth, and Catherine). There is no play by Racine that better answers the forced accusations of Jean Schlumberger, it seems to me, and that I should be more eager to see added to the requirements of our schools. I should make the children learn the whole of Mithridate's long speech to his sons and their two replies, rich (even aside from their beauty) with an inexhaustible moral lesson.

---

[43] *Mais que sert le mérite où manque la fortune?* . . .

> . . . *Trop invincible obstacle, et dont trop rarement*
> *Triomphe auprès d'un père un vertueux amant.*

[44] *Tigre altéré de sang, Décie impitoyable.*

Is any trace found in this notebook (I mean in the preceding one) of the two long readings that held my attention for months at Cabris: the *Simplicius Simplicissimus* of Grimmelshausen and Buckle's *History of Civilization*? Both of them were of great profit to me; the latter an object of infinite meditations, in which I should have indulged earlier in order to strengthen convictions that remained vague for too long.

16 August

Reread some comedies of Musset. *Le Chandelier* [45] is still my favorite. But, Lord, what a nuisance love can be! — in others.

Reread aloud *Il ne faut jurer de rien*.[46] A most exquisite play and almost from start to finish (this "almost" because of some thirty lines of romantic-love ravings in the dialogue of the night rendezvous which can easily be cut in the staging, together with a few inappropriate "my dears").

Cap d'Ail, 21 August

I am amazed to read:

"Must be read with the most extreme care" in the preface to Renan's *Marc Aurèle*, which I find at Malraux's and open at random.

Malraux advises me (I should say: enjoins me) to read:

Gautier: *Mœurs et coutumes des musulmans.*

Pirenne: *Histoire de l'Europe.*

XX: *La Légende dorée des missions* (Grasset, about 1930).[47]

22 August

Long succession of days during which the soul is willing to live in distraction and makes no further effort to get closer to God.

23 August

I ought to confess honestly that I have ceased to know just what that image hides. In this case it is less a matter of a situation than of a spiritual state. One cannot get closer to what is everywhere. It is much rather a question of a transparency of the soul that allows us to feel Him. The majority of men do not know that *state of communion;* but it brings the soul, the entire being, such a delightful felicity that

---

[45] *The Substitute Lover.*

[46] *One Cannot Be Sure of Anything,* a comedy by Musset.

[47] *Manners and Customs of the Moslems,* by Émile-Félix Gautier (1931), *History of Europe from the Invasion to the Sixteenth Century,* by Henri Pirenne (1936), and *The Golden Legend of the Missions,* whose author it has not been possible to identify.

the soul is inconsolable after once having known it and then allowed it to slip away.

This is partly what makes me, without believing in any definite God, really enjoy only the company of pious souls.

Quietism? No; but constantly in a state of effort and stretched toward something indefinable and adorable, toward a higher condition in which the individual is lost and absorbed — to which I see no other name to give but the very name of God.

28 August

At Grasse since yesterday. Late on the day of my arrival, went to see Bunin. Rather disappointing visit, for, despite cordial efforts on both sides, real contact was not established. One esteems too little what the other admires. His cult for Tolstoy embarrasses me as much as his scorn for Dostoyevsky, for Shchedrin, for Sologub. Decidedly we do not have the same saints, the same gods. But during the entire conversation he was charming. His handsome face, though very wrinkled, is still noble, and his eyes are full of enthusiasm. He was wearing dark-red pajamas, open on his chest and affording a glimpse of a fine gold chain on which, I supposed, must have hung a holy medal. He told me that he has just finished a new book, but does not know where or how to get it published. I was somewhat embarrassed to know nothing of his work but *The Gentleman from San Francisco* and *The Village*, a youthful work that, he told me, represents him but little and poorly and which I was quite wrong to like greatly. He almost disowns it. I do not know what he knows of my work, nor was I able to make out on what is based the liking he shows for me.

2 September

Virtuous effort at work, similar to the effort that kept me tense for a month at Syracuse, to result in a fiasco.[48] Doubtless I shall soon tear up the pages I was writing the last few days as I once tore up those that formed a long chapter of *Geneviève* and were no good.

And I prepare to tear up likewise all these "letters to Catherine" written in the last two months, for everything that I expressed in them on the diction of poetry I find, much better put than I had managed to do, in Auguste Dorchain's excellent book on *L'Art des vers*, which I didn't even suspect existed, but find here by chance and read with an almost constant approval. The lines he quotes as examples, with unhesitating competence, are marvelously well chosen.

[48] See *The Journals of André Gide*, Vol. III, pp. 291–6, 343.

10 September

Young Gérald Maurois had very kindly invited me to come and dine with him last night at the Park Palace, where he has been staying for the past two months. We had originally planned merely a game of chess after dinner, for he is busy all day and every day, even Sunday, with his work as a supervisor at the factory. Then, that very morning quite timidly and with a sort of charming awkwardness, he had come to ask if I would not dine with him. I had accepted without fuss, expecting a very simple meal. It was charming; everything was charming, and he to begin with. The meal was served in a small private room opening on the terrace. One has to hide from the public today in order to eat crayfish and meat in abundance. How well he had prepared it all! What a mingling of reverence and trusting lack of reserve in his conversation and manners. With what restrained passion he talks of the situation of France! No arrogance or smugness in his judgments; a fervor without blindness; firmness without intransigence. Simply knowing that such youth still exists can, more than anything else, restore my confidence in France.

I am reading with lively interest Bunin's book on Tolstoy. He explains him wonderfully and at the same time explains to me why I feel so ill at ease in contact with Tolstoy. What a monster! Constantly bucking, revolting against his nature, forcing one to doubt his sincerity at all times, being in turn everything and everybody and never more personal than when he ceases to be himself; arrogant in renunciation, constantly arrogant, even to the point of not being reconciled to dying simply like everyone else. But what anguish in that final struggle, that of a Titan against God, against fate! I admire him perhaps; but I can feel in harmony and in agreement only with the humble, the modest. For me, Tolstoy remains an *impossibility*. Cinelli compared him with St. Francis; what an absurdity! Tolstoy contrasts with St. Francis with his whole being and entire complexity, his ostentation, and even his effort toward a spectacular destitution; forever putting on a show for himself, for him simplicity is but a further complication. Protean, his most complicated "creations" are never more than a simplification of himself; he who is capable of becoming so many persons becomes forever incapable of real sincerity.

I am rereading Genesis for Catherine's intention; and this afternoon, Ecclesiastes and the Song of Songs. To be sure, the last two works contain useless repetitions (harmonious in the Song of Songs) and dull parts; but also, and above all, pages of such beauty, of such solemn grandeur, that I know nothing in any literature that is superior or even comparable to them. If these books of the Bible were architectural monuments, one would willingly make a several days' trip to see them, like the ruins of Baalbek or the temple of Selinus. But they are within reach; and numerous are those who can enjoy only what has cost them dear. Besides, attention is turned away by the reputation of this book for aiming at edification, and by the boredom one consequently expects from it. It is left to priests and ministers; good for converts! A profane person has no concern with being catechized. Is it not "the word of God"? Is it not necessary to "believe" it in order to be interested in it? Some are convinced that the interest I take in it is but a survival of my Protestant formation. Every good Protestant, as is known, "is born with a Bible in his hands." The Catholic hardly reads it at all; no, not even directly the Gospel; the catechism is enough for him, and the prayer-book with "the Gospel for the day."

11 September

To what a degree I miss a piano, *my* piano! . . . On certain days that need, that longing for music, becomes a sort of almost physical pain. The other day, alone at Germaine Taillefer's while waiting for her, I reread the delightful Sonata in B-flat major, a marvel of grace and emotion; then the slow Étude of Chopin in E-flat minor. I noted that it would take me probably but a half-hour to learn it by heart again. To be able to get back to the piano . . . I should enjoy moments of complete happiness. What prevents me from doing so? The physical conditions in which I am living, but, above all, the obsessing fear of bothering the neighbors, a fear that in my case increases with age, becoming almost pathological. As if the neighbors worried about *us*!

12 September

After *Temps nouveaux*, *Esprit* is reduced to silence. (I propose as a motto for Mounier, both for his review and for the friends grouped around him: *Vires acquirit tacendo.*)[49] I leave it to others to be aston-

---

[49] "He gains strength by keeping silent," inspired by Virgil's *Vires acquirit eundo* (Æneid, IV, 175). *Temps nouveaux*, a four-page literary weekly of Catholic inspiration edited at Lyon by Stanislas Fumet, succeeded to the prewar, Parisian *Temps présent*, edited by the same. In July 1941 it published contributions by Claudel, Mauriac, Fumet, and others, but was suspended by the Vichy government at the end of the month. *Esprit*, a Catholic literary and political monthly edited by Emmanuel Mounier, had likewise moved to the "free zone" in 1940 and was forbidden by Vichy in August 1941. Both periodicals were revived in Paris after the liberation, the former as *Temps présent* again in August 1944 and *Esprit* in December 1944.

ished. I am so little inclined, intellectually, toward insubordination, toward refractoriness . . . that I should almost say: This is proper. To begin with, we need order and discipline just as a seriously wounded man needs rest in order to get well. But from the great operation we were forced to undergo I greatly fear that we shall soon come to with our limbs out of place and our neckless heads directly on our shoulders.

14 September

The "*par contre*" which is overused today substitutes abruptly and inelegantly for the "*en récompense*" of the seventeenth century.

"If his hand is not so quick to bestow blessings . . . *en récompense* he possesses far more letters and solidity," Boileau writes exquisitely to Racine.

The opposition is then accompanied with a sort of compensation; this is indeed the latent sense of the word "*récompense*," and it is really possible to reward only what has cost some trouble.

15 September

It is more than difficult for me to believe that the life of the soul can be prolonged beyond the death of the body. But even if I could manage to do so (moreover, I do not go to any great effort in this direction), it is utterly impossible for me to imagine that very hypothetical afterlife otherwise than as the continuation of a trajectory, and this would suffice to free me from worry, if by chance I had any.

One cannot imagine a more beautiful view than the one I enjoy, at any hour of the day, from the window of my room in the Grand Hotel. The town of Grasse opposite me dominated by the cathedral, whose tower breaks the line of the distant mountains, the harmonious disorder of the houses forming a series of terraces on the slope down to the deep ravine separating me from the town. While I am writing these lines the sun is finishing its course and, before disappearing behind the heights of Cabris, is pouring an ineffable golden light over the walls, the roofs, the whole town. A veil of rain has come to hide the mountainous background of the picture so that the cathedral tower, bathed in the last rays, now stands out against a bare sky, so it seems; on the left, another, smaller tower. The dinner hour struck some time ago and yet I cannot leave this sight.

Begin my life over again? . . . I should try at least to put a bit more adventure into it.

16 September

Children of the proletariat say: *"Donne-moi-le"* in obedience to an instinctive logic. According to the accepted rule, they should say: *"Donne-le-moi."* But do we not say, as in *La Parisienne: "Donnez-moi cette lettre"*? [50] Perhaps the first case (*"Donne-le-moi"*) involves but a repugnance for putting the interrogative accent on the "mute" syllable. It seems to me, moreover, that the same is true in English. Departures from the rules, when they cease to be isolated cases and become popular, are most interesting to observe.

19 September

I doubt if the butterfly after having laid her eggs still gets much enjoyment out of life. It flutters hither and thither at the mercy of the perfumes and the breeze. Probably, before laying, it could think (in so far as a butterfly thinks): Ah, how free and light I shall feel once I am delivered of this weight, free of all obligation and all duty. . . . The soul with no further aim, utterly a prey to leisure, is bored.

20 September

Aldous Huxley (*Beyond the Mexique Bay*) notes in Mayan art the absence of feminine forms and then immediately concludes that there is an absense of sensuality in that art. That may be; but the one does not necessarily involve the other, and I have seen in Etruscan tombs paintings of obvious sensuality and even lewdness from which the feminine element was excluded. But this is a quite frequent induction and I am merely surprised that so alert a mind as Aldous Huxley's should have indulged in it. He speaks of a torso of a male divinity, "a marvel of grace and delicacy," worthy, he says, of a place in the British Museum; that torso, he adds, in no wise recalls the ambiguous effeminacy so frequent in Indian sculpture; hence . . . But, of course, the *Ignudi* of the Sistine Chapel do not either! Oh, how easy it is for the uranist to appear frigid or chaste in the eyes of the heterosexual!

25 September

I have just reread — or, more exactly, read attentively for the first time — *La Fanfarlo*.[51] Surprised by the many significant passages in it, so revelatory that Baudelaire did not need to sign them. They also explain the dedication of the *Fleurs du mal* to Gautier.

What a wonderful effort literature made at that time to become art!

---

[50] In the first scene of Henry Becque's comedy *The Woman of Paris* (1885), Lafon says to Clotilde: "Give me that letter." When both objects are pronouns the order is: "Give it me" rather than the vulgar "Give me it."

[51] An early story by Baudelaire.

Why did it have to think it could achieve that only by opposing art to what is natural?

Restrictions!

Obviously, I have never been healthier. . . . None the less, there is hardly a meal at the end of which I would not be willing to eat a large beefsteak.

27 September

At times everything suddenly amazes you and seems strange. One doubts of one's own reality and of what one sees. This evening, after a game of chess with Gérald Maurois, I left the Park Palace of Grasse to return to the Grand Hotel. The half-moon was floating in a cloudless sky. Not a sound, not a breath of air, disturbed the night's supernatural calm. And suddenly the beauty of the sky, the motionless serenity of sleeping nature, my very self and the little shadow I cast on the ground, all seemed to melt into a vast unanswered interrogation that seized me with anguish and desolation. Oh, I might as well have written: with adoration and love! For no real melancholy accompanied that anguish, and the desolation came from not knowing to whom to address my bewildered gratitude.

29 September

After a month of radiant days, this morning a fine rain is falling from a uniformly overcast sky. Opposite me, Grasse is bathed in a sort of translucent syrup in which the green of the near-by palms, the ocher of the distant walls, the pink of the roofs blend in such subtle shades that I wonder if this landscape does not seem to me more delightful thus than in "fine weather."

30 September

I understand, because I share it, the tendency of the aged toward avarice and shall not forgive myself the costly comfort of the very good Hôtel Adriatic, where I nevertheless decided to stay, unless I succeed in working while here. In my youth, urged on by a not very exacting demon, I used to work under any circumstances whatever, anywhere whatever. Today that demon voices certain demands. In order to stay at my writing-table I must like the room. But I have seen too many poverty-stricken people of late not to be constantly aware that the amount of comfort I allow myself would be luxury to them, not to wonder constantly if the work this comfort will allow me justifies such an outlay.

5 October

And so many afflictions one cannot alleviate! One's heart cannot resign itself to that without hardening. That alone, that too hurls us into barbarity.

7 October

My large room at the Adriatic is pleasant. I enjoy being in it. I work in it, and this makes me accept the fact that it costs rather dear. I prefer the nudity of its walls to the reproduction of all the masterpieces in the world, and I am not distracted either by the gloomy appearance of the house opposite on which my two windows open. When I open them, pigeons hasten from the near-by roofs to beg a little of my breakfast bread, then go away disappointed, for my short ration does not allow me to make handsome gifts.

I have just written, as rapidly as possible, two "imaginary interviews," which may be worth nothing, but I shall not reread them until later on when I am sure of my impetus. Then I shall knuckle down again to the preface for Goethe's drama and to the preface for the anthology.[52]

16 October

I have worked all these last few days on going over and perfecting these "Imaginary Interviews" that I am planning to give to the *Figaro*.

17 October

For whoever complains that the sudden turn of national feeling is not based on the central opinion of the country:

Of necessity a turn is always taken on the wing-tip. Not on the wing-tips but specifically on *one* wing. Though a revolution may call itself "national," it always marks the victory of a single party.

31 October

I finish Pearl Buck's *The Mother*. It is a fine book, which I blame myself for having read in translation. Probably what I am about to say of it would be even more noticeable in the original: it is a Chinese

---

[52] The *Interviews imaginaires* appeared serially in the literary supplement of the *Figaro*, then published in Lyon. They were first published in book form by Pantheon Books, New York, in 1943. The preface to Goethe introduced the edition of Goethe's *Drama* published in the Pléiade Collection in Paris in May 1942. Gide's *Anthologie de la Poésie française*, in the same Pléiade Collection, did not appear until spring 1949, though the preface had substantially come out in *Poétique* (Neuchâtel: Ides et Calendes; 1947).

book, but equally, and even more, a Protestant book. I mean by this that the author is visibly brought up on the Bible, whence that sort of austerity, of nudity in the narration; whence that grandeur, that nobility without ostentation, that lofty resignation; the very tone of the narration, often, is Biblical.

And I plunge immediately afterward into *The Good Earth.*

19 November

Diverted from this *Journal* for a month by the articles promised to the *Figaro.*

I know that I am constantly escaping from the image people have of me, but can do nothing about it.

. . . Equally unfit for sulking and for hating.

27 November

I cannot, however, let this by:

"The ground is disseminated with enemy tanks immobilized or on fire." (Italian communiqué of 26 November.)

The vivacity of Stendhal's style is constituted by the fact that he does not wait until the sentence has completely taken shape in his head to write it down. I recall a passage (in *Armance,* I believe) in which he says: "Octave (?) spoke much better since he had got into the habit of beginning his sentences without knowing how he would end them," or something similar. I must have already quoted this somewhere.[53]

7 December

Forsaken this notebook since I began my articles for the *Figaro.* However good they may be, they could not take the place of what I might have said here.

I am writing in the semidarkness of a movie theater while waiting for the showing (announced for eleven o'clock) of anti-Bolshevist "documents." Tickets are two francs apiece, with a special price for soldiers, students of any kind whatever, members of the Legion, etc. The result is that there is a crowd. As always, I had come very early, and even (having read the announcement an hour early) long before the line had begun to form. Hence I was one of the first to get in. But as soon as I had passed the ticket window, I noticed that I had lost my red sweater. Odd how one can attach oneself to objects! (It is a shame that there is nothing reciprocal about this.) Yesterday both my arms were lanced for a full half-hour while trying to force my vein to ac-

---

[53] See *The Journals of André Gide,* Vol. II, p. 33.

cept an injection of "ténébryl" in order to permit an X-ray of my kidneys. . . .[54] The loss of this wool waistcoat caused me just as sharp a
pain; I felt it being torn from my arm. I alerted the police, the woman
in charge of the checkroom . . . but no hope of seeing it again. A
woolen waistcoat today is too good a find.

It had already, on earlier occasions, tried several times to get away.
Consequently I was keeping an eye on it. You are so well aware when
an object is detaching itself from you, wants to leave you like a child
emancipating himself when one has ceased to control him. A moment
of inattention and the trick is played.

The film was most painful; even if all the scenes were fairly taken
and offered only authentic views, the camera's possibility of choosing
and presenting but one aspect of reality invites it to the worst kinds of
deceit. It is essential to arouse public indignation against Bolshevism.
Nothing is easier: here are hideous aspects of poverty, sordid holes,
ragged creatures dying of hunger. And the Red film that offered but
this aspect of czarism would be just as unfair.

The public greatly applauded the upsetting of a statue of Lenin,
then the recruiting of French soldiers, and Italians especially, which
made it easy to understand how the audience was made up. Enough to
disgust one from being interested in the fate of men. The systematic
belittling of the enemy merely debases the victor.

RECOVERED PAGES

La Messugière, Cabris, 1941

These recent months I was absorbed by *The History of Civilization
in England* by Henry Thomas Buckle, the second volume of which is
almost altogether filled with considerations on France. This remarkable work, which appeared in 1861, must have already been translated
into French, but it is in the three-volume English edition (Oxford
University Press) that I was reading and am still reading, for I have
rarely read anything more enthralling. Although tending toward the
greater glory of England, Buckle, with masterly courtesy and impartiality, does homage to France, which he justifies at length, and, while
pointing out on the other hand with appropriate and well-informed
sagacity our shortcomings and the errors that made inevitable the
bloody revolution (which he elsewhere considers as "The most important event of history"), which English discretion, he claims, and
the state's noninterference in spiritual matters succeeded in avoiding,

---

[54] *Ténébryl* is a French product (Laboratoires A. Guerbet) containing
a large percentage of soluble iodine. It is used in urography.

he writes and I cannot read this praise without emotion: "Within the limits I have set myself, I could not do justice to the marvelous activity which the French mind then manifested" (in the eighteenth century) "by carrying on its investigations in all the realms of the organic and inorganic world. . . ." And farther on: "In these two vast fields of science" (chemistry and geology) "we owe the first and most important explorations to the French." And again: "That we owe to France the very existence of chemistry as a science cannot be questioned by anyone for whom the word *science* has the proper meaning." Expatiating later on the research and discoveries of Cuvier and of Bichat (he holds the latter's work, in the history of the human race's intellectual development, to be "as important as that of the greatest geniuses, Aristotle, Bacon, or Descartes"), particularly in zoology, but more generally in all the branches of natural science, it is to Frenchmen, he says, that we owe the loftiest discoveries and speculations of human knowledge. Speaking elsewhere of Lavoisier: before him, Buckle claims, certain partial problems had been more or less clarified by English chemists whose experiments revealed the existence of previously unknown substances; but the still missing connection, the relating of scattered observations, what allowed chemistry to set itself up really as a science, and those perceptions which were later on developed by German chemists, were all given us by "the vast discoveries of Lavoisier"; and he adds: "The credit" (for these discoveries in chemistry) "is so obviously due to France that the whole system, though soon adopted in other countries, was known under the name of French Chemistry" (Vol. II, p. 300). Then Buckle quotes these lines from Thomson's *History of Chemistry*: "This new nomenclature (due, with the entire system on which it depends, to Lavoisier, Berthollet, de Morveau and Fourcroy) penetrated and won out in all the countries of Europe, despite the prejudices and the resistance it encountered everywhere." How can one fail to be touched by such tributes?

Does Buckle overestimate the importance of the role played by France in that epoch of intellectual development? I am not qualified to judge of this; but it strikes me as unbecoming for me, a Frenchman, when a foreigner praises my country, to reduce his praise and say: you are exaggerating. Yes, I read these praises with emotion and I shall be forgiven, at a time when we so greatly need comforting, for having quoted them at some length (Buckle develops them at much greater length still). I was diverted from this, at the beginning of March, by an article of Abel Bonnard entitled "Change in Epoch" which I read with just as great, but quite different, emotion. "The man of the eighteenth century," he says, "thinks as an idle man either because in fact he has no occupation or else because he gives so little of himself to the one he has that he draws none of his general ideas from it; hence the fewer things it embraces, the farther his thought is seen to spread out, and that very extension is in direct ratio to its emptiness." [55] Bonnard may well write subsequently and quite correctly: "There was many a man of noble birth in the seventeenth century who became passionately interested in philosophy, and the effect of this was to withdraw them from society; the men of noble birth in the following century, on the other hand, study only in order to shine in society." But, in the name of men of noble birth and their "itch" for knowledge, is it appropriate, I ask you, to condemn altogether an admirable and worthy effort, the fruitful curiosity of so many modest minds who gave French science at that time an unsurpassed brilliance and fame? Is it becoming to write, thinking only of the dissolute and frivolous nobles of the period: "even when men become enamored" (in the eighteenth century) "of a science, they do so not for the austere joys it eventually dispenses after long study but rather for the surprises and intoxications, the stimulating shocks it provokes at once, and at that time men study much more in order to make their heads swim than to fill their heads" — thus ignoring all the real investigators admired by Buckle and finding no one worth mentioning as eighteenth-century scholars but the ridiculous Duc d'Épernon, who serves as a travesty of them, "so smitten with surgery that he spent his time looking for people on whom to reveal" (he means "exercise") "his talents," overlooking so many authentic investigators whose patient research established the original bases of the natural sciences and of physiology?

"In order to make clearer what I am claiming," Bonnard writes in addition, "it is enough to note that the eternal truths of life to which every poet gives a new expression . . . are found neither in Hugo nor in Lamartine. . . ." Nonsense! But "I should be quite vexed," he has just said, "if anyone took what I am saying as an opinion; it is an observation that I am presenting in all its certainty and all its platitude." Then be vexed, Bonnard, but your "opinion" (for it is one though you object to this) I can in no wise share, however platitudinous your observation may be and however certain it may seem to you. Classical though my tastes may be, I cannot consider romanticism as if it had never existed, and I hold Lamartine and Hugo to be just as important representatives of France and of humanity as Mistral, whom you set up against them (and who has but one shortcoming: that he

---

[55] "It is because that unoccupied man does not even know how, in any particular regard, to work modestly . . ." I hesitate to set down the end of his sentence; it is revelatory, and when we read: "work modestly to maintain the order he enjoys," we understand at once that Bonnard is criticizing in the eighteenth century exactly what Buckle is praising: the spirit of inquiry, of research, and the very idea of progress. [A.]

doesn't write in our language); as "Joseph de Maistre and Nietzsche, Balzac and Gobineau, Proudhon and Péguy," whom you crown later on in a staggering honors-list. It seems to me, and the more precarious our present becomes, that the moment is ill chosen for such voluntary amputations and gratuitous disownings. On the contrary, I enjoy hearing Marcel Arland declare in his preface to a very recent anthology: [56] "French poetry . . . cannot be reduced to its oratorical beauty, to its power of incantation, to the splendor of its imagery, to the depth of its thought, or to the novelty and vigor of the emotions it expresses. This or that aspect, according to the epoch, may predominate in our poetry; but perhaps its noblest virtue lies in having given itself to each one in turn and united them, in its loftiest moments, in an almost miraculous equilibrium." Claiming to reduce France and her past and her culture to being, or having been, merely this or that strikes me as blasphemy. At present the important thing is to find out what we can save of France. Of all forms of love, love for one's country is surely the hardest to define. If there is but one way of dying for one's country, there are many ways of living for it, of loving it; and even mutually exclusive ways, as becomes clear in civil wars. Each of the parties that arise at such a time accuses the other, considering it as an enemy of the country. This involves no misunderstanding, but simply this: that each individual, according to his upbringing, tastes, interests, and favorite ideas, feels drawn to this or that part of the whole, exclusive of all the rest — to certain monuments of our history, to certain partial manifestations of our genius throughout history, or else to specific latent possibilities to which respect for tradition and for *Temporis acti* is opposed. Probably no country has offered a greater diversity of cultures, of aspirations, of tendencies, of manifestations, of creeds than ours. And this is indeed what constitutes her complex beauty. Who can say whether she is better represented by King or League, skepticism or belief, romanticism or classicism? And, more specifically in literature, whereas for many another country almost complete unanimity can be massed around Dante, Cervantes, Camoens, or Goethe, our admiration oscillates between Montaigne and Pascal, Ingres and Delacroix, Bossuet and Molière, Racine and Hugo, and today between Claudel and Valéry. Who would dare to state that our genius used itself up in forming a single one of them? More than any other country in Europe, our country had and cultivated a sense of dialogue (conversation, discussion, controversy, debate). Most likely on the approach of a common danger she can and must unite her energies in unanimity, as we have seen that she can do. But never, save for a short time and at her worst moments, has she listed altogether in

[56] *Anthology of French Poetry* (1941).

a single direction. I was wont to think and say this in peacetime; I think this just as vigorously today, and adverse circumstances have brought about no change. For, as Buckle most excellently says in his chapter on Spain (Vol. II, ch. viii): "Toward the end of the eighteenth century, the French invasion brought that unfortunate country every form of calamity and degradation. Yet it is essential to make a distinction. Calamities may be inflicted by others; but no nation can be degraded but by itself. A foreign nation can bring the horrors of invasion but nothing that need cause shame. For nations as for individuals, dishonor comes only from ceasing to remain faithful to oneself. . . . There is no material suffering from which one cannot rise provided one maintains that feeling of self-reliance, which is the spring and the source of real greatness."

1942

I open a new notebook to begin this new year, leaving the other but half filled. Wrote nothing further in it since tying myself down to those regular articles for the *Figaro,* lacking time and furthermore having no heart to write anything in it.

I have aged frightfully of late. It is as if I were getting away from myself. Oh, without any melancholy! It seems to me that I shall take leave of myself without regrets.

Catherine might have bound me to life; but she is interested only in herself — and that does not interest me.

I have again become interested in work and enjoy a semblance of happiness at my writing-table. My thought takes shape easily, so long as it is not profound; and in my articles I merely touch the surface of thoughts. I remain without opinion in the face of events, wondering at times whether I shall be able to find a place and a *raison d'être* in the new universe that is confusedly taking shape. This I believe: that it can have no relation to this farce of a "national revolution," which I cannot take seriously. The real heartbeats of France are hidden and cannot let themselves be heard. For the moment everything is but temporary outward show, boasting, and deceit. The soil is still too far from firm for anything to be built on it. Everything depends on . . .

It is almost midnight. I am sleepy. Let us put off till tomorrow the continuation of these ratiocinations.

I finish *Sartoris.*[1] Have begun to reread *Egmont* in a volume of Goethe lent by Theodor Wolf, whom I went to see this afternoon.

2 January

In what I wrote of Catherine I intended but very little censure. I am not displeased that that child should develop uncommonly and in a way that is rather baffling for those who are following her. She resembles me much too much not to force me to think that I was like what she is today and that I should have acted likewise without that great love which, almost at the outset of life, raised me so far above myself. But up to now she has shown no love or persistent attention but for herself, and if I add that her voice is getting beautiful and that, on certain days, she can be full of charm and grace, this is enough, in her eyes, to make her accept all the rest. Despite her egotism, she has always

---

[1] By William Faulkner.

shown an interest in others, and in a way of which I am particularly
appreciative: as a novelist, so to speak, and I think now: as an actress.

I had rejoiced immoderately over those lessons I was preparing
to give her in Nice, but I soon had to come down a peg. All her time
is taken up with other lessons (dancing, singing, elocution), which
merely direct her attention to herself. She never gets away from herself from morning to night, and even the little reading she does on the
outside interests her only in so far as she can bring it into some relation
with herself. I had been delighted to see her become enthusiastic
about some sonnets or other by Heredia; she said she wanted to know
others. I took pleasure in giving her *Les Trophées* in a very decently
bound copy I had found at Grasse. But her desire disappeared at once
and I don't believe she ever even opened the volume. I experienced
such disappointments with Marc; it was enough for something to come
from me for the curiosity he had evinced to die immediately. It is as if
first one and then the other had to defend himself against me. It is
better thus, I try to convince myself.

4 January

Now that my pen has almost lost its rust, I should be far better off
just to let it write away. For instance, in doing that preface for
Goethe's drama I write with ease and joy what comes to my mind; but
I am embarrassed by the mass of notes I took and now don't know how
to fit in. This labor of joining together is alone difficult; the thoughts,
once they have cooled off, are recalcitrant and resist the welding. One
no longer knows where to grasp them.

Certain natures, and their nobility can be recognized by this, are
more inclined to accept affliction than felicity.

5 January

Even though it was Sunday yesterday, I had worked more than
eight hours on my preface for Goethe and was about to get back to it
after dinner, but fear of thereby causing myself a sleepless night
hurled me into a neighboring movie-house. I did not stay long; the
theater was three-quarters empty and swept by frigid drafts. Barely
cured of a new cold, I am extremely vulnerable; hastened to get back
to shelter.

Regret at not having been able to see the beginning of a most interesting (German) documentary on the birds of a lake . . . in Pom-
erania, I suppose.

I again dreamed last night that at the piano I recovered the greatest nimbleness I had ever had. I was playing Chopin's first Étude in a

staggering way. Rather like a blind man dreaming that he had suddenly recovered his sight.

By the way, what can possibly be the dreams of a man born blind? I ought to say: of what, of what stuff, are they made?

Charming lunch at the Bussys'. Returned home, immediately afterward, to sleep an hour, but not enough to overcome a sluggishness that is disastrous for work. Nothing to do about it; and rather than spoil my preface, after a few vain attempts, went out again. In a less cold theater than yesterday's the same film on the birds was being shown, but again I missed the beginning. Followed by a long historical film on Ireland, made up of German propaganda and heavily vulgar, like everything that emanates from their dispensaries. But, eager to learn, I had already seen *Jud Suess, Magda, Marie Stuart, Sebastopol.*[2] This last was the only one that, accompanied by Élisabeth, I had seen to the end. Nothing is better designed to bring out the different levels of culture of our two nations. These films seem intended for a public that needs to have sentiments spelled out before it understands, and can read only capital letters at that. Everything is over-pointed up, the action, the dialogues, and the actors' manner of playing. It is decidedly unbearable. The English, it goes without saying, are treated to a real dose.

I should be greatly surprised if such films do not constitute a sort of reverse propaganda in France.

6 January

Not a day goes by without my opening the paper in the morning with the hope of finding news of some amazing event. . . . No, just the ordinary run of things: ships sunk, cities bombed or set on fire; people killed and wounded, always by the thousands . . . a monotonous daily refrain.

Charming lunch with Roger Martin du Gard, both of us as guests of Marc and Nadine, who were at their best. But my tenacious cold

---

2 Produced by the Reich Film Controller, Dr. Fritz Hippler, in 1940 and directed by Veit Harlan, *Jud Suess* (with the famous actor Werner Krauss in the title role) was a sensational anti-Semitic propaganda picture. To emphasize its importance, it was shown simultaneously in sixty-six Berlin theaters in December 1940. *Marie Stuart* (*Das Herz der Königin*) and *Magda* were both directed by Carl Froehlich, with the Swedish actress Zarah Leander in the principal role. *Magda* was based on Hermann Sudermann's naturalistic play *Heimat*. *Sebastopol* was an anti-Russian propaganda film of pseudo-documentary character.

deafens me to the point where I have trouble keeping up with the very interesting conversation.

After a session with the dentist I return to the hotel, where Roger soon joins me. Reading of the preface, at least of the first part. Excellent advice from Roger, who leaves me thoroughly bucked up.

After dinner Alexandre Bachrach, who has come with Bunin to Nice, comes in for a game of chess, the first one with him that I win since playing in Grasse.

I go to bed only after having read some hundred lines of the *Iphigenie auf Tauris.*[3]

After the *Iphigenie,* picked up Lessing's drama for *Emilia Galotti,* which I did not yet know. What I think of it? . . . I should have to make subtle distinctions. . . . Not in a mood for that. And now I want to go back to *Mina* — read at the time of Fräulein Siller, but I have too vague a recollection of it.

Man spricht selten von der Tugend, die man hat; aber desto öfter von der, die uns fehlt. (Lessing: *Mina,* Act II, scene 1.)[4]

30 January

The articles for the *Figaro* have taken all the time I did not give to reading. No desire to note anything in this notebook. The effort I made here to get interested in myself failed. And it's odd how prejudicial paper ruled in squares is to my thought, to my pleasure in writing. (But no other paper can be found today, in Nice at least.) It is so serious that I wonder if, with more pleasing sheets, I might not have continued to keep my journal and if its cessation is not due rather to that external cause, so petty. I have never written anything worth while at any time without enjoying the physical appearance of my writing. A bad pen is enough to hamper my style. . . .

I finished today *Hermann und Dorothea,* which began by disappointing me greatly, but which in its entirety will leave me with the memory of a work that is perfect of its kind, one of the happiest and most accomplished achievements of Goethe. It even seems to me that the tone rises from canto to canto in order to achieve toward the end a sort of half-homely, half-epic grandeur of a most peculiar type, which calmly touches the sublime and constantly escapes the banal while bordering on the prosaic. I don't know anything by Goethe that is more specifically German or that is more notably lacking in our literature. An exemplary book accessible to all ages, to all classes, and

---

[3] Goethe's tragedy, *Iphigenia in Tauris.*

[4] "One seldom speaks of the virtue one has; but much oftener of the virtue one lacks."

to all types of minds, worth consulting for its fine teaching and example. After it one no longer dares poke fun at edifying literature.

"Shall we always look for wit in the things that call for it least?"
(Racine to Boileau, letter dated 30 May without indication of year.)

1 February

Many ways of saying a thing; most often the best form is the one
that comes to mind at once. It is that spontaneous style that delights
us in Stendhal. It always seems that one is taking his thought by surprise as it jumps out of bed before dressing. But there are other ways
of writing well. I do not like thought to bedeck itself, but rather to
concentrate and stiffen itself; the manner of Montesquieu and of
Tacitus. Following Dorothy Bussy's example, I launch into the *Life
of Agricola*. Each sentence is full, heavy, taut. I tarry to weigh every
word; they fill my heart and mouth. At the outset I am seized. What
authority! How much I prefer that sort of wild austerity to grace! I
took the book with me; I read it while walking and, without exhausting its bitter essence, ruminate one of those vigorous maxims in which
the will stiffens:

"*Memoriam quoque ipsam cum voce perdidissemus, si tam in nos-
tra potestate esset oblivisci quam tacere.*"

"*Subit quippe etiam ipsius inertiæ dulcedo, et invisa primo desidia
postremo amatur.*" [5]

6 February

Last night at the movies. The French newsreels fill one's heart
with tears and make one blush. It seems as if the wine of defeat has
intoxicated us; never have we shown ourselves to be prouder than now
that there is so little reason to be. All claims to past fame are spread
out on the screen in an attempt to make the present share in its brilliance. People congratulate, admire themselves, going into raptures
over the splendor and fragile vastness of our "Empire." It is enough to
make one weep.

And, as a conclusion, a mighty row about the bicycle race called
"Tour de France." on which, if you believe them, the entire universe
has its eyes trained. "The most important in the world." Just think: a
five-thousand-kilometer race! And the reproduction "by Belinogram"

---

[5] "We should have lost memory as well as voice, had it been as easy to
forget as to keep silence."

"Besides, the charm of indolence steals over us, and the idleness which at
first we loathed we afterwards love." (Translated by Alfred John Church and
William Jackson Brodribb.)

(that "French invention") of the winner's photo in the newspapers of the world. Oh, by heaven, Germany can well afford to leave us this bauble, if we are satisfied with it!

Beside this a German documentary on radium, which is excellent and interests me particularly since I have just read from cover to cover (without, moreover, understanding much, but with uninterrupted amazement) Gaston Dupuy's little book on radioactivity.[6]

But what is that compared to the glorious "Tour de France"? With what glory, alas, the people are forced to be satisfied today! (I am well aware that this is merely movie propaganda.) And even if "all-round athletes" were involved! But no, France was inferior in all the Olympic competitions; the only laurels she won came from a single event: the bicycle race!

7 February

Texts are not wanting in my *Journal* to show that at the time of the first war I very clearly understood what a Franco-German collaboration might be.[7] I actually longed for such collaboration at a time when it was possible without dishonor. At that time it seemed antipatriotic to think of it. It would have been wise and noble to suggest it to Germany after our victory. Today I have reached the point of not knowing what solution of the present conflict would be least ruinous for France, but I hold the collaboration Germany is offering us as a piece of trickery wholly to her advantage, of which she will be able to make capital when the time comes. There is no question whatever of her helping us to make the most of our good qualities and virtues, but rather of stifling them; and the most lamentable thing about it is seeing France herself lend a hand and help in this.

Those grandiloquent and ridiculous remarks that always make a hit with us (ah, we shall never correct ourselves!). This morning the papers quote with admiration these "sublime words" of M. Henriot in his lecture of yesterday: "If France were to die, all the nations assembled could not raise her coffin." The image is, no doubt, flattering: all those nations assembled for a funeral. No, it all takes place in silence; and since there is no coffin, there can be no question of raising it. The world simply goes on, disregarding. . . .

And now that France is diminished, that she is living solely on hopes and with a precarious and, as it were, problematic existence, there is serious talk of rebaptizing her, of calling her the French Empire! The more one loses footing, the higher one holds up one's head.

---

[6] *Radium et radioactivité*, published by Presses Universitaires in 1941, is a treatise of but 127 pages.

[7] See *The Journals of André Gide*, Vol. II, pp. 113, 213–14, 282–4; Vol. III, pp. 142–3.

National self-esteem takes refuge in those colonies which, even yesterday, when our country was intact, seemed very unwisely spread
out for her size and which tomorrow, like a superstructure out of all proportion, may well make her topple on her side like the *Normandie*.[8]

But will not England, likewise and before us, lose one after the
other her overseas possessions, which constituted her prestige and
glory? After Singapore, the impregnable, shall we not soon see India
and then Egypt escape her? . . .

15 February

I have spent two hours trying to write a reply to Gillouin's accusations in the *Journal de Genève* (No. 33) of the first of February.[9] But
Roger M. du G., to whom I show that article and this outline of a
reply, points out something I hadn't noticed: Gillouin implies that
that "young man of great promise" for whose suicide Gillouin claims
me to be responsible (this is an old story served up again) had presumably killed himself not merely after having read my books, but
even under my direct influence; that frequenting me perverted him,
and even that I directly "depraved" him.

From beginning to end that story is a pure (or impure) invention,
what the English call "a forgery." [10] I know it only through Gillouin,
through Camille Mauclair, and through a vengeful pamphlet entitled
An Evildoer (I am the evildoer), prefaced by "Mgr de Beaumont, fortunately deceased," as it was worded. That avowed apocrypha, attributed to the author of the *Mandement portant condamnation du livre
qui a pour titre Émile (1772)*,[11] should have sufficed to put people on
guard and to keep them from believing it.

---

[8] On 9 February 1942 the greatest ship of the French Line, the *Normandie*, caught on fire at her pier in New York and toppled over on her
side. This entry could not, therefore, have been made on 7 February.

[9] René Gillouin's article on the first page of the Sunday supplement of
the *Journal de Genève*, No. 33, for 7–8 February 1942, was entitled: "Re-
sponsibilities of Writers and Artists." While also scolding Aristide Briand
for his statement on divorce, Léon Blum for his book on marriage, and Jean
Cocteau for his play *Les Parents terribles*, Gillouin directs his attack chiefly
at Gide: "I received a few years ago, and many other writers must have received likewise, a letter in which a father related with a sorrow all the more
convincing for being restrained how his son, a young man of great promise,
had been perverted, dissipated, and finally led to suicide by the influence
of André Gide. To just what extent was André Gide responsible for the
death of that adolescent (and for the demoralization, at the very least, of
many others)? God alone knows."

[10] The words in quotation marks appear in English in the original.

[11] *Pastoral Letter Condemning the Book Entitled Émile. L'Émile* is Rousseau's treatise on education.

Should I cite in return the testimony of those I have saved from despair, of those already close to suicide? . . . What's the use? Gillouin will not let himself be convinced. He will say, if that young suicide exists only in the imagination of Mgr de Beaumont and of Mauclair:

"If it is not he, it must be his brother." [12]

It is better not to start a discussion that I could not carry on to the end and in which the opponent has made up his mind in advance to lay the blame on me.

22 February

That extreme contentment that Chateaubriand's style provides when he is at his best I have never felt more keenly than in his *Vie de Rancé*, the first chapter of which I finish with rapture.[13]

Did Retz himself ever achieve so lively and delightful a style with secret, almost musical overtones that prolong the sentence well beyond the mind's satisfaction? On reading Chateaubriand how can one fail to think of Barrès, who is never so good as when most recalling him?

Verify one's admirations. Was it really so remarkable? How much of it was amazement? Now that this book has ceased to surprise us, let us go back to it. On rereading certain books I am amazed at my original amazement. I am surprised not to have been sufficiently struck at first by certain other things.

The moment when one begins to detach oneself somewhat, when one ceases to cling so firmly to the branch. Soon one will be ready to pick. Is it so hard to die as people think? Doubtless one has only to let oneself go; the mistake lies in hanging on too much to life.

Those who protest most against Rousseau's influence and point out how pernicious it is are the very ones who are most shocked that he should have turned over his offspring to a foundling home. On the contrary, they ought to congratulate him on this, judging that Rousseau never did anything wiser; if indeed his influence was pernicious . . . if indeed he ever had any children.

----

[12] In La Fontaine's fable of *The Wolf and the Lamb* (I, 10) the lamb answers the wolf's accusation of having spoken ill of the wolf last year by pointing out that he is only a few months old; to this the wolf replies: "If it was not you, it must have been your brother."

[13] *Life of Rancé* (1844), the reformer of the Trappist Order.

It is obviously Béranger that Chateaubriand means when he writes: "These lines, which are not so good as those of our great song-writer, but which already marked out the path by which France was to reach an immortality that belongs only to her" (*Vie de Rancé*, chapter iv, p. 195).

13 March

Rancé and his monstrous standards. "That passionate hatred of life," as Chateaubriand says, quoting him thus: "God's intention, when he gives us enjoyment of light, is to deprive us of it." Holy absurdity! He might just as well say: "When God deprives us of light, this is to give us enjoyment of it."

"We live in order to die." Rancé might say just as well and better: we die in order to live. Oh, how willingly I subscribe to this remark of Chateaubriand: "Rancé would deserve to be expelled from the human race," without the restriction and the "if" that he adds!

And "in all his thoughts . . . are found merely repetitions of the same idea." Immediately afterward Chateaubriand holds forth on Voltaire!

3 April

Les Fleurs de Tarbes could or ought to serve as a preface to Jean Meckert's astounding book.[14]

10 April

There was a time when, painfully tormented and plagued by desire, I used to pray for the time when the flesh, subjugated, would let me give myself completely to . . . But give oneself to what? To art? To "pure" thought? To God? What ignorance! What madness! This was tantamount to believing that the flame will shine brighter from the lamp that has run out of oil. Abstract, my very thought goes out; even today it is the carnal in me that feeds it, and now I pray: may I remain carnal and full of desire unto death!

I have always thought that we raise children badly in France, and perhaps this is the chief thing of which I accuse families.

Public garden looted. No guard. The children trample the lawns, break the branches of trees, strip flowering bushes of their buds. And not a parent to put a stop to this absurd havoc, which they don't even much enjoy. It is merely a matter of destroying and of keeping from anyone what ought to belong to all. Is this a question of the French

[14] A powerful first novel of the proletariat, *Les Coups* (*The Blows*), had appeared in 1941 and brought Meckert to Gide's attention.

temperament? Or merely, as I should prefer, of upbringing? Nation unworthy of the liberty they claim; makes one constantly and everywhere long for policemen, keepers of the peace and of order, fences, and "keep off" signs.

Yesterday Catherine announced to me the departure of her singing teacher. I was expecting and hoping that she would offer me those newly free hours which I should be so happy to devote to those lessons she ceased to ask of me for lack of time, in which I was getting ready to give her the best of me.

That she did not ask me to take them back, is not this a clear sign that those lessons did not really interest her? She probably did not see the advantage she could get from them. I was the one who put forth the whole effort of attention, not she, who merely lent herself. . . . I should have been so able and so eager to teach her to recite poetry.

Now she is quite at loose ends, readily returning to that soft state of idleness in which she has always lived until now, not knowing how to create obligations and duties for herself. Yet she has never been more charming, and particularly to me. But I shall go away from her without regret, sadly noting how badly and how little she makes use of my devotion for her.

Oh, if only she could say to me: "I now have some free time; do you want us to make the best of it?" What a joy it would be, it would have been, for me to help her! And as a result I should have no other desire than to remain with her.

From the moment when I realized and convinced myself that *man is responsible for God* . . .

And the wonderful thing is that by believing he was saving humanity Christ did actually save it.

Likewise it may be said that prayer creates God.

It is good to let the child think that God sees him, for he must act as if within the sight of God and make of that his *conscience*.

The considerable number of things I have not said because they seemed to me too obvious, too much of the type that "goes without saying" and not worth saying. . . . And yet when one finally lets oneself go, or forces oneself, to write them, one is amazed to see how many people are still surprised by them and ready to declare that one has never written anything more remarkable.

As I open my *Journal*, my eyes fall on this passage in which I already said (23 August 1926): "The most important things to say are those which often I did not think necessary to say — because they seemed to me too obvious." [15]

It is independently of our will that ideas take shape in us and develop. There exists for them a sort of "struggle for life," [16] of survival of the fittest, and some of them die of exhaustion. The sturdiest are those that feed, not on abstraction, but on life; they are also the ones that are hardest to formulate.

The history of an idea would be interesting to write. It may also be that an idea dies. Yes, it would be a fine subject: the birth, life, and death of an idea. If only I could count on enough time to write it. . . .

11 April

Where had I got the idea that it was all over, that spring had ceased to interest me and would never seize hold of me again? For days now, since the weather has become fine again and the air is warm, I feel that I have the soul of a migratory bird and think only of setting out. I book a berth on the ship leaving Marseille for Tunis on 2 May. Ah, why am I not already there! Everything will have begun already. Again I am going to miss the Overture.

I note in the review *Foreign Affairs* (issue of January 1942), which my new friend Keeler Faus of the U.S. Embassy lends me, as a footnote to a long article "Russia and Germany," signed X.:

"General Karl Adolf Maximilian Hoffmann was one of the greatest German General Staff officers in the last war. . . . His mother was descended from the Du Buisson family. Like him, and like the great Moltke, nearly all the great German army leaders of the past hundred years, with the characteristic exception of Ludendorff, have had some Huguenot ancestry." [17]

Has a list ever been drawn up of the exiled families, of the gifts that France made to foreign countries through the Revocation of the Edict of Nantes?

5 a.m., 5 May

The *Chanzy* left Marseille yesterday at about 11 a.m. I spent almost the whole day lying down; an icy wind was plowing up the sea, which calmed down toward evening and I was able to dine without too much discomfort. Since midnight one can't help wondering if we are moving; one has to be attentive to feel the slight vibration of the engines. The moon still three-quarters full. To the east a few intermittent lighthouses; we must be passing the Balearic Islands. No one on deck. I

---

[15] See *The Journals of André Gide*, Vol. II, p. 387.

[16] In English in the original.

[17] Quoted in English in the original.

take some calomel because my gall-bladder hurts. Lord, how tired I
was yesterday! . . . Let's go back to bed. . . .

10 o'clock

Had coffee at about nine. I had kept a piece of Cantal cheese from
last night's dinner. All the bread one can eat, or almost. The rather
heavy swell had reduced the number of diners; the able-bodied enjoyed what was intended for the absent ones. Already at lunch a much
more abundant fare than for a long time now on land. Animal delight
in at last being able to eat one's fill. I very much need to build myself
up. The last days in Marseille did me in. So many hours chasing from
office to office to get the necessary visas, identification marks and
stamps; had I been alone, I believe I should have given up. But Ballard,
the ever obliging, accompanied me everywhere, kept an eye on me,
palliated my lapses, omissions, or distractions. At the last moment, after
our farewells, he came back to remind me that I had forgotten to check
my trunk: I have to hurry back to the pier and chase from one fantastic
place to another. All very Kafka. I keep thinking of *The Trial*. Feeling
of not yet "having put everything in order." If one had to go through
so many formalities to die. . . . Material for a wonderful tale. "You
can't go away *like that*." . . . But at least then one has no right to take
anything along. That would be one of the finest chapters of the book:
detachment. Roger Martin du Gard is amazed that death, the idea of
death, causes me so little worry. Were it not for apprehension of the
final pangs (perhaps, after all, less dreadful than they seem from a
distance), I really believe I am rather soberly resigned. I have had my
fill on this earth. A certain happy equilibrium is worked out and one
reaches the end of the banquet without much wanting it to go on
longer. Others are waiting for one's place; it is their turn. . . .

I reproach myself for not having sent an interzone card to Jeannie
Valéry from Marseille to tell her at once my delight in seeing Paul
again, more gallant, more real, more charming than ever.[18] And never
have my friendship and admiration for that incomparable personality
seemed to me keener and more unqualified. I experience nothing but
joy in noting his incontrovertible superiority and his widespread influence, which are tempered by the most charming graciousness. I
hold myself to be but very little in comparison with him, but have
learned not to suffer from this. He no longer stands in my way; I have
accomplished my work on a different plane from his — which I understand too well and admire too much not to admit that that work of
mine has no place in his system and no value in his eyes. He is right,

---

[18] Correspondence between the so-called "free zone" and the "occupied
zone" of France was then limited to postcards.

and my friendship even approves him for not "considering" me. His marvelous intelligence, though with nothing inhuman about it, owes it to itself to be strict and exclusive. In comparison with which I seem to myself to be wallowing in approximation. The most wonderful thing is that his mind, without abandoning any of its severity, has managed to preserve all its poetic value, managed to contribute to poetic creation that very severity which might have been thought hostile to art and which, on the contrary, makes of Valéry's art such a consummate marvel. I admire the unflinching direction and victorious persistence of his effort. No one in our time has more effectively or more consistently aided intellectual progress; no one could more legitimately write:

> I know where I am going
> And want to lead you there,[19]

nor was capable of leading so far.

3 p.m.

But, led by Valéry, I should no longer have dared to write. It was my awareness of this that so greatly and for so long stood in my way. I overcame this and went on.

The *Chanzy* is noiselessly continuing its calm progress. The sea is calm. I have slept.

I cannot succeed in getting involved in *The Bishop Murder Case* by S. S. Van Dine (book lent in Marseille by Mme Ballard); no interest, up to now, but that of a well-constructed clockwork. I rest myself from it with *L'Homme devant la science* by Lecomte du Noüy.[20] I read in it: "If mathematics achieve truth, says Vico, this is because the mind makes mathematics: the criterion of truth lies hence in being made: The true is what one makes." This is indeed what allows man to believe in God.

I did well to change notebooks; what kept me from keeping my journal was in great part the square-ruled pages of the other one. Quite surprised on opening this one to find a few pages that strike me as very ordinary as I reread them, which I had forgotten to the point of not recognizing them at all or having any idea as to when I might have

---

[19] The lines:

> *Je sais où je vais,*
> *Je t'y veux conduire,*

are from Valéry's poem, *L'Insinuant.* Gide, quoting from memory, gives them as:

> *Je sais où je vais*
> *Laisse-toi conduire.*

See *The Journals of André Gide,* Vol. III, p. 80, where Gide quotes from the same poem.

[20] This book was published in English in 1947 as *Human Destiny.*

written them. I do not tear them up, out of superstition: fear of bringing the notebook bad luck.[21]

8.30 p.m.

The sun first disappeared behind a thick mass of clouds and I thought it was all over; but it reappeared altogether just above the water, red and dull, so that the eye could watch it sinking whole into the sea.

9 a.m., 5 May

Slight swell. On awakening, Africa is in sight, very close. Then it withdraws and the coastline recedes.

Another great delight in Marseille was the meeting with Jean-Louis Barrault. Marc, who was awaiting me when the train from Nice got in, had taken me to dinner with him and Madeleine Renaud the first evening in a cheap little restaurant near the station, where Barrault ate his meal in a hurry before going to the radio station where he was to read some scenes from *Le Soulier de satin*.[22] Wonderful face instinct with enthusiasm, passion, genius. In his company Madeleine Renaud,

---

[21] Then one of those inner voices that speak out during insomnia, which one would like not to hear but cannot keep from listening to, began:

Realize that it is not a matter of conquests and cease likening to other events in history what has never before been seen. Realize that what the utopians dream of, I do. I have merely the life-span of a single man in which to act. I do not fear using force, even of the most brutal kind, to achieve at once by compulsion what they vainly expect from the good will of others. Good or ill, no will matters; I mean: matters in opposition to mine. I am not a dreamer; I am a realizer. He who has force on his side can override everything. Decency, morality, pity, justice, are merely empty words to me. No consideration, save of a practical sort, stops me. What I intend to achieve your timid imagination cannot even glimpse. It was thought that this was the spreading out of my people because in the beginning I spoke of their vital space; but nothing less than the welfare of humanity is involved. That welfare can be realized only after all things, all peoples, all moral values, are in place, all human activities ordered and subordinated. So long as humanity remains what it still is, the freedom that is granted to men, as you are well aware, will lead not to harmony but to disorder. It is not enough for me to restrict that freedom; I must suppress it altogether. What matters the sacrifice of a few million abject creatures, totally incapable of attaining even the most modest happiness by themselves? This holocaust is necessary to allow us to produce, on this miserable wreckage, a healthy, strong, and joyful race. With such a stake the game is worth playing, don't you think? It is worth the trouble, and even a very considerable trouble. [A.]

[22] Claudel's play, *The Satin Slipper*, which Barrault later staged at the Comédie-Française.

with charming modesty, remains in the background. Neither in him nor in her am I aware of any of the actor's usual unbearable shortcomings. Talented enough to remain simple.

I saw both of them again the day before leaving, lunching with them at their invitation in a very good restaurant on the square where the wide avenue du Prado begins. Barrault urges me insistently to finish my translation of *Hamlet* for him; and I have such confidence in his advice that I should like to get to work at once.[23] I am much pleased to learn that he and Sartre are close friends. In their company, through a keen personal affection, I feel my hopes rejuvenated.

It is good to be able to direct one's admiration toward the future. It would be a source of despair if one had to be satisfied with this renaissance commissioned by order that is offered us today, this mediocrity so willingly accepted.

"That was enough to be aware," is very bad syntax. (The lack of logic that fails to notice the change in subject.) Same type of error: "Mme Britan was enticed out of her house and led to the pile of rubbish *to kill her there.*" (*Un Crime parfait*, p. 119.)

6 May

Sleepless night despite the codoforme and the gardenal.[24] Calm sea. One does not even feel the vibration of the engines; one even doubts at moments that we are moving. This is partly because we are moving very slowly. I get up six times during the night. The moon is in its last quarter; the sky is clear.

The call at Bône was disappointing. The mosaics of Hippo are covered up for fear of bombs. I believe, moreover, that the finest ones have been moved to the Algiers museum.

8.30 a.m.

We are passing Sidi-bou-Saïd. The sea was covered, in the early morning, with those odd little jellyfish that were washed up last year on the beaches of La Croix and the Jouan gulf. We are to reach Tunis in an hour.[25]

---

[23] André Gide's translation of the first act of *Hamlet* had appeared in the Franco-American review *Échanges* in December 1929.

[24] These are French pharmaceutical products, *codoforme* being tablets composed of codeine, aconite, and belladonna, which dissolve in the intestine rather than in the stomach, and *gardenal* being a sedative used to calm spasms, itchings, convulsions, headaches, etc.

[25] This is the end of the *Journal 1939–1942*, published in Paris by Librairie Gallimard in 1946. That edition was preceded by the following note:

"Incomplete editions of this *Journal* have appeared in New York (Schif-

Tunis, 7 May

The packages of tobacco I owe to the generosity of American friends
cause a certain amount of trouble with the customs, and the most
obliging Tournier arrives a bit too late to save me. Lunch at the restaurant of the Tunisia-Palace. Lyric voracity. Ten varieties of hors-d'œuvre
(I counted them!). Everything strikes me as good beyond all hope
after the near-fast of Nice. I devour in an unbelievable way, then go
and sleep for two hours.

4 o'clock

Last night I had gone to pick up Tournier and go with him to a
rather dull lecture by young Professor Astre: "Defense of the Novel."
Sound, but hardly original reflections designed for a not very alert
public. Dinner in the manner of Giono, then long walk along the darkened avenue de France.

This morning I was a half-hour ahead of time at the appointment
with Tournier to accompany him to the Assize Court where he is serving as a juror. Acquittal of an Arab who had unintentionally committed
murder. A rather uninteresting case. Visit to the *souks,* then to the
public library, remarkably well stocked and marked bv perfect order
throughout.

8 May

I give up keeping this insipid report. I might as well set down the
menus of my meals. No interest. It would be better to give my attention to the article for the *Figaro* and try to finish it successfully.

10 May

In a new set, it is the same act of the same play continuing. I am
no longer paying attention. It is already some time since I have ceased
to. I am merely occupying the seat of someone who is taken for me.

15 May

With great difficulty I have managed to put together (but how
well!) a new article for the *Figaro,* about Joyce, Paulhan, and Meckert,

---

frin, 15 June 1944), in Algiers (Charlot, 30 September 1944), and in Switzerland (Éditions du Haut-Pays, 5 April 1945), preceded by a foreword (see
Appendix I).

"Extracts had been previously published by the review *L'Arche,* which
was then appearing in Algiers. We have thought it interesting to reproduce
an echo of the violent reactions they immediately aroused (see Appendixes
II and III)."

The Appendixes will be found on pp. 307–10.

whose novel *Les Coups* had held my attention.[26] I am so far from satisfied with the article that I join to it a letter inviting Brisson to refuse it, if he considers it too ordinary, without any fear of hurting me. The letter will probably strike him as pure affectation; for, however ordinary it may be, this article is still doubtless better than many others signed with the best-known names; but I am less interested in comparing myself with others than with myself, with what I am capable of writing on my best days. Were I X., Y., or Z., I should not have been proud of certain articles. This is the great vice of journalism: forcing one to write when one has no inclination to do so. One is uninspired; the atmosphere is heavy; one's pen scratches; one's thought is involved and the style amorphous. . . . But the article is promised and the newspaper expects it. . . . Hence one writes anyway, though annoyed with oneself for doing so, feeling that it is no good. . . . Then there are always people to tell you that you have never written anything better.

The Kreutzer Sonata recorded by Thibaud and Cortot. A series of false starts and pauses (in the first movement at least). Too many nuances. One would like to have the whole composition swept along by a demoniacal impulse that is not constantly dying in one quarter to start up in another. I am saying this of the interpretation; as for the text itself, I find much rhetoric in it (in the Concerto in D for violin even more!), oratorical pathos, and "just see how I am panting!" School of Pergamo.

The wonderful toccata by Bach played by the Philadelphia orchestra, though written for the organ; but I prefer it on the piano, where the different parts stand out better. It does not seem to me that Bach's music has much to gain from the coloration the orchestra gives it, however well it may be applied (as it is here), which tends to remove (or to hide) that almost mathematical necessity toward which the music tends. This amounts to humanizing it excessively. The music triumphs over that attempt, to be sure; and it may be said that if Bach had known at his time the resources of the modern orchestra, he

---

[26] The article appeared in two installments in the *Figaro* for 30 May and 2 June 1942 under the title *"Aux grands mots les petits remèdes"* ("Little Remedies for Big Words"), which is a pun on the proverb: *"Aux grands maux les grands remèdes"* ("Drastic Remedies for Drastic Ills"). In the form of an imaginary interview, the article treats James Joyce's deformation of words, apropos of Louis Gillet's book on Joyce, Meckert's opposition to ready-made expression and thought, and Paulhan's treatise on rhetoric. Though it appeared in the series of *Interviews imaginaires* in the *Figaro*, the article has not been reprinted in any volume by Gide.

would have taken advantage of them, as he did of the surprising sonorities of certain instruments in the Brandenburg Concertos for instance. But he did not do so, and there is a certain element of treason in bringing out and emphasizing the latent harmonic or melodic possibilities (as Gounod did for the first Prelude of the *Well-Tempered Clavichord*). After this emotional humanization I should like to hear again, in all the abstraction of a blueprint, that celestial edifice which, it seems, can be brought closer to man only by taking it farther from God.

22 May

People then began to understand that certain actors in this enormous drama played their role rather badly and had, after all, hardly studied it at all. Others, on the other hand, knew theirs perfectly and played it up to such an extent that their role seemed to dominate the whole play, so that the play was, as it were, thrown off balance. For the moment they alone could be heard. The other actors seemed to improvise, and this was so bad that at moments the play became incomprehensible; as it sometimes happens for one of our classical tragedies when, for some reason or other, an outstanding actor takes on a minor role, which should remain secondary. . . .

X. asks me: "Don't you understand that everything that is now taking place is but one more scene of the great drama of the *class struggle*? . . ." And this in the same tone as if he had said: "Don't you see that all this is, after all, merely a 'solar myth'?" For a long time people thought they could explain in this way the Greek and all other mythologies. Pierre Laurens used to call them scholars' myths.

2 June

"*Non erat exitus.*" This remark of St. Augustine (quoted by Merezhkovski in his *Calvin*, page 28, note 51) is to serve as an epigraph to the dialogue with Dædalus in my *Vie de Thésée.*[27]

Sidi-bou-Saïd

As soon as I had realized that God was not yet but was becoming and that his becoming depended on each one of us, a moral sense was restored in me. No impiety or presumption in this thought, for I was convinced at one and the same time that God was achieved only by man and through man, but that if man led to God, creation, in order to lead to man, started from God; so that the divine had its place at both ends, at the start and at the point of arrival, and that the start had

---

[27] "There was no way out." Gide did not use this quotation in the finished version of his *Theseus* (1946).

been solely in order to arrive at God. This bivalvular thought reassured me and I was unwilling to dissociate one from the other: God creating man in order to be created by him; God the end of man; chaos raised up by God to the level of man and then man raising himself up to the level of God. To accept but one of them: what fear, what obligation! To accept but the other: what self-satisfaction! It ceased to be a matter of obeying God, but rather of instilling life into him, of falling in love with him, of demanding him of oneself through love and of achieving him through virtue.

8 June

Science, to be sure, progresses only by everywhere substituting the *how* for the *why*. But however remote it may be, there is always a point at which the two interrogations meet and fuse. To achieve man . . . billions of centuries would not have sufficed if chance alone had contributed. However anti-finalist one may or can be, one encounters here something unacceptable, unthinkable; and the mind is forced to admit a propensity, an inclination encouraging the groping, vague, and unconscious progress of matter toward life and consciousness; then, through man, toward God.

9 June

But how slow God is in becoming! . . .

La Marsa, 12 June

The time is approaching, and I feel it quite close, when I shall have to say: I must give up.

The absurdity of all that is maddening. It is enough to make one believe that civilization, our Western civilization, will never recover from it. . . . The fact that that collaboration with Germany, so desirable and so much desired by us at a time when the majority, when public opinion, considered it impious (I mean in 1918), should now be proposed to us, imposed on us by the very ones who once considered it unthinkable; that it should become for us a sign of defeat, a mark of submission, abdication, and abjuration . . . torments one's conscience, or mine at least.

I do not believe in *Liberty* (we are dying of its idolatrous cult) and am ready to accept many a constraint; but I cannot bow before certain iniquitous decisions, give even a tacit consent to certain abominations.

Sidi-bou-Saïd, 12 June

Utter abjection the last few days, but happy to think that it is due solely to the sunstroke I got on the beach of La Marsa during an exciting game of chess with Mme Ragu. Incapable of anything but smoking and wallowing in dejection. Strange country where, as soon as one ceases to be too hot, one shivers. Yet I have managed to read, with a surprise that is not far from admiration, Dashiell Hammett's *Red Harvest* (as a substitute for *The Glass Key*, so strongly recommended by Malraux, but which I cannot find anywhere).

22 June

The trunks of these palm trees seem thick only because they are enveloped in the truncated ends of their dead palms. Excellent image applicable to certain minds.

I have ceased to push myself much to work, aware of writing nothing worth while. Are there still things for me to say? A work of art to achieve? . . . What can I possibly be good for henceforth? What still lies in store for me?

My thoughts escape me like spaghetti slipping off both sides of the fork.

Some Arab children have made a plaything of a little bird. They are dragging it along on a string attached to one leg and are amused by the useless efforts the bird occasionally makes to get away. I hesitate to take it away from them; but the half-dead bird cannot survive; the only point would be to finish it off as quickly as possible, sparing it a longer agony. And I wonder what a sorry "image" of the world can have been formed by this starling fallen from the nest, during this brief span of suffering and jostling? . . .

25 June

In a closet on the ground floor of the Reymonds' villa I discover a very well-set-up library. I take from it a volume of Léon Bloy (sixth and last volume of his *Journal*) [28] and at the same time, by way of contrast, Voltaire's *Dictionnaire philosophique,* where I read at once, with an often very keen satisfaction, a number of very good articles. Struck particularly by the one on Ravaillac, in dialogue form.

1 July

"Just when and from what moment onward will you deign to admit that an adversary who constantly and in all domains reveals so flagrant a superiority deserves to win out?"

---

[28] The last volume of the *Journal* kept by the Catholic writer Léon Bloy is entitled *La Porte des humbles* (*The Gate of the Humble*) and covers the years 1915–17. .

"But then this is the end of freedom of thought. . . ."

"Will *you* be able to carry your liberalism to the point of allowing me to think this freely?"

"To think what?"

"That the path pointed out to us as the most desirable by good Father X., for instance (whom I love and venerate), aiming to restore in us a feeling for the sacred and to obtain from us an intellectual submission, without inquiry or verification, to truths recognized in advance and beyond discussion — that that path is as dangerous for the mind as the path of Hitlerism, to which it is opposed, and perhaps even more dangerous, and I shall shortly tell you why. It is in the name of those accepted and indisputable truths that the Church once condemned Galileo and that tomorrow . . . Does the whole effort of a Descartes, of a Montaigne even, have to be repeated? People had ceased to realize just how and why that effort had been so important, so emancipatory. Despotism can be opposed only by another despotism, to be sure, and it is an easy matter for Father X. to maintain that it is better to submit to God than to a man; but, for my part, I can see on both sides nothing but an abdication of the reason. In order to escape a very obvious danger, we hurl ourselves toward another, more subtle and not yet obvious, but which tomorrow will only be the more dreadful. And thus it is that the seemingly most solidly established civilizations collapse, in a way that soon ceases to be comprehensible. As for ours, a few years earlier we should not have thought it possible; and even today very rare are those who recognize in this so-called recovery and pseudo-revival of France, in this return to the past, in this 'withdrawal to one's minima,' as Barrès used to say, the most tragic result of our defeat, the true disaster: almost unintentional and half-unconscious relinquishment, by the best, of the possessions acquired most slowly and with the greatest difficulty, the hardest to appreciate and the rarest of all. . . .

"I admire martyrs. I admire all those who are able to suffer and die, whatever may be the religion for which they do so. But even if you were to convince me, dear Father X., that nothing can resist Hitlerism but Faith, I should still see less spiritual danger in accepting despotism than in that form of resistance, considering any subordination of the mind more harmful to the interests of the mind than a yielding to force, since force at least in no way commits or compromises the mind."

"Yet if it is in the name of Faith, through Faith, that we succeed in driving the enemy out of France . . ."

"I should indeed applaud the remedy by which we had overcome a great malady. But subsequently how much time and vigilance and effort should we need in order, as Sainte-Beuve said, to 'cure us of the remedy' "?

6 July

Reread with the keenest interest the two *Henry IV's* and *Henry V*
of Shakespeare (read at Saint-Louis in Senegal, but I did not remember them sufficiently); *The Way of the Lancer* by Boleslavki (excellently translated, it seems to me); I have on my table the *Mémoires* of
Rœderer [29] and a typescript of Simenon's *Pedigree,* plus a huge novel
in manuscript by Amrouche's sister. I should like, however, not to leave
Shakespeare before having read also the fifteen acts of *Henry VI* and
Richard II, with which I should have begun.

10 July

This morning, awakening in a thick fog. Sidi-bou-Saïd is bathed in
a fluid, nacreous, sedative milk that is almost cool, a contrast to the
heaviness of the last few days. One might have thought one was in
the Congo. I went out into the garden; the leaves, withered by yesterday's sirocco, are breathing again and dripping. Only the fore-
ground is visible: a few cypresses and the white walls of the nearest
Arab houses, which seem to melt in that silvery vapor. Everything is
soft. The imagination plunges into space and reconstructs with complete liberty a marvelous landscape, as it does with feminine veils.

Around nine o'clock the fog burns off; reality emerges; everything
becomes sharp and hard. Heat settles down; the sun reigns supreme,
and in the vast, reclaimed sky nothing but an ugly broad band, black-
ish and horizontal and looking like a half-erased line in a charcoal
drawing, spread over the entire breadth of the sky, soils the azure
purity. This is the smoke from the electric power-house at La Goulette,
which is now burning alfa for want of other fuel. It encumbers the sky
with its lament.

12 July

The most fragile part of me, and the one that has aged most, is my
voice, that voice which even about ten years ago was still strong,
supple, modulated — that is, capable of moving from the grave to the
sharp as I wished — a voice over which I had complete mastery and
could play as an actor does, which I had, moreover, greatly exercised
through frequent readings to a small, family audience and the habit I
had adopted of reciting poetry while walking. Above all, it was tuned
just right. Now my ear alone is in tune; consequently I have ceased to
sing save in thought.

---

[29] This short title could refer either to the *Louis XII and François I, or
Memoirs for Use in Writing a New History of Their Reigns,* or to the actual
recollections of the same author: *Concerning Bonaparte: Journal of Count
P. L. Rœderer.*

16 July

I ought never to travel without a Montaigne. If I had the *Essais* at hand, I should look up the remark he makes about La Boétie: "I have lived more negligently" (since he left me). Jean Lambert, in his article on Schlumberger (*Fontaine*, number 21), attributes it to St. Augustine: "I had lost the witness of my life," he presumably said in *The Confessions*, "and I feared that I might not live so well." It may be that this remark is there, but is it not the precise translation of these words that I read in the letters of Pliny the Younger (Letter XII, to Calestrius Tiro): *"Amisi vitæ meæ testem. . . . Vereor ne negligentius vivam"*? That sentence, which charms us and makes us reflect, was perhaps but a commonplace in antiquity, one of those banal remarks that were used for each bereavement? [30]

21 July

Their facile assurance disconcerts and pains me, whereas these words of Montaigne (I, 26) comfort me: "None but fools are certain and resolute." And we shall see the most obstinate of today become just as certain and resolute in the other direction, unaware even that they have changed, if only the wind that sways them happens to change.

27 July

I am giving the best of my time to the translation of *Hamlet*. Nothing but this work can take my mind off our anguish. Those who are satisfied today with this wretched "recovery" of France never realized what constituted her greatness of yesterday.

1 August

Yesterday my heart was affected as a result of a novocain injection intended to permit the rather painful extraction of the root of a molar. Good reason to try to keep myself from smoking! After a good night I feel as if still alive. An excellent letter from Roger Martin du Gard makes me feel altogether myself again.

3 August

I read in Sainte-Beuve: *"de les sonder, quoi qu'ils en aient."* (*Causeries du lundi*, Vol. III, p. 276.) [31]

---

[30] Pliny says of the death of an old friend, Corellius Rufus: "I have indeed lost the witness, guide, and teacher of my life. To sum up I shall say what I said to my companion Calvisius when my grief was fresh: 'I am afraid I shall live more carelessly now.'" (*Letters*, I, 12.)

[31] Gide is probably thinking of the naïveté of saying: "to probe them, whatever they may say of it."

Théo R., morning and evening, for more than an hour each time, leans over each of the plants in his garden with the look of concentration of a man to whom great secrets are being told in a language that he doesn't understand very well.

8 August

This morning a card from Saucier to tell me that a client is offering him two hundred thousand francs for the manuscript of *Si le grain ne meurt,* which I sold to B. for forty-five thousand before leaving Nice. I make an effort to consider this very funny.

"It required all the lucidity and the painful relentlessness of our epoch to . . ." writes Jouve.

That illusion that one's own epoch (our epoch) judges more soundly, establishes its roll of honor more fairly than the preceding ones.

Sidi-bou-Saïd, 1 September

Finished the translation of *Hamlet* yesterday. As much as twenty years ago I had translated the first act (La Tortue brought out a very fine edition of it), which all alone caused me more trouble than the five acts of *Antony and Cleopatra.* I thought I had forever forsaken such exhausting labor. I returned to it at the request of Jean-Louis Barrault with an adolescent's zeal and an old man's patient equanimity. For almost three months I have devoted from six to eight hours a day to it and taken relaxation from it only to put into shape for the *Figaro* my "Advice in regard to *Phèdre*" (then in regard to *Iphigénie*). I should certainly not have persevered if my version had not seemed to me greatly superior to all the earlier ones, and especially much more adapted to the stage and to delivery by actors. I had within reach, not so much to help as to encourage me, the translations by F.-V. Hugo, Schwob, Pourtalès, and Copeau. This last one alone seems to show some regard for French; all of them sacrifice rhythm, lyrical power, cadence, and beauty to mere exactitude. I believe that, in this regard, the translations of the last century were preferable.

The great advantage of this work: I could tackle it at any time, always ready for this type of effort, which I was inclined to prolong for three or four hours at a time. Mme Théo urges me vigorously, and with the best arguments in the world, to give henceforth my best attention to my *Journal.* She is doubtless right, but the quality of this journal comes precisely from the fact that I write in it only in answer to some call and urged on by a sort of inner necessity. For some time now I have felt no need to open it again and have lost sight of myself. I become aware again how hard it is to reinterest oneself in something one has abandoned. All my thoughts are elusive; for some time I have been living and feeling only through sympathy; at least my affective faculties are as keen as in the best period of my youth.

Solitude is bearable only with God.

Dr. Misserey, who, a prisoner himself since Dunkerque, is treating Russian wounded in a German *Oflag*, writes me (in pencil) a touching postcard (the third I have received from him). He quotes a sentence of Proust (*Les Plaisirs et les jours* [32]) that, he says, seems to have been written for him: "And then I realized that never could Noah see the world so clearly as from the ark, though it was closed and the earth was dark." A remarkable sentence, indeed, despite its three errors in French in seven words. [33] Only the blind do not notice the night; there are many in France.

September

Still at Sidi-bou-Saïd. Thanks to the charming hosts who are lodging me, I find rest, comfort, calm, and salvation here. From the terrace of the villa I watch the plain as it swoons. Exhausting heat, which I am ashamed to endure so badly. And, for the first time in my life, probably, I am making the acquaintance of what is called nostalgia. I think of the mysterious forest interior at La Roque in which the child I was could not venture without trembling, of the edges of the pond thick with flowering plants, of the evening mists over the little stream. I think of the beech grove at Cuverville, of the great autumn winds carrying away the russet leaves, of the rooks' call, of the evening meditation beside the fire in the calm house on its way to sleep. . . . Everything I owe to Em. comes to mind and I have been thinking constantly of her for several days with regret and remorse for having so often and so greatly been in arrears with her. How often I must have seemed to her harsh and insensitive! How ill I corresponded to what she had a right to expect of me! . . . For a smile from her today, I believe I should forsake life and this world in which I could not overtake her. . . .

15 September

I am rereading *Aurélia* [34] with a great effort of attention and a desire to accept it. Happy to correct the impression of disappointment

---

[32] *Pleasures and Days*, a youthful work of Proust's, first published in 1896.

[33] Gide is referring to "*malgré qu*'elle *fut* close et qu'il *fit* nuit sur la terre," for *malgré que* is a popular variant of the correct *quoique* or *bien que* and the verbs should be in the imperfect subjunctive: *fût* and *fît*.

[34] A short poetic novel by Gérard de Nerval.

and boredom that this poetic tale had given me on first reading and each time I had gone back to it. Happy to admit that Chapter v in particular reveals a complete perfection, a rare and subtle quality, and when one lets oneself go and falls in with it, it is quite moving. A tone previously unheard in our literature, which even Baudelaire but rarely approached and to which French ears were not to open, and could not open, until much later.

16 September

Every night (or almost) I have been dreaming of her, for some time now. And always, in each dream, I see some obstacle, often petty and absurd, rise up between her and me to separate us; I lose her; I set out in search of her, and the whole dream is but the development of a long adventure in pursuit of her. I have related one of those dreams in this notebook, I believe, and I don't know why I chose that one among so many.[35]

Ah, it is better that you are not here! . . . (I am constantly telling myself this). You would have had to suffer too much from the degradation of France.

Finished with great difficulty and great effort my rereading of *Aurélia*. One more beautiful page close to the end ("*Bosquets embaumés de Paphos . . .*"), but one has to wade through such tiresome rubbish to reach it! . . . Engaging, disturbing figure of Nerval; but I cannot succeed in making of him the great poet that Thierry Maulnier sees in him. But Maulnier is making sport of us just as when he magnifies Maurice Scève to excess.[36]

"When he used a word," John Dover Wilson says of Shakespeare in his excellent introduction to *Hamlet*, "all possible meanings of it were commonly present to his mind, so that it was like a musical chord which might be resolved in whatever fashion or direction he pleased." [37] This is what constitutes the force of his poetic incantation and this is what the translator must make a point of preserving. He must constantly fear, by being too precise, to limit the flight of the imagination.

The human soul (and why fear using this word to designate that complex of emotions, tendencies, susceptibilities joined together by a bond that is perhaps merely physiological) has shadowy, changing, in-

[35] See pp. 69–70.

[36] In his highly personal anthology entitled *Introduction to French Poetry* (1939), Thierry Maulnier devotes twice as much space to Nerval as he does to Lamartine or Vigny and more than to Hugo, just as he gives more extracts from the Renaissance poet Maurice Scève than from his better-known contemporaries Ronsard and du Bellay.

[37] The quotation is given in English in the original.

tangible contours, constantly modified and subject to modification according to circumstances, climates, seasons, and all influences, so that
the tensest and most vigilant will has great trouble maintaining in it a
semblance of cohesion. In itself already sufficiently rebellious to description and analysis without that confusion which language contributes by using the same word, "love," to designate two tendencies
of such different nature that they are opposed. Around this word and
by reason of its misuse there has grown up a sort of false mystery,
which would be rendered ridiculous if language turned to another
word to signify love as charity rather than the one used for love as
concupiscence; for desire and for the gift. But such lexical poverty is
itself revelatory; it reveals that slipping from one to the other is always possible. But no matter; many a problem in this domain seems
psychological and is artificially created by an improper use of words.
It would not be useless to study the vocabulary of other languages,
which perhaps do not suffer, in this regard, from the same poverty as
does French.

Tunis, 24 September

As soon as my mind is not busy with a definite piece of work, it
returns to its anguish. Since the translation of *Hamlet* was finished, I
have been unable to get away from useless reflection on the disaster.
I thought I was not very "patriotic"; indeed, it is not so much from the
defeat that I am suffering as from the sagging and warping of the
virtues that characterized the French, from the unconscious approval
of falsehood and the retreat of all integrity. Words themselves are
divorced from their meanings, and intellectual groupings are based
solely on misapprehensions. Every voice of justice is gagged and the
right to think freely is granted only on condition that one refrain from
speaking. "Solely the useful will be considered to be true"; this is the
doctrine of Barrès; it dishonors everything, even religion.

27 September

What France can and must contribute to humanity is the leaven
that makes the dough rise. That is her role, but Germany refuses to let
her play it.

Nations, as much as individuals, grow stupid through laziness.
There is no more harmful doctrine than that of the least effort. That
sort of ideal which invites things to come to us instead of our going to
them disregards the *"vires acquirit eundo"*; [38] and, in this regard at
least, I believe the rule of conduct of Protestant nations to be more
virilizing than that of the Catholic nations, for it encourages effort
more.

---

[38] "It gains strength in its course," from Virgil: *Æneid*, IV, 175.

28 September

                    . . . *So geht*
Der Mensch zu Ende — und die einzige
Aus beute, die wir aus dem Kampf des Lebens
Wegtragen, ist die Einsicht in des Nichts
Und herzlichen Verachtung alles dessen
Was uns erhaben schien und wünschenswert.[39]

No, these last words of Talbot in Schiller's *Die Jungfrau von Orleans* will not be my final words. Probably it will not be granted me to witness the restoration of moral values for which it would have been such a joy to live, but in that restoration I believe firmly.

I cannot succeed in admiring that drama; as artificial as those of Hugo and even in its slightest details, without real depth, without meaning. Even the verse is harsh and the psychological motives are conventional or arbitrary. One does not feel for a moment that any inner need prompted Schiller to write it (such as one feels in *Don Carlos* or *Wilhelm Tell*). It is a well-done exercise (and not even very well done) on a subject that seems to him especially dramatic. That Joan-Walkyrie, a "scourge of God" vowing to exterminate all the English in France, breaking faith with herself as soon as she becomes merciful, and becoming merciful only through the influence of love, then falling to her knees before Agnès Sorel and exclaiming:
                Du bist die Heilige! Du bist die Reine! [40]
How painful and ridiculous! . . . Unacceptable. Not the slightest real feeling in all this.

29 September

Finished reading *Die Jungfrau*. The end is even more absurd than all the rest. Schiller's only excuse is the ignorance still prevailing in his time as to the very documents of the great trial. For fear of doing him an injustice and underestimating him, I want to reread *Don Carlos*, which is incomparably better, if my recollection of it is exact. But how great Goethe seems beside Schiller! How heavy with meaning the least of his works! Each is born of a need, an inner prompting. Schiller's *Die Jungfrau* is unmeaningful and nothing in it seems motivated

---

[39]   . . . *Thus*
      Man goes to death — and the only
      Booty which we carry out of the battle of life
      Is the insight into its utter valuelessness
      And hearty scorn of all that seemed to us
      Lofty and desirable.
[40] "Thou art the holy one! Thou art the pure one!"

save by a childish desire for scenic effect. (I also want to read Kleist's *Penthesilea.*)

1 October

Beside which Shaw's *Saint Joan* (which I am rereading with very great satisfaction) seems a marvel of intelligence, of appositeness, and of ingenuity.

6 October

As a result of my article on *Iphigénie* in the *Figaro* for 30 August, I have received from M. K., a magistrate in Pau, a long letter from which I want to copy some passages here, for I believe them to be particularly illustrative of a state of mind that is tending to spread; these are the last sentences of the letter:

"The writer is responsible for the consequences of his writings. Your proposition [41] is, in my opinion, most pernicious.[42] This is why I have taken the liberty of writing you this letter. I have fought to save my country.[43] Why do you then take the liberty of poisoning it with such false maxims [44] interspersed amid so accurate and so captivating a criticism? You haven't the right to act like this at such a moment when the France of St. Louis needs her lights in order to remain worthy of her tradition. You less than anyone else, to whom has been given the gift of style, which places you above all the Immortals of the moment, except the marshal, who is the magnificent servant of the Word."

What can I reply to that? . . . *Cedant rationes mentis vulneribus corporis.*[45]

7 October

But this morning a letter from Mme Théo containing this sentence: "As for me, I was quite sure that your sentence in the article on *Iphigénie* would draw forth some indignant reply."

---

[41] It is a question of this sentence from my article, "which I was quite amazed to read," says M. K.: "The Christian soul refers back to and relies on God, whereas the pagan soul puts its trust and finds support only in itself." [A.]

[42] Hanged if I should have suspected it! [A.]

[43] He says elsewhere: "A hero of Verdun is writing this, who escaped with a blighty!" [A.]

[44] What M. K. finds to be false in my proposition, as he explained above, is that "one owes one's blood solely to God, and if one sheds it apparently in another cause, one offers it to him alone; this is the sole means of ennobling the sacrifice." Oh, if you wish. . . . [A.]

[45] "Let the mind's reasons yield to the body's wounds."

Tournier gives me Farrère's book *L'Homme seul*,[46] a novel with real characters under fictitious names. I have read so far but thirty pages of it; it is very bad. The portrait it gives of Pierre Louÿs is not at all exact. To attribute to Louÿs "the appearance of an athlete"! Come now! Louÿs had a rare elegance in his gestures, his silhouette, his bearing, but had also a sickly look. He was soft like a marshmallow; his hand melted in yours. His forehead and eyes were instinct with a sort of genius, which compensated for his somewhat too foppish look. He used to stammer at the slightest emotion — that is to say, often — in a turmoil for nothing at all and calm only at rare intervals.

I go on for some twenty pages more and then the book falls from my hands.

9 October

Let myself be kept for dinner last night by Jean Amrouche after a fine game of chess. His friend Jules Roy, the very likable aviator, come in from Sétif, invited us as his guests. After the meal we went to the Halfahouine, which was especially lively on the next to last evening of Ramadan. This morning got up at five thirty because of Suzy's leaving. When I came in last night I had found a short letter from her, since she didn't expect to see me again — such a nice letter that I immediately made up my mind to kiss Suzy good-by. After having got up, unable to go to sleep again and not feeling like doing so, I went out. Radiant morning. I had taken with me the first volume of the *Histoire du peuple d'Israël*, which I had begun reading, but did not open it. Tried in vain to call to mind the whole of Baudelaire's *Crépuscule du matin*.[47] Contemplated at length a group of poverty-stricken children, half covered with sordid rags, obviously homeless. They were lying under a portico, one across another, trying to sleep, but tormented by flies and probably devoured by vermin, occasionally scratching themselves furiously under their tatters. Tunis is full of a poverty that is beyond help. Homeless children seemingly even much more lamentable than the *"besprizornis"* of Sebastopol, who at least seem lively and gay, probably now become valiant soldiers of the Red army. Insouciance of that hopeless youth, stuff of which the "social question" is made. Dream of a society that would not allow of any outcasts.

There are those who would like to ameliorate men and there are those who hold that that cannot be done without first ameliorating the conditions of their life. But it soon appears that one cannot be divorced from the other, and you don't know where to begin. Some days hu-

---

[46] *Man Alone.*
[47] "Morning Twilight" is one of the poems of *The Flowers of Evil. The History of the People of Israel* is by Renan.

manity strikes me as so miserable that the happiness of a few seems impious.

10 October

I puzzled out *Penthesilea,* cursorily at first; now I go back to it, slowly tasting each of its splendid lines one after another with delight and considerable profit. Never before, it seems to me, as much as in Kleist (not even in Hölderlin), had I enjoyed the poetic possibilities of German syntax, with its delays, its turns backward, its sudden drops. At times I think of Malherbe, which is most surprising.

Dr. Ragu lends me a book on Tiberius (translated from the German) which he declares to be a masterpiece and which, he says, "reads like a novel"; but I cannot get interested in it. The mere statement of events tires me. In that vast tangle of the past why choose this rather than that? The most obvious constantly obscures the most important. One seeks a succession, a sequence of facts, a causality that is not accidental or illusory. And, whatever I am told, I always think irresistibly that *it didn't take place like that.* I am tempted to say: of all realms of human knowledge, the one that interests me least is History.

As for collaboration with Germany, nothing would have been more desirable, and for each of the two countries, each one having exactly what the other most lacked. But today events have made it so that the "Gaullist" elements greatly predominate in France, in number and even more in quality. This involves, in my case at least, no discredit for the marshal; on the contrary, he seems to me to be playing as best he can a difficult game, and the future will perhaps prove that even at the moment of the armistice he got out of it with the least prejudice to France (if indeed an event ever *proves* anything). I gladly subscribe to these remarks from the letter I received yesterday from Roger M. du G.: "I confess to being very susceptible to the style and accent of his speeches. It is said that they are written for him; now B., now G., now another are cited. . . . Nonsense! Each of his messages has an authentic ring that belongs indeed to the same man and that generally goes rather straight to my heart. His very mistakes are not lacking in either straightforwardness or natural nobility.[48] It will require perspective to throw light on the secrets of the *Pétain enigma,* and one of my great regrets is that I shall die without knowing . . ." Knowing what? Whether Pétain was not, at heart, the most "Gaullist" of us all; but it was important above all not to let this be seen.

---

[48] Need I add today (1949) that this opinion, which I then shared with my friend, we could neither of us keep for long? [A.]

13 October

One catches cold with a temperature of seventy-seven after days and nights spent in a Turkish bath. I know I shall not escape. . . .

The slow accumulation of very small, modest efforts. I recall the wonderful cry of the man in Dante's Hell (I was not yet twenty when I heard it for the first time, and what a lesson I drew from it for a long time thereafter!):

> *Were I but carrying so light a load*
> *That in a hundred years I gained an inch,*
> *Already had I set out on the road.*[49]

Real old age would be giving up hope of progress. I am not made for contemplative stagnation and enjoy only effort.

I am reading the *Penthesilea* very slowly, letting nothing pass without understanding and feeling it completely, with indescribable rapture. Kleist makes wonderful use of German syntax, and this makes it possible to appreciate its resources, its subtle license, its suppleness. The fine tangle of the sentence, in which he frolics, remains almost impossible in French, where the function of uninflected words is most often indicated only by their position. Enough to form two very different nations.

Finished my reading of the first volume of Renan's *Histoire du peuple d'Israël*. (Five genitives in succession, O Flaubert!) Then made another vain effort to try to penetrate Bergson's thought; hard at *Matière et mémoire* for five days without succeeding in understanding or really getting interested.

Such important events that it seems as if we are on the threshold of a new History. What is needed is a humanity worthy of taking place in it. The world can be saved only by a few.

15 October

Simple, cordial, and charming dinner at the Amrouches'. (How rare it is that one can be equally the friend of husband and wife!) After which Jean Amrouche gets even with me for the game of chess I had won before dinner. On getting home, to finish off a good day, a few excellent chapters of Rabelais. Quite amused to find in the fifth book of *Pantagruel*, Chapter xlvi, the English expression: "will he take a hair of the dog that bit him?"[50] which became with us: *"reprendre du poil de la bête"* and soon took on a very different meaning.

---

[49] *Inferno*, XXX, 82–4. [A.]
[50] Quoted in French.

16 October

Can one speak of "bad taste" except in a middle-class way? But how can one fail to find that the exaggerated sublime of Scene xv of *Penthesilea*, the big dialogue of explanation between Achilles and the Queen of the Amazons, borders on ridicule in a very painful manner? How can one fail to agree with Goethe that Penthesilea's declarations have a comic quality "worthy of a Neapolitan stage"? One irresistibly shares in the laughter that must shake the audience at that point if the play is ever given. A pity that the high point of the drama is so friable; even the quality of the poetry is affected and one is almost amazed, at that moment, at having been able to admire the rest so much.

"Warum lächelst du?"

"Wer? Ich?"

"Mich dünkt, du lächelst, Lieber." [51]

Good heavens! This is not surprising. And Kleist was well aware of it himself when he makes Achilles say:

Deiner Schöne . . .
Ich war zerstreut. Vergib. Ich dachte eben,
Ob du mir aus dem Monde niederstiegst? [52]

17 October

No less ridiculous, no less vulgar in their comic quality, the panting scenes that follow:

"Ich Kann nicht glauben."

"Es spricht von der Dardanerburg."

"Was?"

"Was?"

"Mich dünkt, du sagest was."

"Ich?"

"Du!"

"Ich sagte:

Es spricht von der Dardanerburg." [53]

---

[51] *"Why art thou smiling?"*
     "Who? I?"
   "It seems to me, dear one, that thou art smiling."
[52]   *"About thy beauty . . .*
   "I was distrait. Forgive. I was just wondering
   Whether thou hast descended to me from the moon."
This passage follows directly on the preceding one and is spoken by Achilles.
[53]   *"I cannot believe it."*
   "He is speaking of the Citadel of the Dardanians."
        "What?"
          "What?"

That is unspeakably bad. And it couldn't be good with such a false start. Oh, how disagreeable is that treachery of Penthesilea! And disagreeable that idea of introducing elephants and dogs into that combat with Achilles, which was to be "single-handed"!

> O du,
> Von der mein Herz auf Knien niederfällt,
> Wie rührest du mich! [54]

Not me. I hate the spasmodic: "for in the very torrent, tempest, and as I may say, the whirlwind of passion, you must acquire and beget a temperance that may give it smoothness," said Hamlet. And what a flabbergasting way of killing oneself by striking oneself with a metaphor! . . . . It is enough to make me wonder now whether I did not perhaps exaggerate the beauty, which seemed to me so great, of the first part of the drama. I want to reread it at once.

18 October

That Kleist was unable to perfect his work, that it crushed him, now seems obvious to me. But it would be indecorous, impious to smile at this. His experience seems to me comparable to Nietzsche's, and even more tragic, for with Nietzsche one cannot speak of a failure. All the defects of *Penthesilea*, all its shortcomings, are the effect of that inner drama which they eloquently reveal, and if it were better perfected, that work would be less revelatory, less worthy of moving us. But what moves us, toward the end, is less the beauty of the work than the bankruptcy of the author.

Chacha makes me some verbena tea. When she brings it to me, I ask her: "Has it steeped sufficiently?" And Chacha replies: "Yes, because over the gas it's very fast." Never would a man make such a reply. Specifically feminine illogicality.

19 October

And this morning, in order to understand if possible the working of her mind, I ask Chacha to explain her remark of last night, but with all the respect I owe to her advanced age. It seems clear to me that a

---

> "It seems to me thou saidst something."
> > "I?"
> > > "Thou!"
> > > > "I said:
> He is speaking of the Citadel of the Dardanians."

The speakers in this dialogue are Ulysses and Achilles.

[54]   "O thou,
> Before whom my heart falls on its knees,
> How thou touchest me!"

confusion has got fixed in her mind: the short time the water took to
boil leading to the rest, endowing the water with a sort of attribute of
speed. None of this reasoned out at all, of course; in an uncivilized
way.

At this time when everything is rationed, she wastes gas in an odd
way, putting the water on to boil for no reason at all, then saying,
when she puts it back on the fire: "Oh, it will boil fast; it's already been
heating for a half-hour!"

The Siamese cat, fed almost exclusively on fish in peacetime, now
is quite willing to eat bread. Chacha tells me so this morning: "He
eats anything now!" Then, as if saying: "What a disaster!" she adds:
"Ah, he certainly can be said to choose the right time!"

Twenty times a day, about anything or anyone: "What a poison!"
And about the events of the war: "Ah, all that's very complicated!" I
should have said at the outset that she comes from Martinique.

19 October

Corydon remains in my opinion the most important of my books;
but it is also the one with which I find the most fault. The least well
done is the one it was most important to do well. I was probably ill
advised to treat ironically such serious questions, which are generally
handled as a subject of reprobation or of joking. If I went back to them,
people would not fail to think I am obsessed by them. People prefer
to envelop them in silence as if they played but a negligible role in
society and as if the number of individuals tormented by such questions were negligible in society. And yet when I began to write my
book, I thought that number to be much smaller than it eventually appeared to be and than it is in reality; smaller, however, in France than
in many other countries I came to know later, for probably in no other
country (with the exception of Spain) do the cult of Woman, the
religion of Love, and a certain tradition of amorous intercourse so
much dominate manners or so servilely influence the way of life. I
am obviously not speaking here of the cult of woman in its profoundly
respectable aspect, nor of noble love, but of debasing love that sacrifices the best in man to skirts and the alcove. The very ones who shrug
their shoulders when faced with such questions are those who proclaim that Love is the most important thing in life and consider it
natural that a man should subordinate his career to it. They are naturally thinking of love as desire and of sensual pleasure; and in their
eyes desire is king. But, in their opinion, that desire loses all value and
does not deserve to be taken into consideration the moment it ceases
to be in harmony with, and similar to, theirs. They are very sure of
themselves, having Opinion on their side.

Yet I believe I said in that book just about everything I had to say on this most important subject that had not been said before me; but I reproach myself with not having said it as I should have. None the less, certain attentive minds will manage to discover it there later on.

22 October

I thought I already knew *La Femme de trente ans.*[55] Did Balzac ever write anything worse? It's staggering. (Marquise d'Aiglemont and Charles de Vandenesse.) Especially the story of the privateer: Chapter v, "The Two Encounters."

I then reread *Une Fille d'Ève*[56] (Mme Félix de Vandenesse and Raoul Nathan), in which, amid much claptrap, a few excellent scenes. Then *La Femme abandonnée*[57] (Mme de Beauséant and the handsome Gaston de Nueil). Balzac's case is one of the most extraordinary, one of the most inexplicable, in our literature, in all literatures.

28 October

Have I ever known such a long unbroken succession of fine days? Certain mornings are so gloriously pure that one doesn't know what to do with them. A setting for the full blossoming of happiness. How respond to such a solicitation? One would like to invent a God, so full is one's heart of adoration. Can it be that in such weather men are killing one another anywhere in the world? Any thought that is not full of love seems impious.

6 November

With each cold cured (I am writing this after a week of grippe), with each car or bicycle avoided, I say to myself: well, I have escaped this time!

I note this fine example of cacography in an article by Henry Bataille on Lucien Mühlfeld (*Renaissance latine*, 15 December 1902): "Mysterious retaliation for the intellectuals whose fate here below as it were eternally on the go seems implacable, and why the bitter desire eventually to arrest their fugacity somewhere, sounds perhaps in heaven the punishment of eternal rest." And he adds: "I recall an evening with Rodenbach when we chatted about this." How wonderful it must have been!

The Berlin communiqué of 6 November ends with this admirable sentence: "The command of the Axis armored forces can obviously not

---

[55] *A Woman of Thirty.*
[56] *A Daughter of Eve.*
[57] *The Forsaken Woman.*

everywhere prevent local successes on the part of British tanks, but it is executing a plan conditioned by present enemy activity and is absolutely free in its decisions."

12 November

Occupation of the French "free zone" by Germany and of North Africa by the U.S.A. . . . Events deprive me of any desire to say anything. Always tempted to think that it has no importance *basically* and does not interest me, even were I to lose my head thereby.

14 November

The very small number of mistakes through inconsistency in the *Comédie humaine* makes one enjoy noting them. Marsay speaks of the "handsome blue eyes" of Savinien de Portenduère (p. 359 of *Ursule Mirouet*) and two pages later in a letter of Émilie de Kergarouet reference is made to the "sparkle" of "his handsome black eyes."

Certain dialogues in *Ursule Mirouet* seem to me rather better than those in *Eugénie Grandet*; and, after all, I am rewarded for my perseverance. It is one of the most revelatory "scenes" in the *Comédie humaine* and certainly I missed having read it. Immediately afterward I tackle *Modeste Mignon*, one of the few Balzacs still left me to read for the first time.

15 November

Invitation to Montherlant's *Jeunes Filles*: [58] "I am sure you have never encountered that intellectual windfall: the secrets of a young girl!" Modeste writes to Canalis-Costals (Letter VII). "She asks of you a purely moral and mysterious union. There! Come to her heart when you are unhappy, hurt, tired. . . ." Etc.

Occasionally staggering sentences: "The wind of a mysterious will hurled me toward you as a storm sweeps a rosebush to the heart of a majestic willow." But none the less *Modeste Mignon* is remarkable, one of the best. Dialogues often excellent, or almost.

No more letters to write. Useless: they would not arrive. What an intellectual rest! Since my travels in the Congo I had not enjoyed such tranquillity. I even wonder if that sort of serenity which results from this is not greater than the anxiety of being without news of all those who are dear to me.

---

[58] Montherlant's novel in four volumes (1936–9), *Les Jeunes Filles* (translated as *Pity for Women* and *Costals and the Hippogriff*), recounts the life of the writer Costals, harassed by feminine admirers and loving correspondents. Canalis figures in Balzac's *Modeste Mignon*.

Read *Le Contrat de mariage*; reread *Étude de femme, Autre Étude de femme, L'Interdiction* (one of the best and one that lends itself to reading aloud, as I had learned from experience at Cuverville). *Les Comédiens sans le savoir*, odd, but vulgarly mediocre.[59]

22 November

In Flaubert's *Saint-Julien l'Hospitalier*,[60] I read: "The wall of the valley was too high to climb it." Unacceptable.

26 November

Large posters cover the walls of Tunis. They inform the population that, invaded in cowardly fashion by the Anglo-Saxon pirates and incapable of defending herself, North Africa must gratefully welcome the Axis troops that have come generously to offer to defend her.

If the latter are victorious, this is the version of History that will prevail.

Completely gripped by Balzac again. His *Petits Bourgeois* [61] (unfinished, alas!), of which no one ever speaks, is amazing. "*Avoir lieu de . . .*" [62] I can accept this expression only when impersonal. "*J'ai lieu de . . .*" shocks me even though Littré seems to accept it.

I read in *Les Employés*: "*J'ai tout lieu de penser que le succès couronnera vos espérances.*" [63] But Balzac *makes a character say this* and would perhaps not have written it when speaking in his own name; for, after all, he writes very well and *Les Employés* has an excellent style.

28 November

Yesterday very pleasant lunch at the Ragus', whom I always enjoy seeing, with the young Boutelleau couple, Jean Tournier, and Mme Sparrow.

The events of Toulon are being commented upon and, as almost always, they allow of very different interpretations.[64] Dr. Ragu, in better form than ever, judges them very severely. To him that heroic scut-

---

[59] These are all works by Balzac: *The Marriage Contract, A Study of Woman, Another Study of Woman, The Commission in Lunacy* (see *The Journals of André Gide*, Vol. III, p. 270), and *The Unconscious Comedians*.

[60] *The Legend of St. Julian the Hospitaler*, one of Flaubert's *Trois Contes* (*Three Tales*).

[61] *The Lesser Bourgeoisie*.

[62] "To have reason for . . ."

[63] "I have every reason to think that the outcome will fulfill your hopes."

[64] The French fleet in the harbor of Toulon was scuttled on 27 November 1942.

tling of our fleet seems comparable to the suicide of a disloyal employee cornered by recognition of his crime, escaping punishment and taking refuge in death: an absurd act resulting from an original notorious blunder. I suspect that this interpretation must likewise be Roger Martin du Gard's. This action on the part of the officers of the French Navy explains their attitude at Mers-el-Kebir: an order was given them, doubtless, to sink their ships rather than to let them be of use either to the English or to the Germans. But this amounted to setting one's point of honor above the very interests of the country and I can easily see why reason protests against this. Despite everything, this shows a preference for oneself over the cause, and this leaves the conscience ill at ease. One wonders, without being able to approve. In the dreadful dilemma they had got into, the only choice they had was between suicide and slavery. No loophole possible, no means of escaping. As soon as our fleet failed to decide at once in favor of keeping up the fight, it became useless or dishonored. Accepting the conditions of the armistice was tantamount to a delayed scuttling. Alongside the English, that fleet might have rendered very great services; now it serves merely as an example of the evils of obedience when personal conscience ceases to acquiesce in the commands received.

30 November

The German and Italian forces are occupying Tunis. In the streets a great bustle of trucks, tanks, armored cars, and A.A. guns. From day to day new ships are unloading new munitions and troops. The Americans, whose entry into the city was already announced to take place yesterday, are caught somewhere, not far from Tunis to be sure; but I fancy they will encounter serious resistance, which they have given time to organize. Probably the Axis forces are caught here as in a trap; but when surrounded, they can be expected to struggle for some time before surrendering, and I cannot share the optimism of my friends. Probably the Americans are waiting for air reinforcements to give them a crushing numerical superiority before beginning the battle and are first busy with subjugating Bizerte. It is asserted that the Germans are in great disorder; but I am very suspicious of that tendency of certain people to see their wishes as if already realized. . . .

1 December

Ernst Jünger's book on the war of 1914, *Storm of Steel*,[65] is incontrovertibly the finest war book that I have read; utter good faith,

---

[65] Gide gives the title in French as he does for the second book, but the first one is obviously *In Stahlgewittern. Aus dem Tagebuch eines Stosstruppführers*, which was translated into English in 1929 as *Storm of Steel: From the Diary of a Storm-Troop Officer on the Western Front.*

veracity, and fairness. I greatly regret not having yet read it (and the other one that I was reading at Sidi-bou-Saïd: *Gardens and Roads* [66]) before having received his visit at rue Vaneau (which is mentioned in the latter book). I should have spoken to him quite differently.

I finish *Les Employés*. It is to such books of the *Comédie humaine*, to such "Studies" of Balzac, that I give my most unqualified admiration. There it is (and in *Les Petits Bourgeois*) that he hits his stride and masters his subject most effectively. In *Les Secrets de la princesse de Cadignan*,[67] which I reread next, he is striving toward graces and subtleties that are not natural to him. He succeeds best in the portrayal of wingless creatures and their modest crawling on the ground; that is where he is incomparable, superior even to Gogol. To be sure, it requires great patience to read *Les Employés* through to the end, but the patience is fully rewarded.

2 December

I am rereading with amusement, but little additional profit, Brunetière's book on Balzac.[68] Already I had assimilated everything valuable in it. Brunetière reminds me of Dindiki's [69] manner of progressing, ultra-cautious. His thoughts, tightly tied together, tie him down. He advances in his own footsteps. The views he maintains are not always quite right, but they are always very solidly founded. Dare one say even: the more solidly founded, the less right they are?

3 December

Heard on the radio last night, with great discomfort, the London comments on the speech Mussolini has just made. Can it be that such coarse insults find an echo in the hearts of the majority, and must the radio seek to satisfy that majority? Can they not be made to realize, by means of a victory, as it happens, that one debases oneself by trying to debase a conquered enemy, and that force is not the only way it is essential to be superior?

---

[66] *Garten und Strassen* (1942), a diary of Jünger's months in France as an officer in 1940 containing his reflections on the danger of undisciplined barbarism.

[67] *The Secrets of the Princess of Cadignan.*

[68] *Honoré de Balzac* (1906).

[69] A small climbing lemur (*Perodicticus potto*) that André Gide tamed during his travels in the Congo. In the book devoted to him Gide says: "It is as if he proceeded by syllogisms. If you try to make him hurry, he turns around toward you protesting shrilly, annoyed as if you were interrupting the thread of his reasoning."

4 December

It is not only sounds that waken me, but often tremblings of the earth, of which I do not always understand the cause. My body, my nervous system, is as sensitive as a seismograph, and I am aware of someone's getting out of bed at the other end of the house. I should have liked to find out whether those almost continuous shocks, those vibrations, I felt in the cerebellum these last few nights came from the explosions of the battle going on less than twenty kilometers from here.

"Hold fast to what thou hast. . . ." [70] All those possessions with which I have let myself part! I affected, when I was younger, never to regret anything. But now I am like a tree whose branches have gradually lost their leaves; and the memory of the treasures with which I was loaded sometimes rises to my heart. Pleasures came and lighted on me like migratory birds. In order to welcome everything, I lived with my hands open and was unable to close them on anything. At least I have learned to judge myself without indulgence, and more severely even than would an enemy.

5 December

The fragments of Mussolini's speech given in the Germanophile paper of Tunis are such as to justify the scornful vituperations of the English radio. One cannot imagine anything more stupid, more false, more flat. Impossible that there are not, even in Italy, many people sufficiently sensible and well informed to suffer from it.

The Germans are behaving here, one is forced to admit, with remarkable dignity,[71] which makes the undisciplined swaggering of the Italian soldiers even more scandalous. After 6 p.m. they assumed the right, last night and the night before, to snipe at late passers-by; and this earned them outspoken admonitions from the *Kommandantur*. "They are doing it because of the jitters," says Amrouche, who may well be right; but also the Duce's speech has gone to their heads and they are trying to prove to themselves that they are the masters in Tunisia. Nothing equals the scorn the German soldiers have for them unless it be the hatred the Italian soldiers feel for the Germans in exchange, despite anything Mussolini can say.

---

[70] See *The Journals of André Gide*, Vol. I, p. 16.

[71] Ragu told me that when he had to perform an emergency blood transfusion to try to save a seriously wounded English (or American) prisoner, six German soldiers immediately offered themselves. [A.]

7 December

Yesterday a mild day; not a cloud in the sky, which shines with a pacific splendor, a soft and, as it were, loving serenity such as to make one doubt of the war and of this atmosphere of horror. This morning the sky overcast; at last a little rain, much needed for the sowing, but still far from enough. Finished rereading, for the third or fourth time, the extraordinary *Cousin Pons*, after which I am going to be able to leave Balzac, for he has done nothing better.

One of the most peculiar traits of that child's character, which I have never yet found in any other — at least to such a degree — is his refusal to endure being found at fault. Every error committed by him, and he is constantly committing them, someone else, or the object he is using, is immediately blamed for, so that he never asks anyone to excuse him. Never have I seen him admit to being in the wrong. This is a most unpleasant shortcoming, and an attempt to cure it should have been made at the beginning. But I don't very well see how. Probably by adding to the reprimand a heavier punishment if he does not admit his guilt; but this called for great tact on the part of his parents, which could scarcely be hoped for either from his ever indulgent mother or from his father, ready to get angry over trifles and incapable of ignoring the mother's interventions in order to punish. Nothing is more interesting than to study the functioning of such a mind, all the more interesting since that child is far from being stupid. Victor is much less concerned with others than with himself. His interests come first. His strength lies in feeling no need of being liked; and since he has never felt any real affection for anyone up to now, he has a tendency to doubt the authenticity of others' feelings as soon as they are disinterested, to simplify the moral world until he sees in it nothing but a rivalry of selfish interests. This inclines him to think and claim himself to be a Communist; his mind alone, and never his heart, urges him to this. I have already seen examples of that.

He seeks in life nothing but sweetmeats, never anything that educates or strengthens.

I am rereading *Le Rouge et le noir* [72] with indescribable rapture.

Happy to have learned at last the name of the strange plant of which I am growing here, in seven pots, a large number of shoots. It is one of the thirty-six known species of "Kalanchoe(s)"; crassulaceous, all tropical. It has the peculiarity of reproducing itself not only by seeds (probably) but just as well or better by shoots that spring from

[72] Stendhal's novel *The Red and the Black*.

the edge of the leaves, then break away and, as soon as they fall on the ground, take root. It is this oddity that had caught my attention and that I had observed during last summer. (*Kalanchoe daigremontiana.*)

I believe I recall that Bourget in his *Essais de psychologie contemporaine* [73] (which opened my understanding in my youth) quotes this sentence from *Le Rouge et le noir* for its striking brevity, which he admires: "The children adored him; he [Julien] did not like them" — and I admired it with him. Today I still admire it, but I feel too much awareness and self-satisfaction in the cynicism and some affectation of coldness. One is too well aware that he wants himself to be thus.

10 December
I continue my reading, but painfully and languidly, through the second part. All those variations, willfully subtle, on pride and the possible slights to it somewhat suggest display, ostentation. From my indifference to this outlay of ingenuity I realize that there is no incentive of the human soul that is more foreign to me. It matters little to me that people "fail in their duty" to me. I really attribute but very little value to the consideration of those for whom I can have no esteem. It has occurred to me to envy many things, but never "titles" or "decorations." I doubt if any of the precepts of the Gospel ever touched me as deeply, and ever since my earliest youth, as "My kingdom is not of this world." On the other hand, I have no scorn for such things, but they simply have no real meaning for me, are "insignificant" in the literal sense of the word.

11 December
Finished *Le Rouge et le noir* in the night during a rather heavy bombardment. As for the reflections I noted yesterday, Stendhal himself brings his hero to make them in the last chapters of the book, and this sets off strikingly everything that precedes. One comes again on some very beautiful pages after long, boring passages that, it seems, were written rather perfunctorily. The reader, with Julien, "was tired of heroism" as he says, having become fully conscious of the vanity of that incentive which operates only in relation to "the idea of a public and *of others*" (Chapter xxxix). This at last re-establishes a scale of values. It was high time!

But in the first part there are easily a dozen marvelous chapters distinguished by incomparable novelty, briskness, and boldness such as would make a deep impression on the mind of a sensitive young reader just awakening to life.

---

[73] The *Studies in Contemporary Psychology* appeared in 1883, and a second volume in 1885.

In every street of Tunis many Italian or German soldiers; the former flabby, haggard, and wearing soiled uniforms, devoid of dignity and quick to show insolence; the Germans well equipped, clean, disciplined, appearing simultaneously smiling and resolute, probably ordered to show themselves pleasant and considerate toward the civilian population, to make their domination desirable, and going about it just right. Everywhere considerable munitions and armaments. . . . I fear we may be in for a long siege.

The official communiqués on both sides are most contradictory, each one announcing nothing but victories, retreats on the part of the enemy, and encircling of enemy forces. The mind stifles in this atmosphere of organized falsehood.

Inoffensive bombing-raids of the "Allies." "They don't know how to aim and hardly cause anything but civilian losses. They don't know how to fight"; this is what even their most convinced advocates go about repeating. As for the Germans, *they* know how. *They* are learning something, even at their own expense (and at ours). Meanwhile they will waste much time and lose many men. Victory will find only a world that is bled white, exhausted.

12 December

At last a rather good night, when I did more than pretend to sleep. At once the "animal spirits" revive; everything in me resumes confidence and draws itself up to full height; my inner sky recovers its natural serenity. I disown that pusillanimous state which caused me to set down painful reflections on myself on the 4th of this month and feel myself in no way impoverished. Joy is my normal state; yet without self-satisfaction or excessive assurance, but without any useless malice toward myself either and knowing to what physiological weakness such attacks of self-disparagement are due. One can, however, and must be satisfied with oneself, without overrating oneself, and accept oneself. The important thing is to recognize oneself especially in the best and to stay on the side of *God*.

The number of German soldiers savors of the marvelous. Truly they are "occupying" the city. The Moslem riffraff is obsequious toward them and they for the most part are very dignified. What wouldn't I give to follow them, to talk with them! But this would amount, on both sides, to "compromising oneself." Anything and everything is of consequence today; one is paralyzed with prudence.

14 December

This morning splendid weather, as after a night of love. But it was a severe bombing-raid. Three different times from the living-room window I watched at length the strange illuminations in the sky. . . . A huge fire at La Goulette lasted almost until dawn: an Italian munitions-ship, it is thought. Savage, elementary state of excitement, as irrepressible as it is somehow shameful, results from the havoc and awakens the most darkly primitive in us. And if ever mysticism gets involved in it, what a pretty mess! . . .

The opposing parties in a country are like those teeth of rodents that wear one another down by gnawing; one of them grows indefinitely until it kills the animal if the tooth opposite happens to be missing. It is essential to maintain the opposition.

15 December

The Italian soldiers' sniping, the Anglo-American bombs, the antiaircraft guns, the intermittent din of the German autos, armored cars, trucks, or ambulances rushing by under our windows, and the expectation of all these noises prevented any sleep last night. It is by far the heaviest bombing Tunis has undergone so far. Yesterday alone, ninety dead. Who can tell the number of victims of last night? One is amazed not to see them attack the very vulnerable canal of La Goulette in Tunis. The only plausible explanation is that they don't want to ruin it since they hope soon to make use of it. "Ah, it's all very complicated!" as Chacha says.

The Jewish population harassed, plundered, hunted down; and the refugees from Bizerte in ruins; and all that we must still expect to see. . . .

17 December

At last a calm night. The preceding night, letting the grandmother and the grandson go to the cellar, I had watched the stupefying sight at length. From the living-room windows, beside M. Reymond's room, which I am occupying, one can see as far as the heights of Sidi-bou-Saïd. The broad stars made by the flares lighted up the lake of Tunis and La Goulette, where bombs set fire to a munition-dump, making the horizon waver with a spasmodic red glow. Other bombs fell on the harbor and, not far from us, on the town, their explosions shaking the walls. Showers of tracer bullets from the antiaircraft guns streaked the sky. It would be impossible to imagine more glorious fireworks. For fear of missing any of it, I had gone to bed fully dressed, and never closed but one eye at a time; each time it resumed, I would leap from my bed to the living-room window, my heart beating — not from fear (and this is how I realize that I have ceased to prize life much), but from a sort of amazement and panic horror, from expectation composed of mingled apprehension and hope.

18 December

The *Lettres écrites de la montagne*,[74] which I am finishing reading
almost in their entirety, are perhaps less interesting than the accompanying correspondence, which ought to be published with them but
is not reproduced in the edition I have at hand. Everything about the
constitution and functioning of the Geneva government hardly matters
to us any more, nor, consequently, Rousseau's arguments. What I had
read of this in the edition of the *Complete Works* at Cuverville had
left me with the recollection of being more deeply moved.

The young and very likable Charles Pérez, who had recently offered himself as a secretary, had not been able to work with me for six
days because he was altogether taken up with caring for the wounded,
since he is a Scout serving as a hospital attendant. Certain young Jews
here, whom I know, seem to be making a point of protesting by their
civic virtues, their zeal and spirit of sacrifice, against the abominable
ostracism to which they are subjected. In the *lycée* the Jews are at
the head of all the classes, the hardest workers, and, if perhaps not the
most intelligent, at least the most docile, the most assimilative, the
most zealous. If persecution were to cease, they are the ones who right-
fully would fill the highest positions; and the anti-Semites would have
an easy time of it, new occasions to protest, to exclaim: You see that
we were right to exclude them.

19 December

The electric power station has ceased to function for lack of fuel.
Without news from the radio, one lives in expectation, and hope feeds
on all the rumors: Rommel's army is cut off; a telegram from the Bey
to Roosevelt asks that Tunis be considered an open city. . . . It is a
fact that the Germans have partially withdrawn, liberating several
hotels and restaurants. A large part of the Arab population is fleeing
to the suburbs despite the placards all over the walls of Tunis rec-
ommending and urging calm. The streets are blocked with moving-
vans. The markets are empty and we are beginning to lack bread. Yesterday we dined with no other light than the moonlight, then went to
bed before eight o'clock, worn out by several sleepless nights and, anyway, not knowing what else to do but try to sleep. But we are hardly
in bed when the infernal orchestra begins again. It ceases and then resumes four or five times during the night. But a relatively small number of bombs fall on the city itself, the nearest of them more than

---

[74] Rousseau's *Letters Written from the Mountain* (1764) form a vigorous
protest, promptly burned by the Parliament of Paris, against his political
persecution at the hands of the Republic of Geneva.

two hundred yards from us. Many houses near the harbor (including the one that the Ragus occupied until very recently) have been blown up and several sections of the city have had to be evacuated.

"One man may lead a horse to the water, but twenty cannot make him drink" (found in Boswell's *Johnson*, 9 July 1763, where it is given as an English proverb).[75]

After five o'clock one cannot see well enough to read. We dine as early as six thirty, taking advantage of the moonlight when the night is clear or by the very inadequate light of a candle if the sky is overcast, taking great care to close the shutters and curtains at once for the black-out, which must be very strictly observed. But even candles are getting rare; grocers are out of them, and the little wax taper of Arab make costs twenty francs on the black market. . . . Then, with nothing to do, one lies down fully dressed on one's bed at seven o'clock to await sleep or a bombing-raid. Occasionally I get up and go to smoke a cigarette while walking back and forth in the living-room, striving in vain to scare up some semblance of a thought in my brain.

21 December

What people one meets in the streets! Haggard, ragged, sordid. Where were they hiding until now? Hideous outcasts who seem forever unfit for everything that constitutes human dignity, unfit likewise for happiness and having no possible contact with us but their poverty.

22 December

M. Amphoux, our very kind neighbor, lends me *La Farce de la Sorbonne*[76] by René Benjamin: a sour pamphlet without wit or grace and such as to make Béraud seem to have genius.[77] No more talent in it than anything else I have managed to read by the same author.

"In the eyes of many minds that drag convictions about like old habits . . ." This is the way the book begins. All the rest is of the same quality.

I note in Boswell's *Samuel Johnson*:
"The practice of using words of disproportionate magnitude is, no doubt, too frequent everywhere; but, I think, most remarkable among

---

[75] Gide translates the sentence into French and then gives the original.

[76] *The Sorbonne Farce.*

[77] Henri Béraud (1885–   ), a journalist and polemicist, attacked Gide and the *Nouvelle Revue Française* in 1923 with a series of articles entitled *The Crusade of Long-Faced Men*. Gide noted then that he gave "every impression of being an idiot."

the French, of which, all who have travelled in France must have been struck with innumerable instances." [78] (3 August 1763.)

I am reading the *Émile*, which I had hitherto merely skimmed. I note: "Of the children born, at most half reach adolescence. . . ." Thus in the time of Rousseau, if we can believe him, infant mortality accounted for at least 50 per cent of births.

Having opened the Reymonds' piano for lack of anything to do (for the electricity is cut off, and after five p.m. reading becomes impossible), I note with sorrow that I cannot remember completely any fugue of Bach, any prelude, and can find in my head only fragments of Chopin or Schumann. . . .

The example of Victor makes me realize, by contrast, how vulnerable to suffering sympathy makes us. He who, like that child, loves no one and doesn't care whether or not he is loved is vulnerable only to what hurts him directly. It is a great source of strength (but one which I scarcely admire) to feel no need of the affection or esteem of others. Victor is indifferent, insensitive to censure, and doesn't give a hang what others think of him so long as their judgment in no way endangers his own interests. I do not think that even love later on will succeed in penetrating his self-satisfaction. He is an island living on imports and exporting nothing.

24 December

Events incline me to think I shall be here for a long time more, cut off from those who are dear to me and whom I am not even very sure of ever seeing again; dear friends of whom I am constantly thinking and whose affection is the most valuable of my possessions.

Christmas

I reproach myself for not having copied in a special notebook from day to day the gleanings from my readings that deserved to hold my attention and that I should like to recall in order to quote them at need: for instance, this from Montaigne (III, 12) that effectively depicts the state in which France then was:

"It was a universal conjunction of limbs severally diseased, and each one more so than the other, and for the most part with inveterate ulcers, which no longer admitted of cure or desired it." [79]

Victor enjoys poisoning this life in common, which might be charming, despite the privations, if everyone showed a will. He resists any-

---

[78] Quoted in English.
[79] Translation by E. J. Trechmann, in the Modern Library edition.

thing that is said to him or asked of him, and often with an insolence that would be unbearable from anyone but a child. But it so happens that when he resists like this, he is trying to prove to himself that he is a man.

26 December

NOTICES in three languages (French, Arabic, and Italian) are abundantly posted on the walls of the city. They make known to the Jews that before the end of the year they will have to pay the sum of TWENTY MILLIONS as an aid to the victims of the Anglo-American bombings, for which *they are responsible,* "international Jewry" having, as it has long been well known, "wanted and prepared for the war." (The Jewish victims are naturally excluded from the number of people to be aided.) This is signed by "General Von Arnim, Commander of the Axis forces in Tunisia."

27 December

Been to check on certain results of last night's bombing. A rather large number of bombs fell on the Arab town, rather close to the Porte de France. So long as they were few and far between, they might be imputed to the aviators' lack of skill or to chance; but what can one think when faced with such frequent cases? The victims are many, it is said. Cordons of police or of soldiers keep people from approaching the scene of the disaster; but far around, the effects of the explosions are alarming, and one comes away full of apprehension for succeeding nights.

Despite my resolve to read the *Émile* without skipping anything, I give up. Through his endless dissertations, it is always Rousseau we look for and he interests us the more, the less he reasons. In contrast to him, oh, how wise Montaigne seems! [80] Many of Rousseau's arguments are disconcertingly inept. And yet how sure he is of knowing his business!

I no longer read any book without wondering: If the author were to come back to earth today, what would he think of his own writings?

Most of the axioms drawn from his heart, on which he constructs his religion, his philosophy, and bases his confidence in the excellence of *Nature* have become unthinkable. Nothing has done more to upset them than the study of origins, for which Goethe showed such distrust or disdain. When I read: "What God wants a man to do He does not communicate to him through another man; He tells it to him Himself by inscribing it in his heart" (Book IV), I come to prefer even Bossuet.

[80] Montaigne's essay "On the Education of Children" (Book I, 26) treats of the same subject as *L'Émile.*

31 December

Last day of this year of disgrace, on which I want to close this notebook. May the following one reflect less somber days!

A night of passable sleep urged me to get up well before dawn. The first quiverings of daylight remind me of the glorious settings out by night in the bush when, one's heart full of courage, one is off toward heroic exploits, and everything ahead of one suggests conquest. How many times, on foot or on horseback, preceding the escort of bearers, I have advanced alone on the unknown trail, muffling the sound of my steps in the hope of surprising the game that our escort would put to flight. I then used to savor a joy similar to that of fame itself, but certainly purer and such that the humblest can taste it. I really believe that even today I should not be incapable of it, and my heart feels no less brave than at thirty.

I am preparing to leave Tunis, accepting Dr. Ragu's friendly invitation to join the very kind G. Boutelleaus in settling temporarily at Nabeul while it is still possible to move about without too much difficulty, it seems.

While the successes on the Russian front are being confirmed and strengthened, the military situation in Tunisia seems uncertain and precarious, and this uncertainty may continue for some time. In any case the game will be hard to play and costly. I believe we must expect much worse bombings than those of the last few nights.

Joy of hearing last night on the radio the first act of the second *Henry IV* with an excellent Falstaff and, since I had recently reread it, of recognizing and understanding everything better than I should have hoped.

Yesterday, charming lunch at Mme Sparrow's, together with the Ragus and the Boutelleaus, after which we make our plans for departure more definite.

Doubtless I no longer cling much to life, but I have this fixed idea; *to last.* To make myself and my dependencies last a little while longer: linen, clothing, shoes, hope, confidence, smile, graciousness; make them last until the farewell. In view of this I am becoming economical, parsimonious of everything in order that none of this should give out ahead of time, through great fear that this war may be drawn out, through great desire and great hope to see the end of it.

1943

No electricity. We dine as early as six o'clock, for the gas is likewise cut off while we are sitting down at the table in the light of a single candle. Bombs again fell on Tunis at noon and at five o'clock; the results of the explosions are terrifying. Jean Tournier has been busy with a team of youths the last few mornings extracting corpses and wounded from under the ruins of a block of houses in the Arab town that had been demolished by three bombs early in the week. They counted between three and four hundred victims. It was impossible to help in time those who were calling for help from the cellars where they were walled off. And clusters of corpses, already rotting, continue to be brought out from under heaps of masonry, beams, and rubble.

And this is probably but the prelude to more violent bombings, which keep one from feeling safe anywhere. Hope of escaping narrows from day to day.

Invited by the Ragus, I lunched this first day of the new year at the civilian hospital together with the Boutelleaus. The latter arrive very late: a bomb has just fallen on the house of Mme Sparrow, the eminent Polish doctor who is lodging them. A telephone message (the hospital's exchange is still working) warns the Ragus that Mme Sparrow cannot come. Taken by surprise in her bed, where a severe headache had detained her, she had to rush out in pajamas. The bomb buried itself in the ground without exploding, cutting through the cellar of the building. They are thinking of exploding it, and a police cordon is keeping people at a distance from the block of evacuated houses. The evening before, I had entrusted to Gérard Boutelleau the two notebooks of my journal (the entire year 1942), which Hope Boutelleau had very kindly offered to type for me. Besides, fearing a house-search, I was anxious to put them in a safe place. Gérard B. had the greatest difficulty getting through the cordon of German police and getting hold of the manuscripts. This is what made him so late. It is hoped that the artificially provoked explosion will not do too much harm to Mme Sparrow's apartment. They left us immediately after the meal to make sure of this.

After their leaving we examine at length the plan of fleeing to Nabeul. It is essential to make sure that we are not rushing toward a greater danger: many country houses and farms have been sacked by Arabs and their inhabitants massacred. It is a sort of organized Jacquerie[1] protected by the German army, which is eager to make a good

---

[1] The peasant uprising of 1358 as a result of the English invasion of France during the captivity of King Jean II.

impression on the native population, drunk with its demands. Rather a bomb than butchery.

2 January

Calm night (like almost all those that Chacha thinks it better to spend in the cellar). Got up at daybreak. Glorious, splendid dawn, which I contemplate as if it were to be that of my last day on earth. The lack of electric current deprives us of any news from the radio, true or false; but a violent American offensive against Tunis is expected.

I give up my reading of *L'Œuvre*,[2] the poorest of Zola's books that I can recall. The drama one would like to see spring from the conflict of two æsthetics is miserably reduced to puerile elements. Zola does not seem to suspect any other enemy of naturalism than academicism; and even then he manages to relate the anxieties of his Claude to hereditary taints. The real subject, which might have been wonderful, is not even hinted at. It is a serious mistake to set up against his hero nothing but a valueless opponent, and his artist's conflict offers no real interest. The conversations of his daubers, and even the professions of faith of the best among them, are discouragingly silly. Enough to justify all Zola's detractors.

I am rereading *La Guerre de Troie n'aura pas lieu* (I had seen it on the stage).[3] Soon people will be amazed that an audience could have approved and even swooned over this ballet of sophistries, this dance on the points of irritating paradoxes. I believe the fear of not seeming up to it did a great deal for the success of this play (see *The Emperor's New Clothes*).

Meanwhile five Italian ships have recently entered the harbor and are unloading munitions. Reinforcements are arriving daily by air.

During the next to the last alert Victor was busy guzzling "ftaïrs" in the Arab town; took advantage of the disorder and panic to skip out without paying.

3 January

No, according to other information that seems more trustworthy, the harbor of Tunis is apparently not sheltering any Italian ship at the moment. Easy to verify, moreover.[4] It is less easy to estimate the

---

[2] *The Masterpiece.*

[3] Jean Giraudoux's play, *The Trojan War will Not Take Place*, was produced in 1935.

[4] Yes, asserts a dock-hand: since yesterday a German warship and two Italian warships. [A.]

number of bombs dropped on La Goulette at noon the day before yesterday. A French officer, trustworthy and well informed, claims to have counted seventy-seven, with seven of them on the electric power-house (the damage caused to it can be readily repaired, it is said; but meanwhile we are without light and without radio). From the R.s' living-room windows I could see the wreaths of smoke from the explosions: a broad fringe above the horizon line. The raid was very short and had ended before the A.A. had begun to react.

But I cannot set down here the echo of all the current rumors. It is repeated above all that last Sunday the Americans were on the point of entering Tunis. A very considerable spearhead of tanks is said to have been routed by a handful of German motorcyclists who had set out to meet them and whom they took to be the forerunners of considerable resistance forces. If only those tanks had continued their advance, they would easily have mastered the city. Reported as they are here, such stories seem childish; but many examples are given of the incompetence and lack of dash of the American army, turning tail at the slightest threat and refusing combat so long as they are not sure of being twenty to one. At another point (Tebourba?) a column of tanks, attacked by enemy aviation, is said to have been routed, the men forsaking their wonderful and costly machines intact in order to flee under the olive trees, so that the German army, having seized the tanks, brought them in triumph into town, where everyone could see them. The Americans' equipment is supposedly marvelous, excellent even in its smallest details, but the combat value of the men almost nonexistent; in any case, they are altogether inexperienced, incapable of measuring up to the quality of the Germans, who are sending their best to Tunisia. I fear that there may be much truth in this; and in any case the Allies have to deal with serious opponents, resolute, convinced men, long prepared and disindividualized to the point of ceasing to exist except in terms of fighting.

We are wallowing in suppositions; but one certainty is that a dozen eggs cost a hundred and twenty francs.

The sky is overcast. An icy wind shakes the windows. Fortunately electricity has been given back to us, but my eyes get tired quickly. and, anyway, I do not find any book I like enough to be distracted by it. In order to warm my heart, it would require some friendly presence. I cannot very well imagine what Roger would be like during bombing-raids. Jean Sch. would be too much like a hero of Corneille and too scornful of life. Mme Théo would be marvelous; Dorothy Bussy, courageous and resolute, but too emotive; Simon, probably perfect; Élisa-

beth and Catherine, I fancy, quite up to snuff. . . . I evoke them one
after another . . . and feel lonely.[5]

4 January

Visit from little Charles Pérez, who is continuing to give his attention to the bomb victims as a volunteer in the rescue brigade. He says
that there can still be heard the calls for help of five families buried
under the ruins of the "Foyer du Combattant," a large building of re-
inforced concrete that completely caved in, covering with heavy blocks
of masonry those who had taken refuge in the cellar. . . . Those blocks
can be raised only by powerful cranes that are expected from day to
day. Oxygen is being piped in to the walled-in people to keep them
alive.

Charles Pérez leaves me to go and wash up a bit at his parents';
busy day and night, he has been unable to go home or undress for the
last week.

5 January

No more supplies of food. The Germans and Italians have made
a clean sweep of the stores. Yesterday Amphoux heard one of their
upper-rank officers say laughingly in the restaurant: "If the English
come to Tunis" (I even believe he said: "When the English come"),
"they won't find a thing, *not a thing!*" and this in very good French.
One after another all the shops are closing; already you see no more
than one out of ten or twelve open, their stocks being exhausted. Unable to replace anything, I am making clothes, linen, razor blades,
shaving stick, etc., last as long as possible. The *lycée* has not been
closed for fear of its being requisitioned; but when the professor comes
he has nothing but empty, or almost empty, benches facing him, and
sometimes it is the few zealous pupils who wait for the professor in
vain.

The electricity, which had been given back to us yesterday, is cut
off again. It is said that the Germans will not leave without blowing
up the power-house.

Several trustworthy farmers confirm the lamentable, absurd retreat
of the American forces before the semblance of German opposition.
The sudden appearance of a handful of resolute men forced the withdrawal of those who, very superior in numbers and equipment, would
have had only to continue their advance to become masters of the objective, to seize Tebourba; it is even said: to enter Tunis. And that

---

[5] He is thinking of Roger Martin du Gard, Jean Schlumberger, Mme
Théo Van Rysselberghe, M. and Mme Simon Bussy, Élisabeth Van Rysselberghe, and his daughter, Catherine Gide.

sorry comedy took place, almost at the same time, on several roads. "With their equipment, we'd already be in Algiers," say the German officers, still laughing. What is certain is that the American army gave the German resistance plenty of time to organize. The game will be much more costly now than it would have been if the Allies had taken advantage of surprise. But they gave reinforcements plenty of time to come up, not so much by ship as by planes.

As soon as electricity is restored, I rush to the radio. I stumble onto a broadcast of *"La France Fidèle"* (what can *that* France be? Faithful to what? . . .). I hear: "We know that the marshal has but one aim . . ." and the following broadcast is announced to be in Arabic. Most likely that France is the France of the Tunis *Zeitung*. The voices of the other stations are covered by heavy jamming.

In the still childish, at times almost charming face of Victor one can already make out which features will become vulgar by hardening or thickening.

6 January

Bombs fell last night on the avenue Roustan barely sixty yards from the house of which we are occupying the fourth floor. The explosion blew in a French door of the room in which I was sleeping and broke a large and heavy mirror in the living-room. By an extraordinary stroke of bad luck we had not made sure the windows were unlocked because of yesterday's wind. A rather large bomb-fragment cut through the wooden shutter and knocked out the lower pane of one of the living-room windows.

Late in the afternoon I had gone to get news of Mme Germa-Sparrow, who had kindly served me an excellent prewar tea. The little ground-floor apartment she is occupying, rue Marceau, was preserved as if miraculously. Two bombs fell on the next buildings; they were exploded a few hours later, sacrificing the houses on both sides of hers.

After dinner Amphoux had played us the very beautiful *Concert Royal* (the second) of Couperin, and *Nuages* by Debussy.

7 January

Some fifteen bombs on Tunis last night, but not very near. I had let the grandmother and Victor go down to the cellar. M. Amphoux had come to join me and, since it was not very cold, we were able to watch the bombing for almost two hours seated in front of the large broken window of the living-room.

The bombing resumed a little after five a.m. I suddenly said to myself, I don't know why: the next bomb is for me; dressed in a hurry to go out into the stair well; in my haste had neglected to take the apartment keys; had to wait stupidly, seated on a step, until Chacha and Victor come up from the cellar around six thirty, cursing the absurd false presentiment that had made me leave my bed.

I don't know what I would have given when I was young to have some day the hollow cheeks and prominent cheekbones I admired in the portrait of Delacroix. It was he or Berlioz that I most wanted to resemble.

8 January

My eyes are too tired to allow me to read at length in artificial light. However close the lamp may be, after a quarter of an hour my vision becomes troubled, everything is veiled, and tears come; I have no alternative but to stop. For me this restriction is more painful than all those to which we owe the monotony of our evening meals: always the same bean soup, a vegetable cooked in some vile grease or other (cauliflower, artichoke, eggplant), and an orange for dessert.

The temperature in my room is no more than 45°; but my brain begins to function only above 60°.

Victor, who generally is the last to the table, gets ahead of the others when, like today miraculously, there is chicken, and quickly seizes the best pieces. Each day I wonder more at the extraordinary strength he derives from being able quite painlessly to do without the esteem or affection of others. (When I think that I am still grieved that he should withdraw in the evening without having said good-night to me!) His selfishness gives him a sort of invulnerability. He encounters everything proper and seemly with: "What does it matter to me?" He is taken care of. Curious to know whether puberty, which is slow in coming to him, will awaken any feelings of emotion.

Germans everywhere. Well turned out, in becoming uniforms, young, vigorous, strapping, jolly, clean-shaven, with pink cheeks. The Italian soldiers cut a rather sorry figure in comparison. And the Arabs show themselves full of obsequious regards for the Germans.

Oh good Lord, I am very familiar with those well-known short-comings of the French! They pain me as much or more than anyone else. They have always pained me and there is not one of them (lack of curiosity, triviality, smugness and easy self-satisfaction, vanity . . .) from which I am not careful to protect myself. But not one of my friends has those shortcomings, and they are no less French on that account.

In the streets of Tunis, where I wander aimlessly, what a wretched humanity! Not one face that it is a pleasure to look at. Men and women, Italians as well as Arabs, marked with anxiety, as if withered, wretched. Toward evening many of them carry suitcases, baskets, mattresses, and blankets for the night's encampment. Puny children. Poor cattle, fearful and hunted.

Horses, asses, and mules have been requisitioned. No vehicles but the Italian and German autos, which drive like mad; the French autos are all requisitioned by the army. Electricity is again cut off. I came home and, not knowing what to do, am writing this by the inadequate light of a candle. Chacha is moving about the hall humming lively little tunes. Ah, to know what is happening to Dorothy's eyes, to Mme Théo's knee, to Roger's kidneys, to Jacques's liver, to Marcel's asthma! . . . Are they still alive even? Whom shall I find after all this, and in what condition? . . .

9 January

Victor, who is inclined to help himself before others, feels all the oranges in the dish in order to save out a few for himself. When I ask him if he intends to leave only the poorer ones for the others, he replies: "My taste is not yours and I am choosing according to my taste. As for dates, I prefer the soft ones and you the hard ones. I am free to think it is the same for oranges." And I do not retort that I too like very ripe oranges, for fear of hearing him reply: "In that case you must admit that I am right to help myself first." For if he often lies, he never does so out of politeness.

Victor has this in common with his father: intending to do a certain thing, announcing it loudly, then not doing it. I had never before met anyone so unfaithful to himself, to his own commitments, and so little concerned about it. On the other hand, when Victor declares that he will not do something, especially if it is a favor one is asking of him, entreaties, coaxings, or threats will not get him to do it. *"Fortis et tenax propositi"* [6] in the negative. He is strong indeed; reproaches leave him untouched, and the discomfort and grief of others.

Refusing to do the favor asked of you is a habit to get into; a mere matter of practice, and Victor is giving himself plenty of training. After a short time it no longer requires much effort. Useless to insist; he has said no.

I do not envy Victor, to be sure, and cannot resist occasionally feeling angry with him, nor yet resist admiring him. I have often en-

---

[6] "Strong and resolute in purpose." Gide is thinking of the opening words of Horace: *Odes*, III, 3:

Iustum et tenacem propositi virum.

countered selfish people; they are legion; but unconscious, sly, snide ones. Victor, who never hesitates to lie when he finds an advantage in lying, is utterly frank in this regard: his selfishness is manifest, resolute, cynical; he professes it. Had I known him earlier, I should have enriched with his features the Strouvilhou of my *Faux-Monnayeurs*.

Roosevelt's speech holds out the bright productive prospects of American factories, which, he declares, are now producing all alone more submarines than the factories of Germany, Italy, and Japan combined. Likewise for tanks, cannon, machine guns, and all other war supplies. Fine! He also speaks of the draft that is increasing the American army from two to seven million men (I think). But he doesn't speak, and can't speak, of the military value of those men. It is harder to achieve than machines; long training and practice are lacking. And the flaunting of that numerical and material superiority, if it is not accompanied by a moral superiority, far from reassuring me, worries me. What is the good of giving all those figures? Stalin cleverly hid his, so that the power of the Russian army took the world and Germany by surprise.

10 January

I sleep. I sleep as if to make up now for all the insomnias of my childhood. My siestas, which used to last a half hour at most, sometimes last more than two hours, without any harm to my long night's sleep. I had gone to bed yesterday without supper, my stomach still heavy from the lavish luncheon the Cattans had served me. What a meal! It would have seemed perfect to me if I had been able to divide it four ways. Preceded by a delicious "West Indian punch" (for Mme Cattan comes from Guadeloupe), it began with "breiks" (which are large triangles of very flaky pastry surrounding a soft-boiled egg in the midst of a succulent meat hash; one cannot imagine anything better) followed by copious hors-d'œuvres, which would alone have satisfied me until evening. Then came an extraordinary duck with orange, in a curaçao sauce thickened with minced livers; it was so good that I could not resist helping myself a second time. This was unwise, for I next had to do honor to a loin of milk-fed veal with mushrooms; then to a lobster and vegetable salad *à la russe*. To finish off, to finish me off, two huge cakes, one made with almonds and the other a sort of cream tart covered with thick caramel. All this washed down with four kinds of old and delicious wines: Sauterne, Beaune, Pouilly, and one other, from their best stock. I got them not to open a last bottle of real champagne, prewar Veuve Cliquot, "such as will not be seen for a long time." Dead-drunk and overstuffed, I let myself fall on the couch the Cattans had prepared for me in a quiet room (for I had informed

them of my habit of taking a siesta) with blankets and a hot-water
bottle at my feet. But almost at once a warning from the sirens and
the A.A. guns tore me from my restoring sleep. I feared having to cover
the long way home on foot, weighed down as I was by that too copious
meal; but a providential auto allowed Maître Cattan kindly to take me
home. I was done in.

11 January

All she expected of me and I was unable to give her — indeed, that
was due her . . . there are days when I constantly think of it. Ah, if
the soul, as you were eager to persuade me, is immortal and if yours
still has its eyes fixed on me, may it realize that I feel eternally in-
debted to you. . . . But no, in my case, since I cannot believe in an
afterlife, this is not the form my regret takes; I merely think of all the
attentions I should have had for her, and I await, and shall await, the
smile with which she would have rewarded me. In what a state of
blindness I have lived!

12 January

Confirmation by further eyewitnesses of the American retreat near
Tebourba (in the forest of Mayana) before very small German forces
sent out to meet them. The considerable column of American tanks
was forsaken by the men, who fled wildly, spreading panic, and were
soon pursued by the Germans who had seized the tanks together with
large quantities of munitions and equipment that the Americans had
not taken time to put out of use. Pursuing the Americans in their own
tanks was a sport over which the Germans have gloated ever since.

13 January

Last night a violent storm with a great celestial hubbub, lightning,
thunder, and gusts of wind, which twice sounded like the noise of
bombs exploding. I get up to make sure the windows are closed because they were left open as a precaution against explosions. I hear
Victor shouting: "Chacha! Come and close my window." He is fifteen.
His grandmother is at his beck and call. He will not raise a finger in
favor of the community, and I was the one to climb on a ladder and
paint the hall lights blue. When I asked Victor to do it, he merely
answered: "No," without even raising his head. He was busy at the
moment filing empty cartridges of A.A. rockets, which he is collecting
with the idea of selling them later on to people who want "war
souvenirs."

Yet he claims to be a Communist and even an "atheist Communist,"
for "it is impossible to be one without being the other," he repeats in
imitation of his friend Lévy, who is indoctrinating him. He even has
ready a whole arsenal of arguments to defend his position; for he is

disposed to quibble, not trying to convince his opponent, but rather to "shut him up" and to have the last word, even if he has to repeat the same remark obstinately after the other one has spoken. And indeed he is not stupid. He is sure to succeed.

14 January

We sup before seven, often at six thirty, to allow Chacha, the grandmother, to go down to the cellar earlier and take shelter from possible bombs. I say the cellar, but it is on the ground floor that she settles down, in the employees' coatroom of some office or other. She spends the night in a deck-chair, bundled up until she seems obese (but actually as dried up as a locust bean in winter), at her side her handbag and a suitcase filled with necessities that would allow her to endure being buried for three days. She speaks of "her little storeroom" where she takes refuge as the sequestered girl in Poitiers used to speak of her "dear big black Malampia"; [7] but she admits that she does not sleep well there. She goes there not out of fear, she says, but to keep any family of refugees from taking it over and "leaving lice." And, as if by an irony of fate, the nights when she goes there are regularly among the calmest.

At six o'clock, almost immediately before the evening meal, Victor gets himself a cup of chocolate from his clandestine stock of chocolate bars. He has likewise taken care to make sure of a personal supply of jam. Chacha tells me that since his childhood his mother has always seen to it that there was a box of sweets in his closet.

Coming up from the cellar this morning, Chacha mislays her keys; she looks for them everywhere in vain. For the sake of peace, she eventually offers Victor five francs if he finds them for her. This takes but a moment, for it is a forgone conclusion that the keys fell in the outer hall while Chacha was trying to stop the cat, which wanted to go out. Not for a moment did Victor make a pretense of helping his grandmother in her search until she held out the attraction of a financial reward. (I should have done likewise for darkening the ceiling lights.) Victor charges for the only favors he is willing to do. He told Amphoux, with naïve cynicism, that his father was constantly mislaying the book he was reading and would say to Victor: "A franc for you if you find it for me." I should have liked to ask Victor if he did not take care to hide it first, as Jeanne suspects him of hiding his grandmother's keys. "What wouldn't he do for money?" she says. He tells us this morning at breakfast that he managed, when the State was calling in all gold, to hoard

---

[7] See *La Séquestrée de Poitiers* (*The Poitiers Incarceration Case*), by André Gide.

forty twenty-franc pieces, which are today worth I know not how much, a fortune. His stamp collection is valued by him at sixty thousand francs.

15 January

The new operating schedule for the *lycée* keeps the children in class only in the morning. Several times a week Victor gathers a few classmates in the avenue R. apartment, and the dining-room becomes a gambling-den. The poker and baccarat sessions last from two to six p.m. On the other hand, Victor reads considerably and probably not without discernment. He has just devoured Rousseau's *Confessions* and *Rêveries,* huge quantities of Voltaire and Diderot, writers to whom he is introduced in class; then many detective or other novels at a rate of one a day; for, still having good eyes, he is satisfied with the light of a single candle and reads in bed until late hours. Since he didn't know anything of Zola, I went to get him *Germinal* from the public library. His great friend Lévy, the young Communist who is indoctrinating him, lends him Soviet novels.

16 January

No more bombings. What are the Americans doing? We are waiting; we are getting impatient; we are disappointed. Has the great offensive that was announced been put off until later or has it failed like the advance on Tebourba? One imagines explanations; I was about to say excuses. It is said that they don't want to run the risk until they are assured of an overwhelming numerical superiority. It is said also that they need fuel (and the German radio claims to have sunk the last Allied convoy of tankers). As for that offensive which was so banked on, I now expect the Germans to risk it and drive the American forces back beyond Bône just as the English Eighth Army forced Rommel's army to retreat and take refuge at Tripoli. On the other hand, the too rare French forces seem to be fighting heroically in the vicinity of Pichon and near Kairouan. But the prisoners brought back to Tunis are still angry with the Americans, who apparently left them for a very long time without munitions and supported them insufficiently with their aviation. Those prisoners, it seems, are extremely well treated, even coddled, and so well fed that the Italian soldiers are jealous of them, it is said. As the height of precaution, Hitler promises unconditional liberation to all French soldiers who surrender, as we learn from a circular reproduced on the front page of *Tunis-Journal* (of 14 January) and widely broadcast by planes flying over the "dissident" forces fighting in Tunisia. "The Führer," it says therein, "has decided that the members of the French army who fall into German hands during the fighting in North Africa will not be treated as prisoners of war, taking into account the fact that those soldiers have been deceived by certain of their leaders. Taking account also of the fact that those soldiers were unable to receive news bulletins on the situation of France and on the formal commands given them by Marshal Pétain. The French Government will be called upon to facilitate the transfer of these demobilized soldiers into civilian life" (and doubtless also their shipment to Germany as "volunteer" workers). "The French officers and enlisted men who voluntarily come to our lines in order to submit to their government will be handled in order of priority."

The Vichy radio will probably soon inform us of the results of this propaganda; clever smoke-screen.

I bend over the radio as often as six times a day with that childish illusion that my excessive attention is going somehow to hasten events. In the same way Valéry, the first times he traveled on the railway, used to push the front wall of the compartment with all his might, thinking with that effort, as he told me, to add to the efforts of the locomotive and speed up the train's progress.

17 January

I am reading Goethe's *Achilleis* [8] and enjoying it greatly. Goethe gives Achilles some wonderful maxims; the first rejoinders of Pallas Athena are no less beautiful. Odd that so artificial a work can seem successful to such a degree — at least in spots, for the final canto is extremely disappointing. Goethe was right not to prolong that feat further.

Read much of late despite the fatigue of my eyes. But my brain has ceased to accept any but not very lasting impressions; it seems that nothing more can be deeply inscribed in it. Whence I harvest, after all, but little profit from these readings. I am continuing, as a matter of duty, that of Boswell's *Johnson*. Boswell is considerably more intelligent and stout than Eckermann, but, to be sure, Johnson is less important than Goethe; one is more amused than taught by him, and Boswell is often quite right to stand up to him and to accept his opinions and judgments only with many reservations. Not much of a lesson to be hoped for from conformists. I am eager, as soon as the Boswell is finished, to launch into Gibbon's *Decline and Fall*.

The sight of Victor at the table used to plunge me, the first few days, into stupefaction. Now I have become accustomed to it; nothing about Victor amazes me any more. But on occasion I still fall into a sort of dazed contemplation when he settles down and spreads out, both elbows far from his body and on a level with his face to raise to

---

[8] The *Achilleid* is but a fragment, left unfinished.

his mouth glass, spoon, or fork. He often gets along without the last implement, in the Arab fashion, subsequently sucking his sauce-covered fingers; he uses them also, on the same occasion, to pick his teeth. He guzzles, stuffing in enormous mouthfuls and always helping himself first when the dish is to his liking. His whole person proclaims: "This is the way I am; too bad if you don't like it!" It should be added that he has considerably perfected himself since the departure of his parents, who, however indulgent they were, would never have put up with certain too offensive manifestations of his cheek. In the early days I used to risk a few remarks, but what is the use? He listens only to what encourages him and pushes him farther in his direction. His parents have never given him any discipline, but merely aid, support, protection, and approbation. His father, to be sure, is constantly nagging at him, but always yields to him in the last analysis and at heart, as Amrouche claims, admires him. His mother, made up wholly of weakness, indulgence, and love, forgives him everything. Both of them attribute all the unpleasant aspects of their son to "the awkward age." I do not believe that child has ever been punished. And probably a certain amount of theory entered into his parents' educational system: the decision to ask nothing of him without his understanding and approving it. Whatever you ask of him, he retorts at once: "Why?" He is one more example of those children for whom it would have been better to be long exiled from their families. In any case, I do not think Victor is capable of feeling real gratitude toward his parents. The virtues of his mother, who is one of the finest and worthiest women I have ever met, are incomprehensible to him. As for the affection she bears him, he thinks he has found its explanation in the writings of Freud; and he takes advantage of it. As for his father, he spares no signs of his fierce scorn for him.

It is true: outside of those sudden fatigues that occasionally descend upon me and during which I should like to be able to shout "Pax!" to life, I scarcely feel my age. I do not really succeed in convincing myself when I keep telling myself at all hours of the day: "Poor old fellow, you are past seventy-three!" The bombing alerts, far from depressing me, give me new life. It is not a matter of courage for someone who has ceased to cherish life much; but, in a state of trance, I am at my height. And, nevertheless, I am very curious about what will follow . . . and eager to see family and friends again.

18 January

The Russians have taken back Millerovo; along a vast front they are driving back or encircling the Germans and Rumanians. The English Eighth Army is pushing Rommel's army back in Tripolitania. Gen-

eral Leclerc's heroic advance is winning over the whole region of the
Fezzan. The French forces from Tunisia are engaged in a hard battle
near Kairouan; victoriously, it seems, despite their inadequate equipment. And meanwhile what is the American army doing? What is it
waiting for? Is not this the moment for it to attack while the Germans are busy on so many fronts? Is it going to lose this opportunity?
Must we see in this temporizing a skillful strategy or a blunder, wise
patience or timorous incompetence? Or do they plan to spring into action only when sure of winning, after having let their allies bear the
brunt of the battle? Or, possibly, are they carrying out a wish of
Stalin that the greatest possible number of enemy planes be kept on
the alert far from the Russian front? This is what everyone here is
wondering and this is the subject of all conversations.

19 January

I am reading, or rereading, the three *Unpleasant Plays* of Bernard
Shaw with very keen amusement. *Mrs. Warren's Profession* seems to
me by far the least good.

20 January

"In principle" Victor does not smoke yet. He doesn't mind a few
cigarettes from time to time, however. He likes to smoke them lying
down, but, for fear that his pillow will smell of tobacco afterward, he
lies down on his grandmother's bed. For this purpose he takes advantage of some moment when Chacha is out, and she gives vent to
her indignation only when she finds ashes or cigarette butts on her
bed-table or on her sheets.

An unhoped-for, and probably last, opportunity to return to France:
I am offered a seat on one of the planes that are to repatriate some
officers and civilians. I pretend to myself to be perplexed while knowing full well, at heart, that I shall not accept. The game that is being
played here is too captivating, and my fate is linked to that of these
new friends whose life I have been sharing for more than six months.
It would seem to me that I was deserting. That game, of which I saw
the beginning and which I have followed from day to day, I want to
see through to the end, even if I were to be a victim of it. For I cannot
believe that there are not difficult days ahead. Even if the Germans
withdraw (and this is hardly to be hoped for), the Italians, I believe,
will defend Tunis, "their Tunis," with the ruthlessness that can be expected of them when exasperated by the successive loss of all their
African possessions. Are we going to have to experience the horrors of
a siege and artillery bombardment? Shall we see street-fighting, the
natives revolting against the French, the execution of suspects, looting

of shops and apartments, massacres? . . . I expect everything; I expect the worst, and my imagination is working full time.

22 January

After a series of bad days the sky is again glorious. Last night the full moon was an invitation for bombing-raids. The Germans shroud the city in an artificial fog, which takes on a poetically silver look; walls move farther away and one can barely make out the tops of the palm trees opposite the Residence; everything becomes unreal and late strollers no longer recognize their houses. This morning not a cloud left in the sky; a soft effulgence as on the finest days of my adolescence.

The last two days Victor has hardly shown his face, has said neither good-morning nor good-evening, has looked glum, has not answered when spoken to, and has walked by you without seeing you. I am indeed very silly to be concerned about it.

23 January

But I should like to know whether he would act in this uncivil way and show the same disregard for anyone whatsoever, or whether, as I fear, this reveals a particular hostility toward me. To be sure, he may not like feeling constantly observed and judged by me, and judged very severely. I am the only one to stand up to him. I am very much alone; and despite the great esteem and liking shown me by the grandmother and Jeanne (the old servant and friend of the family) I am ready to feel, in the house of these new friends, as if I were in a very false situation. In the absence of his parents, Victor knows that he is the master here. Is he trying to make me feel this? He is succeeding through his ungraciousness. I am becoming the intruder, and Chacha's constant attentions serve only to antagonize him the more. I doubt if I shall be able to put up much longer with his naggings. But where to go?

The Amrouches were on the point of coming to share my abode by occupying Mme R.'s empty room; but at the last moment they were called upon by the College of Radès. And I also thought of letting myself be taken along by the Boutelleaus, who were planning a well-earned rest for themselves in Fauconnier's country house; but I fear we shall have to give up thinking of this.[9] That country house, like so many others, is requisitioned. Families of refugees have moved into everything that is inhabitable; the hotels are full of German and Italian officers. . . . There remains the Ragus' suggestion of going and camping somehow or other at the civilian hospital, where a bed is reserved

---

[9] The novelist Henri Fauconnier had for many years lived in a beautiful old house at Sidi-bou-Saïd.

for me, the doctor tells me, in the nook next to his office . . . if need
be. Today one has to be satisfied with what can be found, adopting the
proverb: "When you haven't what you like, you must like what you
have." I should be inclined to say that there is no better one, if it did
not encourage resignation rather than action.

24 January

Again tormented by unbearable itchings. Dr. Ragu's treatment had
completely overcome them last June; but here they are again, fiercer
than ever; whence sleepless nights.

Yesterday tea at the house of Maître Cattan, the lawyer, who had
already entertained me so lavishly the week before that I had had to
be satisfied with verbena tea at the next few meals. There were invited also Carteron, the former Minister (who was able to give me
rather recent news of Athens), and the head of the transport service in
Tunisia. Mme Cattan had prepared for us some "breiks" (which seemed
to me less wonderful than the last time), delicate tangerine ices, and
two huge cakes, all of the very best quality and accompanied by chocolate, port, and various liqueurs. The Minister and the "president," obviously very well informed, give details of the bombings of El Aouina
on 22 January. There were two raids, one at noon and the other at
three in the afternoon. From the avenue Roustan balcony I had been
able to see the extraordinary effects of the first one: it seemed like the
sudden eruption of a volcano. Gasoline depots had caught fire, spreading thick smoke over a large part of the horizon; sheltered by the
smoke, the planes (English and not American, it is said) could fly very
low and finish off their work of destruction. People talk of at least
fifteen German or Italian planes destroyed on the ground, having just
landed with reinforcements from Sicily. How does it happen that the
English radio says nothing of so successful an operation? But what
information can be trusted when, even on the spot, people are so far
from agreeing, for instance, about the number of victims? The figures
vary from 50 to . . . 800! The latter figure seems the more probable,
or closer to the truth, for the arrival of that considerable troop movement had gathered a number of people on the airfield, where, furthermore, a number of laborers were trying to put the field back in shape
after it had been plowed up by earlier raids. The only ones spared
were those who managed to throw themselves on the ground in time.
I heard the account given by one of them; but the smoke became immediately so thick, he says, that he could make out nothing around
him and, besides, thought only of fleeing as quickly and as far as possible from the slaughter. Germans, Italians, even Arabs are hiding their
losses as best they can, and it is impossible to check them on any definite basis. The same thing is probably true, on both sides, for the

loss of human life on the Russian front. Solely the very obvious facts, the recapture of towns such as Tripoli, Salzk, Armavir, or Millerovo, are not subject to doubt; even then the Axis press and radio, which cannot deny them, strive to cover them with an advantageous interpretation so as to keep them from seeming like real victories. On what unsteady documentation can the history of today be built tomorrow!

24 January

The Italian newspaper of Tunis, the *Unione,* has reached its fourth issue. It began to appear just in time to have to announce the fall of Tripoli. This is bitter for a paper that runs across the top of its page this patriotic heading: *"Vincere! Vincere! Vincere!"* [10] But one is obliged to admit that it announces this cruel setback much more frankly than the Vichy press or radio.

Amphoux has noted, as I have done myself of late, the increasing number of German soldiers in a state of flagrant intoxication. He says that in the restaurants and hotels their bearing has grown lax and that their familiarity with dubious Arabs whom they lead on to drink and then try to bring in and keep all night in their rooms had, on several occasions already, forced the hotel-keeper to intervene for fear of too great a scandal. "It looks as if they are trying to make the most of what is left them," Amphoux says. They are making a clean sweep of everything they can still find to buy; but the few shops that still remain open (one out of twelve) are almost empty already. None the less there can be seen departing at any time heavy German trucks loaded with packing-cases, the last requisitioned stocks of foodstuffs. Everything suggests that we are heading toward famine. This is expected, and that bread even should soon begin to be short. In front of any shop that still sells something on occasion, there are queues and interminable waits, but those who are wearing any military uniform whatever are always served at once.[11]

26 January

I had been directed to a bathing establishment, the only one still open. I went this morning; the soldiers, the first to be taken care of, are so numerous that the proprietor told me he could admit civilians only on Sunday. "Anyway," he added, "I am going to have to close the establishment for lack of fuel." The bathroom in the avenue Roustan apartment is frigid, and without hot water I cannot, for fear of a cold, allow myself to bathe except in bits, spacing out the operation over the whole day.

---

[10] "Conquer! Conquer! Conquer!"

[11] A decree posted up since yesterday the 23rd, I am told, is to put an end to this military priority. [A.]

Read in succession the four *Pleasant Plays* of Shaw (in English). Amazing cleverness; but at times the dose of Sardou wins out over the dose of Ibsen. How amusing they must be to act! And to see them presented by good actors!

28 January

As a result of their reverses, the animosity between the Italians and the Germans is emphasized. Police in civilian clothes protect those who are molested by Italian soldiers; they bring the soldiers to heel, who then sneak off. Their "inferiority complex" is expressed by arrogance; never have they been so lofty as since they have less reason to be proud; but they are curbed by the Germans, whom they detest the more since the Germans are making them more aware of their scorn. In Libya, in Tripolitania, the Germans were "motorized" and the Italian army was not. ("None the less, when there was a retreat, they always went faster than we," the Germans say, laughing.) Their soldiers are paid less and less well fed than the German soldiers; less well fed even (and this infuriates them) than the French prisoners. The Germans pretend to coddle their prisoners in the hope of enticing our "dissident" soldiers to surrender. Their propaganda is very well directed, although somewhat coarsely at times. In short, everywhere they reveal an incontrovertible surface superiority.

Yesterday, returning after dark from the hospital, where Ragu had treated me with a skillful, affectionate, utter devotion (intravenous injection of "bromical" [12] to try to end the itching, which during the last few days had become unbearable), I brutally fell full length in the filthy mud that covers the ground like oil, hiding its irregularities, since the streets are not lighted. For a moment I feared I had broken my thigh-bone; then, not one of the numerous passers-by having made a gesture to help me, I got up quite restored to youth. To make your blood tingle there is nothing like such a mishap. I suffered much more from the indifference of people than from my fall.

I read with amusement in Johnson's *Rasselas* (1759): "I have been long of opinion, that, instead of the tardy conveyance of ships and chariots, man might use the swifter migration of wings; that the fields of air are open to knowledge, and that only ignorance and idleness need crawl upon the ground"; and a little further: "If men were all virtuous I should with great alacrity teach them all to fly. But what would be the security of the good, if the bad could at pleasure invade them from the sky?" [13]

---

[12] *Bromical*, manufactured by Theraplix in Paris, is a desensitizer used in cases of prurigo, eczema, etc.

[13] In the original, the quotations are given in English.

29 January

When, upon leaving my next to the last year of school, I began to go out and to frequent a few salons, I readily realized that the thing most needed in them is an ear, each person being more attentive to what he says himself than to what others say. Nothing flatters people more than the interest one takes, or seems to take, in their conversation. I paid little attention to mine as a consequence, attributing value only to the written word, and prided myself on becoming a perfect listener. ("You listen with your eyes," Wilde told me.) Thus it is that I was well considered though remaining silent. But now, with age, I am the one who is listened to; but I express myself so badly that I disappoint as soon as I open my mouth. Everything that is dear to me and matters to me remains far this side of my lips, out of reach as it were, and I utter nothing but banalities and nonsense. I am worth something only when faced with blank paper.

I take less and less interest in conversation, in what is called "an exchange of ideas," except with a few rare intimate friends. Most often I strive merely to flatter in order to please, tormented by the desire to be liked. What a weakness! And how I admire those who, like Victor, pay no attention whatever to that! Fortunately it is not the same in my writings, where I override and am very little concerned with "what will be thought of it." At least this is the way I did in the time when one could still write and publish freely. If I had handled my pen as I have my tongue, my writings would be valueless, though they would doubtless have enjoyed a greater, and especially an earlier success.

Avenue de France, in the hope of a little tobacco, queues of one hundred and fourteen dogged people in front of one shop, one hundred and three in front of another. I amused myself by counting them. (At a guess I should have thought I was exaggerating in estimating them above eighty.) Soon we shall be able to die of hunger before finding anything edible to buy in any shop at any price.

I cannot believe that the art of the future will delight in affectation, subtlety, and complication. This war will probably have the effect of divorcing art from realism. Reportage, which will be required to be as documentary as possible, will liberate literature, just as photography has liberated painting, by a sort of "catharsis."

30 January

The German high command is apparently insisting on the immediate repatriation of the Italian fragments of Rommel's army, which is retreating in Tunisia. It is stated that the ration vouchers on Tunis granted to the soldiers (and, I believe, also to the Italian civilians come from Tripolitania) are good for five days only.

How can it be explained that the English radio communiqués have made no mention of the massacre of German planes, four days ago, on the El Aouina airfield? The most important one, it is said, since the beginning of the war in Tunisia.

Ah, how harsh this separation from my loved ones seems to me certain days! How long this wait is! Can I even hope to see them all again? If it may be that, after this perilous passage through the war, I myself am still alive . . . What care I take to save myself for them until that day! It is this, almost as much as curiosity, that still makes me cling to life. Am I going to last long enough to see the following chapter? And how, in what condition, shall I find those I have so long lost from sight? How will they have stood the test? It is doubtless going on for many months more. And I think the worst is still ahead of us; in comparison to it, what we have already endured is nothing.

Hugo writes (*Dieux; Les Voix*).
Jusqu'à ce qu'il s'en aille en cendre et se dissoude.[14]
I fancy he would likewise write *dissoudent* for the third-person plural of the present; but I have not been able to find any example.

2 February
I had asked Maurice Blanc to send me proofs of this book, of which he had the complete text; in principle it was to appear in Switzerland four months ahead of the French edition. After the interruption of postal communications did Blanc dare to overrule this? I hope so. The text entrusted to him contains a last "imaginary interview" that I did not give to Gallimard, which is most especially important to me. There it is that my ratiocination leads; there that I place my confidence. It has not wavered, not changed since the day when, taking my bearings, I tried to formulate my belief. I hid that profession of faith, so to speak, in that very limited edition, not, indeed, in order to hide it under a bushel, but counting that, if indeed it is worth being taken into consideration, certain minds will manage to note it and, proud of their discovery, will be eager to set off those pages much better than I could have done by making them public.[15] Other considerations, besides, kept me from bringing them out at once in France, where everything

---

[14] "Until it goes up in smoke and dissolves" — from the long poem *God*. The proper form of the last verb should be *dissolve* rather than *dissoude*.

[15] I cannot understand what aberration made Blanc set those pages at the head of the volume when I had specified that they should appear as an appendix at the end of the book (and perhaps in smaller type). (December 1944.) [A.] In the 1943 edition of *Interviews imaginaires*, published at Yverdun and Lausanne by Éditions du Haut Pays, a single chapter entitled "Appendix. Extracts" was printed at the front of the volume in the fine-paper copies.

that does not conform and is not recognized as of public utility is suspect. For a long time, I believe, one will not be permitted to think
freely there, or at least to express one's thought freely.

3 February

Yesterday we were again deprived of electricity. Amphoux would
like to convince me that this is to keep us from hearing the Anglo-
American communiqués. Hence we expect some extraordinary news in
the evening, when, after a gloomy candle-lit supper, the electricity restored at last allows us to hear the 9.15 broadcast. Not at all: simply
the Churchill-Inonu interview at Ankara, which rumor already announced this morning.

Joy at recognizing Julien Green's friendly voice in the message from
America. Then, immediately thereafter, the customary display of preparations, the number of new ships launched, their tonnage, the future
crushing superiority of the American fleet and arms over those of the
Axis. . . . After that the least set-back will seem shameful, and victory
will seem a purely numerical and material triumph. The Americans, it
is repeated, will not make up their minds to fight until they are sure of
being ten to one. There is nothing to boast about in this; and some,
who nevertheless cordially wish for the downfall of the Axis, deplore
that ostentation. Material force is changing hands, but it is still force
that is again called upon to win out over human values, to assert itself.
It cannot be otherwise, it will be said, and this alone matters: making
that force serve the spirit. . . . The spirit, in this case, will be well
off to be on the side of material interests. I fear that, in any case and
whatever happens, the spirit will remain, after all, the great loser in
the whole business.

The London radio speaks of two ships sunk in the harbor of Tunis
and of docks set on fire by the raid of the day before yesterday. In
truth, no ship was sunk and that inefficacious raid set fire only to an
old and useless shed. On the other hand, no mention of ten freighters
shipwrecked off Bizerte, nor of the havoc on the airfield of El Aouina.
How can one fail to be skeptical about all the rest they tell?

I finish Johnson's *Rasselas*, the interest of which soon languishes
and peters out well before the end. The volume given as a school prize
that contains it (published in London in 1847) also includes Marmontel's *Bélisaire* and *Paul et Virginie* without any mention of the authors, without even indicating that those two works are translated
from the French.[16]

---

[16] *Belisarius* (1767) by Marmontel and *Paul and Virginia* (1787) by
Bernardin de Saint-Pierre are typical sentimental novels with didactic im-
plications.

In *Dieu,* I wondered at:

> *Over the blue-eyed doe the leopard stretches.*[17]

The "blue-eyed" doe! . . . What daring! I thought. But now I discover in *L'Art d'être grand-père*: ". . . the blue-eyed antelope." It is enough to make one wonder if Hugo did not simply lack observation. I can admit this only with difficulty, for, without being an observer, in the naturalistic meaning of the word, whenever the visionary gives way to the witness, he becomes an incomparable recorder. I prefer to think that he uses the word "blue" as Baudelaire does in *La Chevelure*: "blue hair," and I admit that the dark eyes of the deer species have vaguely azure reflections; furthermore, the word "blue" evokes ideas of sweetness and purity that are most becoming to the victim.

At times I think I cannot any longer endure sitting at the morning and evening meals beside an obstinate boy who seems to have no other concern than to show his scorn flagrantly. Then I convince myself that this is merely a result of his natural caddishness and that I am crazy to be concerned about it.

4 February

On 2 February is definitely effected the crushing of the German army at Stalingrad after a heroic and useless resistance. What must have been the suffering of those sacrificed soldiers, devoid even of hope that their death might contribute to victory? What could they have thought of Hitlerism and of Hitler during their agony? But what does Hitler think of himself?

> *"Awakened, he descends the other slope of the dream."* [18]

While waiting for the French broadcast from London, in the apartment of Amphoux, our very obliging neighbor, we try out the musical broadcasts from various stations. After a Haydn Allegro, of rather languid interest, Amphoux exclaims: "It is not one of his best pages." Already the other evening when he played me the recording of Debussy's *Nuages*, he had said: "You will see, it's a very fine page." The word "page" used this way seems to me characteristic of a surface culture.

I note among the conversations reported by Boswell (under date of 9 April 1778) this remark of a certain Harris (?):

"I think Heroick poetry is best in blank verse; yet it appears that

---

[17] *"Sur la biche aux yeux bleus, le léopard s'allonge,"* from Hugo's poem *God.*

[18] *"Il descend, réveillé, l'autre côté du rêve,"* is a line from *"La Bouche d'ombre"* ("The Mouth of Shadow") in Hugo's *Contemplations.*

rhyme is essential to English poetry, from our deficiency in metrical quantities." [19]

Boswell is indubitably superior to Eckermann. A pity that Johnson remains so inferior to Goethe. His wisdom is wonderfully representative of that of his time, but never rises above it. He has very racy sallies and retorts, but one listens to him without real profit, constantly aware of the limitations of his genius. Constricted, moreover, by the credo to which he constantly renews his allegiance; but one wonders whether without that curb he would have been able to venture very far. He remains a man of letters throughout everything, and one is grateful to him for this. His style is rich, full of images, consistent, rhythmical, and, as it were, succulent; in comparison Swift's seems fleshless. None the less, if Johnson seemed to dominate his time, he did so, I think, especially by his mass. He overwhelmed.

6 February

My dreams are often *auditory* as much as they are *visual;* but it also occurs to me to dream that I am *reading* sentences; they take shape in my mind as if without my knowing it, it seems, since I have the impression of discovering them; they take me by surprise. What an odd comedy one thus puts on for oneself, supplying the subject of the surprise and the amazement likewise. I recall having already noted some examples of this: one is simultaneously the accomplice and the dupe.[20] I also wonder at the extent to which the remarks heard in dream correspond to the characters who make them, characters that are often much more lifelike in what they say and their tone of voice than in their external appearance, which is often vague and uncertain. Often, indeed, it is solely by the remarks they make that I recognize them. At first I don't know who the companion is walking beside me; and suddenly, on hearing him speak, I think: why, it's Marcel! [21] And taking a better look at him, I tell myself: how he has changed! On seeing him, I should never have recognized him; but on hearing him, I know without a shadow of a doubt that it is *he.*

Where could I have been walking with Marcel? It was on the seashore among rocks lashed with spray. "When one is facing the sea," said Marcel, "it is impossible to think of anything." "That is what allowed Hugo to write poetry," I retorted.

---

[19] The quotation is given in English. The speaker is identified by Boswell as Mr. Harris of Salisbury.

[20] See *The Journals of André Gide,* Vol. III, pp. 27–8.

[21] Marcel Drouin.

7 February

A severe cold has been stultifying me since the beginning of this month. Besides, the itching, which the injections of bromical are not succeeding in overcoming, torments me every night. Despite this, I feel in a rather good mood for work and am turning this to account for the preface to my Anthology; [22] but I am too often distracted from it and, besides, soon get tired. What I should once have written in a morning now keeps me busy a week. None the less, I greatly need this semblance of activity to bind me to life, and this is likewise why I cling to this *Journal*.

Victor has been more affable the last few days and it even occurs to him to smile when talking to me, as if he were forgetting himself. He even went so far as to invite me to come and see the big map of Russia that he has pinned up on a wall of his room, marking on it with little flags the wonderful progress of the Russians. (This morning we plant one of the flags on Azov.) He exulted last night because he had discovered in his father's library a little book on *The Social Problem* written by one of his uncles or cousins. No more was required to allow Victor to see in him a "Communist" and to brandish the book in front of his horrified grandmother. She immediately declared that the book was to be looked upon as a youthful indiscretion, for which E. S. had quickly repented. But no, the book dates from 1923. The little I was able to read of it at first seemed to me excellent; and as I assert this to Chacha, she (indulging in what Victor calls "a last-ditch retrieval") insists that she never doubted this, for "all the S. nephews are remarkable men." Alas, the little book, which started out rather well, full of the most generous utopias, does not long stand examination.

8 February

Days of impatient waiting. I am unwilling to share the assurance that the communiqués from London and America are trying to propagate and in which it seems that the Anglo-American armies are putting their faith. These positions in Tunisia which they could easily have taken by surprise, it seems, they have given the Germans ample time to fortify, and from day to day the least advance becomes more difficult and more costly. One tries to convince oneself that these procrastinations are intentional and part of a plan skillfully worked out with the Soviets in order to hold large German forces far from the Russian front, where the Russian army is doing wonders; or simply that the American supplies and reinforcements were not yet considered suf-

---

[22] The *Anthologie de la poésie française,* which did not appear until 1949.

ficient . . . anything rather than to recognize in this stagnation incompetence, lack of punch, apathy. Meanwhile the Germans' discouragement is obvious and their resentment against the Italians is growing. The window of the Italian bookshop, which has been lately exhibiting photographs of the King, the Queen, the Prince of Piedmont, and the Duce, had a brick hurled through it yesterday. By whom? By the Germans? It is thought rather by anti-fascist Italians. The number of these is growing, while among the party members confidence in an Axis victory is decreasing. As soon as one begins to see that the game might be lost, one wishes one had never begun it, aware that it is now too late to withdraw. Nothing can be done about it: they will have to drink the bitter chalice and drain it to the dregs.

This morning the radio announces the recapture of Kursk. There is fighting in the suburbs of Rostov.

Read without much pleasure *She Stoops to Conquer*,[23] very inferior to *The Vicar of Wakefield*, which delighted me even more on a second reading than on the first.

Boswell becomes more and more interesting as he gets away from his idolatry and dares more often to stand up against Johnson and notice the petty sides of his god, whereby the latter nevertheless becomes more human.

9 February

No, I am not superstitious; but I am inclined to seek out what is considered ill-omened, rather in defiance (at least in the beginning) and for the fun of thinking that what brings misfortune to the meek must be favorable to the bold. Thus I never miss an opportunity to walk under a ladder, to travel on a Friday, or to rely on a thirteen. Without at all believing in the mystic virtue of numbers, I always and regularly *count* (and this is often very tiring) the steps of a stairway, at least those between two landings, the number of turns to wind my watch or to raise or lower the rolling shutters in my room. The numbers 7, 13, 21, and 43 are my favorites, which I adopted many years ago for the few physical exercises to which I subject myself from time to time. But this odd thing takes place, which probably nothing but psychoanalysis could explain: I get confused between 16 and 18, wondering if I haven't skipped 17 and not knowing just how far I have got; and I never stumble on any other number, but I often stumble on this one.

I do not believe at all in bad luck and think one can avoid it by refusing to believe in it. In general I hold that there is no situation so

---

[23] By Goldsmith. [A.]

desperate that the ingenious and courageous soul cannot turn it to advantage, but on a plane and in a realm where Hitler and armed force are powerless.

10 February

Sorry need of insulting and vilifying one's opponent, a need equally common to both sides, which causes me to listen so painfully at times to the radio broadcasts, those from London and America as well as those from Berlin and Paris-Vichy. What! Do you really think that all the intelligence, nobility of heart, and good faith are solely on your side? Is there nothing but base interests and stupidity among your opponents? Or perhaps you will tell me that it is good to convince the masses of this, for otherwise they would have less heart in the conflict? It is essential to persuade the soldier that those he is being urged to massacre are bandits who do not deserve to live; before killing other good, decent fellows like himself, his gun would fall from his hands. It is a matter of activating hatred, and one blows on passions to make them glow brightly. It takes brutes to fight brutes; consequently they are turned into brutes.

Recognizing the good points and virtues of the enemy has always been my weakness, and it might make me pass for a traitor among the partisans of either camp. This is indeed partly why I should keep silent today even if I were given license to speak. Today there is room only for falsehood, and it alone is listened to. And everything I am saying about it is absurd. . . .

11 February

. . . for it is not a question of the few decent people I might find in the opposite camp or country, but rather of the principles and ethic animating them, which are weighing on my head and chest, which keep me from breathing, from thinking, from loving, which suppress me. It is against that, not against them, that I am protesting and struggling.

12 February

> *Every insolent victor prepares his fall.*
> *Let us fear common fate and beware of ourselves;*
> *One victory is not all.*[24]

La Fontaine's art lies in stating lightly and as if playfully this overwhelming truth that Nietzsche in 1870 set forth with stirring eloquence,

---

[24] *Tout vainqueur insolent à sa perte travaille.*
Défions-nous du sort, et prenons garde à nous
Après le gain d'une bataille.

These lines are from the "moral" of La Fontaine's fable of *Les Deux Coqs* (*The Two Roosters*).

that we so readily forgot in 1918. If fortune happens to smile on us again, we shall not be any more prudent tomorrow. One does not correct one's errors without first deigning to recognize them.

13 February

There is and always will be in France (except under the urgent threat of a common danger) division and parties; in other words, dialogue. Thanks to that, the fine equilibrium of our culture: equilibrium in diversity. Always a Montaigne opposite a Pascal; and, in our time, opposite a Claudel, a Valéry. At times one of the two voices wins out in strength and magnificence. But woe to the times when the other is reduced to silence! The free mind has the superiority of not wanting to be alone in having the right to speak.

I feel that I spring from French culture and am bound to it with all my heart and mind. I cannot get away from that culture without losing sight of myself and ceasing to feel myself. But I believe that the idea of the mother country, which is so greatly abused in wartime (when it becomes indispensable for leading men to fight and uniting them under a single flag), is hard to anchor solidly in the heart of the vast majority of the untutored, unless by a deceitful simplification. Mystical interests elude them or are almost indifferent to them. It is essential to group individual interests in a cluster around an entity, which is France. This can be done around a tree trunk only by removing its branches.

14 February

In the appendix to Demolins's book on *La Supériorité des Anglo-Saxons*,[25] among some critical judgments, I note this one by Jules Lemaître: "The root of the evil in the French is their lack of individual initiative, whereas among the Anglo-Saxons each man counts on himself." Yes, this is the result of their Protestant formation; and Jules Lemaître is here indicting not so much France as Catholicism. But just try to say this today.

Today, in order to cure this evil, people are "taking a hair of the dog that bit them" — in the original and worst sense of this expression.

15 February

Suffered greatly from the cold the last few days, not so much outside as in this very apartment; my room and the bathroom I share with

---

[25] The title of this book might suggest a current work of propaganda, but in fact *A quoi tient la supériorité des Anglo-Saxons* (*Anglo-Saxon Superiority: to What It Is Due*) was first published in 1897 and translated into English in 1899.

Victor are frigid; so that I cannot succeed in ridding myself of my cold. This Tunisian climate is perfidious: you shiver as soon as the sun leaves you, and in the sun you are too hot; you don't know how to dress, and twenty times a day I take off or put on my sweater.

Nothing to say of events. I make it a rule to write a few lines every day in this notebook as a spiritual exercise, finding, as for prayer, that it is never so useful as in periods of dryness of heart.

The day before yesterday the charming Mme Sparrow had invited me with the Ragus to share a providential roast of pork. After that extraordinary banquet Dr. Ragu very brilliantly defended this disconcerting thesis, which he bolstered with the best arguments: Hitler, without any real personal value, is presumably but the tool of a clever general staff; all his decisions are prompted; but that governing council needs him as an idol set up to rally popular enthusiasm and devotion, he alone knowing how to speak to the masses and stir them. None the less, of late, because of their reverses, the council has presumably kept him from speaking. His silence, like his preceding speeches, is prompted, imposed on him.

It may be that this has become true, and I am willing to accept the fact that the original Führer, such as Rauschning depicts him, has yielded to this second Hitler, a victim of himself and his unwise decisions, at last the captive of his own rash resolves, unable now to escape their sinister consequences and forced to listen to advisers, to submit to more competent men than himself, to sing small. For a Shakespeare of the future there is material for a wonderful drama in this.

None the less the English radio is shouting victory a bit too early. This is unwise presumptuousness, which might not be corroborated by the facts for some time. Such boasting, if it is not followed by victory or if the victory is merely too slow in coming, may seem rather ridiculous. This failing of substituting words for facts is then perhaps not France's monopoly.

16 February

Probably Victor considers as empty, hypocritical pretense any manifestation of cordiality, graciousness, kindness — feelings that I really believe he is incapable of experiencing and that, consequently, seem to him pure affectation in others. If he says neither good-morning nor good-night, this is because he feels no desire to hear these salutations himself, living solely for himself and concerned with others only in so far as they can be of use to him. He does nothing to make himself agreeable, and I admire the fact that in his very caddishness he is utterly natural.

Every evening after supper I lie down on my bed and try to read;

the cat comes and settles on my cold feet, thereby warming them. Then Victor knocks on my door and enters brusquely. "I've come to take MY cat." And yesterday, as I venture to say: "Please leave him here a few minutes more. I'll send him in to you presently," Victor replies: "*No!*" seizing the cat bodily without a word of excuse or farewell. It is *his* cat.

Then on certain days at table, for some reason or other, according to his mood, he loses his frown and talks to you quite naturally. You feel that he does not hold his insolences against you.

Chacha: "Have you been to the movies?"

Victor: "Yes."

Chacha: "Did you have a good time?"

Victor: "What difference does it make to you?"

Then the grandmother bristles and I, to smooth things over: "What was showing?"

Victor: "I don't know. I didn't go."

Chacha: "Then why did you tell me that . . ."

Victor: "So you will let me alone."

The Russians have taken Rostov. (Radio-Vichy considers it more elegant to announce: The Germans have evacuated Rostov.) This has been known since late yesterday, but the Tunis newspaper of today, the 15th, says nothing of it. Among the news from the Russian front (under the general heading of "the anti-Bolshevist crusade") it speaks only of the "slowing up of the Soviet pressure in certain sectors, notably in the western Caucasus and along the lower Donetz," and reproduces a "wire from Berlin" telling of the frightful Russian losses in equipment and ending thus: "As for the Bolshevist losses in men, the 13th of February in this sector they were in the vicinity of one thousand, whereas the Germans lost altogether but eleven men"!!

In an article on the "Military Situation" an editor of *Tunis-Journal* quotes the correspondent of the Berlin D.N.B.: "During a winter offensive one must always let the enemy attack"; and the commentator adds: "This is self-evident" — not perhaps without irony.

17 February

Numerical superiority, superiority in equipment, and in overwhelming proportions; the Anglo-Americans have this and boast of it. They have proclaimed it over and over and seem to rely on it. Their inactivity is going to leave the Russians all the honors of victory and Stalin is beginning to put forward the idea that he has conquered all alone. The communiqués from London now insist on the difficulties of the contest (in Tunisia) put off from day to day, which, they say, will of necessity be very costly. Will this be to exaggerate tomorrow the merits of a victory or to attenuate the shame of a defeat? Whom will they persuade that the contest was easier on the Russian front?

I cannot share the optimism of some who think the Germans will withdraw from Tunis without fighting, that resistance will be made in front of or behind that city, which is said to be undefendable, and that Bizerte rather than Tunis will be the center of the heavy fighting that is foreseen. I expect much worse ordeals, in comparison with which those of yesterday will seem but "a poor rehearsal." It is not even certain that we shall come out alive from the hell I foresee, and the days of semi-happiness that we are still living are perhaps the last.

I picked up Keats's *Odes* again. A half-hour was enough to learn them completely by heart again (at least the *Ode to a Nightingale* and the *Ode to Autumn*). I believe that likewise if I applied myself to piano practice again, I should have hardly any trouble relearning almost all of Chopin's études, the few preludes and fugues of Bach that I used to know by heart, etc.; but I cannot make up my mind to sacrifice the time it would take for my fingers to recover a semblance of dexterity. Besides, the feeling that I am being listened to has become unbearable to me. If I could practice without being heard by anyone and on a good piano, I think I should nevertheless get back to it; and very soon I should be giving many hours to it. . . . The intensity of my practice in the past came from this: disapproval of the virtuosos who play in such a way as to show themselves off at the expense of the composer they are interpreting. Now, I can no longer claim at all, at present, to surpass them. From my practice today I should derive but too unsatisfactory a pleasure; it is better to preserve intact my regret for that lost paradise.

18 February

I finished Boswell yesterday evening. Those thirteen hundred pages can be read almost without a single moment of fatigue or boredom. To what a degree Johnson's robust intelligence is paralyzed or held in check by his religious convictions and his perpetual fear of going beyond them, Boswell implicitly admits himself, though sharing his convictions, and that through them "he had perhaps, at an early period, narrowed his mind somewhat too much, both as to religion and politics." And it is not one of the least interests of this book that it allows us to follow the intentional narrowing of that fine free thought. "He was prone to superstition, but not to credulity," Boswell appropriately says. This is the regard in which his book is most instructive, despite him: we see, by example, how a vigorous mind can remain entangled in dogma.

Same scorn as in Goethe, same lack of curiosity, for problems concerning origins. No more than Goethe does Johnson suspect the lesson that can be drawn from the study of primitive peoples. "One set of savages is like another," Johnson declares [26] (15 June 1784), and he immediately directs his attention elsewhere. The egg that ethnologists will later hatch had not yet been laid; any curiosity in that regard seemed useless and unprofitable.

19 February

I go out early this morning to get a couple of pounds of "date butter"; this is all one can get at a time. The confectioner in rue Amilcar, who sells it, does not open his door until eight o'clock. It is seven thirty and already there stretches out such a queue (almost two hundred customers) that I give up: too much time would be wasted that I can devote to work. I yield my place to the very obliging Mme de S., who has joined me, and hasten away to plunge again into the preface for my Anthology.

20 February

The Allies let themselves be deprived of Gafsa, withdrawing beyond Sbeitla, and were unable to cut off Rommel's retreat, so that now he has joined the mass of the German forces. The lid is becoming heavier, and one wonders if we shall be liberated for a long time. In Tunis itself, those who long for liberation, who are even suspected of longing for it, are arrested. They cannot all be arrested and one wonders what motivates this or that choice. Meanwhile the Arab population is beginning to sing a different tune, it is said, and to turn against those it originally received with open arms, to regret French protection, since the German domination has been strangling and emptying the market to such a degree, since foodstuffs have become rarer, since prices have increased, since even flour has been rationed. Grumbling is increasing and here and there street altercations have been reported, yet they most often take place between German and Italian soldiers. Unfortunately our radio is out of order and I must go and beg for the news in the apartment of our kind neighbor M. Amphoux.

I thought I could no longer endure Victor's glumness and insolences; already I had gone to the Tunisia-Palace to try to secure a new lodging when, today, the charming Patri, professor of philosophy, very kindly came and offered to put me up. But meanwhile Chacha had burst into my room, having somehow got wind of my intention to leave, terrified at the idea of having to remain alone with her terrible grandson. "I beg you, Monsieur Gide, don't leave, don't forsake me! What would I become? I should go away too. Indeed, Jeanne told Victor yesterday that if you leave us she would give up our service and he would be en-

---

[26] In the original, all quotations from Boswell are given in English.

trusted to his grandfather. The vacant apartment would be occupied by the Germans, who would sack everything . . ." etc. I let myself be moved and promised to be patient a little longer. At times, but not always, I curse the beastly idea I had of coming here; then I think anxiously of those I left in France and shall perhaps not see again; I am worried by that increasing obscurity enveloping them, hiding them, stifling them. . . . But at times also I congratulate myself on being at a point where a perhaps decisive contest is taking place or is about to take place. . . .

The American army withdrew, made a disorderly retreat, forsaking tanks, cannon, munitions; and not even pursued by Germans, but by the Italians whom the Germans sent after them. With the killed and wounded, the prisoners and the missing, twenty-five thousand men were presumably lost, says the American radio, which is not covering up the disaster. I did not hear it myself and know only what is repeated to me this morning by V. This at least will keep America from judging us too severely.

21 February

According to X., that American retreat in the region of Sbeitla has but a temporary significance, given the pressure of the Eighth Army in the south. "May this local disaster prick America's pride!" he adds. My personal opinion is more and more hesitant and drifts with the current; I am less and less able to stabilize it in matters that do not concern pure thought, psychology, literature, or art. Doubtless Roosevelt proved to be extraordinarily clever when he succeeded in building a rather considerable army with the approval of his people; but he was unable to inculcate in the soldiers of that army the feeling of urgency that drives the other peoples to fight. Each of his soldiers fights without vigor, careful of his comfort and but little convinced by the reasons given him for having to defend he is not sure just what. He feels neither touched in any of his vital interests nor personally threatened. He lends himself to this adventure, which after all does not concern him; and faced with real danger, he withdraws. It is quite different when one is fighting on one's own soil.

None the less, the details V. gave me yesterday are still unconfirmed. The Americans' retreat is certain, but their losses seem to be monstrously exaggerated. According to Z., that figure of 25,000 which V. gave me yesterday presumably includes their total losses since the beginning of the war and on all fronts. It is when opinions are not better supported and informed that they most readily become "convictions." "The shadows of Faith," as Fénelon says, are what permit religious convictions.

22 February

But V., to whom I make this suggestion, maintains that the figure of "twenty-five thousand" [27] was given by the American radio while announcing the defeat in Tunisia and covers solely those lost in that engagement. He admits, however, that this figure, which he is sure of having heard, was not given again subsequently.

Rereading my *Journal* since the first of January leaves me rather discouraged. Everything I wrote in that other notebook which I finished filling yesterday strikes me as useless and mediocre; I cannot congratulate myself on having constrained myself to write in it every day. It is in this regard that the last notebook differs from the preceding ones, which I opened but intermittently and when the spirit moved. This last notebook became for me the buoy to which the shipwrecked man clings. There can be felt in it that daily effort to remain afloat.

23 February

One reads in a note to Sainte-Beuve's *Port-Royal* (Book III, Chapter vii): "A keen student of mankind has pointed out that sometimes quoting one's own remark as coming from another shows it off to advantage and succeeds better." A device of which he often made use himself, of which he doubtless makes use even here when he speaks of "a keen student of mankind," who is probably none other than he.

I cannot shake off this torpor which dulls my mind and makes it incapable of effort.

"There is no man more different from another than from himself at various times." (Pascal: *Esprit géométrique.*[28])

24 February

Better night (the preceding one execrable), broken by not too many awakenings, which were almost pleasant, for they gave me a chance to become aware of the dreams they interrupted. In each of the dreams food played an important part. Variations on themes of delicacies. Dreamed abundantly of Valéry, and not only of him but also of Jennie and Paule, and of a fourth child still very young, an extraordinarily

---

[27] In English in the original.

[28] This thought is found in Chapter xv of Part III of Pascal's *Opuscules* under the title: "Concerning the Geometric Spirit." Montaigne had already noted that "there is as much difference between us and ourselves as between us and others," and La Rochefoucauld was to rephrase the thought as his Maxim 135: "One is sometimes as different from oneself as from others."

beautiful little girl, about whom he went into raptures.[29] He made
some wonderful remarks, which I promised myself to remember, but
have now forgotten; and both of us were eating sweet "ftaïrs." . . . On
awakening, this dreadful thought greets me: is he still alive?

For the past six days Victor has not spoken to me. It makes me regret the time when he always came to the table with a book, for then
his silence might seem less insulting. This is just what he realized, and
that by not reading he would make his insolence more obvious and I
should feel it more. His behavior toward me, I could swear, is prompted
by his friend Lévy, who wanders about the apartment daily, or almost,
without speaking to anyone, who is inculcating in him the principles
of Marxism, confirming him in his egoism and providing solid founda-
tions for his spontaneous caddishness.

I read one after the other Les Provinciales, Sainte-Beuve's Port-
Royal (at least the two volumes that concern Pascal), Jude the Obscure,
and Rebatet's Les Décombres, which Ragu has just lent me.[30] Pascal
is for the morning; Hardy, for walks (I have gone back to that taste
of my childhood for reading while walking; moreover, I have never
lost it, but it has never been so keen). Rebatet's mediocre book is for
any moment whatever.

25 February

Before twenty, many a man thinks he is clever indeed to discover
that man acts only through interests. And naturally he thinks only of the
lowest, vilest interests. For if he were willing to admit that the most
immaterial chimeras as well as the most sublime imaginations or con-
ceptions can sometimes *interest* man to the point of taking precedence
over vulgar interests, we should not be far from agreeing. But this does
not get us very far toward recognizing that the man who, out of a feeling of duty or to preserve an ideal, gives his life does so because he
takes pleasure in his very devotion to duty and finds satisfaction in his
sacrifice. For, after all, in order to stir a man something is required: desire or pleasure or need. This alone matters: what, for you, precedes all
the rest? As for the motives of self-esteem, La Rochefoucauld exposed

---

[29] Jennie is Mme Paul Valéry and Paule is her sister, Mlle Paule Gobillard. The poet had but three children.

[30] Pascal's *Letters to a Provincial*, generally referred to as *Provincial
Letters*, form a brilliant polemic against the Jesuits, who were trying to get
the Jansenist movement, of which Sainte-Beuve became the chronicler in
his *History of Port-Royal*, outlawed. *The Rubbish* (1942), by Lucien Rebatet, is a work of journalistic pseudo-history. The year before, he had
brought out an anti-Semitic pamphlet entitled *Les Tribus du cinéma et du
théâtre* (*The Movie and Theater Tribes*).

them in such a way that there is no need of going back over them, but perhaps you have not read him. The Church herself is ready to admit that "the will always works toward what it likes most," as Pascal writes (*Provinciales*, Letter XVIII), and "One forsakes pleasures only for greater ones" (Letter to Mlle de Roannez).

26 February

Nothing is more disagreeable than those "arms" of the Périer family which Pascal adopts after the miracle of the Holy Thorn (reproduced on the back of the third volume of the *Port-Royal*, Doyon edition): "azure with an eye in natural colors in the center of a golden crown of thorns." The surrealists have invented nothing better. What can one think of a faith that would order such an aberration? The hideousness of that product is enough to put me on guard. Pascal may subsequently be as great as you wish, there is none the less something distorted in his mind that annoys me; and it is not for his faith that I like him, but for his doubt. The eloquence of the *Provinciales* (which I have just read from end to end) leads to an absurdity, in utter contradiction, moreover, with what his basic fairness laid down originally in regard to that "sufficient Grace that fails to suffice." Then it was that he was right and one could not resist following him. The Holy Thorn distorts everything, tripping up that straight and upright thought, which will never rise again. Let us dismiss that: *Jam fœtet.*[31]

Useless effort to remain within orthodoxy, even when that very intellectual effort drives you from it, and to prove that one has not abandoned it when it would be only decent to listen to and recognize the *"Non possumus . . ."* But this is the source of that anguish in which, subsequently and to the very end, Pascal struggles. This is probably what constitutes his greatness and gives his voice that incomparable quavering, that element of pathos characteristic of a soul at bay.

If he had used his eloquence to fight the Church instead of fighting simply the Jesuits, what wouldn't he have achieved, and for the greater good of France! What wouldn't he achieve today, even in the very name of the Gospel!

27 February

Victor takes his ease at the expense of others. Here is something that depicts him: in the toilet that dirty little beast sits slantwise and has his movement on an angle for fear of getting splashed. And those who come after him are simply lucky if they notice in time that the

---

[31] "By this time [it] stinketh," was said by Martha of her brother, Lazarus (John xi, 39).

seat is all soiled; it is up to them to clean it! His motto: It's always others I bother.

I finish rereading *Jude the Obscure* in English: I had read the translation when it first appeared, when I was still quite young. That book had bowled me over at the time. Today I am full of reservations and react rather violently against it. It strikes me as dreadful, abominable; at any rate inferior to *Tess*, and especially to *The Woodlanders*, *The Return of the Native*, and *The Mayor of Casterbridge*. It is the last named, I believe, that I prefer among all the novels of Hardy.

28 February

However considerable the Russian victories may be, I find it hard to believe that Germany is laid as low as the Anglo-American radio stations enjoy proclaiming it to be. What will they say if the Axis gets the upper hand again in the spring, as seems to me in no wise impossible?

I finish Rebatet's book, read at a great rate. What he says of Maurras and the *Action Française* interested me especially. It is not good writing always to use the strongest word; passion blunts itself in such excess, at least the reader's passion. If one let Rebatet have his way, there would soon be left in France nothing but a handful of frenzied partisans flaying the masses with cudgels. With him I never feel less at ease than when I share his opinion. He seems imbued with this principle formulated by Joseph de Maistre: "One has accomplished nothing against opinions until one has attacked persons."

It is from Sainte-Beuve's *Port-Royal* that I get this quotation. Everything he says of J. de Maistre and with him as a pretext is excellent and most healthily inspired.

What the Count de Saint-Priest says of J. de Maistre (quoted by Sainte-Beuve) might just as well be applied to Claudel: ". . . He never listened; he alone would speak and when one wanted to reply to him he had the faculty of going to sleep at once; but it was dangerous to place too much faith in this, for as soon as one had ceased talking, he would awake immediately and resume the thread of his discourse as if nothing had happened."

3 March

Yesterday, shortly before noon, a more intense bombing than any of last month. I was at the civilian hospital when it began. Dr. Ragu took me out on the terrace overlooking the whole city just in time to see many columns of smoke rise. Far as we were from the explosions, we heard the whistle of the falling bombs. An icy wind was blowing, which made me go in rather soon and I thus saw arrive soon after cars and wagons loaded with wounded. The Arabs were immediately sent to the Sadiki hospital, the Italians to the Italian hospital; the French alone were kept and sent to wards where, as Ragu told me later, a frightful confusion reigned. I regret not having accompanied him on his rounds. In front of the hospital gate was grouped a crowd of poor people, with whom I mingled for a time vainly seeking some face to look upon with pleasure. Nothing but congenitally diseased, deformed, poverty-stricken outcasts, ugly enough to discourage pity. A great anguish of grief weighed upon that sorry humanity. They were waiting to be allowed to approach the victims, and this could not be done until after the latter had received first aid. I saw some on stretchers as they left the ambulance, disfigured by hideous wounds, with only half a face left; others deathly pale and eyes closed, perhaps already dead. . . .

Lunch at the hospital, then returned to town immediately after. Learned on returning to avenue Roustan that all the window-panes in my room had been blown out. About thirty yards from the R.s' house a bomb destroyed the buildings of the registry office.

No more electricity; no more gas; no more water.

I went out again; I wandered in the neighboring quarters that had been hit. Three bombs fell in the courtyard of the school, opposite our windows. None of them exploded, very fortunately, for the pupils were still in class. Other bombs everywhere around did frightful damage; one dug up the pavement of the avenue Jules-Ferry (continuing the avenue de France) in front of the big café, the largest in town, now become the "Wehrmacht Kaffee"; all the plate-glass windows of its façade are blown in. The large movie theater next door, likewise reserved for the Germans, is nothing but an amorphous mass of ruins. If only it had been filled with an audience. . . . But no, these bombs fell only on innocent victims among the civilians, hit no target of a military nature or of any interest to the military operations, it seems. The planes' line of fire remained very far this side of the harbor, in which sizable Italian ships had just entered, and it seems certain that they intended to attack the town itself; as a reprisal, some say, for recent bombings of the city of Algiers.

The appearance of the gutted houses is hideous; the thin sheathing has flaked off, which gave the buildings a rather respectable look, leaving visible everything that an effort was made to hide: a miserable cheap construction of unmentionable materials. The streets are littered with fragments of glass and rubble. In the gutted apartments everything is faded, soiled, tarnished. As one walks, one raises a heavy, whitish, choking dust that brings tears to one's eyes. Disgust is even greater than horror.

It is learned that at the girls' school three women teachers were killed and a rather large number wounded, but the children who had time to get down to the cellar were not touched.

After a cold meal by candlelight I went to bed, unable to see enough to read. Jeanne, considering my room uninhabitable, had made up my bed on one of the two sofas in the living room. At five a.m., alert. At the first explosions I followed Chacha and Victor to the shelter. It serves as a dormitory for many refugees, who have spread out mattresses, most of them directly on the ground. I hear someone near me say: "These bombings will have to come to an end some day!" Yes, but we might come to an end before they do. Die buried under the ruins, die by slow asphyxiation, in a sordid promiscuity, amid the excrements of both soul and body. . . . No, I think I shall not again go down to the cellar.

There is talk of two hundred unfortunate people walled up thus under a crushed building; it is feared that they will not be able to be rescued in time, any more than those of the Foyer du Combattant, whose ever weaker cries were heard for three days. It seems that the rescue squads are very badly organized and that no competent direction takes care of co-ordinating efforts.

4 March

Gérard Boutelleau has just been arrested on a charge of espionage, of clandestine relations with the Anglo-Americans, of sending secret messages, etc. — all things of which it will be easy for him to clear himself, I suppose. There will nevertheless remain a well-founded accusation of tendencies and opinions which will justify considering him as an "undesirable." This is the word used by the Italian officer who came, very courteously, by the way, as Hope Boutelleau tells me, to arrest him the night before last. Since Hope refuses to be separated from her husband, both of them will be taken by plane, within a few days, to Italy; from there I think it will not be hard for them to get to France, for no serious charge can be sustained against them.

Read in succession *L'Affaire Lerouge*, *Le Dossier 113*, and the first volume of *Monsieur Lecoq*, all by Gaboriau.[32] The second volume falls from my hands, for Gaboriau wallows in conventional psychology as soon as he gets away from the field where he is best: police investigation, in which he is an extraordinary pioneer, a precursor of all detective novels. Conan Doyle's are but small beer compared with his. Good train reading, but in his time trains were slower than they are today. At Cuverville some twenty years ago I had already read *Le Crime d'Orcival*, with keen amazement.[33]

[32] *The Widow Lerouge* (1866), *File No. 113* (1867), and *Monsieur Lecoq* (1869) are early detective novels.

[33] He had read *The Mystery of Orcival* only eleven years before. See *The Journals of André Gide*, Vol. III, p. 241.

5 March

I had entrusted to Hope Boutelleau, who offered to type them, two notebooks of my *Journal*. The first fell into the hands of the Italian police. I haven't much hope of seeing it again, but at least the type-script that she had had time to make. As for the second and much more important one, which she had not yet transcribed and had managed to keep from the search party, she hopes to be able to return it to me today; but I am not without fear that some Italian, attracted by the first one, may try to get hold of it. I do not think the police will find anything in it to inculpate me, any more than in the first one; but if merely some . . . bibliophile happens to think of the commercial value of those manuscripts . . .

And will I ever see again the papers I left in Paris? I believe, I hope, that Arnold Naville put Valéry's, Claudel's, and Jammes's correspond-ence in a safe place.[34] I should never be consoled for the loss of Valéry's letters. I had put in a special place everything having to do with Claudel's formal notice regarding *Les Caves du Vatican* (Claudel's comminatory letters, Jammes's horrified letters, and a copy of my re-plies); I attach great importance to that very curious file.[35] Even more important the manuscript relating to Em., in which I had transcribed the unpublished parts of my *Journal* and everything concerning that supreme part of my life which might explain and throw light upon it. Left likewise on my table the confidential notebooks of Luxor. (I wish the publication of these writings; but to be printed only in a small number of copies.) And all the documents relative to the "shep-herd. . . ."[36] Finally all the manuscript notebooks that became the contents of my *Journal* and of my *Voyage au Congo* (many pages of this last work have remained unpublished). Plus many unpublished loose sheets.

This last bombing of Tunis produced such absurd results that one can legitimately hope the Allies, if it has been possible to inform them, will stop there for a time. Only a very small percentage of Germans among the victims. The "Maison Dorée," where the high-ranking Ger-man officers had their meals, was still empty; likewise the big theater of

---

[34] The correspondence between Gide and Francis Jammes was published in 1948, and that between Gide and Paul Claudel in 1950, both edited by Robert Mallet. Most of Valéry's letters to Gide were published by the latter in his *Paul Valéry* (1946).

[35] It was apropos of *Lafcadio's Adventures* that Claudel in March 1914 made the discovery of Gide's homosexuality, and their exchange of letters on this subject is amazingly interesting and revelatory; see *Claudel-Gide Correspondance*, pp. 216–34.

[36] See *The Journals of André Gide*, Vol. III, p. 4.

the Palmarium, which during the show would have provided a holocaust of nearly two thousand Germans, for that theater was exclusively reserved for them. The glass roof fell into the void. Another
bomb, close by, struck the Red Cross depot; it is hoped that three
quarters of it may be salvaged: medicaments and food supplies for the
prisoners. At the moment of the explosions many people (several hundred, it is said) had piled into the cellar of the Palmarium; as if by a
miracle they were saved, the bomb having burst above them, and the
fall of the light glass roof not having pierced the cellar ceiling. I have
just examined those ruins, which exactly frame in the Tunisia-Palace,
more than three quarters occupied by German officers. But at the time
of the raid the hotel was almost empty; and, besides, its few inhabitants
suffered only from fear.

6 March

Amphoux, after marking on a map of Tunis the spots where the
bombs fell, has come to wondering if that scattered bombing was not
intended for the harbor. Dropped from a height of twenty thousand
feet, those bombs could presumably have been diverted from their objective by the rather strong wind that was then blowing. That may be.
The useless havoc may well have been due to a mistake in reckoning;
paltry consolation for the victims! It is said the bombs were only small
four-hundred-pounders. From the results achieved here, one can imagine the dreadful damage caused by the bombs dropped on Naples,
Cologne, Wilhelmshaven, or Hamburg — which, as the radio said,
weighed two or even four tons.

One lives in constant apprehension; but, to tell the truth, this is
hardly a change for me; for even in normal times I never cease to envisage death and do not subscribe to what La Rochefoucauld says: that,
like the sun, it cannot be looked at fixedly.[37]

7 March

The *Journal* notebook (January to May 1942) that I had entrusted
to Hope Boutelleau for typing fell into the hands of the Italian police
at the time of the house search at Sidi-bou-Saïd; the Italian police
handed it over at once to the German authorities, who, I am told, were
concerned by certain passages, and particularly the one ending with
these words: ". . . It is useless to claim that, had we not declared war,
Germany would have respected France, whom she knew, better than
we did ourselves, to be weakened and incapable of resisting her for
long." Alas, I had not waited for this war to think what seemed to me
evident and what even Germany with the best will in the world could

---

[37] *"Le soleil ni la mort ne se peuvent regarder fixément,"* is Maxim 26 of
La Rochefoucauld's famous collection.

not have prevented. Was it not inevitable that a young nation, conscious of its strength and trembling at the recollection of an unjust defeat, injured in its pride by the most blundering of treaties, deprived by it of a possibility of colonial expansion as an outlet for a prolific population crowded within its frontiers, that such a nation should soon strive, as soon as she was back on her feet, to overflow onto ill-defended neighboring lands, insufficiently populated by an aging nation, numbed with comfort, listless and languid? . . . Yes, long before the war France stank of defeat. She was already falling to pieces to such a degree that perhaps the only thing that could save her was, is perhaps, this very disaster in which to retemper her energies. Is it fanciful to hope that she will issue from this nightmare strengthened? I believe she is at present pulling herself together.

The job of excavating is so badly organized that the unfortunate people shut up in a cellar in the rue d'Athènes have just been crushed by a wall that it was thought necessary to blow up with dynamite in order to free them.

Eggs are 96 francs a dozen. Meat costs from 100 to 140 fr. a kilo; oranges, 39 to 42 fr. a kilo. Jeanne served us yesterday a cauliflower worth 50 fr. One is entitled to ONE box of matches a MONTH! Bread costs 5 fr. 55 a kilo, and each of us is entitled to 500 grams every other day.

Each night, sleeping considerably better for some time now (crataegus [38]), despite prolonging my sleep (inadequate light of a candle, which moreover has to be used sparingly, whence reading impossible; nothing else to do but go to bed at eight), I dream of edibles; marvelous. Last night it was a chicken thigh, done to a turn, golden brown, that I could already smell. I was about to bite into it when a noisy truck wakened me.

". . . the harsh and harrying regime of liberty," says Sainte-Beuve in a note to Chapter xx of his *Port-Royal* (on Pascal), in which he skillfully implies that he, Sainte-Beuve, has preserved the delicacy of another age, whereas Cousin, abusing that liberty, attacked it immodestly. The long Appendix to that Chapter xx ("A Further Controversy about Pascal") is most important.

We were barely beginning to get out of the mythological era. Germany and Russia concurrently did much to free us from it, if only by means of the incomparable prestige and value of their respective

---

[38] *Crataegus* is a sedative manufactured by Laboratoire Gmet and recommended in heart cases and for all tension or fatigue.

armies; but also, and principally, they transferred to this present world all the vague aspirations toward a fanciful beyond and, so to speak, materialized human unrest. If only humanity, in its artistic manifestations, can avoid being too much impoverished thereby! Contemporary Russian literature, at least, seems to reveal that this is possible and to stand the test nobly. More and more, better and better, man is called upon to *be sufficient unto himself.*

Another fine example of anacoluthon: "Man is so constructed that by dint of telling him he is a fool he believes it." (Pascal.) Logically one would have to say: "that by dint of being told he is a fool . . ."

12 March

It requires *this* to achieve *that.* You want this, but you shrink from that. Faced with that, which strikes you as iniquitous and cruel, you protest and your white hair bristles, your "few sad last grey hairs." [39] But be convinced that tomorrow those who benefit from the tremendous advantages I am achieving for them (by these measures which seem iniquitous and cruel to you, but which I hold to be necessary) will be no more concerned about those preliminary iniquities than you are concerned today about the ugly origin of certain great fortunes. Wounds of a single day, over which the flesh closes and on which tomorrow's respectability may be founded. They will no longer be thought of, but only the advantages. You would not obtain them otherwise.

"This is what both Stalin and Hitler can say; they are somewhat justified in thinking this. And this is also what I constantly repeat to myself, what my head retorts to my heart. A very bad moment to live through! Happy the periods in history when the heart does not have to protest against what the reason secretly approves!"

"But do you know such periods? Or, to speak more clearly, don't you think that those which seem so to you from a distance do so only because you are not in the midst of them?"

"Yes, perhaps the heart always is led to protest when it happens to enter the kitchen or the pantry and feels nauseated when faced with the preparations of the best that is perpetrated on earth."

"Wait patiently, then, in your study until you are called to the table when the meal is ready. Today you can only get in the way of our preparations with your nosy old conscience."

Oh, if one of these two voices in me could succeed in suppressing the other! But no, at most one dominates for a while. I listen to the echo of the painful conflict that is today laying waste the world.

---

[39] In the original the quotation is given in English.

The din of the explosions tears me from sleep at about nine. And while I am dressing in haste, new detonations much nearer make me rush to the window. In the direction of the harbor I see vast white clouds rising, which filled the sky for more than an hour. A very bright white glow continued for a long time to light up the horizon powerfully, the result no doubt of some tremendous fire. Amphoux, who had joined me in the living-room, judges that it is much closer to us than the harbor. I see another bomb fall on the left, in the direction of the Majestic, certainly less than a hundred yards from our house. And almost immediately afterward people run in the avenue Roustan, under our windows, carrying stretchers and hastening toward the scene. The wave of terror has passed; there is nothing to do but go back to bed, since I am beyond the age of being able to help the victims. But in expectation of a new wave that may perhaps strikes us, remaining on the alert, I do not dare yield to sleep. No one can feel safe from such a blind aim; and why should I be spared? One feels the blast from near-by explosions pass over one like the flapping of a shroud.

How many ruins already in our quarter, where I go walking this morning! Gutted houses, amorphous ruins, collapsed buildings. . . . I learn that last night's big fire consumed the wood stocks of a big furniture factory without taking any victims, it is thought. "Incendiary plates" fell in the rue de Marseille behind the big Café du Colisée, the window of which was blown in. It does not seem that this bombing, which, even more than the preceding ones, threw the population into a panic, did the least harm to the Germans. Did the planes miss their target? What was it? What is the purpose if it all? What sense do these idiotic destructions make? Some go so far as to attribute them to camouflaged German planes; propaganda bombings, they say. In any case, German propaganda does not hesitate to use them.

On the other hand, the damage on the airfield of Gamarth, beyond La Marsa (which they attacked for the first time the day before yesterday) is said to be very considerable. There is talk of a large number of German planes destroyed. At La Marsa itself a rain of small bombs made many victims among those who had not taken shelter.

Read with some impatience and a serious fatigue toward the end *Romance* by Joseph Conrad and Ford Madox Hueffer. Should like to know the latter's role and his share in that collaboration. I naturally attribute to Conrad himself certain excellent parts; but it seems that toward the last third of the book he gave the floor to the other, who is too discursive and finical. It drags on and the judicial misunderstanding becomes boring. Three literary manners are unbearable to me: the

Garibaldi (and this is why I dropped *Nostromo,* though Arnold Bennett, who is a good judge in the matter, considered it to be Conrad's best book), the Musketeer manner, and the *"Caramba!"* manner. If I made a real effort, I think I should find still a fourth. . . . But let's drop it and find relaxation in Gibbon.

14 March

Here I feel farther from those who are dear to me than I could be even in the Chad. And it seems to me that, far from them, my thought falls asleep, that it required their constant attention to keep it awake. Left to myself, to me alone, my thought would perhaps have taken a different course; this is what I occasionally tell myself, well aware that a need of understanding affection has always oriented my life. How often has the fear of hurting kept me from carrying logic to its conclusion! This is partly because I cannot attach value to an utterly abstract and, as it were, dehumanized thought. The reason's inconsistencies are often the heart's consistencies.

But what seemed to me true I have always expressed even if with occasional cruelty to some, though with much more circumspection than one might have thought at first.

15 March

Since yesterday we have had electricity again. Delight at being able to read until eleven! (Gibbon's wonderful *Decline and Fall.*)

16 March

Unable to hear anything on the radio but a self-congratulation of the English Air Force — which at least never attacks anything but military objectives, which it always hits. It seems thoroughly proved that the English aviators are considerably superior to the Americans in daring, and consequently in precision, since the English planes dare to fly much closer to their targets. But for those who have just noted the useless damage caused by the last raid, such a declaration is rather demoralizing. Fine speeches take the place of action. And constantly (Voice of America) boasting of the importance of their production! This is to let it be known that the extraordinary Russian successes are not due solely to the value of the Red army but just as much to the new equipment furnished Russia by America. It is said that Stalin asked for the recall of the U.S. Ambassador to Moscow, who was insisting too indiscreetly on this point. Stalin's annoyance can be only too well understood.

16 March

The very pleasant young German officer, a student of art history and friend of Ernst-Robert Curtius, whom I went to see yesterday at the

Rose de Sable, told me that in Rome, where he began his military service and was stationed more than a year, the books of the Pléiade Collection [40] are so sought after that the few booksellers who still have
some ask up to two thousand francs (in our money) for them (quoted
up to four and five thousand francs in New York, Keeler Faus wrote
me at the beginning of the war). It was that collection, created and
edited so intelligently by Schiffrin, that Jean Schlumberger and I had
such trouble getting accepted. We had to insist and to struggle for almost two years before reaching an understanding. "I don't see what
you consider so remarkable in it," X. persisted in saying. Initiative in
admiration is an extremely rare thing; here, too, nothing but followers
are found. I recall a conversation with the chief bookseller (I might as
well say the only one) of Dakar, during my first stay in French West
Africa, who said to me of the Pléiade books: "No, sir, our clientele
doesn't like those books; they have no chance of success. No, the
colonists don't want them." Then, taking out a hideous large illustrated
edition of some then popular author: "Here, this is what they like."
If I saw him again today, probably he would assert that he never said
such a thing, or even that he was one of the first booksellers to sell and
to recommend to his clients the Pléiade Collection; but I am sure that
my memory is not wrong on this point.

The charming F. V. Arnold is the first, and only, German to whom
I have spoken in Tunisia. I hesitated to meet him, then decided that
my reticence was absurd. We did not speak of the war. He told me
simply, in the beginning of our conversation, how embarrassed he felt
by his uniform. He enjoys declaring his great admiration for Thomas
Mann's Lotte in Weimar,[41] then takes out of the breast pocket of his
military tunic a tiny edition of Goethe's Divan, no larger than a ciga-
rette-lighter, which, he says, helps him over many difficult periods. He
also speaks enthusiastically of Jünger. The war can never make me
look upon such representatives of Germany as enemies; but he knows
and feels himself to be an exception and expects to be crushed in a
world in which he will be unable to find a raison d'être.

Read with very keen interest (and why not dare to say with admiration) The Maltese Falcon by Dashiell Hammett, by whom I had

    [40] A series of French classics, well printed on thin paper and leather-
bound, which is now published by Librairie Gallimard. A single volume contains all of Montaigne; another, all of Rimbaud; Balzac's Comédie humaine
appears in several volumes. In the summer of 1939 Gide's Journal 1889–
1939 came out in this series in a volume of over 1,300 pages.
    [41] Published in 1939, this novel was translated the next year as The
Beloved Returns.

already read last summer, but in translation, the amazing *Red Harvest*, far superior to the *Falcon*, to *The Thin Man*, and to a fourth novel, obviously written on order, the title of which escapes me. In English, or at least in American, many subtleties of the dialogues escape me; but in *Red Harvest* those dialogues, written in a masterful way, are such as to give pointers to Hemingway or even to Faulkner, and the entire narrative ordered with skill and an implacable cynicism. . . . In that very special type of thing it is, I really believe, the most remarkable I have read. Curious to read *The Glass Key*, which Malraux recommended so strongly to me, but which I cannot find.

I notice in one of Gibbon's notes (Guizot edition), Chapter iii; A.D. 117), of Hadrian (in regard to Antinoüs): ". . . We may remark that, of the first fifteen emperors, Claudius was the only one whose taste in love was entirely *correct*." [42]

A writer's integrity consists in not giving out as his own the ideas he has gleaned here and there in others.

19 March
. . . All the slight infirmities of great age, which make such a miserable creature of an old man. Glandular restorations, I suppose, succeed on a much smaller scale. With changes in temperature, for instance, the organism now reacts only too weakly. I have to have recourse to a whole series of drawers and vests, which I take off and put back on twenty times a day. If occasionally I try to escape that bondage and convince myself that it is becoming a mania, I am sure to suffer: I catch cold and am down for some time with a cold. Just now I am wearing, one over the other, three pairs of drawers, and at times, in order to remain motionless for some time in this frigid room, have to pull on my pajama trousers over my trousers or wrap the lower part of my body in a blanket. My mind almost never succeeds in forgetting my body, and this is more harmful to work than one can say. Besides, the unbearable itchings constantly keep my mind from soaring. At night those itchings become worse; it seems as if they stand guard to keep sleep from approaching me; and I don't know what position to take for sleeping: first one part of me, then another, gets numb. Since I have got much thinner, an insufficient cushion of flesh fails to keep me from being indiscreetly aware of my skeleton. One has to go on living, however, constantly reminding oneself that it all might be much worse. . . .

---

[42] The quotation is given in English.

Victor continues to soil the toilet seat with his dung. This morning the cleaning woman complains mildly that she has to clean up that filth; whereupon Jeanne scolds Victor, who protests, as always, with an obstinate: "I didn't do it." And Jeanne (she alone still has a semblance of authority over that overgrown child of sixteen) tells us that when he was younger, he often happened to "do something big" (as she says) in his trousers through laziness or carelessness. The surprising thing is that he was willing to remain soiled until evening when Jeanne didn't do anything about it. Curious to know (but it is a quite footless question) what a severe and rigorous upbringing might have made of that child, who has an undeniably bright mind but a strange lack of affective qualities. Curious to know if in his denials he would have gone so far as to let an innocent person be accused and condemned in place of him; for example, the cleaning woman for having broken the lock on my trunk or drunk the rum locked in his grandmother's closet. . . . I am told that his mother from the very beginning met his lies, even the most shameless of them, with indulgent and almost amused smiles. How much she herself, who is all affection, abnegation, and honesty, will soon have to suffer from the shortcomings and vices that she so unwisely tolerated and even, one might say, cultivated in her son!

20 March

An opportunity arises to return to France; presumably such a chance will not be repeated for a long time. Three or four hours' flight and the plane lands you in Naples, but it takes no less than six days thereafter, I am told, to reach the frontier. One can take along only two thousand francs and a little Italian change. Would I be permitted to take along also some manuscripts? I doubt this very much and cannot accept the idea of seeing them confiscated. And once there, would I find a possible place to live? At Cabris I run the risk of bothering my friends considerably. All the hotels will be full. And under Italian domination what modicum of liberty can one expect?

No, I cannot make up my mind to leave and abandon, at the moment of the supreme ordeal, the new friends with whom I had lived these dark months and who showed themselves to be so affectionately thoughtful. Courage fails me as I think of it; I have now taken sides with them. Probably we have dreadful days ahead of us, and it is with them that I must live them.

That liberation of France which the Anglo-Americans promise us, that liberty will prove to be for us, I fear, the occasion of serious upsets and of lasting internal dissensions, of which I shall presumably never see the end.

21 March

It is in fields of grain and not under olive trees, like anemones, that these huge red tulips grow, just like poppies at home. The last few days they have covered the flower stalls in the shade of the fig trees in the avenue Jules-Ferry. Not quite the same, I believe, as the beautiful wild tulips around Brignoles.

Since the day before yesterday, radiant weather. I am making slow progress in reading *Chance*, the least good of Conrad's books that I know (and I know a rather large number of them). Its finical slowness seems even more tiresome after the lively gait of Dashiell Hammett. Odd to think that it was precisely this book that brought Conrad his first real success. Hardly to the public's credit!

26 March

The offensive opened a few days ago and the battle is raging in the south. But after the first success, which already suggested a breakthrough of the "Mareth Line," the entrance into Tunisia, behind which Rommel's army had taken its stand, a German counterattack had almost immediately driven the Anglo-American forces back to their original position. Meanwhile that "Maginot Line" of Tunisia, or rather that "Siegfried Line," had been turned on the north, and Anglo-French forces, after having taken Gafsa, are advancing to cut off Rommel's retreat. We are awaiting news with an anxious impatience. A speech by Churchill implies that the struggle will be long and difficult.

According to Amphoux, there is an element of comedy in all this. The Allies are apparently not at all in a hurry to win and, whereas their crushing numerical superiority would have given them victory long ago, they prefer to wait; for England and America fear Stalin as much as Hitler and would like to have to deal, when it becomes necessary to make a treaty, only with exhausted forces among the Allies as well as among the enemies. Consequently Churchill's and Roosevelt's speeches enjoy exaggerating the difficulties of the struggle (according to Amphoux) in order to explain at one and the same time this delay and the little aid that they are contributing to Russia. This may be; and I admit that the Allies have every interest in drawing out the engagement, risking in the present battle the least possible of their forces, prudently economical and eager to reserve the best of them for tomorrow. However this may be, everything suggests a still rather long struggle. The Germans are preparing lines of defense at the base of Cape Bon, where they are preparing to withdraw and to resist as long as necessary in order to allow their troops to re-embark. The last few days many civilians have been sending their families back to France. It is expected that Tunis will be fiercely bombarded, and trenches are

being dug along the avenue Jules-Ferry, which prolongs the avenue de
France. Yes, we shall certainly be in the thick of it!

But I cannot share the indignation some feel upon seeing civilians
get theirs also. That indignation would be justified only if all the mo-
bilized men had deliberately agreed to fight; but they are obliged to.
They did not choose their fate.

27 March

Victor reads a great deal. I do not know whether or not he reads
intelligently, but in any case he reads good authors. Of late he has devoured a considerable quantity of Voltaire, of Rousseau, of Diderot,
and today he is tackling Montesquieu. He is engaged in sorting; he is
informing himself.

An odd failing I have discovered in this child consists in implying
that he had long known what he has just discovered. François de Witt,
I recall, used to excel, if I may say so, in this failing; and I was much
amused to read in Sainte-Beuve that his grandfather Guizot used to
do likewise, giving out as his own the most recent information he had
received and taking great care not to point out his sources in order not
to reduce his credit.

Certainly I appear to Victor as an utter hypocrite, for he cannot
accept as authentic any feelings he is incapable of experiencing. He
attributes to others, and to humanity in general, the considerations of
self-interest that guide him, and he thinks that my affectionate gratitude
toward his grandmother is simulated. (He was very much amazed to
learn that I share with her the daily expenses of the house.) This allows
him to indulge in a scorn that he takes pleasure in making me feel. His
inner landscape is one of those in which it would be most painful for
me to live, and mine one of those in which he would feel most out of
his element. I should like to be able to keep an eye on that child in
his career. So little bothered with sentiments and scruples, certainly
not lacking in personal value, ready to trample on everything that
cannot be of use to him, eager for gain and pursuing his advantage
through everything, he cannot fail to succeed.

He does not yet seem very developed from a sexual point of view.
I should likewise be curious to know what advantages and disappointments this new and yet undeveloped appetite holds in store for him.
I told him one day, considering the inelegance of his table-manners,
that he "was getting ready to be a magnificent cuckold." This was intended to nettle him. He didn't seem to be much moved by my joke,
but he probably does not forgive me the continual sallies I made at his
expense when we were still conversing; he was in no wise corrected by
them, never rose up in protest, but stored up my rebuffs as secret

grievances, anxious to make me pay for them some day; incapable of generosity, but building up a capital of resentment.

It is that constant, somewhat Quixotic need, almost an *idée fixe*, of correcting, of reforming, not only myself but others that often made me so unbearable, first to Pierre Louÿs, then to so many others, but that would make me, I think, so good a citizen of a real republic. How could it have failed to make Victor take a dislike to me, accustomed as he is by his parents to have everything his own way, never reprimanded by them, but adulated, turning his desires into laws and never encountering anything but indulgence for his shortcomings? How could he have discerned, through my continual thrusts, the interest I took in him, for which, besides, he cared nothing? For him I was simply the spoilsport. A Protestant, of course! . . . In that quarrel with Victor I had all the wrongs on my side; almost all.

If there returns to France a period of well-being, soon enough for me still to take advantage of it, I promise to treat myself more generously. I have always been very "close" about myself, and this has often made me look like a miser; I was really a miser only when I alone was concerned. I was eager to prove to myself that I could be satisfied with little. But now that I have proved that and know where I stand, I think I shall cease holding my appetite, or even my greed, in check. I managed to be an ascetic; I remain a sensualist. There are certain elegances less suitable to the young than to old men and I should like not to leave too unprepossessing an image of myself. Just now I am making everything last, linen, shoes, suits; I have to! But it seems to me that nothing will be too good for me afterward. . . . I am writing this without believing in it too much. For probably such a general poverty awaits us after the war that it will encourage me, I suppose, to even more parsimony than in the past.

Moreover, I have no great hope of surviving this period of horror.

Besides, there is no great hardship in wearing frayed clothing when one knows one could afford new things, or when one even already has them in one's closet. One is a prisoner in indigence, but what fine credit one deserves for living in a jail while having its key in one's pocket, with the possibility of leaving it when one wishes! . . . I have never experienced poverty save as an outsider, a dilettante, just enough to be able to understand what the pangs of real need can be to some.

29 March

Events seem to be about to take a precipitous turn: the famous 'Mareth Line" fell to the Eighth Army the day before yesterday, with

six thousand prisoners already and a large amount of equipment. There
is announced, besides, a considerable advance on Gabès and a continuous advance on the northern Tunisian fronts. The German army, it
seems, has only to surrender; otherwise it will not escape being massacred, it is said. But it is probable that it will continue to fight and
try, by a last-ditch resistance, to protect a partial retreat and re-
embarkation, under a murderous shelling.

Nine hundred tons of explosives dropped on Berlin last Saturday,
the London radio announces. The havoc must have been frightful. One
can hardly imagine it in view of the fact that less than a hundred tons
at the very most caused all the devastations in Tunis.

31 March

Yesterday Victor deigned to break his silence for a moment to announce to us the occupation of Gabès. This morning there is talk of
an English landing at Sfax. People coming from Bizerte assert that the
Germans are abandoning the town. Kairouan, it is said, has presumably
fallen into Allied hands.

Poor dear Chacha, the grandmother, was knocked over by a German truck (they go at breakneck speed, do not sound their horn at
corners, and accidents are numerous). She was brought home, her face
swollen and covered with blood, but, as far as one can tell before a
medical examination, without any serious injuries. Fortunately, the accident took place close to the house. At first she lost consciousness, and
did not come to until she had been taken into a pharmacy. Although
accompanied, she had the courage to climb the four flights without
help, worthy mother of gallant Dr. R.; and, just like her daughter
during the most painful moments of her brain tumor, Chacha had the
moral strength to smile and, without ever complaining, tried only to
reassure others, as if to excuse herself for the trouble she was causing us.

Before handing over to Mme V. my *Nourritures*, in which I write
an inscription, I glance over again the last part of the volume, those
Nouvelles Norritures which the most recent edition adds to the original
ones; and I hardly recognize myself in them.[43] Of all my books it is the
most uneven, the least good. I am aware of the intention and the trim-
ming in it. However close to me the first ones, *Les Nourritures terrestres*, may still be, so that I can still quiver anew as I reread them
and revive my emotion from sentence to sentence, these last pages,

---

[43] *The Fruits of the Earth* of 1897 and *New Fruits of the Earth* of 1935
were first published together in a single volume by Gallimard in 1942.

although much more recent, have withdrawn from me to such a degree that if I had not signed them, I should doubt that they were really by me (aside from a few "chance repetitions" and certain songs that I used in *Perséphone*[44]). I have ceased to feel in it that accent of sincerity which doubtless constitutes the chief value of my best writings.

1 April

Postal exchange with France resumes today, we are informed. There are many who take this good news as an April fool's joke. However that may be, I send cards to Marcel Drouin, Roger Martin du Gard, Mlle Charras, and Yvonne Davet (most likely those cards will first go to Berlin to pass the censor) and two letters to Mme Théo and to Dorothy Bussy, which, through diplomatic channels, will, I hope, arrive much sooner.

3 April

Went out yesterday, toward evening, with Patri and Flory. The Germans and Italians in uniform have left the city. The streets and avenues of Tunis are clear and silent. Even the sparrows are silent, which ordinarily in the evening rejoice in the branches before going to sleep. Deceptive calm: every day the Axis troops are receiving considerable reinforcements by plane. Doubtless they are preparing for a desperate resistance. The future of our old world is at stake.

4 April

In his latest speech Eden speaks of the definitive disarmament of Germany. It is essential to take away from her not, as he says, "the possibility of arming again," but rather, but better, the need, the very desire, to do so (surveillance, as we have seen, is impossible). Do not parch with thirst whomever you would keep from drinking.

6 April

Books recommended by . . . others are rarely to our taste, and a few recent experiences warn me of this: very rare are those whom literature interests. Amphoux lent me the day before yesterday a novel translated from the English which, he said, had made him laugh uproariously: "You will see; I have never read anything wittier or more enthralling. It is both an adventure story and a very subtle and won-

---

[44] *Persephone*, an opera in three tableaux, was written for Ida Rubinstein, with whom Jacques Copeau collaborated on the staging; Stravinsky provided the music, and Kurt Joos the choreography. First presented at the Théâtre de l'Opéra in April 1934, *Perséphone* was published the same year by Gallimard.

derfully successful caricature of the Irish character." The book soon
fell from my hands and I didn't dare tell Amphoux that I had never
read anything so ordinary, so trivial, or so insipid. "Not worth mentioning," [45] and I have already forgotten both the title of the book and
the name of the author.

Incontrovertibly better, *Bahia of All the Saints* [46] by Jorge Amado,
a Brazilian novel that Flory lends me with a warm recommendation.
But I have been unable to get interested in this purely linear narrative (I mean without depth), solely discursive, though recognizing in
it certain qualities of presentation, but very ordinary ones.

A recommendation by Dr. Ragu has considerable importance for
me. I get along very well with him and there is probably no one in
Tunis whom I more enjoy seeing. The Ragus keep open house for their
friends, and two or three times a week I go there to dinner at their
constant invitation. The doctor is most intelligent, most cultivated, most
informed; curious of everything, or almost everything, he reads a great
deal, devouring book after book with a youthful avidity; ever accustomed to sleep but very little, he prolongs his studious sessions
until three a.m. It took me rather long to realize that in his reading
he seeks above all to inform himself and in an almost exclusively historical domain, the very one in which I have the least desire to join or
to accompany him and for which my brain is most obtuse. He is, consequently, most inclined to read chronicles and memoirs; and I really
believe that literature arouses his curiosity only in its relations to history. Yesterday I saw Hemingway's *Farewell to Arms* on his table; he
was unable to get interested, he told me, in that book which had seemed
so remarkable to me. And I see him on the other hand become enthusiastic over works that I judge severely, like Schiller's *Jungfrau von
Orleans*, which he considers admirable. He was unable to get interested
in Buckle, which I had gone to get for him at the library, any more
than in Gibbon, I fear; for him they are "outdated." He confessed to
me his ignorance in natural history, botany as well as zoology, and the
little attention he had ever given it. He is smitten with Maurras (of
whom Bainville, according to him, is but a pale reflection) and discovers in his dreary poems qualities that I cannot discern; I should be
worried about my blindness on this point if I did not think the doctor
suffering from a certain literary daltonism. What I like in him is his
faculty for enthusiasm and the great interest he takes in all forms of
life, his amused receptivity, his broad understanding of people, and,
beyond all that, his kindness.

---

[45] In the original the expression in quotation marks appears in English.

[46] *Baía de todos os santos* is the original title of this novel, which has not
been translated into English. Gide gives the title in French.

10 April

Documentary value of literature: this alone matters to them. They would judge painting more soundly and, even without any special competence in the matter, would at least know that exactitude or, in a portrait, resemblance plays but a small part in the value of a picture. But reporting is far from having purged literature as much as photography managed to free painting of certain adventitious values. People suspect that qualities of technique alone confer on a canvas chances of survival and that what the painter represents, what is called the "subject," matters relatively little. But in a book everything is more mingled, confused, and the "subject" matters much more. Yet the interpretation of the subject, the resemblance with the thing represented, its profound resemblance, and the personal mark of the writer who sets it forth and sets himself forth, his style — all this enters into play, constitutes the value of the work and keeps it from falling into oblivion in a short time. To create a lasting work is my ambition. As for the rest: success, honors, acclamations, I make less of them than of the slightest particle of true glory: bringing comfort and joy to the young men of tomorrow. Oh, not limit life to oneself, but help to render it more beautiful and more worthy of being lived! I do not believe in any other afterlife than in the memory of men; just as I believe in no other God than the one that is formed in their minds and hearts, so that each of us can and must contribute to his reign.

Dr. Guttierez told me this morning that during the four years he occupied, before Amphoux, the apartment next to the R.'s, not once did Victor's father, whom he often met on the stairs, address a bow, a smile, or a word to him, though he was meanwhile on the best of terms with Mme R., the doctor, his colleague at Sadiki hospital. How can Victor, who so closely resembles his father, endure being to such a degree the prisoner of his heredity? In his stubborn silence toward me there is perhaps less resolve than surrender to his natural inclination.

Oh heavens, yes, I am well aware in what sense I could say with Valéry that "events do not interest me." None of the things I cherish spiritually is dependent on this war, to be sure; but the future of France, our future, is at stake. Everything that still concerns our thought may disappear, sink into the past, cease to have for the men of tomorrow anything but an archaic meaning. Other problems, unsuspected yesterday, may trouble those to come, who will not even understand what constituted our reason for existing. . . . (I am writing this without really thinking it.)

But at last events are ceasing to crush us. The deeds of Leclerc's division are rehabilitating the French army. The British Eighth Army produces an air of heroism that makes one's heart beat faster. On our radio set, now repaired, I anxiously listen to the news, hear it again in German, in English, in Italian, on the alert for a bit of information not given in the other language, and as if my attention could hasten the future.

11 April

I have patiently reread from end to end the interminable *Vanity Fair*. I should not have time enough in France; here nothing exerts any pressure on me; everything is leisure for me, while waiting. (And I want likewise to go back to a Walter Scott.) But I wonder if in my youth I had gone on reading the Thackeray to the end, or if the translation of it I read at twenty was not considerably cut. The number of idle reflections rather unfortunately *date* this novel, and only certain chapters remain remarkable. *Henry Esmond* seems to me much better (if I can judge at least by my memory of it).

Rather disappointed by a rereading of *The House of the Seven Gables*, which I take up immediately afterward. Less sensitive to the poetic aura with which Hawthorne can envelop our outer world than to the often exasperatingly slow progress of the narration. It is a voyage in a coach, with frequent stops at inns, that makes me think of Vigny's lines:

> *Farewell, slow voyages, distant sounds to hear . . .*
> *. . . the wheel's delays.*
> *A friend along the way, and hours forgotten . . .*
> *The hope of late arrival among untrodden ways.*[47]

That means of locomotion, indeed, had its charm; but the habit of speed makes me particularly sensitive to "the wheel's delays." Moreover: literature that reflects. And what I enjoy most, in American literature of today, is its direct contact with life.

13 April

The Protestant missionaries in French Equatorial Africa and the Cameroon were more scrupulous in general than the Catholics as to the means utilized for converting the Negroes, the Catholics more concerned with the number than the quality of the new converts. Yet at Yaoundé (I believe), Maistre told me he freely turned to cinematographic representation of miracles; he did not understand how I could

---

[47] *Adieu, voyages lents, bruits lointains qu'on écoute . . .*
> *. . . les retards de l'essieu.*
Un ami rencontré, les heures oubliées . . .
L'espoir d'arriver tard dans un sauvage lieu.
These lines are from *La Maison du berger* (*The Shepherd's Wain*).

consider that practice as dishonest. It took unfair advantage, I told him, of the naïveté and ignorance of the spectators who were unable to recognize the trick devices he was using. But Maistre firmly believed in the reality of miracles and could not recognize any imposture in their artificial reconstitution. Solely my incredulity fed my censure, he considered; if I admitted that the miracle had taken place, I should consider its *re-presentation* as legitimate. For him, a believer, the question did not even arise.

Gibbon brings out one of the causes, which I had not noted, of the gloom cast over society by Christianity. "Those persons," he writes, "who in the world had followed . . . the dictates of benevolence and propriety, derived such a calm satisfaction from the opinion of their own rectitude" (see Goethe), "as rendered them much less susceptible of the sudden emotions of *shame,* of *grief,* and of *terror*" (italics are mine) "which have given birth to so many wonderful conversions." And he adds very judiciously: "As they emerged from sin and superstition to the glorious hope of immortality, they resolved to devote themselves to a life, not only of virtue, but of penitence." (Book I, Chapter xv.) [48]

. . . But to feel unutilizable for this great action that is about to begin; to feel one's intelligence not so much reduced perhaps as slowed down, without sudden impulses to counter, without retorts, still an excellent spectator, but not a participant in the struggle, and too acquiescent in the event whatever it may be. No indeed, not for honors, not for money, not even for personal protection shall I be made to say what I do not think; but I am less and less sure of what I think or that reason should be all on my side. I even believe that the cases of total and fundamental error are rather rare or at least rather rapidly put out of countenance. People could be found who think that if Galileo was right to be convinced that the earth turns, at least he was wrong to say so, because of the harm that might cause the Church. This is also what certain Communists told me after my return from the U.S.S.R.: "We know all that as well as you, but sh! It is essential first of all to say or do nothing that might harm the party." In the last resort, did not the "*téjés,*" as Stendhal called them, get the better of Pascal? [49] Besides, Pascal's arrows have become blunted, and his shafts do not carry so far as they once did. I did not always feel on his side when I recently reread the *Provinciales.* But when faced with injustice and oppression, it is difficult for my heart not to rise up. I shall prob-

[48] In the original the quotations are given in English.

[49] Stendhal called the Jesuits "*téjés*" because of Société de Jésus, the name of their order.

ably not relinquish indignation until I relinquish life. It is said to be
the very "wrong side" of love, but I believe that for certain natures
this wrong side wears out less rapidly than the right side.

A "nature" like mine is utterly unfit for politics. Not that I am totally devoid of the spirit of intrigue; but only with difficulty convinced
that all the wrongs are on the side of the adversary, I am more inclined to busy myself with understanding him than with combating
him. Consequently I am worth nothing in discussion, leaving my position to follow the other, being thrown off the scent and soon having
no idea where I am. It's lamentable.

16 April

Reread *King John,* a most imperfect drama, but containing three or
four scenes that count among Shakespeare's finest ones and certain
series of admirable lines. It also contains the line that served as an epigraph for Conrad, which I had not yet been able to locate:

So foul a sky clears not without a storm.

17 April

This morning I reread with delight numerous parts of the *Well-
Tempered Clavichord,* of which F. left me the first book yesterday. I
believe that of all of them the slow Fugue in C-sharp minor is my
favorite; it is almost the only one that I can readily imagine interpreted
by a chorus of human voices. But as I go over them, there are at least
a half dozen that strike me as no less beautiful. Literature has been unable to produce anything so perfect.

19 April

The bombing of the night of the 17th, which seemed by far the
most terrible, has presumably had no victims, we are told, and caused
but very little damage. It kept us awake a large part of the night. Far
as we were from the places where the bombs fell, the house was shaken
by them. Probably the windows and doors of the avenue Roustan have
been blown in, and I imagine that poor Chacha must have thought her
last hour had struck. Sorry to have had to forsake her in that ordeal.
Last night, likewise interrupted by continual alerts, but for a bombing that, if it was not any lighter, was at least farther off. The bombs
of the night before also seemed much more powerful than those previously dropped on Tunis. Probably until the day of liberation almost
all our nights will be similarly upset.

Dazzled by *Richard II,* of which I had but too vague a recollection.
Wonderful, the second scene of the first act — Mowbray accused by
Bolingbroke (Harry Hereford, Lancaster), with a rather long series

of rhymed verses. Wonderful, the profession of love for England by
John of Gaunt, the King's brother, on his deathbed (Act II, Scene i) —
which I ought to learn by heart. . . .

Art — called upon to disappear from the earth; progressively; completely. It was the concern of a choice few; something impenetrable
for the "common run of mortals." For them, vulgar joys. But today the
chosen few themselves are battering down their privileges, unwilling
to admit that anything should be *reserved* for them. By a somewhat
silly magnanimity, the best of today desire: *the best for all.*

I can imagine a time coming when aristocratic art will give way to
a *common* well-being; when what is individual will cease to have a
justification and will be ashamed of itself. Already we have been able
to see the Russians reviling whatever manifests an individual feeling,
no longer admitting anything but what can be understood by anyone
whatever; and this may become anything whatever. Humanity is
awakening from its mythological numbness and ventures forth into
reality. All these children's baubles will be relegated among the obsolete; those to come will not even understand any longer how for centuries people could have been amused by them.

> . . . *Withdrawing himself into some obscure retirement and pa-
> tiently expecting the return of peace and security.*
>   (Gibbon, Chapter xvi.)

20 April

I finish *Richard II.* Odd play in which no further curiosity as to
events maintains one's interest after the second act; nothing further but
poetic ground swells. Most amazing sketch of the King's flabby character. Those two great families of Shakespearean characters: the men
of action and the irresolute men, whom he opposes to one another in
many of his dramas. And often the irresolute man is the center of the
play, of which the very subject becomes his deterioration and retroces-
sion before the other, better equipped than he for life. The first often
gifted with the most exquisite qualities; the other stronger because less
scrupulous. Whence, so often, the sacrifice of the best.

Did Freud know and cite the Duke of York's slip when saying to
the Queen, after having just learned of the death of the Duchess of
Gloucester:

> *Come, sister — cousin I would say — pray, pardon me.*
>   (Act II, Scene ii.)

As soon as I have read it, I reread *Richard II* almost entirely. One
of the least perfect, the least constructed of Shakespeare's dramas, but
one of the strangest, one of the heaviest with poetry.

What to do with such a line:

Rouse up thy youthful blood, be valiant and live,
which I cannot succeed in scanning satisfactorily.

Days as if stolen from life. . . . It is now already eight spent in this retreat, rather gloomy despite the extreme kindness of my hosts and companions in captivity. They have been cloistered for almost six months, not even daring to show their faces at the window or especially to appear on the balcony in full view of the neighboring terraces, even less to risk themselves in the streets, where one is exposed to mass round-ups. That my own person is sought by the German authorities is not thoroughly proved. Arrested as a suspect? Suspected of what? No, but perhaps a lawful prize as a witness likely to talk and whom they prefer not leaving to the English. This is what was suddenly told me, and that I should do better to "hide out," as so many others were doing, without further delay. Even though I find it hard to convince myself that, if it came to that, my person or my voice could be of any importance, it was better not to run the risk of a forced voyage and sojourn in Germany or Italy.

Numerous hostages, undesirables or suspects, have been sent back to France of late; but many of the planes transporting them have been brought down on the way and no convoy is seen off without anxiety.

Pierre Laurens — peevish and powerless, dreadfully jealous of the friendship his brother bore me and using every means to undermine it. He did not succeed in this; but Paul, animated by a very keen "family spirit," who, all kindness, intelligence, and charm, trembled at his younger brother's brutality, hid from him in order to see me, setting clandestine rendezvous like a guilty man or a lover, in which he would complain at length of that constraint upon his feelings and thoughts, console himself for his own weakness by the account of those despotic abuses of authority and of many unjust accusations, bring me from Pierre cutting remarks in the manner of Léon Bloy, with an odd mixture of suffering from injustice and admiration for a temperament more imperious than his. Withal, Pierre was not incapable of generosity, enthusiasm, veneration, which he would readily have converted into genius if only a little talent had allowed him to make it effective. The penury of his own means would not forgive his colleagues any success on their part.

Mme. X., the companion of my captivity, tells me a remark her daughter made at the age of twelve. Since she had shown a curiosity about where and how children are born, her mother had not felt justified in lying to her and had replied quite bluntly: "In their mother's belly." Some time after, the child had shared her new knowledge with two girls of her age; one of the two claimed, fortified by what her mother had told her, that she had been born in a bottle of cologne, and the second one had issued from a rosebud. A discussion ensued, which one of the parents busy in the next room had happened to overhear. "It is not possible," the first one maintained, "that roses should produce children. No, roses produce roses; cats produce kittens; mammas produce little girls, and papas produce little boys."

The only books I took into my retreat were Gibbon and Shakespeare. X. lends me *Ivanhoe*, which he has just finished. (It just happens that I had promised myself to read or reread a Walter Scott, but preferably any other one.)

I have a horror for this papier-mâché and Viollet-le-Duc style. I seem to recall that *The Antiquary* is less historical. . . . Worth looking into, for, all the same, there are great qualities of narration and dialogue in him; it is understandable that Balzac was fecundated by him.

23 April

All night long from ten o'clock on, the distant cannonade made the ground tremble with a vague continuous grumbling. A sort of anguish, mortal as well as physical, kept me awake and as if on the watch until daybreak, trying to imagine the inferno and wondering if it is worse on the German or the English side. . . .

We are living here without electricity and consequently without any news from the radio; often without water, almost without alcohol or gas or oil, on our almost exhausted remaining supplies, barely kept alive by meals that become less adequate every day, brought in from the outside by the family of the incomparable Flory's wife.

24 April

Speak from a distance or else keep silent.[50]

These lines from La Fontaine might serve very well as an epigraph if I happen to publish the pages of this *Journal* in America.

Malraux certainly did not fail to notice that I mangled the name of Amenophis or Amenopis (I said Amenopsis).[51] I did not fail to notice either that he had noticed it, but he was too courteous to correct

---

[50] *"Parler de loin ou bien se taire"* is the last line of La Fontaine's fable *L'Homme et la couleuvre* (*The Man and the Snake*).

[51] In the XVIIIth Dynasty there were several kings by the name of Amenophis (Amenhotep). Amenophis III (reigned *c.* 1414–1379 B.C.) began constructing the Temple of Luxor.

me. That was two years ago. I had promised myself to tell him this; unable to do so, I write it here.

With no other pastime but reading, my eyes are very tired. I ought to rest them by doing nothing; but I go on just the same, though with an ever increasing effort. . . .

Many are those who are counting on the hour of our liberation for the 2nd of May. Why precisely the 2nd of May? No one knows, but they assert it so definitely that eventually one almost believes them. The radio announced yesterday, as it was repeated to us, a "general advance along the whole front from Cape Serrat to Enfidaville."

27 April

Uninterrupted grumbling of artillery all night long, a bit nearer, it seems, than the night before last. It is like a tight, coarse-grained weft on which is superimposed at daybreak the delicate embroidery of the roosters' crowing. One would like to be able to make out whether the voice of the cannons has a German or an English accent. What an inferno it must be over yonder! All that youth mowed down. . . .

"Tut, tut; good enough to toss; food for powder, food for powder; they'll fill a pit as well as better; tush, man, mortal men, mortal men," says Falstaff.

Can there be a more wretched humanity than the one I see here? One wonders what God could ever possibly come forth from these sordid creatures, bent over toward the most immediate satisfactions, tattered, dusty, abject, and forsaken by the future. Walking among them in the heart of the Arab town, I looked in vain for a likable face on which to fix my eyes and pin some hope: Jews, Moslems, south Italians, Sicilians, or Maltese, accumulated scum as if it were thrown up along the current of clear waters, capable, however, of disturbing backwashes, at the mercy of any agitator; perhaps events will stir it up anew. . . .

But it is two weeks already since I have left my room. I am letting my white beard grow; I am waiting for the liberation before shaving again. Unable to go to sleep until shortly before dawn; but, without itching and without too much nervous anxiety, I became resigned to my insomnia and remained with my eyes fixed upon and lost in the black abyss occasionally broken by distant, fitful glows. Last night the cannonade could not be heard, but during rather long periods of time the ground was all shaken by a prolonged, as if seismic shudder.

What can our friends in France suppose when they hear an "escapee" from here announce on the Paris radio that Sfax is devastated, Sousse destroyed, and that in Tunis "not a stone remains on a stone"?

28 April

"Whoever at forty is not a misanthrope never loved men," said Chamfort (or Rivarol?).[52]

Yet it is too easy to say to those who profess to love humanity and sacrifice themselves for it: this is because you haven't really looked at it; it is scarcely lovable. They might well reply: you are the one who has not been able to discover it under its lamentable appearance. The creatures who seem to you commonly abject are deformed, crushed, and prostrate under the weight of an evil society. You who are concerned with horticulture are well aware, however, that there is no plant so humble that it is not capable of flowering, provided that circumstances contribute to this, that the ground, one's care, the climate . . . Just consider what rosebushes become in bad soil and without sun and attention. You accuse people; I accuse only their poverty and those who caused it and maintain it for their own profit. — It is essential to know whether one is for the greater number or for the choice few. Their interests seem opposed. But are they really? . . . This is not merely a question of humanity, of humanitarianism; art and culture are the stake.

Fired with enthusiasm by the two *Henry IV's*. With *Henry V* I had to come down a peg. It is one of Shakespeare's least good plays, mediocre and even definitely bad in spots, saved solely by the King's admirable address before the Battle of Agincourt.

The finest subjects for drama are suggested to us by natural history and particularly by entomology. My *Saül* [53] was inspired by the odd discovery I had made of the chrysalis of a hawk-moth; it preserved its perfect form with the minute indication of the butterfly that was to issue from it; yet I noted at once that it was not capable of any of those slight quivering movements under the influence of tickling which reveal the latent life of ordinary chrysalises (at least the ones belonging to these butterflies). At the first pressure of my fingers the fragile envelope broke, which preserved but the form of the original animal; under this very thin and fragile sheathing many little cocoons had usurped all the space; they belonged to a sort of sphex, doubtless. . . . And I did not understand how the original animal, now devoured, had been able to find strength enough to achieve this deceptive pupation. Nothing revealed on the outside its total disappearance and the victory of the parasites. Thus, I thought, my Saül would say: "I am utterly suppressed."

---

[52] This maxim is found in Chamfort's *Journal de Paris*, No. 178.
[53] Gide's drama on Saul and David was first published in 1903.

And I learn this morning that the caterpillars of the *Lycænidæ*, after an initial period of vegetarian feeding, are carried off into an anthill by the ants, who enjoy the bit of honey secreted by their dorsal papillæ just as they do the milk of the aphis. But, deprived of vegetable food, those caterpillars change their diet and soon devour the entire nest of ant-eggs. Too bad for the ants! Thus it is and only thus and only in the anthill that the development of those caterpillars can reach completion.

Amazing "subject" of a drama! Not of a La Fontaine fable, but of a drama, and here is the first act: the caterpillar, a future butterfly, gets itself invited to the ants' house; all this, naturally, in the world of men and transposed to our scale.

Again in *Henry VI* (Part I) I find a scene (between Talbot and his son, Act IV, Scene v) entirely in rhyme from line 16 on. Likewise the following scenes until the end of Act IV. Beautiful, but with a somewhat facile sublimity: a dialogue almost like that of Corneille.

Curious to hear Dorothy B. defend this line:

> Before the wound would prove incurable
>   (*Richard III*, V, i.)

or

> Vaughan, and all that have miscarried.

1 May

Disobeying orders, I went out yesterday without even meeting anyone on the stairs, either on my way out or on my way in. During my half-hour I wandered in the neighborhood without any pleasure: broiling sun, heavy air, everything seemed ugly to me, both things and people. I almost got run over crossing a street. No pleasure; pleased to return to my grotto.[54]

3 May

The Anglo-Saxons are losing a few positions won by a first advance; it appears as if their superior numbers are yielding to courage. The Germans feel more involved in this supreme resistance than they are in the attack.

The Eighth Army remains inactive in front of the mountainous mass of Zaghouan, and the other army has not been able to go around it. Most likely the movements are agreed upon in advance, but do not always succeed according to plan. There is convergence of efforts, to be sure, but also rivalry, it is thought, and respect for precedence, so

---

[54] Probably a reference to *The Poitiers Incarceration Case* (1930), where Gide recorded the sequestered girl's strange affection for her "dear little grotto."

that it would be inappropriate for one general to harvest the laurels reserved for another general or for the English forces to offend the American forces, which have hardly distinguished themselves up to now. Whence procrastinations and delays, which would be hard to explain otherwise. Thus we seek reasons and encouragements in this exhausting period of waiting. . . .

4 May

Fatigued by several nights of sleeplessness, I feel at moments as if at the end of my tether and aged to the point of despair.

6 May

I have just reread one after another nine of Shakespeare's ten historical dramas (the only one that remains is *Henry VIII*) with an almost constant admiration. I am learning by heart a number of La Fontaine's *Fables*. Stultified, aged, feeling my thought at its lowest ebb.

Yesterday afternoon the most violent bombing that Tunis has known yet; although rather far from the places that were hit, the house was quite shaken. They began again last night, from ten o'clock until two thirty, without interruption; an unbelievable number of bombs fell all around the city. The A.A. reacted but very little.

7 May

Explosions and fires in every direction on the periphery of the city. I counted more than twenty fires. They are not the result of the Anglo-American planes. The Germans, hunted down, before evacuating the city are blowing up their depots. This is a way of breaking camp. Thick columns of smoke tragically darken the sky.

Toward evening the fires multiply. Heavy black clouds spread over the city. Through the incessant noise of explosions, strange, incomprehensible cracklings of machine guns rather near. It is beginning to rain. The main roads whose intersection can be seen from our terrace, so busy the last two days with the traffic of half-tracks, tanks, and vehicles of all sorts, are now deserted; they emptied all of a sudden; their silence is impressive.

8 May

While I was writing these lines yesterday, the Allies were already entering the city. This is what everyone said yesterday evening. This morning, awakened at dawn by a dull, constant, indeterminate sound, which seemed like the roar of a river. I dressed in haste and soon I saw the first Allied tanks approaching, cheered by the people from the

near-by houses. You can hardly believe that what you have been so long
waiting for has taken place, that *they* are here; you don't yet dare believe it. What! Without any further resistance, battles, or fighting? . . .
It is over: *they are here!* The amazement increases even more when
we learn from the first of these liberators to be questioned that these
tanks and these soldiers belong to the Eighth Army, the very one that
we thought was held in check in front of Zaghouan, that glorious army
which came from the Egyptian frontier after having swept Libya,
Tripolitania, conquered the Mareth Line and the Wadi Acarit Line,
and whose progress we had followed from day to day in southern
Tunisia. How are they the first to get here? Which way did they come?
There is something miraculous about it. One imagined the liberation
and entry into Tunis in many ways, but not like this. In haste I close
my bag, my suitcase, and get ready to return to the avenue Roustan.
No more reason to hide. All the hunted people of yesterday come out
of the darkness today. People embrace one another, laughing and
weeping with joy. This quarter near the nursery, which was said to
be peopled almost exclusively with Italians, displays French flags at
almost every window. Quickly, before leaving my retreat, I shave the
four weeks' beard and go down with the companions of my captivity
into the street, where they have not dared appear for exactly six
months. We enter the wildly rejoicing city.

Odd: in this city where every language was spoken, today nothing
but French is heard. The Italians are silent, are in hiding, and one
meets but a few rare Arabs.

In General Giraud's proclamation, which is posted on every wall, a
comminatory and inexplicit sentence fills them with fear. Their conscience is not at ease; is that vague threat aimed at them? [55] They are
not hiding, it might be said, but are in no wise taking part in the
celebration, remaining shut up in the Arab town. So that this frantic
swarming of a cheering mob is made up in great part (and in certain
quarters almost exclusively) of Jews. Everyone is shouting: *"Vive la
France!"* As soon as one of the tanks stops, it is surrounded, besieged
by a crowd; children climb in and sit down beside the conquering
heroes. And, as if by the sky's approval, all yesterday's clouds have
disappeared; the weather is splendid.

10 May

Unable to note anything yesterday. I run hither and thither, go to
see friends, mingle with the crowd. By evening I am dead-tired; fur-

---

[55] "As for those who abetted the enemy in his work of misery and pain,
they will be pitilessly and promptly punished. I give you my formal assurance of this. There is no room among us for traitors." [A.]

thermore, electricity is cut off, the Germans having blown up the power-house before getting out, so that, unable to write, I go to bed as daylight wanes. The sky is uniformly pure. Series of radiant days, among the finest I can recall, among the finest possible; and the most innumerably starry nights. But the city is still in a state of siege and all traffic is forbidden after eight p.m.

Close behind the Eighth Army, the First Army has made its appearance in the city, together with French forces, Zouaves. It seems that the Eighth cut the ground from under the feet of the First; come from the Enfida (having, however, left a deceptive screen of their forces in front of Zaghouan), they presumably took advantage of the breach painfully, dearly, and most courageously opened at Mateur by the French infantry and American armored units. All that will be known later on and I have no need to note here what belongs to history.

The Germans were surprised by the suddenness of the last advance. The order was received all of a sudden, most unexpectedly, to clear out, to leave without taking anything but the bare necessities, to destroy, before leaving, anything the new occupants could take advantage of, and likewise personal papers and souvenirs. It was a frantic flight toward Cape Bon, but many found their retreat cut off, whence the great number of prisoners. A desperate resistance was attempted at Hammam Lif, and during the whole morning of the 8th the cannon was heard rumbling; then that last island was crushed by artillery fire.

Yesterday the entire victorious army was drunk. Little improvised bars opened everywhere, where unscrupulous merchants unloaded their stocks of adulterated products, the Germans having previously made a clean sweep of all the decent wines, liqueurs, and other drinks. Toward evening trucks passed by, gathering up and taking back to their units all those who were incapable of standing upright. Dragging on the ground, victory soils its wings.

What beautiful weather! A sort of light joy is floating in the air. One breathes freely. The daily bread ration has just been increased from two hundred to five hundred grams a person. Milk reappears on the market. Since people expect supplies in quantity and since restrictions are about to end, they finally take their reserve supplies out of cupboards, open cans, and dare to eat all they want. Packages of American or English cigarettes rain upon us, and bars of excellent chocolate. Each meal becomes a feast. One regrets not being able to hear on the radio, for lack of electricity, the Berlin, Rome, or Vichy communiqués. How will this dreadful setback be announced? As late as the day before, the official bulletins nourished confidence and hope, spoke at most of a few "purely local operations." I managed to get a copy of *Tunis-Journal* for 7 May, suddenly stopped as it was being printed, in which I read: "Several Anglo-American actions against the north and central (*sic*) sectors were repulsed, the Berlin communiqué announces." Will they try again to "minimize" the importance of their defeat or will they proclaim general mourning as when Stalingrad was recaptured by the Russians? Germany is clever enough to clothe this defeat in all the colors of victory. We could hope for nothing better, she says, and were well aware from the outset that we had to yield to greater numbers. But we were counting on resisting one month and we held out for six months; this goes beyond all our hopes. The Allies are congratulating themselves; we are congratulating ourselves more than they. In any event, this liberation of Tunisia, this reconquest of the entire African coast, must demoralize Germany. Already undermined by the Russians' victories, she must already envisage the collapse of her hopes.

I am preciously preserving a stillborn issue of "*Die Oase,* Feldzeitung der deutschen Truppen in Afrika," dated 9 May!

13 May

Radiant days. . . . I sleep in front of the casement window in my room (opening on a narrow balcony) wide open on a sea of stars; going to bed very early, I get up at dawn. Sleep somewhat bothered by mosquitoes.

Day before yesterday, dined at the Ragus' with Mme Sparrow, Hope Boutelleau, and two English officers whom she brought, both charming. I take pleasure in noting their names here as a reminder: Captain Chadburne and Dr. Gidal, photographer for the Eighth Army. Perfect agreement, in two languages, with each of them on each of the points of literature that is brought up. Gidal talks to me, with great perspicacity, of Stefan George, to whom he prefers Rilke, and for excellent reasons. The names of Kafka, Steinbeck, Faulkner, Aldous Huxley, etc., are brought up.

The American auto taking us home stops at the "grade crossing" where the first British tanks broke the last German resistance on the 7th. The road is blocked by an endless file of trucks and half-tracks filled with German prisoners being brought back from Hammam Lif, where, the day before, a dreadful battle was waged before the surrender of the Axis troops. We get out of the car to watch this fantastic procession, and, using flash-bulbs, Gidal takes a few pictures of some of these vehicles: they are German "police wagons." He who expected to seize others is himself seized. I am told that certain groups of prisoners were singing. Of course! This was the only hope left them of escaping this nightmare and ever seeing their families again. Others were weeping, it is said. I thought that a larger number would kill themselves or get killed according to orders. The Italian army surrendered almost at once as a unit, and that surprised no one. The German forces, without further munitions, without a possibility of reinforcement, without a possibility of retreat and re-embarkation, driven to the sea and to despair, finally agreed to yield; in the absence of Rommel himself, von Arnim is taken prisoner.

The Berlin or Rome radio, to save face, may well relate that the Axis armies fought to the last man, to the last cartridge, in a last heroic resistance. That may protect patriotic honor and pride; but it is not true. "Unconditional surrender," however surprising it may seem, was accepted almost at once. The bitter struggle of Hammam Lif was the last battle waged; after it all useless resistance ended and von Arnim sent word that he was surrendering.

But, above all, what I am writing here must not be taken to decrease the worth of the German troops. They gave proof, up to the last few days, of extraordinary endurance, discipline, and courage, yielding only to superior equipment and numbers. Probably also, in the last days, to the suddenness of the Allied advance, which is transforming the retreat into a rout. It is only natural that von Arnim, seeing the game irremediably lost, wanted to avoid an inevitable and useless massacre. In what I am saying I am taking to task solely the radio's camouflage.

This African campaign, which was to be triumphal and triumphant, adds up, for the Axis, to a tremendous loss of men and of war material. Besides, confidence in the Führer will doubtless be considerably shaken as a result, and the Führer's confidence in himself. While all the conquered peoples now under the German yoke will derive from this great setback to the oppressor an extraordinary encouragement to resistance. It is possible to hear in it the announcement of a general collapse.

Ragu would like to persuade me of the important role I should presumably soon have to play here; he claims that I am qualified to assume it. I believe he is wrong both about me and about the weight my voice might carry. Even less fatigued, I should not feel in any way qualified for political activity, whatever it might be. Aside from the fact that I do not understand clearly enough the interplay of nascent dissensions, I am too uncertain myself to propose some equitable conciliation or other and could not speak without betraying or forcing my thought. I neither can nor will interfere with or take a part in the struggle that is ahead. I fear that, for a rather long time, bitter rivalries will divide France, at least the liberated part of her. I am totally incapable of seeing what "declaration" I might make that, if I remain sincere, would not be of such a nature as to displease almost equally all the parties.

14 May

From all sides it is reported to us that the American troops, just as much as the English or French forces, fought admirably. The delays with which one could justifiably reproach them at the outset were but measures of prudence so long as they were insufficiently equipped. It was essential not to begin the combat until having full assurance of being able to carry it through to victory. The event dissipated whatever doubts might remain and proved the wisdom of that procrastination, whereas precipitation might have compromised everything.

Dull boredom of an English Sunday in Tunis; the fogs of London would be more appropriate. But the soldiers seem resigned to this Sunday idleness. The two movie theaters that have reopened, not reserved for the army as during the German occupation, are invaded by civilians. Still, never before had so many uniforms been seen in the streets. The initial days of drunkenness and rejoicing (when there was nothing left to sell or to give them but frightful adulterated drinks, the Germans having emptied every cellar) are followed by a period of prohibition, based on rigid rules. Then there are rows of bare knees along the sidewalks, on the house steps, on the few benches along the avenues, tommies who, smiling after all, are discreetly waiting for night to fall.

Unbearable Tunisian climate; frequent changes in temperature; as soon as one ceases to be too hot, one shivers, not knowing how to cover oneself. A bad cold adds the finishing touch to my subnormal feeling. I now think only of leaving, but where shall I go?

Amrouche, doubtless, will accompany me first to Algiers, where he hopes to find a post; with Suzanne Amrouche, he is the one I shall most regret leaving. Then the Ragus, then Victor's grandmother, and Jean Tournier, and Amrouche's friends. All have been indefatigably kind to me. The Florys, Patri, Hope B., Guttierez, Cattan, Mme Sparrow, Amphoux . . . with them, thanks to them, I went through this time of ordeal almost easily. Perhaps the future will allow me to show them my gratitude. Leaving seems to me like an uprooting.

19 May

Reread *The Tempest*; amazed to recognize everything in it so well. Strange drama, which leaves one more unsatisfied than any other by Shakespeare, probably because no other awakens such lofty demands. Nothing unexpected in these symbol-characters: each of them, in order to represent the better, becomes superlative. Once the situation is established, the action unfolds without trouble, without digression or hitch. Everything is a matter of course in this exemplary display at the door of the theater, where everyone, full of his role, adheres to it and maintains it, as correct as in a tintype. Only the relationship between Ariel and Prospero remains disturbing and devoid of rigidity:

> "Do you love me, master? No?"
> "Dearly, my delicate Ariel."

It is charming, but it remains a bit brief.

20 May [56]

Great joy upon seeing Jean Denoël again; but made considerably gloomy by his tales. The French losses were tremendous and due, apparently, to the stupid routine (as in 1914) of certain military leaders, to their outdated conception of courage, of honor, and of some false gods or other. Some of them led their men to slaughter, without advantage of any sort and as if in answer to the call of a tradition. Mere common sense should have kept them from launching that attack without artillery preparation; besides, it was clear that it was to be useless. Alas, these are the same men who are in a fair way to govern us tomorrow. It is easy to understand that the hearts of some are filled with indignation and revolt.

Denoël, enrolled in a "surgical unit" and called upon to attend to a great number of people, and especially of very young children mutilated, maimed, gashed by the mines with which the Germans laced every bit of ground they gave up.

I am told that they hid their explosives even in corpses, which explode in your face as you go to bury them. Even more horrible: a wounded man shouted to the ambulance man approaching him: "Look out! Don't come near me: the bastards have mined me!"

22 May

No school edition, at least in those I have been able to see (and I should be curious to consult on this subject the big edition of La Fontaine I left in Paris, wondering if perhaps it is not more explicit [57]) alludes to the most amazing faculty frogs have of swelling up their gullet like a goiter, like pigeons in the mating season, and of projecting on one side of the mouth, as I have seen done by camels in heat, a sort of huge blister, or growth, a vibrant and yapping apparatus that is indeed one of the strangest things one can imagine.[58] The article

---

[56] In the original this entry is dated "29 May," which must be a misprint.

[57] No mention of that peculiarity in that edition either (June 1945). [A.]

[58] "In the male, two *vocal bladders* can issue from a crevice that extends back to the shoulder; such pouches are sometimes as large as a hazelnut." Brehm (June 1945). [A.]

"Frog" in the big Larousse dictionary makes no allusion to it either. And yet it is that odd characteristic which explains and motivates the fable of *The Frog Trying to Be as Big as an Ox*. No doubt but what La Fontaine was able to contemplate one day, as I did myself at La Roque, this extraordinary spectacle: on a broad lily pad floating on the surface of a pond, two frogs illustrating and miming that fable in exemplary fashion. One of them a mere spectator, and the other swelling up to the bursting-point, his way of courting and manifesting his desire, with oblique glances at the other one:

> *Look carefully, sister!*
> *Tell me, is this enough? Have I not achieved it?*

In the ignorance of this fact, that fable may seem arbitrary and somewhat absurd. This is its justification, which ought to be pointed out to children to show them that here again La Fontaine proves to be an observer and remains close to nature, probably much more than any other writer of his time.

I am not at all among those who rather disdain those first fables of La Fontaine. The subsequent ones, more amply developed, have quite different qualities; but the initial ones have a density, a weight, a substance *à la* Breughel that delights me; and particularly that gem *The Wolf and the Lamb*. Not a word too many; not a line, not one of the remarks in the dialogue, that is not revelatory. It is a perfect object. But the taste for perfection is being lost, and I foresee a time when it will even cause people to smile indulgently as one smiles at children's games, when the *"quod decet,"* harmonious ponderation, the nuance, and art, in short, will yield to qualities of impact and to practical considerations, when the fact alone will matter. "Somber pleasure of a melancholy heart." [59] it will be all up with you! Here begins the virile age, the era of reality.

22 May

"Yes, we could have entered Tunis much earlier, it is true, but at that time we were not in a condition to maintain ourselves there: we considered that it would be deplorable to run the risk of letting ourselves be driven out soon after by the German counterattack that would not have failed to follow almost at once. We wanted to act when we were sure of the result, and preferred to wait and to make you wait rather than risk inconsiderately our soldiers' lives and yours."

This is what is told us this morning by W., who has just moved up to the American consulate here and with whom I lunch at the Ragus'.

---

[59] *"Jusqu'au sombre plaisir d'un cœur mélancolique"* is a line from the next to the last poem in La Fontaine's *Amours de Psyché et de Cupidon* (*The Loves of Psyche and Cupid*), Book II.

Jean T. waited until this last moment to tell me that he doesn't think he can lend me more than fifteen thousand francs out of the fifty thousand that he had led me to hope for.

Now this obliges me to turn elsewhere and to put off my departure, which I had set for Tuesday, letting Soupault reserve a seat for me in the Algiers plane. Even the loan from J. T. (and, in this emergency, I reduce it to ten thousand, to his greater relief) is going to require formalities at the registry office and, because of the week-end (it is now Saturday), we shall have to put them off until Monday. Had I been informed earlier, I should have made other plans. This will teach me not to rely on too vague promises.

23 May

Always frightful mental confusion on the eve of departure. You take leave of friends, and they all want to see you once more. This morning the Amrouches, the Florys, Pistor, and a captain of the Leclerc division who wanted to be introduced to me, young Guy Cattan, were crowded into my room while Bourdil, Amrouche's brother-in-law, was hastily finishing my portrait. I try to find the pleasantest thing to say to each one of them. Meanwhile, while still posing for Bourdil, I start with Amrouche a game of chess, which he wins without difficulty, for I have lost my presence of mind. Besides, I have been playing much less well for some time now and my attention soon wanders. And I don't know yet whether it is really the day after tomorrow, Tuesday, that I am leaving; nor at what time; nor what I have a right to take with me in the plane; nor how nor when the rest of my luggage will catch up with me. How much simpler with death; the sudden command to leave *everything*.

On checking up, I find that I do not leave until Thursday. Horrors! I shall have to repeat all the farewells.

I meet Jean T. at the registry office. The loan must be made in the presence of the lawyer whom we had already gone to see. Reading the official document that I must sign, in which I learn that I shall have to begin by subtracting from that sum of ten thousand francs five hundred francs that go to the state for legalizing the transaction. It is implied that I shall have still other expenses for registry or something of the sort, without counting the lawyer's fee . . . so that, of those ten bank notes, I shall retain but nine. . . . This is ridiculous. I refuse to go through with it. The game is called off. The few hundred-franc notes that I still have will be enough till I get to Algiers, where I shall take the necessary steps.

Captain Alaurant asks me timidly to write a line in his travel diary, and I shall do so most willingly, happy to express in this way my admiration for the lofty achievement of the Leclerc division, which he symbolizes in my eyes. After that heroic crossing of the Fezzan and their victorious advance, no sooner arrived in Tunis and back in civilized life than he has his car stolen, with all his effects, his supplies, his papers, etc. . . . I accompany him to the Residence to inform Soupault of his case and, if possible, to help him recover his car.

Soupault very kindly takes both of us to dine at the mess, together with Lieutenant Bénard. Soupault's charm, wit, and adaptability put everyone at ease. Only at moments some cracks in the conversation provide a glimpse of the profound political divergences under the cordiality of the remarks.

Algiers

So at last I have left Tunis! On this Thursday, 27 May. We left the El Aouina field at seven o'clock; the trip, which was to last but two hours, took more than twice this, with stops at Zaghouan and at Le Kef. I had not slept all night, and after a choppy trip I reach Algiers in a rather lamentable condition. The charming welcome of the Heurgons and an excellent lunch instill new life in me.

Great joy upon finding Saint Exupéry.

In our old world the Americans get themselves liked by everyone everywhere. With such a ready and cordial generosity, ever smiling and so natural, that one gladly accepts being obliged to them.

"Make yourself liked" was the watchword launched by the German newspaper in Tunis during the beginning of the German occupation. The newspaper (which was not for sale and circulated only within the army) added: "even by the French." This watchword did not succeed, any more than it did in France itself, and was soon replaced by: "Make yourself feared." Behind the feigned politeness, one remained too well aware of the need to dominate, which their smile did not succeed in camouflaging.

At the Heurgons' I yield to the intoxication of a new library, reading one after another a little Leopardi, then a little Dante, then a little Stendhal, then a little Virginia Woolf: wandering at random in a garden.

Before writing an affectionate inscription in it for Amrouche, I reread this morning my *Tentative amoureuse*, into which I put much more of myself than I remembered. All in all, a little book that is very revealing of the epoch (even excessively so) and of myself.[60]

---

[60] *The Attempt at Love* was first published in 1893.

Add, as a postscript to my notes on Christ's last words: Have these remarks ever been made before? I don't know. But I do know that I have never read them anywhere.[61]

2 June

It is high time to change notebooks.

17 June

"But those masters" (David, Gros, Guérin, Girodet), "too much extolled in the past and too much scorned today, had a great merit . . . of beginning to restore in the French character a taste for heroism." (Baudelaire, *Exposition Universelle de 1855.*)

Algiers, 26 June

I dined, then, yesterday evening with General de Gaulle. Hytier, who accompanied me, had come to pick me up in a car at about eight. The auto took us to El Biar, directly to the villa whose terrace overlooks the city and the bay. We moved into the dining-room almost at once and took our places, Hytier and I, on the two sides of the general. On my right sat the son (or the nephew) of General Mangin; I did not catch the names of the other guests, two of whom were in civilian clothes, all of the general's entourage. We were eight in all.[62]

De Gaulle's welcome had been very cordial and very simple, almost deferential toward me, as if the honor and pleasure of the meeting had been his. People had told me of his "charm"; they had not exaggerated at all. Yet one did not feel in him, as one did excessively in Lyautey, that desire or anxiety to please which led him to what his friends laughingly used to call "the dance of allurement." The general remained very dignified and even somewhat reserved, it seemed to me, as if distant. His great simplicity, the tone of his voice, his attentive but not inquisitorial eyes, filled with a sort of amenity, were such as to put me at ease. And I should have been completely so if I did not always feel in the company of a man of action how remote the world I inhabit is from the world in which he operates.

I had just read with very keen interest, and why not say with admiration, many pages by him that were excellent, even capable of making one like the army, presenting it not as it is, alas, but as it ought

---

[61] See, for instance, *The Journals of André Gide,* Vol. III, p. 36.

[62] Jean Hytier recalls that the two civilian guests were Gaston Palewski (1901–   ), who was named director of de Gaulle's private cabinet in July 1943, and René Pleven (1901–   ), then Commissaire aux Colonies after having organized the colonial resistance in Africa; he has been several times Minister since 1944 and in July 1950 became Premier.

to be. Reminding him of the remark he quotes to the effect that Jellicoe had all the qualities of Nelson save that of knowing how *not* to obey, I asked him how and when, in his opinion, an officer could and should take it upon himself to disregard a command. He replied most appropriately that this could only be at the time of great events and when the feeling of duty entered into opposition with a command received. Some of the guests then entered the conversation to compare military obedience to the obedience required by the Church. One could have continued much further than we did. The conversation soon dropped and I did not feel strong enough or in the proper mood to start it anew.

After the meal the general suggested to me that we take a little walk on the terrace. This amounted to offering me the opportunity of a private conversation, and I took advantage of it to speak to him at some length of Maurois. In the general's writings a sentence had somewhat surprised and hurt me, I told him, the one in which he states that he met Maurois only once and hopes never to see him again. I tried to explain Maurois's attitude, which, I said (and this was going rather far on my part), would have been very different if he had been better informed. I added: his eyes will soon open when he talks with the friends who are at present expecting him here. Maurois is wrong because he has been deceived. He thinks it is his duty to remain faithful to the marshal, and he is all the more inclined to think so because that duty pains him and, in acting thus, he is setting all his former friends against him.

The general's features had stiffened somewhat and I am not sure that my rather vehement defense did not irritate him. (Less sure, and this is worse, that my arguments were all valid, it seemed to me after having seen Maurois again.)

We spoke next of the advisability of creating a new review to group together the intellectual and moral forces of free France or those fighting to free her. But this was not carried very far either. He then told me how much he suffered from the lack of men.

"Those who ought to surround you," I told him, "are, alas, under the wooden crosses of the other war." One has to play out the game with the hand one has. The trumps are not numerous.

We joined the rest of the company again and all went back into the drawing-room. The rambling conversation began to languish and I think everyone was grateful to me for breaking up the gathering soon. I thought sadly of what that interview might have been if Valéry had been in my place with his competence, his clairvoyance, and his extraordinary *presence of mind*.

I had spoken to the general, during our brief private conversation, of the resistance in Paris and particularly of that session of the Academy in which Valéry opposed addressing congratulations to the marshal as some academicians proposed. The general was thoroughly informed about it all.

He is certainly called upon to play an important role and he seems "up to it." No bombast in him, no conceit, but a sort of profound conviction that inspires confidence. I shall not find it hard to hang my hopes on him.

27 June

Some English officers back from Pantelleria bring us details about the surrender of the little island. It is untrue, they say, that the island was running short of water, of food, and of munitions. In the Italians' place, we would have resisted for six months, perhaps a year. Sheltered in deep caves, the small civilian population and the military defense could have held out as we held out at Malta, and the number of victims of the bombings was negligible (not more than sixteen, they say). Everything that has been said on this subject, according to them, is untrue; except this: that the rock of the island is so hard that the most powerful bombs merely scratch it. The defending forces surrendered through lack of endurance, because they had had enough and knew that a longer resistance on their part would be useless, because they had lost all hope.

Algiers, 7 July

Charlot has lent me the December 1942 issue of the *Nouvelle Revue Française*, in which I enjoy reading an excellent article by Fernandez on Tocqueville. I do not enjoy underestimating an adversary and I should have liked to be able to think better of Drieu's article and Chardonne's *Dialogue*.[63] I made an effort (but in vain), for it is absurd and unbecoming to see intelligence, honesty, courage, and nobility all on one side, your own, and on the other side nothing but cowardice, stupidity, or disloyalty. Consequently that systematic debasement of

---

[63] The article by Ramon Fernandez, inspired by a new edition of Tocqueville's *Souvenirs*, ends thus: ". . . this book provides the occasion and model for those solid and subtle reflections which used to guide public life and of which we have lost the habit through the exaggeration of modern propaganda." Drieu La Rochelle's article, entitled *"La Fin des haricots"* ("The End of All"), deals with the writer as a political leader and his political responsibility; incidentally it ridicules the French war effort. Jacques Chardonne's "Dialogue" discusses an imaginary dialogue with the Germans, who are exaggeratedly praised. "It is not only the Occidental man of the present who is threatened," says Chardonne; "Germany is defending his past and his roots against the horrible coalition of the Bolshevik Russian and the American, those two bastards of Europe. And if life has a meaning, victory will go, not to the greater number or to the power of machines or money, but to the superior man."

the adversary, toward which propaganda too often strives, is extremely painful to me. I have often expressed this, but, I believe, without convincing anyone. And I now have come to the point of wondering whether, in order to elicit certain reactions from the crowd, it is not necessary first to discredit the enemy. Perhaps; but personally I cannot take part in that game. This is in great part why I am so ill adapted for politics and am so hard to convince of the role that I might assume in the "psychological war."

8 July

Here are new issues of the N.R.F. (January and February), containing a very interesting and satisfying *Bilan* by Drieu [64] and a remarkable *Lamennais* by Fernandez. The review, altogether, is holding up, despite the absences, as well as possible. To be sure, I am glad to have withdrawn from it, but I recognize the cogency of many of Drieu's arguments. My heart much more than my reason disapproves them and I was not far from subscribing to them; but I think that I should have rapidly and bitterly reproached myself for having done so.

Idleness, from which I should suffer more if I felt within me anything whatever to say that I have not already expressed and better than I could do today. I expect from events no profound modification of my being. But the intense curiosity I have about them comes from the fact that the very justification of that being, its foundation, yes, its *raison d'être,* are at stake in this dreadful game.

It does not seem to me that one can correctly speak (as the radio does) of a "fierce defense"; this word must be reserved for attack.[65]

---

[64] "Balance-Sheet" by Drieu La Rochelle begins by summing up the achievement of the *Nouvelle Revue Française* during the two years of his editorship and then turns to a justification of his political position: "I am a fascist because I have measured the progress of decadence in Europe. I have seen in fascism the sole means of limiting and reducing that decadence . . . disapproving of the intrusion of empires foreign to our continent such as those of the United States and of Russia, I have seen no other recourse than in the genius of Hitler and of Hitlerism." Russia strikes him as the only effective military force among the Allies and at the same time as the age-old enemy of Europe, against which Hitler alone can protect the Continent. If he loses, says Drieu, Russia and the United States will eventually clash and fight to the bloody finish of all Europe.

Fernandez's article on Lamennais was inspired by Claude Carcopino's study of 1942.

[65] Although the word *"acharné"* has primarily an active connotation, in conjunction with *"défense"* it would normally be translated as "stubborn" or "desperate."

15 July

Little Edith Heurgon is beginning to walk. Never before had I had an opportunity to witness this marvelous sight: the first steps of a little child. Supported until now, he begins to realize that he can stand up without aid and advance alone. . . . Humanity has barely reached this point, still staggering and seized with dizziness at the thought of the space to be covered, not fully balanced, not fully weaned from the milk of beliefs.

17 July

Lavish light, splendor. The summer asserts itself and forces each soul to happiness. I cannot keep myself from adoration, from joy. Everything is a nuptial urge and one would like to embrace a god. This is the season when Pasiphaë goes to meet the bull in the meadow. Last night Diana covered Endymion with her whiteness.

The day before yesterday, explosion in the harbor; it was a freighter loaded with munitions that blew up. The loudest detonation I have heard. A very large number of victims. Hangars on the quai next to it caught fire, as did a ship filled with fuel oil, which darkened the pure sky with torrents of thick black smoke after the huge mushroom of yellow vapors thrown up at first by the explosion.

19 July

By the suffering I felt at not being able to approve the things that were done and said in the name of France I was able to measure my love for my country.

Called upon to sign a wondrously bound copy of the *Nourritures terrestres* (the big edition called *à la Gerbe*, "revised and corrected by the author"), I am amazed to discover at the first glance that it is richly studded with crude typographical errors, often making sentences incomprehensible or ridiculous. In five minutes I pick out half a dozen of them. And I wonder if the same errors are found in the edition of my complete works. "*Planètes*" for "*plantes*"; "*pics*" for "*pins*," etc.

25 July

A passable night, though still interrupted by rather frequent awakenings, is enough to give back to my mind some of its liveliness. Disposed to work as in the blessed days of my youth. But such nights are rather rare; most often I get up at dawn only half rested, fearing fatigue and effort. The obstacle comes especially from the useless congestion of my brain, from anxiety not to fall behind, not to be in arrears, not to fail in any obligation. . . . It is only when free of all foreign preoccupations that one can create a work that matters. I feel bound, claimed, mortgaged, through and through.

9 August

I have just read *L'Intérêt général* [66] to the Heurgons (in three evenings, for my voice gets tired very rapidly). Very pleasantly surprised to find my play better than my recollection of it, influenced by the unfavorable judgment of the friends who had read it. I do not think I shall have to disown that work over which I have labored so long and which has given me so much trouble. It seems to me that it can brave the stage, and I do not despair of seeing it staged during my lifetime, if the present torment is not prolonged too much. I prefer not to publish it until afterward, unless this would mean waiting too long; but I think that it at least deserves to be published. I should like to offer it to the Comédie-Française rather than to some experimental theater where it might seem too subversive. At the Comédie-Française I think it would keep the appearance of a comedy of character, as I claim it to be, as it is, whether successful or not, rather than that of a social satire (as it aimed to be at first, and this remains its weak point, for I have not been able to efface altogether all the traces of that first disastrous intention).

11 August

The beginning of Chapter xxxviii of *Henri Brulard* implies it rather clearly: Stendhal was not, strictly speaking, "musical"; what he liked was singing, *"bel canto,"* or more exactly, the beautiful singer, not the music. He confesses. "I have no taste for purely instrumental music"; but he most unwisely adds: "Solely vocal melody seems to me the product of genius."

Alexandrines are extremely rare in Saint-Simon. I notice this upon discovering two a very short distance apart:
"*mais non pas tout, ni quand et comme elle voulait . . .*"
"*et préparer ainsi la perte ou la fortune . . .*" [67]
at the end of two consecutive paragraphs. This is the result of chance. Generally, no style is less musical than his, or less concerned with

---

[66] *Robert or The Common Weal,* a five-act play by André Gide, was written originally as a social satire in 1934–5 and, translated into Russian, was about to be played in Moscow when his *Return from the U.S.S.R.* appeared. Completely rewritten in 1938–40 as a comedy of character, it was first published in 1944–5 in Numbers 5–8 of *L'Arche* and later issued as Volume VI of *Théâtre complet d'André Gide* (Neuchâtel: Ides et Calendes; 1949).

[67] *"but not everything, nor when and as she wished . . ."*
"and thus prepare loss or good fortune . . ."

grammatical or syntactical correctness; in him everything yields to the movement of passion, of thought. He is not at all embarrassed to write: "Every type of amusement was forbidden in Vienna and strictly observed"; and that sort of bold anacoluthon is very frequent in him. (For the thing that is "strictly observed" here is the prohibition and not the amusement.) The thing suggested indirectly in one sentence suddenly becomes the very subject of the next sentence. By virtue of the very incorrectness and the surprise that this provokes, this often has a marvelous effect. Each sentence, each word, lives, vibrates, gets out of hand, preserving the mark of his impetuous genius.

It is characteristic of a born writer to bend language to his own purpose; but no one ever did so with such offhand boldness or for a happier result.

Let us leave it to Italy to learn at her expense what it costs to fight on the side of Hitler.

Fez, October

The old ivy upholds the wall, which had long upheld it.

Thought a great deal of Sheng Cheng-hua these last few days, with a smarting recollection of that awkward, absurd sentence with which I must have hurt him so cruelly at our last meeting. How could he have explained it to himself when I cannot explain it myself and fail to see in it an evidence of ill will, of spitefulness, which was certainly very far from my heart. . . .

I had received from Cheng two charming long letters, filled with emotion and inspiring emotion, which I have preciously preserved and hope to find some day in Paris. I owed to my books the feelings he manifested toward me. For Cheng was very cultivated. Still very young, he had come from China to Paris for his education, but had not, I believe, mingled much with the students, who must have seemed rather vulgar to him, to judge from the refined delicacy of his own manners, from his reserved and charming discretion. One felt him to be from an excellent family; and how out of his element he must have felt among us!

He had come to announce to me his marriage, to tell me that he wanted to introduce his young wife to me before returning to his distant country. By what aberration, what confusing bewilderment, what slip of the tongue, did I then ask: "You have naturally married a Japanese?" I saw the expression of his features change at once, his smile disappear, his lips tremble. He stammered: "A Japanese! . . . Oh, Monsieur Gide, how can you . . ." The harm was done. I could not recall that unfortunate word, which I tried in vain to explain, to excuse. I had recently frequented a number of Japanese, who had just filmed my *Symphonie pastorale*; whence, doubtless, that sudden and temporary confusion, utterly unforgivable. I immediately realized that I had dealt our nascent friendship, so trusting on his side, a perhaps mortal blow; and I have not forgiven myself for it even today.

What has become of him? Shall I ever see him again? If I write down these lines, it is with some hope that they may some day come to his attention and that he will know that the memory I still have of him is as it were preserved in my heart.

Fez, October

Si Abdallah, converted to Islam and a Sanscrit scholar, gets me to read the books of René Guénon. What would have become of me if I had met them in the time of my youth, when I was plunged into the *Méthode pour arriver à la vie bienheureuse* [68] and was listening to the lessons of Fichte in the most submissive way possible? But at that time Guénon's books were not yet written. Now it is too late; the die is cast. My sclerosed mind has as much difficulty conforming to the precepts of that ancestral wisdom as my body has to the so-called "comfortable" position recommended by the Yogis, the only one that seems to them suitable to perfect meditation. To tell the truth, I cannot even manage really to desire that resorption of the individual into the eternal Being that they seek and achieve. I cling desperately to my limits and feel a repugnance for the disappearance of those contours that my whole education made a point of defining. Consequently the most obvious result of my reading is a sharper and more definite feeling of my Occidentality; in what way, why, and by what means I am in opposition. I am and remain on the side of Descartes and of Bacon. None the less, those books of Guénon are remarkable and have taught me much, even though by reaction. I am willing to recognize the evils of Occidental unrest, of which war itself is a by-product; but the perilous adventure upon which we thoughtlessly embarked was worth the suffering it now costs us, was worth being risked. Now, moreover, it is too late to withdraw; we must carry it further, carry it to the end. And that "end," that extremity, I try to convince myself that it is *good*, even were it achieved by our ruin. I should probably need the "comfortable" position in order to bring my thought to maturity. Meanwhile I am persevering in my error; and I cannot envy a wisdom that consists in withdrawing from the game. I want to be "in it" even at my own expense.

---

[68] The title *Method for Achieving Blessed Life* is not mentioned in Henri Bremond's eleven-volume *Literary History of the Religious Sentiment in France*, though it may well represent such a document as *Christian Method for Ending One's Life in Holiness and Making Oneself Happy in This World and the Next*, by a Priest of the Mission of St. François de Sales.

Fez, November

What would have happened *if* . . . Everyone is free to fashion imaginary events in his own way and according to his own opinions; whence facile convictions. This is what puts me on guard against History and urges me to prefer greatly "natural history," in which we have a constant check on facts and can always refer back to them; in which the "if" becomes an instrument of experiment, allowing new observations. Who, for instance, would dare to maintain that the butterfly is the same creature as the caterpillar if the fact of the metamorphosis had taken place but once? . . .

Anti-Barrès: I note in *The White Devil* by Webster (first scene):
We see that trees bear not such pleasant fruit
There where they grew first, as where they are new set.

In *Hamlet*, from one end to the other of the drama, nothing bolder, nothing more skillful, than that sort of shift which takes place from scene to scene by which each decisive action on the part of Hamlet is preceded by a sort of try-out of that action, as if it had some trouble fitting into *reality*. Already at the very beginning of the drama, in the dialogue with the ghost; then in any one of Hamlet's ways of behaving, toward his mother, with the King, with Ophelia . . . first he outlines the action, awkwardly. And we find this everywhere, in the double apostrophe of greeting to the players, so disconcerting, yet less so than the pantomine preceding the performance of *The Murder of Gonzaga*. Before the successful realization, there is always a failure.

25 December

I cannot maintain the criticism I made of the use of "*j'ai lieu de* . . ." which struck me as improper.[69] Corneille makes a wonderful use of it. This morning I read in *Sertorius*:
Vous n'avez aucun lieu de rien examiner.
(Act I, Scene i.)

Odd use of the word "*moindre*":
De suivre les drapeaux d'un chef moindre que vous
(Act I, Scene i.)
Ils étaient plus que rois; ils sont moindres qu'esclaves
(Act III, Scene i.)

The English and the French have never more clearly defined their differences (and I was about to say their opposition) than in their drama. As a foil to Corneille's drama, I am reading *The White Devil*

---

[69] See *supra*, p. 133.

and *The Duchess of Malfi* by Webster (already read in French some time ago), then *The Broken Heart* by Ford. I am amazed that the surrealists do not stand in admiration before *The Duchess of Malfi*, whose excess of horror seems designed for their liking, and all those ingredients of phantasmagoric sorcery. . . .

I ceased keeping my *Journal* since leaving Tunis and feel no desire to resume it, but I should at least have noted my readings.

In German: *Don Carlos*, several tales by Gottfried Keller (*Spiegel, das Kätzchen* seemed to me the best).[70]

I should have liked to take advantage of my idleness here in order to plunge into Gibbon again; but the edition offered by Brown's library is much less good than Guizot's (in the Tunis Public Library), enriched with notes and most interesting commentaries.

Reread *David Copperfield* (which I remembered remarkably, anyway), but it is not my favorite among Dickens's novels. He seems to me to have outdone himself in *Great Expectations* and to be at his best in the nightmare of *Martin Chuzzlewit*; he cheapens himself in my opinion when he tries to flatter his public by a display of facile sentimentality. In the horrible he is almost the equal of Dostoyevsky, and that is when I prefer him. He does not amuse me at all in *Pickwick*.

Stevenson's *Kidnapped* somewhat disappointed me on rereading.

Large amount of Conan Doyle during the period of profound depression at the beginning of my stay here (Fez). Some of those Conan Doyle novels are rather ordinary; but there are others (*The Valley of Fear* and especially *Elias B. Hopkins, The Parson*) much superior to what I had reason to hope.

In that series of gardens beneath the Medina forming a sort of lake of verdure in which a single house (Brown's, which I am occupying) is lost, I saw the orange harvest; it followed the even more beautiful harvest of pomegranates; then the *Arundo donax*, those huge plumed reeds which edge the roads and form thick gardens in summer were cut; and suddenly the enclosures lost their mystery. But after the first rains the barley germinated under the olive trees, and never had a more captivating color been seen except perhaps that of the last lingering leaves on the grapevine under the broad glassed-in bay where I sat working or trying to work; they blazed and turned incandescent before the rain suddenly dulled their splendor.

Not only the cutting of the reeds but also the falling of the leaves now allows one to see the ground, which during the summer was hidden by a thick tangle of foliage. In winter everything proves to be simpler than one thought.

---

[70] *Mirror, the Kitty. Don Carlos* is Schiller's play.

1944

Potted pork, *pâté*, cold cauliflower with French dressing, as much butter as one wants. Allice shad, mashed spinach with hard-boiled egg; boiled potatoes. Knuckle of ham (excellent). Jams and cake. . . . This (or the equivalent) is what I find served at my table every day. I should be satisfied with a third. And Si Haddou excuses himself for not being able to vary the menu more. Very good wine; and since the water is not sure and typhoid is to be feared, I drink the wine straight. After each meal, an infusion.

Needless to say, I touch but a few of all three dishes. For instance, at noon today, having taken some allice shad, I left the knuckle of ham, which I am delighted to see again this evening. Ham is an exception to Si Haddou's self-imposed rule never to serve left-overs. I reprimanded him on this point, but achieved nothing.

The sad thing, when faced with so many and such excellent things to eat, is to be alone at table. For Si Haddou joins in the meal only when some guest is with him and it would not be gracious for him to withdraw. But ordinarily he remains away, through discretion, modesty, and fear of being in my way. After the noon meal he appears for a moment, just long enough to ask me whether I do not want to "walk up to town"; after the evening meal he comes to wish me good-night.

Who could tell with what attentions he surrounds me? It is impossible for me to desire anything but what he gets it for me at once. He tries to divine my tastes in order to forestall my least desires. Every morning, before going to the fonduk, he asks: "Do you need anything?" And on returning from the fonduk: "May we do your room?" for he accompanies Mohammed in his household duties and never lets him make my bed alone for fear that I may not be quite comfortable.

I reproach myself for not doing sufficient honor to the meals, excessively copious, in which he contrives to offer me all the best and rarest things he has managed to find. But I am not a heavy eater and adapted myself very well to the scarcity in Tunis or to the monotonous meals of Rabat. But the inappreciable thing for me here is the constant warmth maintained in the room where I spend the whole day by the small stove, which I fill and light every morning on getting up, which I light again as the daylight wanes, and for which the sun substitutes in the afternoon. The kindness of M. Robert, the farmer friend of Si Haddou, furnished me with a superabundant supply of firewood and of vine stubs. My sensitivity to cold has become such that, without this means of heating, I should probably not have been able to get through the winter.

Every day I take myself by the shoulders and force myself to go for a walk, sometimes rather long. Unfortunately the outskirts of Fez are scarcely inviting and discourage curiosity: the country is all open and does not even offer the surprise and amusement of new plants. Everywhere the same little marigolds, which began to flower in about mid-January; clumps of scilla, of which nothing is left now but clusters of leaves. I still walk along at a good pace, but get tired quickly.

The example of Cardan, whose autobiography I am now reading in a German translation, urges me to speak more of my health. The condition of my liver and kidneys has greatly improved by itself and, altogether, I should be very well were it not for this tendency toward a cold and an almost constant hoarseness. The most unsatisfactory thing is sleep. Every evening I go to bed in apprehension of the few hours of anguish, often really painful, that I shall have to live through before being able to go to sleep. And again I am tormented by itchings, often unbearable, the whole length of my legs or between my toes. As for my mind, I feel it to be as active as in my best days, and my memory, which I am diligently exercising, has never been so good, at least for the poetry I am asking it to retain; for I believe that for the little details of life it is weakening; this is partly because I grant them less and less importance.

On my walks I always take along a book; but it often happens that I return without having opened it, having preferred to let my mind wander aimlessly or to recite, all along the way, the most recently learned of La Fontaine's *Fables* (of which unfortunately I find only the second volume here): *La Mort et le mourant, La Fille, Les Souhaits, Les Deux Amis, Le Paysan du Danube, Le Rat qui s'est retiré du monde, Le Rat et l'huître,* the long *Discours à Mme de La Sablière,* which opens Book X, and the fable of *Les Deux Rats,* which follows it.[1]

In the garden of the Villa Brown the lavender iris have been in flower for the last twelve days; recently, a few rare jonquil-narcissus; in the wild state, oxalis, fumitory, arisarum, hawkweed; this is all, I believe.

Reading is invading the hours that were filled, even last week, by the polishing and typing of the extracts from my *Journal* that I am giving to *L'Arche,* which are to appear immediately afterward in a

---

[1] *"Death and the Moribund," "The Girl," "The Wishes," "The Two Friends," "The Peasant from the Danube," "The Rat Who Withdrew from Society," "The Rat and the Oyster," "The Discourse Addressed to Mme de La Sablière,"* and *"The Two Rats, the Fox, and the Egg"* figure in Books VII–XI of *The Fables.*

volume published by Charlot.[2] I am reading especially German and
English, but have just devoured one after another eight books by
Simenon at the rate of one a day (this was the second reading for
Long Cours, Les Inconnus dans la maison, and *Le Pendu de Saint-
Pholien*).[3]

I have long ceased to keep my *Journal* (since I left Tunis, for I
consider as naught certain pages in the interval). This was in great
part because of the unbearable square-ruling of the last notebook
(there were no others to be found), which forced me to write my lines
too close together. But each time that I resume my *Journal* after a
rather long interruption, I should like it to be in a somewhat different
tone, and yet not an unnatural one, as when one changes interlocutors.
And furthermore, I should like indeed not to repeat constantly the
same things. Now, I long ago looked at myself from all angles; at least
it seems so to me; and have inventoried my spiritual furnishings. No
further great discoveries to be hoped for from introspection. Events
will take care of providing me with the element of surprise and I
remain extremely curious of what is going to take place.

An attempt at a Moroccan nationalist insurrection, which seemed
rather threatening, has just failed, it seems; it miscarried. Certain demands that were made seemed to me justified and I hope they will be
taken into account. De Gaulle's position is strengthened thereby, I
believe, both in regard to the Sultan and in regard to Churchill, and
the meeting at Marrakech has had a most happy effect.

Fez, 29 January

Feeling, as I wrote the day before yesterday, my mind as alert as
on the best days I believe to be an illusion, which I can maintain only
so long as I do not put my brain to the test; I should soon see, with
use, that, like my body, it gets winded much more quickly. As if to
mock my presumptuousness, I was seized yesterday with one of those
sudden fatigues which leave me for a rather long time almost incapable of effort either physical or intellectual. And nothing, abso-

---

[2] The monthly literary review *L'Arche* was founded in Algiers in late
1943 under the patronage of André Gide, with an editorial board consisting
of Maurice Blanchot, Albert Camus, and Jacques Lassaigne; Jean Amrouche
was editor-in-chief. The first issue appeared in December 1943 and was at
once compared to the former *Nouvelle Revue Française*. In 1945 *L'Arche*
was transferred to Paris, where it continued to appear until the summer of
1947. The Algerian, later also Parisian, publishing house Charlot published
the review.

[3] *Ocean Voyage, Strangers in the House,* and *The Hanged Man of Saint-
Pholien* are all novels.

lutely nothing, can explain the feeling of exhaustion that I then experience. The only thing that keeps me from getting alarmed over such weaknesses is that, more or less violent and prolonged, I have always been accustomed to them. During my youth they were accompanied by headaches, from which I completely ceased suffering subsequently. But already as a mere child my uncles and aunts used to call me "the erratic one," attributing to whims my apparent changes in mood, which were due merely to the variations of my inner temperature, if I may express it thus, or, as people would say today, of my pressure. For I remain, on the contrary, very constant in intention. But how bothersome it can be in any undertaking not to be able to count on oneself. What a fear in commitments! This is what makes me flee society people and keeps me at a distance from the world, despite the often very keen amusement I take in frequenting my fellows (and even more, I believe, those who differ from me).

2 February

Matters are getting worse in the Medina of Fez. Arab scouts and Senegalese have been called out to quell the nationalist insurrection that has been threatening for several days. The insurgents hurled themselves in great numbers with cudgels and side-arms against the Senegalese, who shot at them. On both sides some were killed. The official figure is one hundred victims.

In view of the isolation of the Villa Brown, where, besides, the telephone has been cut off, we considered it prudent to decamp. Guy Delon (Si Haddou) consequently moved to the fonduk. I accepted the kind offer of shelter that had been passed on to me from M. Robert, the very likable farmer who had already provided the wood for the stove at the villa. The atmosphere of his family and of the three parachutists on leave whom he is lodging is altogether comforting and I could not wish for anything better.

The air here is much keener than in the gardens around the Villa Brown and in the foothills below the Medina. The wind blows without obstacle on the vast plain where the Roberts' farm is placed (and it is impossible to say why it should be here rather than there). Large orchards of almond trees (all very distinct varieties, some with particularly beautiful broad flowers) and of olive trees, under which graze large flocks of Astrakhan sheep and pigs. Many tiny orange-colored marigolds. Very few other plants are at present in blossom, aside from a few rare narcissus. At times one sees little white stiltbirds ("oxpeckers") join the flocks. Landscape without drama or surprises, but beautiful in its extent and its profuse light. I go back somewhat chilled to M. Robert's office, to read and write, comfortably seated beside a fire of vine stubs and eucalyptus logs.

It is reported to us that yesterday the insurgents at Rabat were for a short time masters of the French city, where they carried about on the end of a pike the severed head of a sixteen-year-old French youth.

At Fez itself the revolt is not completely smothered and new clashes are expected. The gates of the Medina are closed and guarded by the Senegalese. This makes a sort of covered pot in which discontent simmers. Deprived of water, electricity, and food supplies; it is hoped thus to force them into submission and lead them to terms. . . .

6 February

After several almost sleepless nights I make up my mind to use the new soporific that Denoël had sent me from Rabat, hypalène,[4] which, besides, did not begin to act until very late, after a long period of very painful anguish. Deprived of sleep, I am not good for anything. The gears of my brain get choked up; the springs of my will relax. But upon issuing from the fountain of youth that sleep is for me, I am not too much aware of my age and can believe myself to be still hale. The outer world recovers its savor for me and I take a new interest in life.

During the hours of sleeplessness I go over this or that series of verses, beginning for instance: *"Iris, je vous louerais,"*[5] and am not satisfied until I reach the end. That fear that my memory may fail me urges me to keep it in training without respite. A sort of avarice is involved in this, which differs only in its objective from the need that the old feel to hoard; after all, just as ridiculous, just as useless. Feeling everything slip away, one clings to trifles. But almost as much as the miser's false treasures, it remains external to oneself and is not integrated. . . .

If I had not abandoned the piano, *The Well-Tempered Clavichord* would be better than La Fontaine's *Fables*; closer to serenity.

Been to see *The Moon Is Down*, based on Steinbeck's novel. Excellent film in the main and for long episodes. One of the best I have seen for a long time. Certain dialogues are remarkable and as exemplary as one could wish. They irresistibly raise the question: would I be capable of heroism? The way in which the mayor of the little Norwegian village achieves it strikes me as utterly correct psychologically, and everything he says is perfect.

---

[4] *Hypalène*, a product of Laboratoires S.I.T.S.A., is a combination of barbituric acid with other ingredients, but with no narcotic agents.

[5] "Iris, I should praise you," is the opening line of La Fontaine's "Discourse to Mme de La Sablière," at the head of Book X of his *Fables*; it contains more than 170 lines.

Denoël appears to be greatly affected by the appendix to *Attendu que* . . . ; [6] and I am affected in turn, not by that appendix with the too conspicuous title: *Dieu, fils de l'homme*, but by the sorrow it causes him. And yet I cannot regret either having written those pages or even having divulged them. What I have expressed in them is close to my heart, and in regard to the religious question I can be neither "indifferent" nor merely skeptical. It is as a "believer" that I speak and that I set up my reason against their faith. Abandoning my reason, I should doubtless easily recover certain emotional accents that would touch Denoël as much as those of my *Numquid et tu* . . . ? I know how to achieve them; I have the recipe for that false profundity. Every cry of distress finds an echo in pious souls; every recognized need for supernatural help. Every cry such as: "O Lord, save us or we perish!" What separates us from such souls is the claim, which they consider impious, of doing without divine aid. Denoël foresees in it a drying-up of lyricism. To him that sort of smugness of the soul seems antipoetic. And doubtless in the "shadows of Faith" lyricism readily spreads its wings. . . . But the lyric state is not far from seeming to me a childish state, which the adult soul somewhat scorns. I could still lend myself to that game (and I should even be perhaps caught in it); but this could not be without some pretense and some sort of dishonesty.

7 February

An order has reached me to return to Algiers at once. The telegram comes from the Ministry of the Interior: a precise and urgent summons constituting an official mission, with which I must comply. I had not taken quite seriously an earlier telegram from Amrouche, calling me equally urgently: I thought that, considerably worried about my fate and exaggerating the danger of the uprising, he, as a friend, wanted to provide me a way out, leaving me free to take advantage of it if need be. On receiving the second telegram, I went to see General Suffren, and this morning I am informed by telephone that arrangements have been made for me to return to Algiers tomorrow evening by the plane which will come to get me at Meknes. So be it.

---

[6] *Considering that* . . . , published in Algiers by Charlot in 1943, contained much of the material issued the same year as *Interviews imaginaires* (*Imaginary Interviews*) in Paris, Yverdon, and New York editions plus two dialogues entitled *"Dieu, fils de l'homme"* ("God, Son of Man"). Those dialogues were subsequently included in the New York edition of *Pages de Journal, 1939–1942* (Pantheon Books, 1944). They express Gide's mature and personal religious credo.

8 February

No pleasure in being back in Algiers, but great delight on finding the Heurgons and Jean Amrouche. The latter came to meet me at the distant airfield of Maison Blanche. I was chilled despite the radiant sun. Slept during a large part of the flight, which seemed to me interminable. From Fez I had gone to take the plane at Meknes, where General Suffren's car had taken me. Having arrived much too early at the airfield, I was able to talk at length with the new official (I don't know his title) who regulates the departures; he had arrived the day before from Agadir to assume his new duties. Victim of an accident to a mail-plane on the Toulouse-Casablanca line (I believe), which turned over and then caught fire, Félix (this is his family name) managed to save the mail, but got out of it himself only with very serious burns. During eight months in the hospital the constant attentions of a surgeon (I am angry with myself for not having noted his name) made him by successive grafts a new and acceptable face and a semblance of strange hands, with which "I can do everything," he says with a smile of subdued pride. That was twenty years ago. "In the beginning all that was left of a thumb remained stuck to the hand. There was no resistance left, you see. It took more than two months to separate it. But later on . . . Well, just put your finger there." And he pinches my index finger in a sort of nutcracker. He laughs. "I can even type with this"; and he points to the remains of a finger emerging slightly from the stump: "Just enough." Then he adds: "What you see there are the nails." They form a bizarre squama in the middle of the back of his hand.

Then he tells me of his sons, eight and ten years old. "Oh, they are strapping fellows, you can take my word for it. And well brought up, I assure you. The older one already has twenty hours in the air. Good little boys. And because of them it is worth while going on living."

"I hope they are proud of their father," I say.

"Oh, as for that, they're very fond of me. . . ."

Sudden and profound liking such as I often experienced in Russia. I leave him with tears in my eyes.

Denoël had sent me an issue of *Confluences*, in which I have been able to read Mauriac's article on Charlie Du Bos, which he had told me about.[7] My mind refuses to accept such mystical assertions. It is not lack of understanding on my part, but refusal to assent and protest in the face of that "flattering error" which "sweeps away our souls," and in which I am too much aware of the self-indulgence. Copeau

---

[7] "Charles Du Bos and His Creator," a nine-page article by Mauriac, appeared in No. 25 of *Confluences* (September-October 1943).

and Charlie made it possible for me to understand the subtle trap that selfishness or pride can set for us with holiness as a bait.

I find here *The Moon Is Down* by Steinbeck, which I am reading avidly. All the best of the dialogues has been put into the film, which, for many reasons, seems to me better than the novel.

What calls me back here is a dispute about *L'Arche* between Amrouche and Robert Aron. They are counting on me to settle it, to cut it short if need be. First I must inform myself, listen to the disputants, read the copies of the letters they exchanged, consult various outsiders. . . . It is endless.

Compared with Lucretius, Virgil seems honeyed and too full of grace. Harsh strength is not natural to him; he seems rather stiff in it and thereupon readily indulges in rhetoric. As soon as he lets himself go, it is toward the affectionate mood. Then he is charmingly suave. But what a masculine energy in Lucretius, what austere nobility in his impiety, in his undaunted free thought! . . . Understanding him much better than I dared to hope encourages me to return to Latin.

Excellent preface by Bergson.

20 February

It seems that the Americans are repeating in Italy the same errors as in Tunisia. Enough to make one wonder whether experience ever teaches much to anyone, so that each time the lessons of experience lose out to accustomed routine and especially to the prompting of temperament.

> *One follows one's first footsteps*
> *On the first occasion.*[8]

Just as at Tebourba, their army on the way to Tunis could have entered by surprise (it was asserted), so it apparently advanced all at once to Frascati; then instead of going on unexpectedly to Rome, it is said to have waited, according to orders or some rule or other, and let pass the extraordinary opportunity. Forced to withdraw subsequently, the Germans having recovered from their surprise. At least, this is what is reported by people back from the front, who seem to be well informed.

They speak also of a certain bridge south of Rome that it was sup-

---

[8] *L'on reprend sa première trace*
A la première occasion.
These lines are from La Fontaine's fable *"Le Loup et le renard"* ("The Wolf and the Fox"), which is Number 9 in Book XII.

posed the Germans had blown up, so that the advance guard had received the order (so it is said) to await the arrival of the engineers before crossing the river. The engineers were to rebuild the bridge. But it so happened, as luck would have it, that the bridge had remained intact. But that didn't make any difference! The army obediently waited just the same. The engineers did not come along until four days later, during which the German artillery had plenty of time to blow up the aforesaid bridge.

Let it be added that the very bad weather bothers the invaders much more than it does the Germans, entrenched in positions prepared long ago. In short, they are not advancing. It is all more costly than had been foreseen; and now there is talk of using as reinforcements certain troops that were being saved for the landing in France, and this would require that landing to be delayed.

I am limiting myself to reproducing here some echoes of "opinion." At most I shall add that it strikes me as rather sensible, on this point at least.

On the way to Gao, 3 April

Maison Blanche. Waited in vain for the happy accident that would have kept me from leaving. Raynaud and Morize accompanied me to the airfield, whence we take off at 7.30. Very cloudy sky.

I must have dropped off for scarcely a half-hour, and already we are flying over an utterly different country: sand-colored, covered with strange signs, with a sort of mysterious writing, inhumanly and incomprehensibly beautiful; elementary; nothing living or even merely vegetable mars it.

9.30

Blue-white sky. It is beginning to be sumptuously hot. Half-hour stop at El Golea. Conversation with two very likable mail and radio directors of that place. One of them comes from the Congo. Beautiful harmony of the palm trees on the pure sand; it gives me a sensual pleasure to encounter this again.

Arrival at Gao at about five thirty (Algiers time). One has to turn one's watch back two hours to agree with the sun.

Unable to note anything during the trip. Flew over a stupefying landscape. Almost mystical beauty.

At Gao everything is swooning with heat. After sunset the thermometer goes down but a few degrees; not below 96° except a few hours before dawn; the only moments in the day when one can breathe.

Neglected to bring along quinine, whence fever for the first three days. The light would be unbearably bright without these Zeiss sunglasses that Captain Morize gave me. The pith helmet, which I was nevertheless advised against bringing, is equally indispensable.

The waters of the Niger are at their low-water point, and the vast river now offers but a number of tiny shallow arms, which the flocks ford at nightfall. Summer spreads out over the plain. Incapable of movement, of will, of thought, I let myself be annihilated before that profuse splendor.

Excellent hotel, which I leave only for the shade of the market arcades, where the natives display unknown spices, pungent-smelling aromatics, numerous odd commodities. Naked children hold out their hands, offer their smiles, the trusting and naïve felicity of their eyes. Beauty of the women. The unconcern of paradise. Strangeness.

The meals are excellent, served out of doors in the large courtyard of the hotel. The menus observe the Good Friday fast. At dinner the insufficient lighting does not allow me to make out very well the dessert that the tall Negro waiter offers me. I question him; and, very dignified, imperturbable, he replies: "*Des pets-de-nonne.*" [9]

A very pleasant lady, who has just got out of the plane here on her way back from Fort Lamy, says to me: "Oh, Monsieur Gide, you wrote in one of your books a little sentence that I constantly repeat to myself in the difficult moments of my life (they are many): One must never close a door altogether." To this I can but smile in rather silly fashion. [10]

Gao

Large white-bellied guinea hens; definite crossbreeding, since a little later I see completely white ones. Many small and very tame finches (?). In the trees (silk-cotton trees) the martins known as "gendarmes" hang their nests from the branches (the entry is from the bottom). I observe them at length: with one peck they clip off the buds and cut all the new shoots; not surprising if the trees, after such treatment, are so puny and wither away. I am told also that the too dry wind scorches their foliage.

> They did all that in their power lay
> and then fell unheralded.
> Victory had been theirs today

[9] Literally meaning "nuns' farts," this is the traditional name for delicate sweet fritters.

[10] Gide never wrote such a sentence. But as an epigraph to Book II of *Les Caves du Vatican* he had used these words of the Cardinal de Retz: "Since one must never deprive anyone of the possibility of return."

had all on them depended.
For they did what in their power lay
  through hardships uncounted,
Giving their bodies — nay,
  their very souls undaunted.
All is over. Gone are they,
  their names unrecorded.
Such love in vain cast away? . . .
  No, it cannot be wasted;
But rather, beyond their survey,
  God is formed of these new-dead.[11]

I cannot succeed in despising the joys of the flesh (and, besides, scarcely try to). A mishap to the plane that was to take us back (a providential mishap, I shall say) allowed me to enjoy one of the keenest the evening before last; all my memories of Gao radiate around it.

Had I carried quinine with me and taken some at once, I should doubtless have held up better; but I was unable to find any until the third day; that is to say that the kind Mme Pinson was good enough to give me some.

Algiers, 30 April

I find in Rabelais, whom I am reading with assiduity and for the first time from beginning to end, these words of Gargantua (Chapter xliii):

". . . True military discipline forbids you to make the enemy desperate. That only revives his spent courage and increases his strength. The only salvation left to disconsolate and exhausted soldiers is to be denied all hope of salvation. How many victories have been wrenched out of the victors' hands because they lost control, sought wholesale

---

[11] *Ils ont fait tout ce qu'ils ont pu*
      puis sont tombés sans gloire.
  Si rien qu'à eux il n'eût tenu
      on eût eu la victoire.
  Car ils ont fait ce qu'ils ont pu
      restant des jours sans boire
  Mais bien plutôt, qu'à leur insu
      de leur âme très méritoire.
  C'en est fait. Ils ont disparu
      sans laisser de nom dans l'histoire.
  Tant d'amour en vain répandu? . . .
      Non, je ne puis le croire;
  Mais bien plutôt, qu'à leur insu
      Dieu se forme de leur mémoire.

carnage and destruction to the last man? Rather open all possible ways and roads to the enemy; build them bridges of silver as avenues of escape." [12]

Words that seem very wise and that probably would have been so at the conclusion of the last war; but one doesn't dare quote them today, so incapable of improvement seem the Germans.

Montesquieu (*Grandeur et décadence*, Chapter ii) speaks admirably of that "negligence resulting from victory" against which it will be essential to forearm ourselves.

"What makes wolves emerge from the woods? Lack of meat." (Rabelais: *Third Book*, xiv.)

". . . Preferring [the Romans] to consider the whole nation criminal and assure themselves a useful revenge." (Montesquieu: *Grandeur et décadence*, Chapter vi.)

Today, 21 May, I finished *Thésée*.[13] There still remain large parts to rewrite, and particularly the beginning, for which I had not yet managed to find the proper tone. But now the entire canvas is covered. For the past month I have daily and almost constantly worked on it, in a state of joyful ardor that I had not known for a long time and thought I should never know again. It seemed to me that I had returned to the time of *Les Caves* or of my *Prométhée*. Furthermore, exalted by events and the recovery of France. The friends surrounding me here have been perfect. I owe them much and without them should never have been able to bring my work to a happy conclusion. I should like to dedicate my *Thésée* to each of them in particular (besides, they are not numerous), as a sign of my gratitude.[14]

I also owe much to the beautiful books of Charles Picard; to those of Glotz, so sensitively intelligent (to mention only the moderns).[15]

". . . Among the Greeks, as among the Hebrews, wherever the foreign element mingled most intimately with the native element, in Attica as in the tribe of Judah, there was formed the cream of the na-

---

[12] This and the following quotation from Rabelais are taken by kind permission from the translation by Jacques LeClercq of *The Complete Works of Rabelais* (New York: Modern Library; 1944).

[13] *Theseus* was not published until 1946, first in New York (Pantheon Books) and then in Paris.

[14] Indeed, when the work appeared, it was dedicated severally to Anne Heurgon, to Jacques Heurgon, and to Jean Amrouche.

[15] Charles Picard (1883–   ), known as an authority on pre-Hellenic religions, has written extensively on Crete, as has Gustave Glotz (1862–1935), professor of Greek history at the University of Paris and author of *The Ægean Civilization*.

tion." (Glotz: *Greek History*, p. 286.) Most interesting remark and of wide application.

Nothing amuses me so much as work, not even the noble game of chess, in which I get beaten every day by Jean Amrouche. Delighted to learn that Minos was already addicted to it, if we are to believe the archæologists.

"In those days of old, Minos was at ease and the gods were cramped." (Glotz, p. 560.)

"Sometimes they [the Romans] would make a peace treaty with a prince under favorable conditions; and when he had fulfilled them, they would add others such that he was forced to begin the war again." (Montesquieu: *Grandeur et décadence*, Chapter vi.)

The young people who come to me in the hope of hearing me utter a few memorable maxims are quite disappointed. Aphorisms are not my forte. I say nothing but banalities, nothing but platitudes to them; but, above all, I question them; and that is just what they prefer: talking about themselves. I listen to them and they go away delighted.

"No state so greatly threatens others with conquest as the one that is in the throes of a civil war. Then everyone in it . . . becomes a soldier.

". . . Furthermore, in civil wars there are often formed great men because in the confusion those who have merit stand out; everyone places himself and assumes his rank instead of being placed, and often quite wrongly, as in other times." (Montesquieu: *Grandeur et décadence*, Chapter xi.)

Finished *Le Tiers Livre. Lucien Leuwen*, which I had long been planning to reread, seems to me superior to *La Chartreuse* and to *Le Rouge et le noir*, as to its beginning at least; [16] for after the first pages are passed (and they could not be more captivating), one gets lost in a thick tangle of conventions (because it is essential to combat them, but why are they not simply omitted, overridden?). Annoying like Marivaux.

"He [Lucien] did not have enough vanity for the vexation of being afraid to give him the courage to . . ." (p. 222).

Labyrinth of psychological preciosity.

---

[16] *The Third Book* by Rabelais is the sequel to *Gargantua* and *Pantagruel. Lucien Leuwen* is by Stendhal; the first part of it has recently been translated by Louise Varèse as *The Green Huntsman.*

"In a free state in which the sovereignty has just been usurped, everything is called a rule that can establish the unlimited authority of a single person; and disorder, dissension, bad government are the names of everything that can maintain the reasonable freedom of the subjects." (Montesquieu: *Grandeur et décadence*, Chapter xiii.)

"There is no more cruel tyranny than the tyranny that is exercised under cover of the laws. . . ." (Chapter xiv.)

"Justinian, who destroyed those sects by the sword or by his laws, and who, forcing them to revolt, forced himself to exterminate them, let several provinces go to waste. He thought to have increased the number of the faithful; he had merely decreased that of the living." (Chapter xx.)

6 June

ALLIED LANDING IN NORMANDY.

Tipasa, 12 June

I am finishing, in great gulps, *Sense and Sensibility*; less enthralling doubtless than *Pride and Prejudice* or than *Emma* (as far as I can remember), but with an admirably deft draftmanship and perfectly filling its frame. Comparable to certain portraits by Ingres, or rather by Chassériau. The sky is rather low, rather empty; but what delicacy in the depiction of sentiments! If no major demon inhabits Jane Austen, on the other hand a never failing understanding of others. The element of satire is excellent and most delicately shaded. Everything takes place in dialogues, which are as good as they can be. Certain chapters reveal a perfect art.

Finished, the same day, Malraux's *La Lutte avec l'ange*,[17] in which I recognize what he read to me at Cap Martin, in other words almost everything. I had hoped that he would bring his narrative to a more nearly perfect state. There is still much to criticize in it and, however gripping it may be, it is still very far from what it might have, and ought to have, been. Often, too often, he does not use the words that are called for, and many a sentence remains so imperfect, so ambiguous, that one would like to rewrite it or else say to him what as a child, he relates, he would have liked to say, hidden behind a desk in the Academy, to the "Great Writers": "Come now! Begin that over again, now." I could cite many a sentence whose syntax is indefensible (among others, the one with which the father's notes begin; I stumble on it just as much on a fourth reading as on the first; and the descrip-

---

[17] Malraux's unfinished novel, *The Struggle with the Angel*, bearing the sub-title of *The Altenburg Walnut-trees*, first appeared in Switzerland in 1943.

tion of the first men carrying the gassed men out of the contaminated zone). The excessive use of abstract terms is often prejudicial to the narration of action. One must not try simultaneously to make the reader visualize and make him understand.

I plunge into *Twelfth Night*, forsaking *The Longest Journey*, in which I cannot manage to get sufficiently interested. Last month I patiently read *Howards End*, of which I retain almost nothing but a great esteem for Forster.

Without being too impolite, I should like to take leave of myself. I have decidedly seen enough of myself. I no longer even know whether or not I should still like to begin my life over again; or else, I should do so with a little more daring in affirmation. I have sought much too much to please others, greatly sinned through modesty.

25 June

Odd example of anacoluthon that I encounter in Buffon (*The Eagle*): "He is too heavy to be able to carry him, without great fatigue, on one's wrist."

It was with her that I had promised myself to achieve happiness. For each of us two the drama began on the day when I was obliged to realize (and when she realized likewise) that I could accomplish myself only by deviating from her. Yet she did nothing to draw me backward or to hold me back; she merely refused to accompany me on my impious way, or at least on what she considered to be such.

Ever ready to belittle herself, to efface herself before others. If the word "modesty" did not exist, one would have to invent it for her. Never was she heard to say: "As for me, I . . ."

Where have I written that La Fontaine "rhymed meanly" or some such asininity? . . . To be corrected. He rhymed perfectly, if I don't mind.

"I am at ease with myself only when I am doing my duty." (Diderot: *Lettres à Sophie Volland*, 8 October 1760.)

This is very well said; but the trouble is that one doesn't always know what one's duty is.

For the last few days I have been applying myself to Latin again, with much more pleasure and much less difficulty than I should have thought, and reviving my first raptures by going over again rapidly the second book of the *Æneid*. It seems to me that I understand everything much better than I did then. And I now hold the key to Latin verses:

it is enough to place the accents properly, without too much concern
for the longs and shorts; then everything comes naturally. It is simple.
Why was this not taught me at school instead of trying to teach me
when a syllable is strong or weak, which comes out quite naturally
when the verse is properly scanned? But it is first essential to get rid
of that absurd habit, which was still prevalent then, of pronouncing
Latin words "in the French manner" — that is, by always putting the
accent on the last syllable, which distorted everything.

I give about three hours a day to Virgil. While walking, I continue reading *Humphrey Clinker*; and in the intervals, Rabelais's *Quart
Livre*.[18]

5 July

As soon as Siena is liberated, General de Montsabert rushes there
to offer his army corps to St. Catherine. I leave it to others to consider
that gesture sublime. As for me, I think it must have made some very
ill at ease, Jews as well as Protestants or skeptics. The skeptics might
have taken part with amusement in what seemed to them a mere pretense. But I can imagine an ardent Protestant refusing that gift of his
soul, over which his general has no right. Will he then be banished
from that society, considered as a renegade and a traitor? . . . And
now those young men are divided who hitherto rushed toward victory
with a common impulse. I expect other examples soon of a compromising bigotry, which will not fail to make certain minds rise up in revolt.

I receive *Peace and War*, the official publication of the documents
concerning "the foreign policy of the United States" from 1931 to 1941.
That publication closes before the revival of France. One's mind reviews with amazement the various stages of that extraordinary story.
Mussolini's vaulting lack of restraint and overweening conceit dragging
the Italian people along in his ruin prefigures the fate of Hitler and
the German people. They are still resisting, whereas the former are
bitterly crestfallen. What Shakespeare will some day portray the im-
mensity of this disaster?

It is essential for the salvation of humanity that Germany should
feel the wind of defeat flatten her out. At the time of the preceding
war, through that serious error of not carrying our victory to the very
heart of Germany, the Germans did not feel conquered. It is essential
for the future that the smugness of that arrogant people should be
crushed and that the oppression of force should be made known to

---

[18] *The Expedition of Humphrey Clinker* (1771) is by Tobias Smollett;
Rabelais's *Fourth Book* continues the adventures of Pantagruel.

those who, through force, claimed to dominate the spirit. *"Et debellare superbos."* [19]

It is often when it is most disagreeable to hear that a truth is most useful to utter, and when it might encounter the keenest opposition. But there is often danger in not blowing with the wind.

Fatal doctrine of autarchy. Presumptuous absurdity! *Needing one another* was the great harmonious strength of the Argonauts. Not one of them was "sufficient unto himself."

Vicit iter durum pietas.[20]

Of how many men may it not be thought that it is through mediocrity that they are good!

Sabotage of the pronunciation of our beautiful language by the radio announcers. Is there no one to tell them that it is inappropriate to say: *"Hol-landais, voie fer-rée"*? Let them consult Littré and they will see how one should pronounce. [21]

Probably one has to have run the risk of losing those acquired and transmitted possessions in order to appreciate their importance. All that seemed due to us which we had inherited without trouble, and we no longer knew that those whose heirs we were had won it in open competition and often at the price of their life.

I am reading with great interest and profit John Stuart Mill's treatise *On Liberty*, which Raymond Mortimer sent to me through the offices of the very kind Gill, with Mill's *Autobiography* and *The Memoirs of a Justified Sinner* by Hogg, one of the most extraordinary books I ever read. [22] I bless Mortimer for having introduced me to it. Can it be that it has not yet been translated? And if translated, that it is so little known? I should like to get Roger, Mauriac, Breton, Green, and many others to read it. [23]

Every day, two or three hours of Latin: Sallust or Virgil.

----

[19] "And to tame in war the proud." Virgil: *Æneid*, VI, 854.

[20] "Love has vanquished the toilsome way." (*Æneid*, VI, 688.)

[21] The doubled consonants in these words should be pronounced as if single.

[22] In the original the words "I ever read" appear in English.

[23] Gide did indeed write a provocative preface for *The Private Memoirs and Confessions of a Justified Sinner*, which added interest to the republication (only the second in a hundred years) of that psychological thriller (London: Cresset Library; 1947) and prompted its translation into French.

15 August

Yes, it is indeed a liquidambar (I was able to get close to it) whose flowers I was admiring in the next-door garden, under the windows of my room. Why so rare, that charming little tree?

. . . *bonum publicum simulantes pro sua quisque potentia certabant*.[24] (Sallust: *Catilina*, XXXVIII, 3.)

Great fatigue of the eyes, which forces me to limit my readings.

Read especially Latin of late; some progress, but I must still almost constantly have recourse to the translation (Sallust and Horace). Reread for the tenth time *Polyeucte*; exasperation now dominates admiration.[25]

Algiers, 5, 6, or 7 September

Having nothing to do, my mind empty, my eyes tired. . . . Never yet has a wait seemed so long to me, and doubtless just because events are occurring in rapid succession. A special order for Rome is to reach me soon and send me to Italy, when it is in France that I should like to be already, that I could be . . . Ah, how eager I am! I fear I may not have enough breath at the last moment to climb that final slope, not have time left to embrace the few people whom I should nevertheless like to see again before closing my eyes forever. Six times a day at the radio I listen to the same news I had already read in the morning newspaper, as if my attentive impatience could hasten events. . . .

The best hours in the day: the three or four that I spend in the company of Sallust or of Virgil, whom I already understand much better and, at times even, almost without difficulty.

14 September

And Warsaw? . . . Not a day passes without my thinking anxiously of its agony. Its sufferings involve untold and untellable things, some underhanded political interests withholding the needed aid. . . .

19 September

Strange use by Mauriac of the verb *atteindre*: ". . . *ses tuyaux atteignent à salir même un clair ciel de printemps*," [26] already encountered in *Le Baiser au lépreux*. And I find again in *Préséances* (p. 181):

---

[24] ". . . under the pretext of working for the public good, everyone strove to gain power for himself."

[25] *Polyeucte* is Corneille's tragedy of the early Christian martyrs.

[26] *Préséances*, p. 71. [A.] ". . . the factory chimneys go so far as to soil even a clear spring sky."

"Si même il atteint à me comprendre . . ." and p. 248: *". . . à aucun moment . . . elle n'atteignit à se créer une illusion. . . ."* [27]

2 October

Eric Allégret, back from Paris in six hours by plane, brings me a large bundle of Paris papers. They date from yesterday and the day before, and we marvel at having such recent news.

Unfortunately not Paulhan's *Lettres françaises*, which would interest me above all. [28]

Excellent article from the *Manchester Guardian* (28 August 1944) reproduced (without cutting, I believe) by the *Documents de la quinzaine*, [29] which are sent me. (Concerning Mr. Eden's policy.) "Some think that after this war Germany will give up the ambitions which led her to such a catastrophe. It is certainly more likely that the Germans will give less thought to their defeat than to the series of victories that brought them so close to success." Etc. I am saving the article.

Read by Mauriac one after another: *Le Baiser au lépreux*, *Préséances*, and *Les Chemins de la mer*. I had previously read *Le Nœud de vipères*. [30]

Then I plunge again into Cæsar's *De Bello Gallico*.

After Sartre's remarkable *"Le Mur"* (which, besides, I recalled very well; one could not forget it), I reread *"L'Enfance d'un chef."* Reread next *"La Chambre,"* which I thought I preferred; but no, I set the two others even above it. [31]

10 October

I am awaiting with apprehension my call to Paris, where many of those I should have taken the most pleasure in seeing again will not be, I fear; where I shall encounter nameless and numberless difficul-

---

[27] "If indeed he reaches the point of understanding me . . ." and ". . . at no moment . . . did she succeed in imposing an illusion upon herself" might translate these unusual uses of the verb, which generally can be rendered by "reach," "attain," or "achieve." *The Social Hierarchy* (1921) and *The Kiss Bestowed on the Leper* (1922) are both novels.

[28] Founded in clandestinity by Jacques Decour and Jean Paulhan, who had been editor-in-chief of *La Nouvelle Revue Française* from 1926 to 1940, *Les Lettres françaises* appeared openly as a weekly literary journal immediately after the liberation of Paris.

[29] *Fortnightly Documents.*

[30] *Roads to the Sea* (1939) and *Vipers' Tangle* (1932) are novels.

[31] "The Wall," "The Childhood of a Leader," and "The Room" are short stories in the collection *Le Mur* (1939) by Jean-Paul Sartre.

ties, troubles, and fatigues that I don't know whether I shall be strong enough to bear, any more than the inevitable cold. I am not risking any project and filling frightfully empty days as best I can with the assiduous study of Latin and with reading.

11 October

Great pleasure on seeing Vildrac again, with whom I lunched yesterday at the home of the very kind Mondzains. The conversation went on afterward until almost six o'clock. Vildrac seems to me to apply to events a very reliable and unprejudiced judgment, something that is becoming extremely rare at present.

According to Ehrenburg, literature is a "combat weapon." And soon painting too, I suppose, as it already was in the U.S.S.R. Not a canvas in that exhibit I saw at Tiflis that did not have an educative and edifying (I was about to say edificatory) meaning; nothing but daubs, but active ones and which in their eyes were probably more valuable than all the productions of our gratuitous art. Their sole justification lay in their timeliness.

28 October

After Sallust, finished Cæsar's *De Bello Gallico*. I now have got to the point of understanding Virgil better; almost easy to reread, but often very hard to decipher. (Every day a minimum of four hours on Latin.) I glance through Quintus Curtius with great amusement.

Activity or passivity in the practice of love distinguishes men much more than the very object of their desires.

The motto of Hitlerian Germany: *"Man hat Gewalt, so hat man Recht,"* remark of Mephistopheles toward the end of the *Second Faust.*[32]

Virgil. Certain passages hard to decipher. I want to get to the point of at least rereading him readily.

After a certain age one does not so much choose one's friends as one is chosen by them.

Laws and censorships compromise freedom of thought much less than does fear. Every divergence of opinion becomes suspect, and all but a very few rare minds force themselves to think and to judge "properly."

---

[32] "One has power; therefore one is in the right."

12 December

"Who cares about the ravings of solitaries!" exclaims M. Gilbert Mury in an article against Montherlant (*Action* of 27 October 1944). The Nazis do not think otherwise. O Dante! O Pascal! And we see that vicious doctrine infecting the minds even of those who claim to be opposed to it.

Yesterday 11 December, finished the complete reading of the *Æneid* (without skipping a single line) and immediately afterward I reread at one sitting Book VI, easily, almost readily, with delight.

13 December

Then, rather disheartened by Ovid, I plunge into the *Georgics*. Did Virgil ever write anything more perfect than certain long passages? And even, in connection with the most practical advice, so many wonderful lines in which feeling and spirituality animate and magnify even the commonest gesture.

> *Pater ipse colendi*
> *Haud facilem esse viam voluit, primusque per artem*
> *Movit agros,* curis acuens mortalia corda
> *Nec torpore gravi passus sua regna veterno.*
>
> (I, 121–4.) [33]

22 December

I read, at random, the short introduction to Denis de Rougemont's *Journal d'Allemagne*. It could just as well serve as a preface to my *Pages de Journal*. Yes, that is precisely right. I even rather like what he says of "timely stylizations," against which the sincere notations of the intimate diary are opposed, which "translate the relations of an individual with *collective passions.*" And he adds: "Tomorrow perhaps there will be nothing but manifestoes, epopees of propaganda." And that "tomorrow" is today.

On page 24 of this book D. de R. speaks of one of his students who is preparing a study of Barrès and writes: "*The earth and the dead* is almost the *Blut und Boden* of the Nazis." I should say!

---

[33] "The father himself has willed that the path of husbandry should not be smooth, and he first made art awake the fields, *sharpening men's wits by care,* not letting his realm slumber in heavy lethargy."

1945

Benda's *Belphégor* is far inferior to *La Trahison des clercs*.[1] The most disconcerting confusion throughout the book, not indeed in the ideas the author sets forth, but in the choice of windmills at which he tilts. He quotes the best and the worst one after the other and seems to attach as much importance to Aurel or Tancrède de Visan or Jean Florence or Bersaucourt as to Nietzsche or Claudel. No discrimination; everything is grist to his mill; this greatly harms his thesis. I have fought the same dragons as he. If he had deigned to read me a little more carefully, he would have been aware of this, and I dare believe that my *Enfant prodigue*, my *Porte étroite* or my *Symphonie pastorale* have done more, for instance, against Belphégor than the unmethodical battue of his treatise. But he does not like to be helped. Everything is game to him, and whoever accompanies him on his hunt is likely to get some lead in his rear. In my writings he could find abundant sentences to justify his ideas (like the very spirit behind those writings). He prefers to pick out only the things to which he is opposed.

Why, in preference to the paltry lines of . . . Gondinet:

> *Why am I saddened by the song of a dove,*
> *By a wilted flower or a falling leaf?* [2]

does not Benda quote Hugo's lines, which seem written for his thesis:

> *The sighs of an oboe or the sound of rustling leaves*
> *Fix my mood for a day . . .*[3]?

He speaks excellently of the Comtesse de Noailles, but why doesn't he mention Francis Jammes?

As for what he says of society "salons" . . . that is just what keeps me away from them.

---

[1] *Belphégor: Essay on the Æsthetics of French Society in the First Half of the Twentieth Century* (1919) aims to prove that "French society of the present asks works of art to make it experience emotions and sensations; it has no intention of deriving any sort of intellectual pleasure from them." *The Great Betrayal*, as *La Trahison des clercs* was entitled in England (*The Treason of the Intellectuals* in the United States), first appeared in France in 1927 and is the most widely known of Benda's books.

[2] *Pourquoi suis-je attristée au chant d'une colombe,*
Pour une fleur fanée, une feuille qui tombe

are lines from Act I of the opera *Lakmé*, of which the libretto was written by Edmond Gondinet and Philippe Gille.

[3] *J'en ai pour tout un jour des soupirs d'un hautbois,*
D'un bruit de feuilles remuées,

are lines from Hugo's poem "Enthusiasm" in *Les Orientales*.

15 January

The U.S.S.R. . . . I should astonish many people by telling them that there is probably no country in the world where I should more like to return (aside from "wild" countries, virgin forest, etc.).

Some think that I have a bad recollection of the trip I made there (in 1936, I believe) and that the two pamphlets I subsequently published are the result of a disappointment; this is absurd.[4] I wrote them in the same way and in the same spirit as I pointed out, on my return from the Congo, the colonial abuses that had sickened me down there. And those who became angry over my criticisms of the U.S.S.R. were the very ones who had most applauded when the same criticisms were directed against the by-products of "capitalism." There they admired my perspicacity, my need to disregard camouflage, my courage in denouncing. In Russia, they suddenly said, I had been incapable of understanding anything, of seeing anything. And if some admitted the justice of my observations, at least they considered them untimely. At most a few imperfections were admitted among comrades, but the time had not yet come to speak of them. One had to realize the overall success and close one's eyes to the temporary, inevitable deficiencies. . . .

Outside of those "deficiencies" I liked everything there. Nowhere yet more beautiful landscapes, nor, to inhabit them, a people with whom I felt more readily in a state of sympathy, in a state of communion (though I did not speak their language; but it seemed that that mattered little, so easily was that sympathy established through looks and gestures).

I am speaking of the people, of the "masses"; for what made me suffer there was seeing the social classes taking shape again despite the vast and bloody effort of the revolution, convention winning out over freedom of thought, and falsehood over reality.

Doubtless Stalin was very clever to give all his attention, first and above all, to the Red army; events have justified him flagrantly; and it matters little now that he did this by relaxing in other regards. For was it not love of the land and of individual property, often a religious feeling also, that, much more than clinging to Marxist theories, made the Russian forces so valiant and victorious? Stalin grasped this and showed that he had grasped it when he opened the churches again. . . . But I think that the justice of some of my accusations will be readily recognized; in particular the one about the oppression of thought. What I said of this remains true, and that oppression is begin-

---

[4] The journey was made in 1936 and resulted in *Retour de l'U.R.S.S.* (*Return from the U.S.S.R.*) and *Retouches à mon Retour de l'U.R.S.S.* (*Afterthoughts on the U.S.S.R.*).

ning to be exercised, in imitation of the U.S.S.R., in France. Any thought that does not conform becomes suspect and is at once denounced. Terror reigns, or at least tries to reign. All truth has become expedient; that is to say that the expedient falsehood is at a premium and wins out wherever it can. Solely "right-thinking" people will have a right to express their thought. As for the others, let them keep silent, or else. . . . Doubtless one can overcome Nazism only through an anti-Nazi totalitarianism; but tomorrow it will be essential to struggle against this new conformism.

The spectacle that the H. children, unintentionally and without knowing it, provide me is instructive. Faced with certain examples of aimlessness, I come to realize how much I have been helped in life by the method, early applied, of always beginning with the most repellent, the most difficult, devoting the newest of my strength to whatever cost the greatest effort. In the beginning I did this through instinct; it soon became a mania.

30 January

No longer tempered by light, nor checked by the outer world, the insomnia-sufferer's thought indulgently unfolds its branches and stretches them to the point of enormity, of monstrosity, in the night.

And, unable to go to sleep, I imagined a letter to Camus, who I am told, has just given to *Combat* my article on Benda under a title invented by him: "Justice before Charity" (or something similar), which emphasizes too much the quotation from Malebranche that Benda made and that I also used. There would be a great deal to say on that subject, and it seems to me of great importance.

5 February

Developed (insufficiently) the above-mentioned ideas in an article entitled "Justice or Charity," which I send to Amrouche for some weekly, since it is too long for the *Figaro*.[5]

12 February

. . . *by their fruits ye shall know them.* (Matthew vii, 20.)

The entire system of Linnæus derives from that word of Christ.

Sufficient unto the day is the evil thereof. (Matthew vi, 34.)

I have already noted that the Vulgate gives "*malitia*" and Bossuet "*malice.*" Compare with I Corinthians x, 13:

---

[5] The article did, however, appear in the daily *Figaro* for 25 February 1945; it is reproduced in the volume *Feuillets d'automne* of 1949 (*Autumn Leaves*).

*There hath no temptation taken you but such as is common to man:
but God is faithful, who will not suffer you to be tempted above that
ye are able.*

Wonderful parable of the tares and the good seed (Matthew xiii,
24–31). Those who want to gather up the tares (always numerous, and
numerous those who approve them). Christ stops them. ". . . lest
while ye gather up the tares, ye root up also the wheat with them."
Let them grow together, both in the outer world *and in ourselves.* You
cannot judge in advance what those rank weeds might become that
you take too readily for tares. Inexhaustible lesson.

> *Aucun ne doit périr, mais tous . . .*
> *En retournant aux cieux en globes de lumière,*
> *Vont rejoindre leur être à la masse première.*

Remarkable use of this word, which Littré would probably have
cited if he had thought he could find it in Delille (who seems to me
rather unjustly disparaged). (Translation of the *Georgics*, IV.)

15 February

. . . *animosque ad sidera tollunt.*[6]

The Germans too, to be sure; the Germans especially. And the
Americans not at all.

17 February

Hector's widow, alas, and wife of Helenus! [7]

The Greek fable, after Troy, loses its symbolic meaning but takes
on a psychological and poetic value, to the great advantage of dramatists. There is no longer occasion to seek the hidden meaning of those
stories; they have ceased to have anything mythical about them; their
admirable pathos must suffice for the ingenious poet.

I am making an effort in Latin; rather ridiculous obstinacy, doubtless; every day I give to it from four to six hours and even more; but
a good teacher would teach me more in an hour than I can succeed in
acquiring alone in half a month of vague gropings. Forced to disregard
many little unsolved problems. Virgil alone brings me a real reward;
and solely in regard to him do I note a real progress; I am now rereading very long passages almost without difficulty and readily.

I wanted to go back to St. Augustine. Mystical nausea. Fit to vomit.

Reread Cæsar and Sallust. Horace's epistles. Cicero's *Pro Archia.*

---

[6] "Their spirits soar to the stars." Virgil: *Æneid*, IX, 637.

[7] *Veuve d'Hector, hélas! et femme d'Hélénus!*
is a line in Baudelaire's poem *"Le Cygne"* ("The Swan"), in the *Fleurs
du mal.*

25 *February*

To find out right with wrong, it may not be. (*Richard II*, Act II,
Scene iii, line 145.)

28 *February*

Handbook of the rotter:
> *Teach others kindness*
> *You may need their services.*

What an advantage in life to feel no need of the esteem or affection
of others!

3 April

That veneration which you nourish for your saints I bestow on
those martyrs and should like to see their name celebrated, their story
told, not in a fabulous "golden legend," but simply according to first-
hand evidence. This would show the effort of Faith to arrest the progress of knowledge, and belief in the dogmas of the Church opposed
to the research of science. A Vanini (who even knows his name today?)
denounced by the clergy as tainted with atheism, condemned to the
stake after having his tongue torn out, on 9 February 1619. According
to the terms of the sentence, he was divested of all his clothing but his
shirt, a noose was put around his neck, and a sign hung on his shoulders with these words: "Atheist and blasphemer of the name of God."
Called upon to retract, Pompeio (this was the name Vanini had taken,
having found refuge in Toulouse after an initial condemnation concerning the *Dialogues*, which he had published during his sojourn in
Paris) refuses. And as the magistrate in charge of the case repeated to
him: "The court has ordered that you ask pardon of God, of the King,
and of justice!" "There is no God," exclaims Vanini; "as for the King,
I have in no way offended him; and as for justice, if there were a God,
I should pray him to hurl his thunderbolt at the Parliament, as wholly
unjust and wicked." And with a voice "that the cold caused to tremble
since he was without clothing in the midst of winter, he did not cease
to deny God aloud and the divinity of Christ, proclaiming that there
was no other God than nature, that Jesus was a man like him, that the
soul did not exist by itself, and that death led to nothingness; this was
also why," he said, "it was sweet and welcome to the unfortunates
who, like him, were tired of fearing and suffering. For them it was liberation, the end and remedy of all their ills." Such was his belief, such
his doctrine. And as if he had feared that the Parliament flattered itself that that doctrine would perish with him, he added that he was
sure that it would continue to live in the books he had written to dis-
seminate it. Aware of setting an example, he exclaimed at intervals that
he was dying as a philosopher. When he reached the scaffold, amidst

the vociferations of the crowd, he said: "You see, a wretched Jew is the reason I am here!"

The witnesses, the story adds, did not dare report the rest.

When he was attached to the stake, the executioner, having thrust the pincers into his mouth, tore out his tongue down to the roots and threw it into the fire. At that moment Vanini uttered a cry of pain so strong and so heart-rending that those present shuddered. A reverend Jesuit, relating this fact later, considers it "very amusing."

I read the above in the little book by S. Zaborowski: *Les Mondes disparus* [8] (Alcan, without date), p. 15, footnote.

Set down this third day of April at Biskra, where arrived yesterday. Should be verified. Useful to recall today.

17 April

Back to Constantine yesterday evening from an expedition in the south.

By auto to El Kantara (an hour's stop to initiate Mme Théo to the charms of the oasis, and subsequently no oasis seemed to us so beautiful), then arrival at Biskra for lunch, by auto to El Oued, then Touggourt, and back to Biskra by train and likewise to Constantine.

Reread the *Æneid* all along the way and every day.

Naples, 17 December

Landed here the day before yesterday, Robert Levesque and I. Found here again Professor Caccioppoli, with whom the unforgettable evening at Sorrento in 1937.[9] Feast at the house of his mother (a daughter of Bakunin) with his wife and his brother.

The next day (yesterday) excellent lunch at the Pasquiers' (director of the French Institute in Naples) together with Maurice Ohana, who plays remarkably, after dinner, Bach, Scarlatti, Albéniz, Granados, Chopin's Barcarolle and fourth ballade.

Fatigue and intense gloom. We leave the Patria hotel for the Sirena, scarcely better (requisitioned for the English army) to await the airplane call.

Last days of 1945

Finally at Luxor for the last four days. At Cairo the marvelous Abbé Drioton explains the museum with reassuring competence. That museum, besides, tires me less since I have made up my mind not to try to admire everything. Faced with Egyptian art (with very few exceptions), I become nothing but resistance and opposition.

---

[8] *Worlds of the Past.*

[9] That evening is not described in *The Journals of André Gide;* see Vol. III, p. 358.

1946

T hat turn of mind (that vicious turn of mind) that people used to blame in me was what saved France. An attitude of insubordination, of revolt; or even initially and simply an attitude of inquiry. . . . So that, as if by chance, my former accusers suddenly and all together turned up on the wrong side: Béraud, Massis, Mauclair, Maurice Martin du Gard . . . without a single exception so far as I know — and it could not have been otherwise.

Academy? . . . Yes, perhaps, accept becoming a member if without solicitations, grovelings, visits, etc. And immediately afterward, for my first deed as an Immortal, a preface to *Corydon* declaring that I consider that book as the most important and most "serviceable"[1] (we have no word, and I don't even know if this English word expresses exactly what I mean: of greater usefulness, of greater service for the progress of humanity) of my writings. I believe this and it would not be difficult to prove it.

The most useful . . . I do not say the most successful. Its very form hardly satisfies me today, nor that way of avoiding scandal and attacking the problem through a feigned proxy. It is partly because at that time I was not sufficiently sure of myself: I knew I was right, but I did not know to what a degree. . . .

Aswân, 15 January
It is essential before beginning the game — nay, even before shuffling the cards — to make sure that they are not marked.

I am reproached for my oblique gait . . . but who does not know that when the wind is contrary, one is obliged to tack? It is easy to criticize for you who let yourselves be carried by the wind. I take my bearing on the rudder.

I am with difficulty convinced that it is restful (for me at least) to do nothing. But I easily convince myself, conquered by fatigue, that what I do at such times is worthless. None the less, sometimes a few moments are enough to save a day from being zero. The important thing is not to consent to despair.

---

[1] In English in the text.

Aswân, 19 January

Shortly before the war, as an experiment or as a game, and on the advice of . . . Naville perhaps, I had amused myself by risking a rather large sum in the purchase of securities that, I was told, were to go up considerably. What were those securities? Entrusted to what bank? Impossible to recall. I suddenly thought of this again last night with a sort of curiosity that became all the more anxious since I was not quite sure of not having dreamed it all. I must check, if possible, on my return to Paris. And I mention it here as a reminder.

It is when one says: "not a day left to lose!" that one utilizes one's time most stupidly. Nothing excellent can be done without leisure.

21 January

The Ponte Santa Trinità (in Florence) destroyed . . . a marvel of harmonious equilibrium, of slimness and of bold grace, which moved me as much as the most imposing architectural feats of Egypt. I like what exalts man and not what bows him low and humiliates him.

Were I to open my shutters in the morning on
> . . . *the flowery shores*
> *Watered by the Seine . . .*[2]

it would be a delightful surprise. These black boulders of granite breaking the course of the Nile are beautiful; but I do not admire them any the more for having, originally, been more amazed by them. I shall not try to put order into my thoughts. What's the use?

Nothing bothers me so much as the fame of a landscape (for the work of art it is not the same at all: admiration gives it stuff and density; its surface is nourished by successive interpretations; here I am bothered only when fashion enters into it — as it did recently for Emily Brontë and today for Kafka; but when this or that Greek or Latin writer is involved, what a joy to share the emotion of Goethe or Montaigne!). Before these black rocks of Aswân too many imbeciles have swooned. . . .

The letter from Mme X. that the hotel porter gives me this morning exasperates me, for it says: "We must have certain sensations in common, those that you must have irresistibly felt here when faced with the black rocks on these pink mornings." No, madame, faced with

_____

[2] The opening of the famous *Vers allégoriques à ses enfants* (*Allegoric Lines to her Children*) by Mme Deshoulières (1638?–94) reads:
> *Dans ces prés fleuris*
> *Qu'arrose la Seine*
> *Cherchez qui vous mène,*
> *Mes chers brebis:*

these black rocks, I felt nothing at all. I am a gentleman; and the emotions I might have had politely made way for yours.

Yesterday, a round of inspection of the hotel. A Serbian, who was employed at Luxor at the time when we were there, offers to guide us. The father of six children from three different marriages. He speaks six languages equally well; one of his sons is a law student in Cairo. He served for a long time on the Côte d'Azur. We encounter in the hall the pastry chef, an extremely lively, elegant Piedmontese of noble manners, and I was about to say a "thoroughbred," who manages to find, in impeccable French, a few words of praise neither empty nor platitudinous to show that he has read some of my books and considers himself quite honored by my handshake and the attention I show him. We go down together to the kitchen. The chief baker is Rumanian. The chief cook is Greek. Another is Czech or Lebanese. All the nations are mingled here, all faiths, all languages. And the same for the guests and those who pass through. The kindly old lady who asked me the time this morning is Danish and married to an English lawyer from the Transvaal; she lives in Cairo. Egypt is a magic carpet, a crossroads, where the Jew becomes perhaps the most permanent and purest element. He is much in evidence. The young and likable assistant manager (?) of the hotel speaks ironically of the number of Egyptian *nouveaux riches* who now form the hotel's chief clientele, and he is sensitive to their vulgarity and lack of culture. And just as in the Rouen Assizes I would irresistibly imagine the stupid jurors taking the place of the accused, and the latter in exchange sitting on the jury bench, I could not keep myself from reversing the roles here and thinking how much better the shapeless appearance of these *nouveaux riches* would suit lackeys, and imagining in their place the distinguished and elegant servants of the hotel.

I have made a great but useless effort to express this, nevertheless so simple, more simply.

Through a great anxiety to be brief (always, and ever since my childhood, the fear of not being listened to until the end), I generally present but the outcome of thoughts. Let him understand who can or who will. It will perhaps happen, later on, that an attentive reader will bring out this or that sentence of mine which first went unnoticed, and that, in connection with the row that is kicked up today (for which Sartre is not solely responsible) over certain "existentialist" declarations and manifestations, he will protest in amazement: "but Gide had said it before him. . . ."

I broadcast my seed. And let the seed wait if the season is not propitious! The best is often waited for the longest.

24 January

I am continuing my reading of Forster's *Passage to India*. If I understood it better, I should be reading with rapture, I believe; for the book strikes me, in so far as I can judge, as a marvel of intelligence, of tact, of irony, of prudence, and of cleverness. But too many things escape me, and perhaps I attributed too much to him, filling to Forster's advantage all the blanks resulting from my lack of understanding; for everything I understand seems to me of the best quality. I like, and even more than what he says, what he suggests and insinuates, as if incidentally and without committing himself, in apparently inoffensive sentences that force the reader to a sort of complicity. How I like, for example: "There was a moment's silence, such as often follows the triumph of rationalism"[3] (p. 205, Penguin edition).

Those wise precepts of Boileau that we were made to learn by heart, in which the classical tradition was crystallized in alexandrines — it would not be without interest to take them one after another, seizing them by the nape of the neck and making them pass judgment. The fact that I consider them excellent is what most outmodes me, for today I should like to be told which of our young writers still pays any attention to them. They are disregarded; and of all those precepts I wonder if the most scorned is not the one urging us to

Put our work back on the table twenty times.[4]

To this is opposed the advice that Barrès gave to Maurice Martin du Gard (as the latter, the journalist, once told me) to get into the habit of writing *"currente calamo"* without ever striving to perfect. This takes training. One practices carelessness. One acquires certain qualities of nimbleness and of virulence; and the sentence goes forward without anything further "that weighs or comes to rest," often getting ahead of thought, the "dull brain" that "perplexes and retards." . . .[5] This already amounts to slipping toward the "automatic writing" of the surrealists, which is supposed to reveal the mysterious functioning of the intellect. Like any experiment, this one was worth trying. Furthermore, I am now writing this *"currente calamo,"* after reading some remarks of the likable Dupertuis, professor of French in the Aswân school. When he was a graduate student, he used regu-

---

[3] In the original the quotation is given in English.

[4] Distorting Boileau's famous line somewhat, André Gide quotes it:
   Vingt fois sur le métier remettre notre ouvrage.

[5] Gide here borrows from the opening lines of Verlaine's *"Art poétique"*:
   De la musique avant toute chose,
   Et pour cela préfère l'impair
   Plus vague et plus soluble dans l'air,
   Sans rien en lui qui pèse ou qui pose.

larly to go over with some friends, out of a spirit of abnegation, the proofs of the *Cahiers de la Quinzaine*.⁶ He testifies that Péguy's manuscripts that passed through his hands never had the slightest erasure (one suspected this); the sole corrections were a few occasional interlineations.

31 January

On the Nile. I let myself be taken (oh, very willingly!) by Robert L. to Wadi Halfa. Left Aswân by auto at about 11 a.m., but the *Lotus* did not weigh anchor until 1 p.m., escorted on both sides by two supplementary boats attached to its sides, one taking the place of the second class and the other loaded with Egyptian scouts. (This reminds me of the railway car filled with Komsomols accompanying us to Ordzhonikidze.)

Landscape more extraordinary than beautiful, but startlingly strange. Almost mystical exaltation. Villages the color of the soil, of the sand, of the rock; villages that I suppose to be Coptic, inhabited by apprentice stylites. Harshness that the Nile fails to soften.

Night almost without sleep. On awaking, along the still half-lighted bank, palm trees with their trunks submerged by the overflow caused by the dam.

Robert L. shows to one of the leaders of the scouts a Bagdad review, received at Aswân the day before our departure, containing a photograph of me, together with a rather long article. This serves as an introduction. Some of the scouts speak French; the review passes from hand to hand.

"The author of the article says that today you occupy the place of Goethe," the leader explains to me; and as I make a tentative gesture of protest, he thinks he has to add: "Oh, *Maître*, that is less than the truth!" At times he calls me: "*Maître*" and at others: "Monsieur André" (which he pronounces: Handraï!).

A vast country ruined by the backing up of the waters. Paradox. This submerged land nevertheless permits hasty sowing, I believe, when the level of the water goes down in the summer before the flood, and a harvest of wheat. But I do not think the palm trees can bear the prolonged foot-bath.

What can the inhabitants of these villages live on? Around the mud houses not a blade of grass, not the slightest vegetation. It is the reign of the Holy Ghost.

---

⁶ *The Fortnightly* was published between 1900 and 1914 by the poet Charles Péguy.

Started out wrongly. Just as at the time of my escapade to Gao.[7] Just as always. . . . I shall have to take leave of this earth dissatisfied, having known almost nothing of it. That absurd laziness which led me to return to the same places because it cost less effort. I look with a sort of despair at a map of the unknowns. . . . Regret for all I might have seen, should have seen, borders on remorse. Wadi Halfa, the terminus of this journey, should be a point of departure. It is from Khartoum onward that I should like to go up the Nile. . . .

I would lean over the bridge at Saint-Louis, would remain raptly watching the schools of tiny fish peopling the waters of the Senegal, so thick that it seemed they could have supported you, and occasionally shaken by sudden and inexplicable panics. And the crabs, the legions of crabs on the beach. . . . I see again on the banks of the Logone (one would have thought them covered with flowers) the beds of multicolored birds. . . .

The banks of the Nile between Aswân and Wadi Halfa are deserted; its waters are empty. A paltry swarm of large dragonflies escorting the ship before reaching Abu Simbel; the only living things I saw during the whole journey.

At Aswân itself, however, many glider hawks and many grayback crows. On the Elephantine island, some wasps' nests and a few hoopoes. A tiny stiltbird runs along the shore looking as if it had escaped from a bas-relief. A single variety of butterfly, in great abundance on Kitchener island.

Marvelous hotel of Wadi Halfa. Simple and perfect comfort of the rooms. One could not imagine anything better for a rest. But I must leave again. . . .

The air is keen, almost frigid. Little electric radiators in the rooms.

On the walls of the drawing-room, excellent color-reproductions of Manet, Renoir, Van Gogh, etc.

Between the tables in the dining-room, sparrows snap up crumbs.

Staggering temple of Abu Simbel; yet nothing to say of it but what has already been said.

Wadi Halfa

In all these Sudanese: what a bearing! What decorum! What dignity!

Back to Aswân the 4th.

At Luxor the 9th (of February).

---

[7] In April 1944.

I should give all the "black rocks" of Aswân for the austere desolation of Thebes.

Often I am gnawed by a feeling (which sometimes gets to the point of anguish) that I have something more important to do (than what I am doing and am concerned with at present). If I had to die in an hour, should I be ready?

Assiduous, daily rereading of the last books of the *Æneid.* From three to four hours every day. These last books seem to me today to be in no wise inferior to the first.[8] Or at least, if perhaps less perfect in form and more scattered in interest (more confused, especially in Book XII), constantly revived by charming inventions, in which pity is mingled with horror, tenderness with heroism, the sentiment of glory and human dignity with fright.

24 February

At Nag Hamadi, where I find the same charming welcome from Dr. and Mme Girardot, of whom I had such a pleasant memory. Unexpected meeting with Jean-Paul Trystram, whom I take a keen and deep pleasure in seeing again. He is going to Afghanistan to take up a post as professor at Kabul; he accompanies us in a jaunt through the sugarcane fields and to the dam.

Yesterday evening I receive this letter from an unknown named Bernard Enginger; it is so significant that I want to set it down here:

For five years I have been wanting to write you. At that time I discovered your *Nourritures terrestres*; I was seventeen. I could not tell you how it upset me. I have never been the same since. I want to tell you of my respect and my admiration. Hundreds of letters like this one must have reached you. That is not the only thing I wanted to write you.

I struggled against you for five years. Your Ménalque knows enough to say: "Leave me." That is too easy. I struggled against that spiritual tyranny you exercised over me. I loved you, and certain passages from your books helped me to live in the concentration camps. In you I found the strength to tear myself away from a middle-class, material comfort. With you I sought "not so much possession as love." I cleared everything away to be new for the new law. I liberated myself. That is not enough. "Free for what?" That is the dreadful question. At last I detached myself from you, but I have not found any new masters, and I remain quivering. The terrifying absurdity of the Sartres and the Camuses has solved nothing and merely opens horizons of suicide.

---

[8] Exaggeration. [A.]

I still live with everything you taught me. But I am thirsty. All young people are thirsty with me. You can do something. And yet I know that one is alone, always.

I do not expect from you a convenient solution for my little problem. That would be too easy, a collective solution. Each one must find his way, which is not the same as his neighbor's. But a glimmer from you might indicate the direction to take. . . . If there is a direction.

Oh, *Maître* . . . If you only knew the confusion of all our youth. . . . I do not want to waste your time. I have not said everything I wanted to say. There would be too much to say.

This is an appeal I am throwing out to you. Forgive my awkwardness: I know that you do not like sympathy.[9]

None the less, I want to tell you of my tremendous admiration and the hope I put in you.

Believe me, *Maître,* faithfully and respectfully yours,

BERNARD ENGINGER
Hotel de Paris, Cairo
(until 27 February)
on the point of leaving for
Pondichéry

At Suez he will take the same ship as Trystram, who is going to Afghanistan by way of India. I entrust to him a first hasty letter, which scarcely satisfies me. Then, after deliberation, write this, without much hope of still being able to reach B. E. at Cairo — and that is why I make a copy:

DEAR BERNARD ENGINGER,

Rushed by Trystram's departure, I wrote you too hastily yesterday evening. This is what I should rather have said to you:

Why seek "new masters"? Catholicism or Communism demands, or at least advocates, submission of the mind. Worn out by yesterday's struggle, young men (and many of their elders) seek and think they have found, in that very submission, rest, assurance, and intellectual comfort. Indeed, they even seek in it a reason for living and convince themselves (let themselves be convinced) that they will be more useful and will achieve their full value when enrolled. Thus it is that, without being really aware of it, or becoming aware of it only too late, through abnegation or laziness, they are going to contribute to the defeat, to the retreat, to the rout of the spirit; to the establishment of some form or other of "totalitarianism" which will be hardly any better than the Nazism they were fighting.

---

[9] Obvious allusion to a sentence in my *Nourritures:* "Not sympathy, but love." [A.]

The world will be saved, if it can be, only by the *unsubmissive*. Without them it would be all up with our civilization, our culture, what we loved, and what gave to our presence on earth a secret justification. Those unsubmissive ones are the "salt of the earth" and responsible for God. For I am convinced that God is not yet and that we must achieve him. Could there be a nobler, more admirable role, and more worthy of our efforts?

PS. — Yes, I am well aware that I wrote in my *Nourritures*: "Not sympathy, but love." But I too, and before anyone else, following my own advice, "left my book" and went beyond. Even in regard to oneself it is essential not to come to a stop.

22 November

My seventy-seventh birthday; I get up a little before six o'clock with the sudden resolution to begin to keep this journal again, interrupted since . . .

If that resolution does not hold beyond a few days, I shall tear out this page; for it is useless to leave a trace of such an uncertain commitment; without importance; Yvonne Davet, without suspecting it, has done a great deal, by the cult she has made of me, to disgust me with myself. I can understand Schwob covering the mirrors in his apartment; [10] my image, that reflection of me that I constantly encounter, thanks to her, is becoming unbearable to me; I bump into it; I bruise myself on it. Consequently I reproached myself yesterday with not having peremptorily suppressed the row that the zealous Amrouche is organizing on the radio for my birthday. Yes, I should have opposed it clearly as soon as he spoke to me of it. I told him, to be sure, that I did not like it, but too weakly for him not to think he could nevertheless disregard me. I lack firmness in defense, not through lack of will, but through a sort of modesty (I don't care if this word causes smiles), which keeps me from making my point of view, my opinion, my plan, prevail over those of others. For many people this will remain incomprehensible, for I believe it extremely rare for pride not to accompany notoriety. Yet this is my case; and Clouard was very perspicacious when he entitled an article: "Gide or the Fear of Being Right." That was very long ago; but that has remained one of the few constant elements in my nature; and it is this that makes me worthless in politics: I understand the adversary too well (at least so long as he remains sincere and does not try to deceive me).

I return to that broadcast of yesterday evening: it seems to me definitely indecent to bother friends with a request of that kind, which

---

[10] See *The Journals of André Gide*, Vol. I, p. 110.

it is very hard for them to sidestep gracefully. Amrouche went about it so well that even Roger Martin du Gard, who generally refuses, thought he had to play his part (I am going to write him a note of apology), while probably wishing me, with Amrouche, in hell; for nothing is more disturbing than that sort of obligation. None the less, his message was charming and moved me in proportion to the effort he had gone to in order to write it. I have not yet been able to make myself acquainted with those of Malraux, Schlumberger, Paulhan, and Camus. . . . Yesterday evening, having remained alone with Mme Théo (while the Herbarts went to the Pléiade concert), was unable to hear anything on the radio set that had been moved in for that purpose, either of the concert or of the broadcast that was to follow it. I hope to see the written texts.

Received a visit from the charming Chevaliers, father, mother, and young son, whom I did not yet know. They were to take a plane at 9 p.m. to return to Karnak, where I had taken such pleasure in seeing them. Would that I could accompany them! The rehearsals of *Le Procès* keep me in Paris, where I run the risk of seeing death come with the first frosts; but Barrault's undertaking interests me too much for me to be willing to be distracted from it.[11]

Yesterday afternoon, intolerable chore of autographing the "complimentary copies" of *Hamlet*.[12] Nothing more exhausting.

I am entering my seventy-eighth year in rather good condition, altogether; with still enough curiosity to want to continue to live; not too tired or fed up with myself; not loving myself much, but finding myself easy to live with, accommodating.

The other evening Catherine and I amused ourselves by wondering in whose skin she and I might like to live; and, everything considered, concluded that we should not gain anything by changing.

It is time to go and light Mme Théo's fire.

23 November

A sumptuous armful of roses. It is Mme Voilier transferring to me some of the attentions she used to shower on Valéry. Red carnations brought by Dominique Aury. She came the evening before last, accompanying Amrouche. Mme Théo remembers (quite appropriately to congratulate her on it) her excellent article on Simenon, which came out in *L'Arche*. She is kind enough to take Mme Davet off to dinner

---

[11] The adaptation to the stage of Kafka's novel *The Trial* by André Gide and Jean-Louis Barrault was staged by Barrault with great success at the Marigny Theater on 10 October 1947.

[12] Gide's complete translation of *Hamlet*, after being pubished in New York in 1944 (Pantheon Books), appeared in Paris in a Gallimard edition in 1946; Gide is referring to the Paris edition.

with her in order to allow her to hear on her radio the broadcast that Mme Davet was unhappy not to be able to hear.

A most unexpected telephone call: it is Colette wishing me a happy birthday and expressing her desire to see me again. She was touched by what I said of her in my *Journal*; I wondered if she had known of it. Doubtless I shall respond to her call, but knowing well, alas, that immediately after the first effusions we shall have nothing to say to each other.

Opening by chance Rouveyre's book on Léautaud,[13] I fall upon this: "A. G. has confided to the *Virginia Quarterly Review* that if he were to withdraw to a desert island, he would take along the following books: *La Chartreuse de Parme, Les Liaisons dangereuses, La Princesse de Clèves, Dominique, La Cousine Bette, Madame Bovary, Germinal, Marianne.*" [14]

I protest: I had been asked to designate my ten favorite *French novels*. If, in exile, I could take along only ten books, not one of these would be among them.

25 November

I have always had for Léautaud an almost keen affection; consequently I am hurt by a certain remark of his, quoted by Rouveyre from a letter addressed to him in which Léautaud speaks of my "hypocrisy," my "duplicity," and my "little deceits." . . . Very curious to know on the basis of what anecdotes that opinion could have been formed. As a result of what ill-natured gossip? . . .

Perhaps Léautaud, reading the wholly affectionate praise I make of him in the pages sent recently as a contribution to the revival of the *Mercure de France*,[15] will think that I wrote them as a sort of reply to his accusations, so that that very praise will appear, in Léautaud's eyes, as one more "little deceit." What an odd process of *deformation* can take place, unconsciously or almost, in the minds of the most perspicacious and best-informed! Thus it is that any portrait of another comes to resemble the painter as much as the model or more. . . .

---

[13] *Choix de pages de Paul Léautaud* (*Selected Writings of Paul Léautaud*) by André Rouveyre appeared in 1946.

[14] *The Charterhouse of Parma* is by Stendhal, *Dangerous Relations* by Choderlos de Laclos, *The Princess of Clèves* by Mme de La Fayette, *Dominique* by Eugène Fromentin, *Cousin Betty* by Balzac, *Madame Bovary* by Flaubert, *Germinal* by Zola, and *Marianne* by Marivaux. In the original article, first published in 1913, Gide had included also *Le Roman bourgeois* by Furetière and *Manon Lescaut* by the Abbé Prévost.

[15] Those pages, entitled "*Le Mercure de France*," appeared in No. 1000 of the *Mercure*, which bore the date 1 July 1940–1 December 1946; they are reprinted in *Feuillets d'automne* (*Autumn Leaves*).

With what a shock had I read in Benda's *Exercice d'un enterré vif* [16] that, as a result of something or other, I had gone a fortnight without being willing to shake his hand!

And how I like, on the other hand, Vallotton's exclamation when, after having drawn my "mask" for Remy de Gourmont's book,[17] he met me for the first time at the *Revue Blanche*: "Good heavens, my dear Gide, from my portrait I should never have recognized you!"

But no; knowing Léautaud, I am inclined to believe rather that he was unable to consider sincere the sentences, the pages of my *Journal* which do not fit his view. He looks upon all genuflexions as pretense, and all reverences; and my *Numquid et tu . . . ?* , for instance, seems to him a proof of stupidity or of hypocrisy: whoever thinks or writes such a thing without being stupid is acting a comedy. This is perhaps enough to make Léautaud tax me with duplicity, without there being any reason to look further. I prefer that; for it hurt me that he could believe in some ill intention toward him.

26 November

Scum of the Earth seems to me the best possible illustration of Sartrism (if not of existentialism proper). Incoherence and absurdity. I am reading this book and taking a very lively interest in it. I believe I have read almost all the books of Koestler (not *Spartacus* or *The Gladiators*, which I had taken with me to Egypt and which bored me) beginning with his *Spanish Testament* (I must reread it), which probably remains his best. Read in English *Darkness at Noon* and *The Yogi and the Commissar*. Reread the latter in French (at Brussels). It seems to me that nothing better, more cogent, has been written on (or, rather, against) Stalinist Russia. It has an extraordinary eloquence and persuasive force, and through the mere exposition of facts presented with utter fairness. And what do I care about his attacks in the beginning of this last book! [18] I am ready to admit that he is right. At

---

[16] *Exercise of One Buried Alive*, Benda's journal of the four years of enemy occupation, was published in Geneva in 1945.

[17] *Le Livre des masques* (*The Book of Masks*) was a series of studies of writers, each one illustrated with a portrait by Vallotton.

[18] In "The French 'Flu," the second essay included in *The Yogi and the Commissar*, Koestler ridicules the English literary public's weakness for anything French, taking as examples — the essay first appeared in November 1943 — Gide's *Imaginary Interviews*, Aragon's *Crève-Cœur*, and Vercors's *Silence of the Sea*. After stating that "Gide's writings have always shown a touch of esoteric arrogance; there is a thin rarefied atmosphere about him and his books," he finds "the same ethereal boredom" in the *Imaginary Interviews*.

most I could claim extenuating circumstances (both for the virulence of his attacks and his attitude of mind at the moment when he formulated them and for what motivated them — that is to say, the apparent unseasonableness of my writings). For everything that he says my approbation is too great to keep me from thinking that we should both have reacted in the same way before the same instigations. I am convinced that there is no basic misunderstanding there, but simply a temporary one, so that I disregard it and let my congenial feeling alone subsist, for which he probably does not give a fig; but that doesn't matter. It is perhaps better that we should remain strangers to each other. But I have rarely read books that went more directly to my heart than his.

27 November

I am finishing Koestler's book. The very last chapters seem to me much less good — that is, as soon as he abandons reporting, in which he excels. Everything he says seems to me right, but the metaphors he uses to illustrate his reasonings are clumsy. He loses his footing in the abstract and clings to images. And then this, which seems to me most important, he does not say: that one can fight an enemy only by borrowing his arms, his methods, and even his *psychology*, with the result that today we have conquered Hitler, while everywhere Hitlerism is triumphant.

28 November

Nothing more difficult to translate than a title, the moment it ceases to be very direct. And the cleverest thing is often to disregard it, without seeking an equivalent. This is what was done for *Darkness at Noon* (though I do not see exactly what stood in the way here of an almost literal translation). But *La Lie de la terre* (I do not know what the English title was) seems to me inadmissible.[19] At most one can say: the dregs of a nation, of a people, of something, in short, capable of running out.

1 December

The extraordinary prestige that actors enjoy often comes from this, which is added to their own worth: the mass of the public is not capable of understanding and appreciating a masterpiece of dramatic art through mere reading; but only when *interpreted*.

Olivier in *King Lear*. I have no doubt that he is admirable in it, and I should have enjoyed applauding him. . . . But I renounce this with disconcerting facility. I renounce anything and everything: pleas-

---

[19] *Darkness at Noon* was translated as *Le Zéro à l'infini* (*Zero to the Infinite Degree*) and *Scum of the Earth* as *La Lie de la terre* (*The Dregs of the Earth*).

ures, travels, epicurean delights, and without effort, without regrets.
I have had my fill. "Next gentleman." I withdraw. No merit in this; I
am yielding to a natural tendency. Furthermore, weakened by a *filthy*
head-cold, and my heart likely to give in since (it was the day before
yesterday) I ran after the bus that was to take me to the Martin du
Gards'; ran like a child, and I am not one any longer, as I was made
aware immediately: on the platform, which I painfully and just barely
reached, I thought I was going to faint. Then it takes me a week to
get back to normal and re-establish myself one or two rungs lower.
But a good pretext to refuse any solicitation from the outside. Were
it not for the obligation to go and get the majority of my meals in a
restaurant (a compulsion that is becoming more a nuisance every
month), I should go days and weeks without leaving the apartment.
It is in work that I take the greatest pleasure, and I rail against whatever distracts me from it. Whether of ivory or of crystal, now it is that
I should like to take refuge in a tower surrounded with impassable
moats and with a postern to which only a few intimate friends would
have a key. But it so happens that those who besiege me are intruders,
and my friends are those who respect and protect my retreat and
isolation. How to make the others understand, however well inten-
tioned they are (like the editors of *Franchise*,[20] from whom I receive
this morning an excellent and most urgent letter), that they disturb
me frightfully and that if they have any consideration for my writings,
they ought to leave me in peace to allow me to go about my work.
There still remains much for me to do; I am convinced of this at every
instant of every day.

2 December

Finally let myself be taken to *King Lear* last night. No effort to get
there. Enid MacLeod comes to pick me up in an Embassy car, which
is to bring me home likewise. Élisabeth, though having already seen
the play the day before yesterday, accompanies me. Everything is ar-
ranged in the best possible way. But as soon as I am in the box (exactly facing the stage) or very soon after the curtain goes up, a mortal
boredom begins to numb me, a rather special sort of boredom that I
hardly ever feel save in the theater. There are pauses, suspenses, slow
moments, preparations of effects, that are unbearable. Like a child at
the Châtelet, I wait for the set to be changed.

As for Olivier, he is without contest a great actor. The fact that
he can, with the same success, impersonate one after the other the
dashing young officer of Shaw's *Arms and the Man* and old Lear is

---

[20] A Leftist group of anti-Communist tendencies, which founded a
weekly newspaper that lasted for but two numbers.

amazing. And the whole company surrounding him is definitely above average, completely homogeneous; excellent ensemble. But shall I dare write here what I think of *King Lear?* Yesterday's production strengthens my opinion: I am almost on the point of considering that play execrable, of all Shakespeare's great tragedies the least good, and by far. I constantly thought: how Hugo must have liked it! All his enormous faults are evident in it: constant antitheses, devices, arbitrary motives; barely, from time to time, some glimmer of a sincere human emotion. I cannot even very well grasp what is considered as the difficulty of interpretation of the first scene: difficulty of getting the public to accept the King's naïve stupidity; for all the rest is in keeping: the entire play from one end to the other is absurd. Only through pity does one become interested in the tribulations of that old dotard, a victim of his fatuousness, his senile smugness, and his stupidity. He moves us only at the rare moments of pity that he himself shows for Edgar and for his sweet fool. Parallelism of the action in the Gloucester family and in his: the bad daughters and the wicked son; the good Edgar and the kind Cordelia. The white hair in the tempest; the brutality unleashed against weak innocence . . . nothing that is not intentional, arbitrary, forced; and the crudest means are employed to seize us by the guts. It has ceased to be human and become *enormous*; Hugo himself never imagined anything more gigantically artificial, more false. The last act ends with a gloomy hecatomb in which good and evil are mingled in death. Olivier's company handles it as a sort of final apotheosis *à la* Mantegna: living tableau, skillful grouping; everything is there, even to the architecture of arcades framing in the admirably ordered ensemble. Art triumphs. One has only to applaud.

The enthusiastic audience acclaims Olivier and his company.

Strange part played in that drama by papers and missives, presented, stolen, falsified; up to seven times, if I counted aright.

7 December

Lunched yesterday at Carboni's with Stephen Spender and Henri Hell, both at their most charming. I had invited them, but Spender insisted on paying the bill in the name of UNESCO, which he represents and of which Huxley (Julian) has just been named the head. I send the latter, as an epigraph for his program, the last line of Book II of the *Æneid*, which Spender notes down — a line that I had already quoted in my article for America, giving it a symbolic meaning:

Cessi; et sublato montis genitore petivi.[21]

------

[22] 19 October 1942. [A.] See *supra*, pp. 130–1.

literal translation of this line. It has not been possible to identify the "article for America." Possibly a reference to the Bryce Memorial Lecture he gave

". . . and, taking upon myself the entire weight of my patrimony, I strove toward the heights." Is not that just what UNESCO proposes?

Unsatisfied if I cannot begin my day by the eagerly awaited reading of some fifty lines of Virgil.

8 December

Saint-Évremond's pages on Virgil (*Des traductions*) I put among the best he has written, and nothing better has been written on the great Latin poet. I reread them aloud the other evening to Roger Martin du Gard. Achilles, too, weeps in the *Iliad* (I want to find the passage), but it is not the same thing. And I dislike also the tearful in Racine, however admirable the lines may be at that point. Anti-heroic aspect of Æneas' piety. (Regrets that the character of Mezentius "*contemptor deum*" was not developed further.) And perhaps Virgil was yielding not only to his gentle natural inclination, but even more to the desire to please the suite of Augustus, the court.

Sunday, 15 December

Forsaken this *Journal* for the past week; too busy. Yesterday I felt "played out" . . . of what? Of everything. Yes, truly, I have had enough, both of others and of myself; my heart not up to it, my will weakening. . . . An excellent visit from Roger, after dinner, put everything back in place. Already comforted by his mere presence, like that night at Hyères-Plage when, tormented by the beginning of a most painful otitis and unable to bear it, I went and got him out of bed at three in the morning, for the mere solace of feeling my hand in his. Lively conversation for three full hours; profound mutual understanding.

18 December

"Cold wave" for the last three days over all Europe, the papers tell us; and Pierre H., who took a plane Friday the 13th (lucky fellow!) for Marseille, writes that it is 21° above on the Côte d'Azur. At 20° above I fold up. In order to "hold up" I stiffen myself, hang on, and my whole will is used up in this. In the morning I should give almost anything to remain in bed and bless the necessity of going to light Mme Théo's fire, which forces me to get up. The feeling of *duty* confers a sort of benediction on every deed accomplished: one feels like a moral being:

ERRATUM

Page 270, first line of footnote should read:

[21] "I gave way and, taking up my father, sought the mountains" is the

doesn't matter. And all that, without any need of turning to mysticism, remains human (in me at least). Amazing aptitude for happiness.

18 December

In the heavy mail brought me by my article on the French language, in the *Figaro* of 10 December, a very long, too long letter signed Gabriel Daures (?) and dated from Lourdes contains pertinent remarks and confessions: he has never been able to get interested in novels. ("The popularity of the novel seems to me one of the surest signs of the present obvious and headlong decline of letters. . . .") Thus it is that he "has never had the courage to tackle *Les Faux-Monnayeurs.*" He most enjoys in me the stylist: "For me, you are the Racine of prose," etc. I should not speak of all this were it not for a few lines as a postscript that bring an unexpected judgment, ringing so new (for me) that I do not resist transcribing them (partly because of the commentary they provoke, which I want to set down): "Quite astonished by what you say in the last issue of *L'Arche* about *Corydon.*[22] I should like to reread that work, my memory being bad (except for the memory of impressions). But it so happens that I recall that, on my now very old reading, I had the feeling of an *artistic* achievement. I used to put in the place of importance among your works, and among our French masterpieces (with most of your 'essays'), *La Porte étroite*, *Amyntas*, *Corydon*, without analogy in our literature; I should say in any literature if I were not so utterly ignorant in foreign literatures."

And I transcribe this passage not so much for me as for Roger Martin du Gard, who greatly disapproved, to be sure, that recent publication of new *Pages de journal* (in which, by declarations of a political nature, I unnecessarily make myself vulnerable to attacks and criticisms), but congratulated me unqualifiedly on what I said of *Corydon.* "You did quite right to return to the subject and to express at one and the same time what you think of the major importance of that book and of its imperfection." I believe that Roger was particularly grateful to me for admitting that it was a book that did not come off. But what I must now add is that when I wrote that page in my *Journal* it seemed to me the most elementary prudence to make concessions on the plane of the successful achievement. "I grant you that the book is abortive, and this is a pity, but grant me that what I say in it is important." There was a sort of tit for tat in this, which was perhaps not altogether sincere on my part; for that book, which I worked over, meditated, returned to and rewrote, and "tempered" more intensely and over a longer period of time than any other, and which it was so especially important to succeed, in view of its temerity . . . I

---

[22] 19 October 1942. [A.] See *supra*, pp. 130–1.

do not consider it as quite so much a failure as I said on that page; oh, far from it! And this is why those few lines from an unknown both surprised me pleasantly and made me ashamed of my pretense.

28 December

Bossuet speaks of the "points of faith that one must believe explicitly in order to be saved" (*États d'oraison*, II, 19). He would turn over in his grave upon seeing the Church so accommodating today and hearing people speak of its evolution. He wants it to be immutable, and all the "variations" belong to heresy.[23]

In Geneva: Preface for the *Anthologie.*
Scenario of *Isabelle.*[24]

"Je n'ai point connu qu'elle ait dans l'âme aucun ressentiment de mon ardeur." (*Amants magnifiques*, Act I, Scene ii.) And farther on (Act II, Scene i):
"J'en ai, Madame, tout le ressentiment qu'il est possible (des soins qu'on a pris pour moi)." [25]

---

[23] Bossuet had, indeed, written a work of theological controversy entitled *The History of the Variations within the Protestant Churches*. See *The Journals of André Gide*, Vol. II, p. 337.

[24] Gide's *Anthologie de la poésie française* did not appear until 1949. His *Isabelle* has not yet been released as a film.

[25] In reading *The Magnificent Lovers* by Molière, Gide is struck by the now obsolete use of the word *ressentiment* in the sense of "awareness" or "recollected feeling"; today the word means chiefly "resentment."

1947

Buchet's book that Y. D. had sent me when I was in Egypt has just come back to her today.[1] Had I already read it? A note to his essay on Valéry, which I remembered, makes me think so; but up to that note (p. 133; that is to say, close to the end of the volume) everything seemed to me unfamiliar. Rather absurd criticism; for, after all, taking into account only my *Journal*, it is easy for him to prove that I am merely an erratic individual, incapable of producing any work; easy, but not quite fair. He argues as if I had been the author only of that *Journal*; and this allows him to talk of a "perpetual frustration" and of my vain and constant effort to hide this. At most he mentions *Paludes*; of the other books not a word.

I was very much behindhand with contemporary drama, if not with the drama of Marcel Achard, yet I did not yet know either his *Colinette* or *Une Balle perdue*, which I have just read with a certain rapture, partial with *Colinette* and almost constant with *Une Balle perdue*.[2] (Neither *Malborough* which is inexistent, nor *Voulez-vous jouer avec moâ?* which is rather disappointing.) As for Salacrou's drama, unbelievably uneven, I informed myself attentively of six plays. Excellent scenes in *Un Homme comme les autres* and the first two acts of *La Femme libre*. *L'Inconnue d'Arras*, alas, does not justify its claims; this is a pity.[3] At present I am absorbed by Stève Passeur. Too early to speak of him. . . .

I consider Sartre's *La Putain respectueuse* as a sort of masterpiece. I did not at all like his last two long and boring novels; but *La Putain* . . . since the excellent stories of *Le Mur* he had written nothing stronger or more perfect.[4]

---

[1] *Écrivains intelligents du XXᵉ siècle* (*Intelligent Writers of the Twentieth Century*) by Edmond Buchet appeared in 1945. Its three parts are entitled: "Marcel Proust or the Power of the Abnormal," "André Gide According to His *Journal* or Intelligence against Life," and "Paul Valéry and the Limits of Intelligence."

[2] *Colinette* (1942), *A Wasted Bullet* (1928), *Malborough Goes to War* (1924), and *Will You Play with Me?* (1923) are all comedies combining a comic gift of nonsense with a peculiar poetry.

[3] *A Man like Anyone Else* (1936), *A Free Woman* (1934), and *The Strange Woman of Arras* (1935) are all comedies by Armand Salacrou. The last named, employing an expressionistic technique, was overpraised by its producer, Lugné-Poe, and by some of the critics.

[4] The play *The Respectful Prostitute* was first presented in Paris in 1946; the stories of *The Wall* came out in 1939. The novels are *The Age of*

Individualism:

Mme Théo's clock, stopped for three months now, suddenly began again this morning by itself, *sponte sua,* and without anyone's having touched it. We hear it strike eight o'clock; it is noon.

Odd inadvertence:

> *I was about to throw myself into his arms . . .*
> *But he did not open his.*
>
> (Fleuret: *Jim Click,* p. 80.)
>
> *. . . the sublimities of ignorance.*

(Claude Bernard, quoted by Renan in his *Discours à l'Académie.*)

> *Neuchâtel, November*

A Swedish interviewer asked me if I did not regret having written any particular one of my books (I do not know whether he was think-ing of *Le Retour de l'U.R.S.S.* or of *Corydon*). I replied that not only did I not disown any of my writings, but that I should certainly have bade farewell to the Nobel Prize if, in order to obtain it, I had had to disown anything.[5]

(Letter that was not sent, but it is worth setting down, since errors are hard to kill.)

SIR:

Allow me to protest against the article *"L'Italia di Gide"* that ap-peared in your paper [6] with the signature of Massimo Rendina. He in-tensifies the suspicion I have always had in regard to interviewers. I cannot point out all the errors contained in his article and particularly in what he makes me say: for I did not know Carducci, or Pascoli, or Benedetto Croce. It was not in Paris but in Florence that I frequented d'Annunzio. I do not recognize any of the remarks he attributes to me regarding the latter, or regarding the existentialists and Sartre.

AUTUMN LEAVES

> *Neuchâtel*

I shall be able to say: "So be it" to whatever happens to me, were it even ceasing to exist, disappearing after having been. But just now I am and do not know exactly what that means. I should like to try to understand.

Reason (1945) and *The Reprieve* (1945), the first two parts of *Roads to Freedom.*

[5] André Gide was in Neuchâtel in November 1947 when informed that he had been awarded the Nobel Prize for Literature.

[6] *Il Giornale dell' Emilia-Bologna,* 14 December 1947. [A.]

Please, leave me alone. I need a little silence around me in order to achieve peace within me.

What a nuisance you are! . . . I need to collect my thoughts.

"Free thought. . . ." X. explained to me that true freedom of thought had to be sought among *believers*, not among such as me.

"For, after all, your mind is fettered by logic."

I granted that it required a special freedom of thought to believe in miracles and all the rest, and that I could clearly see that his mind did not object to admitting what seemed to me (and to him) contrary to reason. That is the very essence of Faith. Where you can no longer observe or prove, you must *believe*.

"And if you refuse to believe," he concluded, "stop telling me and claiming that you love freedom."

Basically I was well aware that I was not a "free thinker."

Faith moves mountains; yes, mountains of absurdities.[7] To Faith I do not oppose doubt, but affirmation: what could not be is not.

Hence I shall refuse to consider finality in nature. According to the best advice, I shall everywhere substitute, systematically, the *how* for the *why*. For instance, I know (or at least I have been told) that that substance the silkworm discharges while making his cocoon would poison him if he kept it in him. He purges himself of it. To save himself he empties himself. None the less the cocoon, which he is obliged to form under threat of death and which he would be unable either to imagine or to fashion otherwise, protects the metamorphosis of the caterpillar; and the caterpillar cannot become a butterfly unless emptied of that silky poison. . . . But I am indeed forced at the same time to admire the way in which the *how* joins the *why* in this case, fusing with it so intimately and with such a tight interweave that I cannot distinguish one from the other.

And likewise for the mollusk and its shell. Likewise constantly and everywhere in nature the solution is inseparable from the problem. Or rather: there is no problem; there are only solutions. Man's mind invents the problem afterward. He sees problems everywhere. It's screaming.[8]

Oh, would that my mind could let fall its dead ideas, as the tree does its withered leaves! And without too many regrets, if possible!

---

[7] See the PS. at the end of this section. [A.]

[8] After using here the vulgar expression: *"C'est marrant,"* Gide adds this footnote: "This is the first time I have used this frightful word; do not even know how to spell it. . . . But it is the only one that fits."

Those from which the sap has withdrawn. But, good Lord, what beautiful colors!

Those ideas which one first thought one could not possibly do without. Whence great danger of basing one's moral comfort on false ideas. Let us check, let us verify first. Once the sun turned around the earth, which, as a fixed point, remained the center of the universe and focal point of God's attention. . . . And suddenly, no! It is the earth that turns. But then everything is upset! All is lost! . . . Yet nothing is changed but *the belief.* Man must learn to get along without it. First from one, then from another, he frees himself. Get along without Providence: man is weaned.

We have not reached this point. We have not yet reached this point. It requires much virtue to achieve that state of total atheism; even more to remain there. The "believer" will probably see in it nothing but an invitation to license. If this were so, hooray for God! Hooray for the sacred falsehood that would preserve humanity from collapse, from disaster. But cannot man learn to demand of himself, through virtue, what he believes demanded by God? Yet he must nevertheless get to this point; some, at least, must, to begin with; otherwise the game would be up. That strange game that we are playing on earth (unintentionally, unconsciously, and often unwillingly) will be won only if the idea of God, on withdrawing, yields to virtue, only if man's virtue, his dignity, supplants God. God has ceased to exist save by virtue of man. *Et eritis sicut dei.* (Thus it is that I want to understand that old word of the Tempter — who, like God, has existence only in our minds — and see in that offer, which has been characterized for us as fallacious, a possibility of salvation.)

God is virtue. But what do I mean by that? I should have to define; I cannot do so. I shall manage to do so only subsequently. But I shall already have accomplished much if I remove God from the altar and put man in his place. Provisionally I shall think that virtue is the best the individual can obtain from himself.

God lies ahead. I convince myself and constantly repeat to myself that: He depends on us. It is through us that God is achieved.

What rubbish all that literature is! And even were I to consider only the finest writings, what business have I, when life is here at hand, with these reflections, these carbon copies of life? The only thing that matters to me is what can lead me to modify my way of seeing and acting. Merely living calls for all my courage; merely living in this frightful world. And I know and feel that it is frightful; but I know also that it could be otherwise and that it is what we make it. If you point out the present horror in order to bring about a protest through indignation, through disgust, bravo! But if not, up and at the demoralizers!

There might very well be nothing; nor anyone. No one to notice that there is nothing, and to consider that natural.

But that there is something, and, whatever it may be, the strange thing! I shall never cease being amazed at this.

Something and not complete nonexistence. It required centuries of centuries to produce that something, to get that, whatever it may be, from chaos. Even more centuries to obtain the least life. And even more for that life to achieve consciousness. I have ceased to understand, and from its very beginning, that progress, that history. But more incomprehensible than all the rest: a disinterested feeling. Faced with that, I am amazed, I stand in awe. People are doubtless wrong in going into raptures over the maternal or conjugal or altruistic abnegation of animals; it is possible to explain it, to analyze it: there is really nothing disinterested in it; everything follows its inclination and its pleasure. I grant this, but only to admire all the more those sentiments when I find them refined in man and capable of gratuitousness. Before the least act of self-consecration, of self-sacrifice, for others, for an abstract duty, for an idea, I get on my knees. If it is to lead to this, all the rest of the world is not useless: all the vast misery of men.

They do not recognize a serenity acquired outside of their teaching. I am speaking here of the Catholics; any doctrine that strays from their Church *must* lead to despair.

"By speaking thus of that serenity on which you pride yourself you put it on show; by putting it on show you compromise it. It must be read in your features and in your deeds, not in sentences that you do not know why or for whom you are writing. . . ."

Get along without God. . . . I mean: get along without the idea of God, without a belief in an attentive, tutelary, and retributive Providence . . . not everyone can achieve this.

The blinded bat is nevertheless able to avoid the wires that have been strung in the room where it is now flying without bumping anything. And probably it senses at a distance, in the nocturnal air, the passage of this or that insect on which it will feed. It does not fly at random, and its gait, which strikes us as whimsical, is motivated. Space is full of vibrations, of rays, that our senses cannot perceive, but that are caught by the antennæ of insects. What connection between our sensations and their cause? Without a sensitive receiver, nature is mute, colorless, odorless. It is in us, through us, thanks to us, that number becomes harmony.

The wonderful thing is that man has been able to construct instruments capable of making up for the insufficiency of his senses, of catching imperceptible waves and unheard vibrations. With our senses we already had enough to satisfy us; the rest is excess. But whether or not we wish it, that rest is there. Man has rashly enlarged his receptivity and immoderately increased his power. A pity that he is not more up to it! He behaves badly. Lack of habit perhaps (let us hope so); all this is so new! He trespasses and is overwhelmed.

When I had learned that little bows of ribbon were called rosettes (how old was I then? five or six . . .) I got hold of a large number of them, in my mother's workbasket; then, having closed myself in a room far from others' eyes which might have broken the charm, I laid out on the floor a whole flowerbed, a whole garden of them. Were they not flowers? The word said so. It was enough to believe so. And I strove to do so for a whole quarter of an hour. Did not succeed.

On a childish plane this marked the defeat of nominalism. And perhaps after all I lacked imagination. But above all I recall very well having said to myself: "What a fool I am! What is the meaning of this comedy? There is nothing there but bits of ribbon, that is all . . ." and I went and put them back in my mother's little basket.

The harshness of the epoch is such that we find it hard to imagine (or, rather, are unwilling to admit) that there could have been such a tragic one at any other moment in history. Better informed, we should perhaps get to the point of being convinced that, quite on the contrary, the exceptional was the long period of toleration in which we lived before the unleashing of the horrors (which decidedly feel *at home* on earth) — so natural seemed to us that intellectual freedom, so lamentably compromised today. Now a time is returning in which all will be traitors who do not think "properly."

Some, it is true, are still resisting; and they are the only ones who count. It matters little that they are not very numerous: it is in them that the idea of God has taken refuge.

But the temptation that it is hardest to resist, for youth, is that of "committing oneself," as they say. Everything urges them to do so, and the cleverest sophistries, the apparently noblest, the most urgent, motives. One would have accomplished much if one persuaded youth that it is through *carelessness* and laziness that it commits itself;

. . . if one persuaded youth that it is essential — not to be this or that, but — to be.

One constantly flatters oneself; or at least one has a tendency to flatter oneself. Self-indulgence is a trap into which I have such a great fear of falling that I have often been able to doubt the sincerity (the authenticity) of impulses, which none the less were natural to me, the moment they tended in the direction I might have hoped they would. (My sentence is frightfully complicated, but impossible to express this more simply.) Yet I had to admit that those impulses, those "spiritual states," were natural when I found them, exactly the same, in my daughter as a mere child; in particular a certain basic optimism, which in me I had feared to be the result of *will*.

As Catherine was asked, somewhat foolishly it seems to me: "Where do you prefer to be? In Saint-Clair" (where she then was) "or in Paris?" she first evidenced a great surprise: she could hardly understand that such a question deserved to be asked; then she eventually replied ingenuously: "Why, in Saint-Clair, *since I am there*." (She must have been hardly more than five at the time.) And suddenly I recognized in her the very basis of my own nature and the secret of my happiness; a "so be it" shown likewise in the great difficulty, if not impossibility (in that child as in me), of producing and nourishing regrets.[9]

Take things, not for what they claim to be, but for what they are.
Play the game with the hand one has.
Insist upon oneself as one is.

This does not keep one from struggling against all the lies, falsifications, etc., that men have contributed to and imposed on a natural state of things, against which it is useless to revolt. There is the inevitable and the modifiable. Acceptance of the modifiable is in no wise included in *amor fati*.

This does not keep one, either, from demanding of oneself the best, after one has recognized it as such. For one does not make oneself any more *lifelike* by giving precedence to the less good.

PS. — It strikes me today, as I take out these pages again, that I was wrong to tear out those at the beginning of this notebook. However imperfect they were (I was recovering from an illness), they replied in advance to the remarks made me by a friend in whose wisdom I have great confidence; he never speaks uselessly and never says anything that is not sensible. He protests that these detached pages, which I have just given him to read, are much less subversive than I seemed to think at first; that even many eminent representatives of the Church

---

[9] For an earlier version of this story, see *The Journals of André Gide*, Vol. III, p. 83.

of today would be willing to subscribe to them, and he cites a few names that I am careful not to reproduce. Already X. and Y. had told me this, maintaining that I didn't know very well the present state of the Church, the intelligent flexibility of its credo. I granted him that I was not at all "up to date" and that, for greater convenience doubtless, I confined myself to what Bossuet taught: that the moment *Variations* were involved, these could only be the *Variations of the Protestant Churches* (according to the title of his admirable work), from which the Catholic Church was distinguished by "its character of immutability in faith."

"To be sure," he continues; "yet it is constantly evolving. You would like to dry it up by making of it a perfectly finished thing; it is living and replies to new demands. Remember the fine pages by Chesterton that Claudel had translated and that you yourself made me read in in the old *N.R.F.*[10] The Church, he said, is never motionless; and he compared it to a chariot hurtling at full speed on a narrow crest and constantly avoiding new dangers on both sides. "There is no doubt," my friend continues, "that enlightened Catholics would not be bothered at all by your recent assertions. What they call God you are free to name Virtue if you wish; simply a question of words; it is the same thing. The idea of God, the need for God, torments you; *they* ask nothing more in order to recognize you as one of theirs." And since, nevertheless, I protest that there is some misunderstanding, since I look for something that will make them reject me after all, I return to those opening pages, the first ones written in this notebook, those imperfect and torn-up pages: they concerned eternal life: a sort of premonitory instinct urged me to emphasize them, to speak of that first, and I now realize that it was indeed essential to begin with that.

That the life of the "soul" is prolonged beyond the dissolution of the flesh seems to me inadmissible, unthinkable, and my reason protests against it, just as it does against the incessant multiplication of souls. (May 1948.)

---

[10] Claudel translated a few pages entitled "The Paradoxes of Christianity" from Chapter xii of Chesterton's *Orthodoxy*, which appeared in the August 1910 issue of the *Nouvelle Revue Française*.

1948

I have not kept a journal for more than a year. I have lost the habit. I did not exactly promise myself to resume it, but all the same I should like to try; for in the state in which I am at present, I fear that any other attempted production will be destined to failure. I have just re-read with disgust the few pages I had written at Neuchâtel; they smack of effort, and the tone strikes me as stilted. Doubtless they were not written naturally and they betray an anxiety to escape certain re-proaches, which it is absurd to take into account. My great strength, even in the past, was being very little concerned with opinion and not trying to construct myself consistently; writing as simply as possible and without trying to prove anything.[1]

6 January

Interrupted yesterday by the arrival of the mail. My morning is spoiled. And every day it begins all over again. "Here lies P. V., killed by others," the epitaph Paul Valéry wished for. "Others" . . . ah, if only I could get myself to pay a little less attention to them! And yet most often I reply to scarcely more than one letter out of six (there are such unbelievably absurd ones!). But as soon as I do reply, I cannot do so with indifference; and, thereupon, it takes time. . . .

Every morning I get up with very little strength to squander; I should like to save a little for myself. But then I should have to suc-ceed in convincing myself that what I am writing can still be worth something. These last few weeks I got to the point of completely sacrificing meditation and reading, even that of Virgil, whom I had not failed a single day since Algiers, washing my mind of all stains, find-ing in him a sort of appeasement, of comforting, and of ineffable serenity. I had nevertheless been led to diminish the doses consider-ably, but at least unwilling to go to sleep before indulging in fifty to a hundred lines of him. And for weeks on end I went back through him methodically, but at times also amusing myself by opening him at ran-dom, with what delight at finding my way so easily! and yet at con-stantly discovering new reasons to admire him, and more intelligently, which nothing but a more rapid reading allows. (Despite the pious and piteous and pitiable character of the hero, and all that Saint-Évremond, and so justly, thinks of him.

---

[1] Yet it is these pages, reworked, that I wish to put into this *Journal*, just as I once brought back into my *Journal* the "green notebook" of *Num-quid et tu . . . ?* [A.]

Extemplo Æneæ solvuntur frigore membra;
Ingemit, et duplices tendens ad sidera palmas . . .[2]
thus it is that Virgil *first* presents him to us.)

To be sure, I feel much closer to Lucretius, but do not enjoy the same delights in his lines; an unequaled suavity. And what can be said of the very composition of each book of the *Æneid*? of its position in the whole? of the relationships of the books among themselves?

On the occasion of Tristan Bernard's death many of his amusing witticisms were cited, but never, so far as I know, this one, which I feel it a duty to preserve:

In '41, I believe, when I was in Nice, he gave a lecture at Cannes, which I regret not having been able to attend. Before beginning, I was told, he presented himself before the audience: "I believe it a duty to warn you that I am myself a member of that people which has been often called 'the chosen people.' . . . Chosen? . . ." He repeated the word with ever increasing doubt; then suddenly, as if having discovered the key: "In short, chosen by lot — by the carload lot." [3]

Most of the witticisms that are repeated are deformed, often simply because the intonation is not there. There are very few that are not differently interpretable whether one turns or inclines them to right or left. It often seems to me, when I hear some such repeated intentionally, that that is not at all what their original author meant. This is what often makes intolerable certain of Benda's *utilizations*, stupid if one doesn't go so far as to consider them unfair (sallies of Valéry, for instance, that Benda takes, or pretends to take, seriously, and which he uses to prove that . . .). When an intelligent man makes an effort *not* to understand, he naturally succeeds much more cleverly than a fool. How can one discuss (and what is the use?) with someone who has made up his mind to find you at fault? A pity! I should so much enjoy talking with him, nicely, arm in arm, as we none the less did a few times in the past. I recall in particular a lunch at Lady Rothermere's; she was concerned then, together with T. S. Eliot, with the *Criterion*. Benda and I were side by side at table. It seemed to me (I thought) that I got along so well with him! Both of us were talking, as in a private conversation, of Péguy first, then of Chopin. Ah, how intelligent, just, and sensitive and sensible everything he said of music in general and of Chopin in particular seemed to me! It was as a re-

---

[2] "At once Æneas' limbs grew slack and chill;
   He groaned, and raising his two hands to the stars . . ."
                                        (*Æneid*, I, 92–3.)

[3] This is an approximation of the original pun, which plays on "elected by vote" (*en ballottage*) and "driven from pillar to post" (*en ballottage*).

call of that conversation that I wrote, much later: "Like Chopin by notes, one must let oneself be guided by words . . ." etc. — a sentence that he now uses as an arm against me, pretending to see in it a confession of something or other that is detestable; for he enjoys only being opposed to something. And now that the *Action française* is not there to exercise his pugnacity, he attacks those who are utterly amazed to see him rise up as an adversary. I could not get over learning (in his *Exercice d'un enterré vif*) that at the *N.R.F.*, as a result of something or other, I had gone more than a fortnight without being willing to shake his hand! Such psychological aberrations befit a very poor novelist; and I am convinced that the failure of *L'Ordination* and of *Les Amorandes*, and the resentment he felt at this, have much to do with the elaboration of the thesis (in many ways so right, but constantly distorted by passion and bias) that he sets forth in *La France byzantine*.[4] Since he has to see an enemy in me, he takes care not to speak of my visit to Carcassonne (at the beginning of the war), of the long conversation that followed the meal together, of which I had such a charming recollection. . . .

Not so much intellectual shortcomings as flaws in character. A pity! On so many points I should agree so well with him!

8 January

Read little of late. Worth noting, however, Zweig's *The Right to Heresy: Castellio against Calvin* [5] (excellent translation), to be considered as a pendant (or as a counterpart) to Renan's article (1848) on *Clerical Liberalism*.

"One is very close to burning in this world the people who are burned in the other" (compare the story of Claudel's flaming *crêpe*).

The wonderful lectures by Leriche at the Collège de France on *La Chirurgie de la douleur*,[6] which I had long been wanting to read (told of them by Simenon!) but could not succeed in getting. It goes without saying that, through ignorance, I am constantly losing the thread, but the little that I can grasp and retain is so instructive! Com-

---

[4] *Les Amorandes* (1922) and *L'Ordination* (1926) are Benda's unsuccessful novels. *Byzantine France, or The Triumph of Pure Literature* (1945) is an essay, similar in spirit to his earlier *Belphegor*, attacking Gide, Valéry, Alain, Giraudoux, Suarès, and the surrealists and leading to an attempt to define "the original psychology of the man of letters."

[5] *Castellio gegen Calvin: oder, Ein Gewissen gegen die Gewalt* (1936), by Stefan Zweig.

[6] The twenty lectures given at the Collège de France by the professor of medicine, René Leriche (1879–   ) were published in 1937 and translated into English by Archibald Young in 1939 as *The Surgery of Pain*.

pared with this, the poetical or pataphysical[7] elucubrations of X. or Z. (to name no one) seem a strange twaddle.

Not yet finished *The Managerial Revolution* by Burnham, so warmly recommended by Roger Martin du Gard; to tell the truth, it rather bores me. (I shall get back to it.)

New plunge into Simenon; I have just read six in a row.

And Sartre's *Réflexions sur la question juive.*[8] Altogether somewhat disappointed after all the (perhaps excessive) good that Pierre Herbart had said of it. The thesis advanced here is the very one that my friend Schiffrin defended: the characteristics of the Jews (I mean those that you anti-Semites hold against them) are characteristics acquired through the centuries, which *you* have forced them to acquire, etc. I recognize here certain arguments of the long conversation I had with him, which have ceased to shock me. Today that conversation seems to me clever and specious rather than correct, despite the deep and close affection I have always had, and increasingly so, for Schiffrin, in whom, I must add, I recognized but very few of what might be considered Jewish *shortcomings,* but merely their good qualities. Likewise in the case of Léon Blum, for whom my esteem (and why not say my admiration?) has only increased during the long time our friendship has lasted,[9] but especially since tragic events have given him an opportunity to reveal his worth more amply. (I am thinking particularly of the sinister — and for him glorious — Riom trial.)

9 January

And it so happens that yesterday afternoon's mail brought me a stirring letter from Blum. If this journal is ever divulged, that surprising coïncidence will seem "faked" and the above paragraph written as an afterthought. Nothing of the sort.

Our relations are very spaced out, yet without there ever having been exactly any distance between us; but we live and operate in different domains (or rather on different planes), where tangent points are rare. After all, he seems to me to have remained (for he always was so) much more utopian and even mystical than I am willing to be. Interesting to note that, between the Jew and the Christian, it is on

---

[7] In a "neo-scientific" work, *The Deeds and Opinions of Dr. Faustroll,* the humorist Alfred Jarry had created the term "pataphysician" to indicate one who displays great metaphysical and mathematical reasoning to demonstrate an inherently absurd proposition.

[8] This little book, published by Paul Morihien in 1946, was issued in New York in 1948 by Schocken Books as *Anti-Semite and Jew* in a translation by George J. Becker (Baltimore: William Wood & Company; 1939).

[9] Since the deaths of Valéry and of Marcel Drouin, he remains the only surviving friend of my generation. [A.]

his side that Hope and Faith are to be found. But I have rarely encountered in a Christian such personal disinterestedness and such *nobility*. I am very grateful to him for not holding against me the rather harsh passages of my *Journal* about the Jews and about him (which, by the way, I cannot disown, for I continue to think them utterly correct). He disregards them and has never spoken to me of them. Just like all of us, he has, to be sure, his shortcomings; and his seem to me most particularly to be Jewish shortcomings. But to what a degree his good qualities, even (or especially) those that I believe specifically Jewish, prevail! In my eyes he is an admirable representative both of Semitism and of humanity; just as he managed to be, in his official and political relations with foreign countries, an excellent representative of France (whatever the nationalists may think of this) and for the greater honor of our country.

I return to Sartre's book. However right certain of his most important affirmations seem to me (for instance, that "it is anti-Semitism that creates the Jew"), only apparently paradoxical, it remains none the less true that anti-Semitism is not (or not solely) an invention made up out of whole cloth by hatred and the need of motivating and feeding hatred. Psychologically and historically, it has its *raison d'être*, on which Sartre, it seems to me, does not throw sufficient light.

When I was in Tunis in '42, I had occasion to talk with several *lycée* professors, "Aryans" themselves. Each of them independently told me (and this would have to be verified) that in each class and each subject the best pupils were Jews. They were constantly at the head, and over the head, of the others. Even though this does not necessarily mean that the Jews have a better mind than the "Aryans," but perhaps merely that the qualities of the latter, more profound, develop and manifest themselves more slowly, I should be rather inclined to believe this and am very wary of precocity. . . . None the less: the die is cast and now hearts are already sown with the seed of fierce passions, which will merely await an opportunity to come to the surface, even if need be in violence, with that sort of permission and right to injustice which theoretical anti-Semitism provides them.

From Sartre's whole book, often pasty and diffuse, I retain this excellent passage:

"The Jews are the mildest of men. They are passionately opposed to violence. And that obstinate mildness they preserve amidst the most frightful persecutions, that sense of justice and reason which they set up as their sole defense against a hostile, brutal, and unjust society, is perhaps the best of the message they hold for us and the true mark of their greatness." Bravo, Sartre! I feel cordially in agreement. But there is none the less a "Jewish question," painful and obsessive, and far from being settled.

We are stifling (the modern world), and tomorrow it will be worse, in a dense forest of insoluble problems, in which, I fear, force alone — and the most intentionally blind, the most monstrous and absurd, the most brutal force — will be called upon to make light, to cut clearings, to win out.

I am writing this while striving not to believe it, preferring to shout "Fire!" before the house burns down and in order, if possible, to prevent it from burning.

10 January

In 1857 (*Étude sur Étienne Quatremère*), Renan already speaks of "the undermining of the world by immorality, charlatanism, and triviality."

13 January

Finished *Touriste de bananes*,[10] one of the less successful novels of Simenon. One is rather vexed with him for this, since in it he spoils a marvelous subject, through haste and, one might say, impatience. Simenon's *subjects* often have a profound psychological and ethical interest, but insufficiently indicated, as if he were not aware of their importance himself, or as if he expected the reader to catch the hint. This is what attracts and holds me in him. He writes for "the vast public," to be sure, but delicate and refined readers find something for them too as soon as they deign to take him seriously. He makes one reflect; and this is close to being the height of art; how superior he is in this to those heavy novelists who do not spare us a single commentary! Simenon sets forth a particular fact, perhaps of general interest; but he is careful not to generalize; that is up to the reader.

It was in great part, it was especially, the fear of bothering neighbors that made me give up piano practice.

19 January

However different Valéry, Proust, Suarès, Claudel, and I were from one another, if I look for the way in which we might be recognized to be of the same age, and I was about to say of the same team, I think it is the great scorn we had for the things of the moment. And it was in this way that the more or less secret influence of Mallarmé showed in us. Yes, even Proust in his depiction of what we used to call "the contingencies," and Fargue, who of late has been writing in the newspapers to earn a living, but still with a very clear conviction that art operates in the eternal and debases itself by trying to serve even the noblest causes. I wrote: "I call journalism everything that will interest less tomorrow than it does today." Consequently nothing

---

[10] *Banana Tourist.*

seems to me at once more absurd and more justified than the reproach that is directed at me today of never having managed to *commit myself*. Indeed! And it is in this regard that the leaders of the new generation, who gauge a work according to its immediate efficacy, differ most from us. They also aim for an immediate success, whereas we considered it quite natural to remain unknown, unappreciated, and disdained until after forty-five. We were banking on time, concerned only with forming a lasting work like those we admired, on which time has but little hold and which aspire to seem as moving and timely tomorrow as today.

Nevertheless, when there was a need to *bear witness*, I did not at all fear to commit myself, and Sartre admitted this with complete good faith. But the *Souvenirs de la Cour d'Assises* have almost no relation to literature, any more than the campaign against the Great Concessionary Companies of the Congo or the *Retour de l'U.R.S.S.*

22 January

Gandhi's victory, his pacific triumph, seems to me one of the most surprising facts of history. Pierre Herbart, who has come to spend two days with me, is as much moved by it as I. We spoke of it at once and at length. Is it appropriate to deplore the fact that such a miracle of unanimity among a whole people cannot be achieved, or even sought for, by a Latin or Anglo-Saxon people? Subject of infinite discussion. But the wonderful thing is that that unanimity should take place in favor of a renunciation. Strange example of a virtuous "totalitarianism."

24 January

No shame as a result of facile sensual pleasures. Sort of vulgar paradise and communion through the basest in man. The important thing is not attributing any importance to them, or not thinking oneself debased by them: the mind is in no wise involved in them, any more than the soul, which does not pay much attention to them. But, in the adventure, an extraordinary amusement and pleasure accompany the joy of discovery and of novelty.

25 January

Harmony! Harmony!
Language that genius invented for love!
Which came to us from Italy, and to her from heaven! [11]

---

[11] The lines:

Harmonie! Harmonie!
Langue que pour l'amour inventa le génie!
Qui nous vins d'Italie, et qui lui vins des cieux!

are from Alfred de Musset's elegy *Lucie*.

One cannot imagine anything more vapid. Enough to justify Valéry's scorn and hatred for Musset.

"A barber's assistant with a pretty music box in his heart," François de Witt sententiously uttered about Musset (we must not have been more than sixteen); I can still hear him, on the road from La Roque to Val Richer. (He had read that remark somewhere or other.)

It is a very frequent failing to hide one's sources, or one's tributaries, as would a stream of very small volume that might think it could thus increase its importance. Great minds have never feared to testify to others' contributions to their work, and with gratitude.

It is a failing of our epoch to give too much value to originality. There is not one of the great writers of the seventeenth century who was not (and did not admit to being) an imitator. But in our day what is most prized in music, painting, or literature is new departures, even if they lead to nothing, with hardly any concern left for that transmission, that continuity, of which real culture is made.

30 January

Gandhi has just been murdered by a Hindu. Pierre has just rung me to tell me. Two days ago already a bomb had been thrown at him. It was too beautiful, it was unbelievable, that mystical victory in which spiritual ardor held brutality at a respectful distance; my heart is filled with admiration for that superhuman figure; filled with sobs. This is like a defeat for God, a step backward.

All the asininities people manage to bring out on the subject of *sincerity* when aiming to throw it into disrepute; this is only too easy, by pretending to confuse it with cynicism, exhibitionism, etc. Even Valéry said some wonderful stupidities on the subject.

Mme Théo told me this of Catherine. She was only a few months old when she had to undergo a little operation for an inflammation of the eye, which was very painful, at least for a few moments. She screams, then suddenly stops; and the doctor exclaims: "Well, by Jove! that is really out of the ordinary: a baby who stops crying as soon as it has ceased suffering!"

That example of *sincerity* on the part of my daughter delights me.

There are many things that I find more interesting than myself.

When the fruit is ripe, it will leave the branch by itself. If you try to tear it off, you will only strengthen it by putting it on the defensive; and your fingers will smart. Leave religions alone, then, and let the sap gradually withdraw from them.

But no, please understand that this is an experiment I must make myself. No one else can attempt it in my place. It would not have the same meaning.

Du style d'idées by Benda.[12]

Almost always I am in agreement with Benda against the apocryphal "ideas" he attributes to me (or to Valéry). In him scorn is almost always based on a misunderstanding; and his strength comes from the fact that he doesn't care a bit.

11 April

The *Malatesta* that Montherlant has just sent me, which I finished reading last night, seems to me a very mediocre work.[13] Mediocre to the point of making me regret the very cordial letter thanking him for this *Malatesta*, which I was probably quite wrong to write and send to him before reading it. Decidedly I cannot maintain my esteem for so wary a man, however good a writer he may be.

Malraux too is following the fashion: just as Mauriac would, he writes (*Psychologie de l'art*): "*Aussi* différentes que soient leurs recherches . . ." where in my opinion "*Si* différentes . . ." or "*Pour* différentes . . ." would be far preferable. Grévisse, in his excellent *Bon Usage*,[14] points out the error and says some good things about it.

Curious to know what "competent" connoisseurs think of the so remarkable *Magdalen with the Vigil Light* reproduced in colors in *La Psychologie de l'art*.[15] Authentically by Georges de Latour? I cannot believe it.

8 June

There is nothing to do but pick up the thread, without explanation and as if nothing had happened. Summer (after frigid days, now we have warm, glorious days . . .) helps me return to life. Yes, suddenly I caught myself enjoying life again. Last night, in a sort of joyous intoxication and new lease of life, I could not resign myself to going to bed until after midnight, and this morning I was awake before seven

---

[12] An essay by Julien Benda appeared in 1948 with the title: *Concerning the Style of Ideas; Reflections on Thought, Its Nature, Its Realizations, Its Moral Value.*

[13] Henry de Montherlant's four-act play on the subject of Sigismondo Malatesta appeared in early 1948.

[14] *Good Usage: Course in French Grammar and Language*, by Maurice Grévisse.

[15] The first volume of André Malraux's *Psychology of Art*, entitled *The Imaginary Museum*, appeared in Geneva in 1947; *The Magdalen with the Vigil Light*, on p. 149, is from the Tesch Collection in Paris.

o'clock. I should have worked admirably if my whole morning (it is now half past twelve) had not been taken up by correspondence, like every day, or almost — and almost exclusively letters of refusal or excuse. That puts you in a sort of cantankerous state of mind, at least in a defensive state from which your friends run the risk of suffering. It wrinkles one's forehead and heart, and I am dreadfully sorry not to have been able to give a better welcome to Jef Last, who was considerably affected by my insufficiently cordial reception. He might have attributed it to some cooling of my friendship, whereas I was simply out of patience. How painful it is not to be able to *suffice*! I lack time and strength. I went through a long period of almost constant fatigue in which I longed to get out of the game; but impossible to *withdraw*. And just as in economics "bad money drives away the good," bores and intruders usurp and take over the field as masters; all that remains is theirs.

The worst is allowing people to think: "Yes, since the Nobel Prize, Gide has *become distant*." After that there remains nothing but to go and drown or hang oneself. And it so happens that since the warmth has returned, I have ceased to have any desire to do so. But before that, on certain days, I felt as if already completely detached; this, however, held me back: the impossibility of getting anyone to understand, to accept, the real reason for a suicide; at least, this way I shall be left alone and in peace. But go away on a trip . . . already on the steps of the train, what a relief to feel out of reach, liberated! But go where? I think of that little hotel that Alix told me about (I noted it down) in a fishing village on Lago di Garda. If only I were sure of finding room there. . . . Constantly called upon, I must put off from day to day; and constantly I hear the eldest of the Fates whispering in my ear; you haven't much time left.

. . . If I were not constantly and absurdly disturbed, it seems to me that I could write marvels, with the aid of the warmth. . . . I am resuming interest in life.

I am writing all this at full speed, with the fear of not being able to finish, but with the constant preoccupation of much more interesting things I should like to say: in particular the discovery I made the day before yesterday in Charlie Du Bos's *Journal*. . . .[16]

11 June

What an extraordinary monument! One has no sooner entered it than every possible exit closes. (Ah, if only I had a little time to myself to speak of it!) Even the most refractory, like Jean Schlumberger, are

---

[16] The critic Charles Du Bos died in 1939 leaving extensive manuscripts and typescripts of his *Journal*, which his widow began to publish in 1946.

caught. He admitted this to me yesterday; but I do not recall to what substantive he added the adjective "heady." As soon as one consented to lend oneself to it, to give oneself to it, to forget the rest of the world and physical realities, nothing was more engaging, charming, intoxicating than Charlie's conversation. No remark, except vulgar ones, fell flat with him. It was like a game, absolutely gratuitous, in which I used to amuse myself like a child, inventing new pretexts for subtleties. I had imagined the various "tempi" of prose writers. I might just as well have launched him on the odors, the irradiations of the poets; their temperature, their varying degrees of porosity. . . . He immediately blossomed out and held forth for hours. To such intellectual games he brought a sort of genius; but the most wonderful thing is that he took them seriously. . . .

A few sentences in that extraordinary *Journal* (where our relations are mentioned every six pages) have thrown a new light on his sudden change of attitude in regard to me. It was a sort of revelation for me, the day before yesterday. They can be read on page 356 of Volume II, under date of "Tuesday, 28 April 1925" — and he adds with his customary attention to detail (the preciosity of useless exactness and honesty): "9.25 a.m." I give up transcribing at length the endless sentence, the beginning of which is already directed against me, in regard to the sale of my library. . . . Then he gets to this, following a new parenthesis: "(here it is indispensable to be altogether sincere)" — "all this subterraneously nourished by my resolution, no less formal and no less well kept, of hiding from him the disappointment I experienced as a result of his total abstention regarding me during the period of choosing an editor for the *N.R.F.* . . ."

This took place soon after the death of Rivière. Yes, we suspected all right, or some of us did, that Charlie would have wished nothing better than to succeed him; but we were utterly convinced (it is enough to read his *Journal* to see the justice of our fears) that Charlie's "editorship" would have led the *N.R.F.* to ruin. (I can still hear Jean Schlumberger's saying: "He will put us in the soup.") I had seen our friend Ch. D. B. at work, noted his lack of "common sense," his total incapacity when faced with difficulties of a practical nature, at the time of the Foyer Franco-Belge.[17] Du Bos chief editor of the *N.R.F.*! This was not even considered. His candidature was not even proposed. I knew all this and suspected that he had felt some disappointment. But I had not been aware of the profound and lasting bitterness left by that blighted hope. It was the "turntable" that suddenly directed

[17] At the beginning of the war, in 1914–16, Gide was assistant director of the Foyer Franco-Belge, a charitable organization, and Du Bos was in charge of one of its sections.

against me his *Dialogue avec André Gide,* begun in enthusiasm.[18] (Very much worked up likewise against Gallimard and the neighborhood of the *N.R.F.*) Odd to see a mind so concerned with equity and fairness at the mercy of the most distorting passions, and so accessible to flattery!

I admire all the more the excellent pages (in *Approximations,* I believe, but I don't know in which volume) where Charlie speaks of the social question with extraordinary wisdom, pertinence, and even competence, which I was far from expecting of one so remote from contingencies. . . .

Constantly interrupted; impossible to write anything consecutive, anything worth while.

Great pleasure in working with Jean L.; put the last touches to the *Anthologie.*

In the *Annales du Centre Universitaire Méditerranéen,* great pleasure in finding the course of lectures by Father Valensin on *L'Art et la pensée de Platon.*[19] He signs Auguste Valensin, for he dislikes that sort of insulator that his cassock might constitute in his relations with the public, with others; and one is most grateful to him for remaining as much as possible on the human plane, for putting himself on our level. Equally grateful for tackling without being frightened certain ticklish questions. He speaks of them very well with the decorum one might expect of his cassock, and with a sort of boldness one did not dare hope for. None the less he is forced to cheat a bit without intending to and without knowing it. For, after all, that victorious chastity he proposes was not a pagan ideal, not even, it seems (or only exceptionally), according to Plato, who seeks above all the harmonious well-being of the City and, as Valensin says: "A single purpose dominates everything: to make sure of fine types of humanity." So that the question remains altogether urgent, which he scamps and ought not to avoid: That superabundance of pollen which bothers the adolescent, how is it going to manage to expend itself? Does he hope that abstinence will completely resorb it? He is well aware that this is not so, or only very exceptionally, and with a view to some ideal of holiness that Christianity alone can legitimize. . . . It is on this precise point that we find him cheating: the demands of the flesh are overlooked, the necessary relief of the glands, for which there are but a few solutions, not mentioned and understandably so: masturbation or spontaneous emissions during sleep; and with what erotic dreams? Here Plato himself cheats by purifying all that, which remains altogether real, and

[18] Du Bos's very valuable *Dialogue with André Gide* appeared in 1929.

[19] *The Art and Thought of Plato* was a course given at the Mediterranean University Center at Nice.

material, and . . . practical. I maintain that the order of the city is less
compromised by the sought-after contact between young males (it is
of less consequence) than when the libido immediately directs the desires of those adolescents toward the other sex. I cannot believe that
those relationships of adolescents such as antiquity offers, either among
themselves or with elders, remained chaste — that is to say, unaccom-
panied by relieving emissions. And if Plato does not speak of this, it
is because of propriety and because, the thing being taken for granted,
it became useless and indecorous to speak of it. Plato is well aware that
when Socrates eludes the offers and provocations of Alcibiades, he is
offering a sort of almost paradoxical ideal, which simultaneously evokes
admiration and smiles because it is not natural and can serve as an example for but a few. He thus rises above humanity, you will say; but
with a view to what mystical reward or satisfaction of pride?

And when Valensin writes: "Consequently the question is answered:
Plato cannot be annexed by the partisans of vice" (this pejorative
word already involves a judgment that is not appropriate, for no *vice*
was involved, properly speaking, in the eyes of Plato's contemporaries);
"he condemns the behavior of the vulgar Venus. He condemns it to the
same extent that he approves and encourages that of the celestial
Venus," he is speaking as much of heterosexual relationships as of
homosexual ones. Plato opposes virtue and indulgence in pleasure,
whatever pleasure it may be.

Torri del Benaco

The Jews likewise, from being the oppressed, became the op-
pressors, as it happens, apparently necessarily, when religious convictions have the support of power — or, to express it more simply, have
the power.

"As certain resounding incidents indicate, the punishment inflicted
on Vriel de Coste, the excommunication of Juan de Prado, that of
Spinoza even, the Portuguese Synagogue of Amsterdam did not take
long to exercise a jealous surveillance over the opinions of the faithful,
nor the pious zeal of the community to become intolerance." (Charles
Appuhn: *Introduction to Selections from Spinoza.*)

Text of the excommunication pronounced against Spinoza on 2 July
1656: "May he be cursed by day and by night. . . . May God never
forgive him. We order that no one have commerce with him by speech
or in writing, that no one ever give him the least sign of friendship, or
approach him or live under the same roof as he, that no one read a work
written or composed by him."

3 September

These last days of life seem the most difficult to live through; but
this must be an illusion, for one has only to leave it to time, and to

gravity. . . . Valéry used to get angry at the fact that more importance is given to the last moments of a life than to all the rest; this in relation to last-minute conversions. I believe that not even he escaped the devotion of his family; but I have so much respect myself for the sentiments that, in such a case, motivate one's relatives that I prefer to beat a retreat, as perhaps Valéry did too. And what more would that prove than, most likely, a great conjugal love, which is certainly worth sacrificing something to; that something, after all, not having so much importance when it is given the lie by the entire work. But the use that is then made of it! The contradiction of the entire work that people try to see in it. . . . This is what must stiffen you.

An extraordinary, an insatiable need to love and be loved, I believe this is what dominated my life and urged me to write; an almost mystical need, moreover, since I consented to its not being satisfied during my lifetime.

Torri del Benaco, 7 September
I believe I am sincere in saying that death does not frighten me much (I am constantly thinking of it); but I see the summer go by with a sort of despair.

Never before had I seen such a long series of such beautiful, such splendid days.

Here since the 22nd of July, I believe; first with Marc (in the Hudson bought from Pierre, with a stop at Locarno and crossing of the Gothard), then with Pierre. In August, unbearable heat and suffocation. Besides: otitis and weakness of the heart. The heart is hardly any better, it seems to me (no pain, but insufficiency and a constant feeling of insecurity such as the skater experiences when venturing onto ice that he feels to be thin and ready to break under him).

Two wonderful and amazing storms:
Fluctibus et fremitu assurgens Benace marino.[20]
But since the beginning of September the air is light; the midday heat is no longer excessive; the mornings and evenings are cool. To the daily splendor is added a constant feeling of death near by which makes me keep repeating to myself that these fine days are the last for me. I am writing this without bitterness.

"Humanity's return to its ancient errors, supposedly indispensable to its morality, would be worse than its complete demoralization."

---

[20] "You, Lake Benacus, surging up with waves and a roar like the sea," is from Virgil: *Georgics,* II, 160. Benacus is the modern Lago di Garda, on the shore of which stands Torri del Benaco.

I gather this sentence from the pasty verbiage of Renan's *Examen de conscience philosophique.*[21] (The date is not given. . . .)

Wonderful concert (on the radio) devoted to Paganini. At first I hesitated to recognize him, somewhat too stuffed and stifled by Brahms.

Arrived at Grasse on 15 September, in the evening. I let Pierre hasten to Les Audides and do not go myself until the morning of the 16th. The pleasures of seeing old friends again; but already death has slipped between me and things (people a little less), and the union can no longer be effected. I have taken leave; I have my leave; there is no occasion to reconsider. And there is even added a sort of æsthetic disapproval of this *postscriptum,* which does not fuse with the whole, but remains outside as an appendix, an extra. . . . The Catholic will claim that this overtime is granted me by God, in his infinite kindness, to allow me an exemplary conversion. . . .

18 October

Went to get Mme Théo at Cabris to bring her back to Nice, leaving the modest but very pleasant Pension des Cigognes, insufficient for Mme Théo.

Strange negligence of people: I carefully spelled out the address of Les Cigognes for the use of a few rare correspondents: "16 rue Maccarani." Out of ten envelopes the mail brings me, not one copies the address correctly. Five ways of misspelling the name of the street: Maccaroni, Macarini, Macariani, etc.

Mougins, 30 October

. . . When science got to the point of specializing, requiring a patient apprenticeship and, consequently, making impossible those great universal busybodies of the eighteenth century . . . See the beginning of Butler's *Life and Habit.*

Paris, 15 December

Last words. . . . I do not see why one should try to pronounce them louder than the others. At least I do not feel the need of doing so.

---

[21] The *Philosophic Self-Scrutiny.*

1949

. . . **B**ut don't believe that. I recall having gone months, long series of months, without working, without being able to work at all. To such a degree as not to understand just why I did not utterly collapse. You see, what saved me was a certain obstinacy, a certain strength in cling-ing that kept me from letting go. Yet I have lived at least ten years of my life, if they were put end to end, in the belief that all was lost and that I should never again manage to say anything. Besides, on two occasions I tiresomely persisted on the wrong track. I spent as much time spoiling *L'Intérêt général* and then *Geneviève* (of which I de-stroyed almost everything) as in successfully completing *Les Faux-Monnayeurs.*[1] Everything that I wrote then, *invita Minerva*, remained unspeakably mediocre.

But doubtless it is not bad to find something to blush over in one's life, and without having to look very far.

I note in Proust: *"Cela ne me souciait pas davantage."* [2] Indefensible, I believe. But no matter. Cailleux's book urges me to plunge again into *Le Temps perdu*, or, more exactly, into *Le Temps retrouvé*, with an even greater admiration than in the past.[3]

I pick out this gem from *Les Lettres françaises* of 28 April 1949:
"An ancient legend relates that two women had come before a very wise judge; they were disputing over the possession of a certain infant. The woman who wanted to pass herself off as the mother answered the judge: 'Cut the child in two.' She spoke thus because the child was not hers. . . ." (Ilya Ehrenburg: *Speech at the Congress of Peace.*)

Hospital in Nice

Each time that this or that great poet speaks to me intimately, in-dividually, and reveals to me what the majority of his readers had

[1] Neither the play *Robert or the Common Weal* (1944–5) nor the tale *Geneviève* (1939), which closes the cycle of *The School for Wives*, is gen-erally considered among Gide's major works; whereas *The Counterfeiters* (1926) forms the cornerstone of his reputation.

[2] "That did not concern me any more." *Soucier* is a personal verb and one would expect the sentence to read: *"Je ne me souciais pas davantage de cela."*

[3] Gide's friend Dr. Roland Cailleux recorded in *Une Lecture* (*A Read-ing*) his impressions on reading Proust. *Le Temps retrouvé* (*The Past Re-captured*) is the final part of the long work known in English as *Remem-brance of Things Past.*

perhaps not been able to hear in him, each time I reveal that secret he
entrusts to me, many people protest, accusing me of reading it into him:
That is not at all what he meant. — But it is! But it is! Perhaps he did
not mean *solely* that; but he meant that *too*, and I am not at all betraying him by discovering that secret intention, which only fits his general
meaning. Is it Virgil or I who fills with profound meaning these few
words that he makes Nisus address to his Euryalus:

> *Nisus ait: Dine hunc ardorem mentibus addunt,*
> *Euryale, an sua cuique deus fit dira cupido?* [4]

That I see more in them today than Nisus himself could see there
is possible and likely; but I am not betraying him, or Virgil, whose
theology, or logic, or genius, remains almost as vague and uncertain as
mine. But how I like that god that our very ardor fashions. I look for
a good translation of that little sentence and can find nothing better
than what Pessonneaux offers: "Is it the gods who inspire in my soul
the ardor I feel *or does a violent desire become a god for each of us?*" [5]

("Or does not every violent desire become a god for each of us?")

The admirable conciseness of the Latin will always leave the in-
evitably explicit interpretation of the French far behind. Nisus takes
care not to assert. It might be that . . . perhaps . . . It is enough for
him that it might be, in order to forge ahead.

15 May

I cannot really believe that it can take place without suffering (dis-
pense with suffering); that would be too easy. One would bow out
and everything would be said. No applause would have authority to
recall you to the stage. . . . I tell myself that most often the trouble
comes from the fact that people hang on tightly. I consider it very
beautiful, at times, to see people cling to life and be unwilling to let
go (there are admirable examples of this, such as the case of Guillaumet [6]); but not always; not when one has lived; and in certain cases,
like mine, it is proper to consent.

Spiritualistic to an unbelievable degree, he never went to pray, or
weep, or meditate over the tomb of his parents. For that goes far back,
that disregard for matter which keeps it from holding his attention. It
is as if he did not believe in it. I say "he," but that "he" is I. No logic in
this; it is instinctive and spontaneous. I can find no better example of it
than this: when at Cuverville I was present at the lugubrious delivery of

---

[4] "Nisus cries: 'Do the gods, Euryalus, put this fire in our hearts, or does
his own wild longing become to each man a god?' " *Æneid*, IX, 184–5.

[5] Émile Pessonneaux's translation of Virgil dates from 1857.

[6] See *The Journals of André Gide*, Vol. III, pp. 157–8.

my sister-in-law — I mean by this that I had to help the doctor in the dreadful operation to which he consented only after making sure that the baby's heart had stopped beating (he would have had to have recourse to a Cæsarean, but he did not have the surgical instruments) — I had to hold my sister-in-law's legs while he extracted what was already nothing but a corpse. . . . No, I cannot relate that; nothing more painful can be imagined. And I recall that later on, in the night, the two of us alone and face to face beside that recumbent woman looked at each other. He was sweating. "We are assassins," he said. "But when the child has ceased to live, one tries to save the mother." (The pangs had lasted thirty hours.) Although she had not been put to sleep (it was still contrary to principles; there has been progress since), she was lying unconscious. Near her a jumbled mass of bloody, soiled remains. . . .

When the morning came, "Get that out of the way," I naïvely said to the gardener's wife when she at last came to see "how everything was." Could I suppose that those amorphous fragments, to which I pointed while turning away with disgust, could I suppose that in the eyes of the Church they already represented the human and sacred creature they were preparing to clothe? O mystery of the incarnation! What was my amazement, a few hours later, when I saw *it* again, which for me already had "no name in any language," cleaned up, dressed, bedecked with ribbons, lying in a little cradle in preparation for the ritual entombment. No one, fortunately, had been aware of the sacrilege I had been on the point of committing, had already committed in thought, when I had said: "Get that out of the way." Yes, quite happily that thoughtless command had been heard by no one. And I remained a long time lost in thought before *it;* before that little face with the broken forehead carefully hidden; before that innocent flesh which, if I had been alone, yielding to my first impulse, I should have thrown onto a manure pile near the afterbirth, and which now religious attentions had just saved from the abyss. . . . I told no one what I experienced then, what I am relating here. Was I to think that, for a few moments, a soul had inhabited this body? It has its tomb at Cuverville, in that cemetery to which I do not want to go back.

Half a century has passed. . . . I cannot say, to tell the truth, that I exactly still see that little face. No, what I recall precisely is my surprise, my sudden emotion before its extraordinary beauty. I had never before seen anything, I have not since seen anything, comparable. The faces of the dead can be beautiful. Death often brings to our features a sort of calm and serenity in the renunciation of life. But that little corpse had not lived; its beauty remained utterly inexpressive. Some (some mothers especially) go about exclaiming over the beauty of the newborn. As for me, I do not believe I have ever seen a single other one that did not seem to me almost hideous, I confess, shriveled, grimacing, flushed. . . . This one (it was partly to this that he obviously owed his beauty) had not known the pangs of being born. And it was probably not enough that his features were beautiful (my sister-in-law was beautiful; my two other nephews and my niece were among the most beautiful children I have ever seen), but besides, altogether bloodless, the substance of which he was made did not seem like human flesh, but rather some ethereal substance, some translucent and nacreous paraffin, some immaterial pulp; it seemed like the flesh of a Eucharistic host. A bow of blue satin (it would have been pink, the gardener's wife told me, if the baby had been a girl) on the right side of a delicate lace bonnet, as in the portrait of an infant by Sustermans (I believe), further emphasized the paleness of that face and of that uninhabited forehead. That little cranium had been emptied of the brain matter, which had indeed been thrown on the manure pile with the scraps from that frightful operation, the mucus and the placenta.

This tale aims to prove what? That the soul is at a loss where to take refuge when its carnal support disappears? The Church provided for this when she enjoins us to believe in "the resurrection of the flesh."

As for the soul, it goes without saying that I believe in it! Why, of course I believe in the soul. I believe in it as in the glow of phosphorus. But I cannot imagine that glow without the phosphorus that produces it. In any case, I am not indulging in theories here. Theories and ratiocinations annoy me. *Animus, Animum, Anima.* . . . Such discriminations make me dizzy, for I have reached the point of not even distinguishing the soul from the body. I cannot conceive of one without the other. In writing this I am merely suggesting a personal attitude of mind that explains in my own eyes, without in any way justifying or excusing it, what I said earlier about the tomb of my parents; and this too: that I did not even dream of spending the night sitting by the bedside of my dead wife. It was all over. A telegram announcing her end had suddenly recalled me to Cuverville from Chitré in Poitou, where I was staying with a woman of my acquaintance. I had left my wife, a few days earlier, in a precarious state of health, to be sure, but not an alarming one, so that I had left her without fear. She was not only what I loved the most in the world; but it even seemed to me (it still seems to me today) that it was in relation to her that I lived, and that, really, I depended on her. Likewise I had been the tragic occupation of her life. And now it was over.

I can see her again on her deathbed. With no more of that smiling amenity left which always tempered her gravity, she seemed like a Jansenist painted by Philippe de Champaigne.

I left there those mortal remains. *"Et nunc manet in te,"* I said to myself; or at least (for I had not yet discovered these significant words in Virgil's *Culex* [7]) I felt urgently that henceforth *she* lived on only in my memory. And if I return now to that image of the phosphorus and its glow, it is to say that solely because of, and by virtue of, its glow the phosphorus matters to me, that solely the glow matters to me. . . . Oh, perhaps I should not speak in the same way if I had loved her carnally. And how explain that? — it was her soul that I loved, and yet I did not believe in that soul. I do not believe in the soul separated from the body. I believe that body and soul are one and the same thing, and that when life has withdrawn from the body, it is all over with both at once. That arbitrary, artificial distinction between the soul and the body — my reason protests against it: I believe (I cannot not believe) in their inevitable interdependence. So I may well say that the soul alone matters to me; but it cannot produce and manifest itself, and I cannot understand and apprehend it save through the body. And it is through the body, despite all mysticism, that any manifestation of love becomes possible.

In writing this I am well aware that I am not throwing any light upon what remains the great mystery. But you do not throw any light whatever on it either by trying to give to the soul an existence distinct from that of the body. It even seems to me at times that it is because of you and your distinctions that I cannot understand anything about it, and that perhaps everything is simpler than you make it out. You shift and disperse the problem without solving it at all, and immediately you come up against many an impossibility.

> *Chanterez-vous quand serez vaporeuse?* [8]

writes Valéry in an admirable sob, which is tantamount to saying: "Alas, great soul that I loved, I know that, without the vibrant body, the soul is absent." Now, that soul that I know to be unable to exist without the body, how could it then be immortal? I have already written, I don't recall where, that there is probably no word of the Gospel which I earlier or more completely adopted, subordinating my being to it and letting it dominate my thoughts: "My kingdom is not of this world." So that "this world," which, for the mass of human beings, alone exists — to tell the truth, I do not believe in it. I believe in the spiritual world, and all the rest is nothing to me. But that spiritual world, I believe that it has existence only through us, in us; that it depends on us, on that support which our body provides it. And when I write: "I believe that . . ." there is no question whatever of an act of faith. I say: "I believe" because there is no other way of expressing

---

[7] "And now (she) remains in you" is found in line 269 of *The Culex* or *The Gnat*, a poem of doubtful authorship often attributed to Virgil's youth.

[8] "Will you sing when you are vaporous?" is a line from *Le Cimetière marin* (*The Cemetery by the Sea*).

the establishment, by my reason, of that obvious fact. What have I to do with *revelations*? I want to appeal solely to my reason — which is the same and was the same at all times and for all men.

Beneath which sprawls at ease my constant sensuality.

I believe that there are not two separate worlds, the spiritual and the material, and that it is useless to oppose them. They are two aspects of one and the same universe; as it is useless to oppose the soul and the body. Useless is the torment of the mind that urges them to war. It is in their identification that I have found calm. And that the spiritual world prevails in sovereign importance is a notion of my mind, which depends intimately on my body; both conspire and agree in order to achieve harmony in me. I will not and cannot try to subject and subordinate one to the other, as the Christian ideal aims to do. I know by experience (for I long strove to do so) what it costs. On whichever side, body or soul, victory inclines, the victory is artificial and temporary and we have eventually to pay the expenses of the conflict.

16 May

Yes, I know: all the indications are excellent (except that of the white corpuscles), so that I do not know how to explain the overwhelming fatigue of the last three days. In the morning I have difficulty "getting out of the sands"; quicksands. I feel at the bottom of a slope that it is not at all certain I shall climb back up. Yet I am writing these few lines in order to help do so. . . .

17 May

Goebbels's *Diary*:

"In reality, we are carrying the torch that is lighting humanity" (p. 105). What is more dangerous than an ideologue in action!

I also note this sentence (p. 118): "Schlepalberger . . . always answers me, when I urge him to action, that he lacks the legal justification for acting. *We could obtain it for him.*" Good Lord! That is indeed the worst of it.

Read the whole book with a most lively interest.

Nuremberg Journal (G. M. Gilbert), lent by Roger Martin du Gard.

"There would never have been a Hitler without the Versailles Treaty" (p. 225 and *passim*). How did it happen that at the moment of signing the aforesaid treaty there was no one of sense to put us on guard? The absurd imprudence of certain clauses of that treaty is obvious. No one, at that time, to point out that obvious *fact*. Some trace in my *Journal* of my convictions at that time? But yet there were a few of us to think that; a few rare inoperative individuals.

"You are making Hitler's bed. You are making Hitler necessary, to be expected, inevitable. . . ."

Roger Martin du Gard, to whom I communicate some reflections on this subject, tells me that he thinks he indeed noted conversations of ours at that time which show to what a degree we were in agreement on all these points, and our consternation over the absurd clauses of that treaty, which was the Pandora's box that subsequently many of the ills escaped from which we soon had to suffer, from which we have not ceased suffering.

Ut sementem feceris, ita metes.[9]

23 May

Too worn out, these last few days, to have a desire to note anything. But without pain or distress. And I almost got to the point of accepting ending up thus in a sort of numb daze. I do not at all know yet whether or not I am heading toward a convalescence. It is not when a member is dead with cold that one suffers; it is when life returns to it. Today, restlessness . . . analogous to the twinges and tinglings in fingers as they revive.

27 May

Accumulation of days in the hospital; vague mass of more than a month; hesitating between better and worse. Succession of days filled almost solely with reading. Sort of desert morass with the daily oasis, charming beyond all hope, of the regular visits of the incomparable friend that, during this long period of purgatory, Roger Martin du Gard was for me. His mere presence already provided me a link with life; he forestalled all the needs of my mind and body; and however gloomy I might have been before his coming, I soon felt quite revived by his remarks and by the affectionate attention he paid to mine. I do not know whether I could ever have been more aware in the past of the ineffable blessing of friendship. And what an effacement (even excessive) of his own interest, of himself! No, no! Religion achieves nothing better, or so naturally.

The *Anthologie* so long awaited has finally appeared.[10] *Grosso modo*, very satisfied; and especially, perhaps, at not having made my personal taste, it seems to me, prevail unduly. I hope to have brought to light a number of exquisite little poems that deserved to be known and that I did not see quoted anywhere.

---

[9] "Whatsoever a man soweth, that shall he also reap." (*Galatians* vi, 7.)
[10] The printing of his *Anthology of French Poetry* was finally finished on 31 March 1949.

This morning I find a stumbling-block in Jammes's particularly well-turned-out poem: *"Il va neiger dans quelques jours. . . ."* What is the meaning, what could be the meaning of:

> *. . . and the numbers*
> *Which prove that beautiful comets will pass*
> *In the night cannot force them to pass.*[11]

Yes, it is exquisite, charming, and all the more idiotic since it passes itself off as profound. But all Jammes is there, all the absurdity of his *belief*. Those very "numbers" belong to God's order; are God. Those lines signify, vaguely, that God (the God of Jammes) is always in a position to perform a miracle, not to feel bound by the laws that he properly instituted. It is Joshua, with the aid of God, capable of stopping the sun. Such a remark strikes me as outrageously impious, and is saved only by its unconscious poetical incongruity. Jammes's God would be free to keep a certain triangle from having its angles equal to two right angles? . . . Absurd! Absurd! Absurd like an unjustified challenge to authority. Useless to insist. None the less, this little poem is one of Jammes's best.

31 May

At Saint-Paul at last! Shall I dare confess now that I had but a feeble hope of leaving the hospital alive? Here, what calm! Night has fallen. No other sound than the croaking of the frogs in rhythm. Then, as if in response to some mysterious signal or cue, all fall silent at once; then all burst out again in chorus.

1 June

In order for a convalescence to succeed properly, it requires the complicity of spring.

I note in La Rochefoucauld this maxim that I had not hitherto noticed:

"The wise man is better off not taking sides than he is on the victorious side."

And this one too:

"Quarrels would not last long if all the wrong were on one side."

---

[11] The lines:

> *. . . et les nombres*
> *Qui prouvent que les belles comètes dans l'ombre*
> *Passeront, ne les forceront pas à passer.*

are from the poem "It is Going to Snow . . ." which Gide included in his *Anthologie*.

3 June

Reread *Le Cabinet des antiques* and *Le Père Goriot*, and *Honorine* (one of the best-written), in which Balzac uses the word *compatissance.* Curious to see if it is in Littré.[12] It seems to me that *compassion* suffices.

Strange need to transform into reflexive verbs (?) those which it would be much more natural to use in the simple form:

". . . *Un lac où se passe une tempête.*" "*Personne ne peut me prouver que l'amour se recommence.*" "*Enfin ses grands yeux se remuèrent.*" (*La Grande Bretèche.*) ". . . *Des mansardes où se séchait le linge en hiver.*" (*La Vieille Fille.*) "*Les tempes se miroitaient.*" (Ibid.) "*Ces deux amants s'escomptaient l'avenir.*" (Ibid.)

And even after a piece of gossip at second hand he adds: ". . . *se disait-on*" for "*disait-on.*"

"*Cette peur s'augmente.*" (*La Vieille Fille.*)

". . . *Ces inexplicables soifs qu'ont les malheureux de se plonger les lèvres dans leur calice amer.*" (Ibid.)

4 June

Some days it seems to me that if I had at hand a good pen, good ink, and good paper, I should without difficulty write a masterpiece.

10 June

Hugo enjoys rhyming two diphthongs, one counting as two syllables, the other as one. I note in passing:

> *Qu'un vin pur fasse fête aux poulardes friandes!*
> *Et que de cet amas de fricots et de viandes . . .*[13]

I had noticed others.

---

[12] *The Cabinet of Antiquities, Old Goriot,* and *Honorine* are parts of *The Human Comedy.* The noun *compatissance* figures neither in Littré nor in the Dictionary of the French Academy; it is obviously formed from the adjective *compatissant,* which means "compassionate," "expressing compassion."

[13] *Let a pure wine honor these dainty fowl!*
And of this mound of victuals and meats . . .
are lines spoken by Aïrolo in Hugo's comedy *Mangeront-ils?* (*Will They Eat?*), Act II, Scene iii.

Ces ~~dernières~~ lignes
insignifiantes
datent du 12 juin 1949.
Tout m'invite à croire
qu'elles seront les
dernières de ce Journal.

André Gide

25 janvier 1950.*

---

* "These insignificant lines date from 12 June 1949 [*sic*]. Everything leads me to think that they will be the last of this *Journal*. — André Gide. — 25 January 1950."

APPENDIX I

Foreword to *Pages de Journal*

[NEW YORK AND ALGIERS EDITIONS]

IN THESE PAGES from the journal that I kept, quite irregularly by the way, during the somber months following our defeat, I do not recognize that I have any right to change anything. I am not pretending to be any more courageous than I was: it was not until about March 1941 that I began to hold up my head somewhat again, and again took heart. A certain book by Chardonne that I read at that time contributed to this by opposition and acted on my mind like a reagent. Then only did I realize just where we stood, and in the first article I wrote on this subject for the *Figaro* I made clear what I would not accept being. The contemplation of one's very swoons becomes an encouragement as soon as one recovers from them. Blessed be he who permitted and favored the restoration of our dignity. Today this recovery seems to us beautiful in proportion to the depth of our fall.

I should like these pages, and especially those of the beginning, to be granted but a relative value: if altogether they contain a lesson, let it be in the manner of an intellectual itinerary by marking the stages of a slow progress out of darkness into light.

Rabat, 3 September 1943

APPENDIX II

Proceedings of the Provisional Consultative Assembly

[*Algiers, 7 July 1944*]

QUESTION NO. 27

The President: I shall read question no. 27.

M. Giovoni asks the Commissioner for Information:

"Is it possible to print in Algiers remarks such as these which I shall quote without superfluous comment:

" 'It is through the privations it involves, and only thereby, or almost, that the great majority will feel the defeat. Less sugar in one's coffee and less coffee in one's cup; that is what they will feel.'

" 'Is there one among them [the farmers] who would not willingly accept Descartes's or Watteau's being a German, or never having existed, if that could make him sell his wheat for a few cents more?'

" 'The patriotic feeling is, moreover, no more constant than our other loves.'

"These remarks are by M. André Gide and were printed in the April–May issue of the review *L'Arche*.

"Clemenceau is often spoken of. His remark is often repeated: 'The country will know that it is defended,' and there was no question of an Almereyda or a Lenoir.

"If Clemenceau were here, the author of these foul writings would be already arrested, brought before the military court under the law that punishes traitors with death in wartime; the managing editor of that review would be brought before the same court; the review would be suppressed and the paper that is allocated to it would be turned over to the few patriotic newspapers and reviews of Algiers. What does the Commissioner for Information think of this?"

The Commissioner for Information: "These lines are taken from the *Journal* in which André Gide sets down, day by day and quite spontaneously, his impressions, his reflections, and his emotions.

"The world has noted with great satisfaction how few were the French writers of value who took sides with Vichy. Almost all of them, and Gide among them, understood the real duty of France and, refusing Vichy's paltry blandishments, prepared our country's return to

a major position in world literature. Hence tomorrow the world is sure to find France's contribution, intact and pure, to that literature."
M. Giovoni: "I knew that the rights of literature would be invoked, but I believe that when the fate of our country is at stake, a well-known writer must not publicly indulge in certain speculations colored with narcissism and egocentricity.

"André Gide has placed himself 'above the fray'; the sounds of the battle do not reach him. He has seriously insulted the farmers and peasants of France by accusing them, in almost the same terms as the traitor Flandin once did, of 'sordid materialism.' He has insulted the patriotism of the French and has today misjudged the French peasants as much as he once did those of the U.S.S.R. In short, this artificial writer who has exercised such a murky influence over young minds indulges in defeatism in the midst of the war. His craze for originality and exoticism, his immoralism and his perversity make of him a dangerous individual.

"Today literature is a weapon. That is why I demand prison for André Gide and public prosecution of the managing editor of *L'Arche*."

APPENDIX III

Letter from Mme Berthe Zuckerkandl,

Clemenceau's niece, then eighty-four years old,
who died in 1945

(*this letter is reproduced at the request of Mme Zuckerkandl*)

30 avenue Clemenceau
El Biar

9 July 1944

DEAR MONSIEUR GIDE,

We were all shocked on reading the latest report of the Consultative Assembly. The ominous fool who made himself ridiculous by daring to attack your work had the impudence to make use of Clemenceau in order to pass off his false patriotism and his totalitarian attack on intellectual freedom. I lived many years with Clemenceau. I have known the heights and the depths of his soul. To be cited as a witness by this presumptuous imbecile would have made him furious, and this Giovoni would have felt the Tiger's claw. . . .

Clemenceau, "the man in chains," fought unflinchingly throughout his life against obscurantism. As for the real nature of the peasant, Clemenceau, despite his love of the soil and his friendship for those who till it, would have been in agreement with you.

Innumerable were the anecdotes that he and his brother Paul enjoyed telling about the narrow egotism of the peasantry, which excluded any community of feeling based on the recognition of spiritual values. How many times have I heard Clemenceau exclaim:

"The soil! Nothing but the soil! . . ." They recognize nothing but the soil and money!

I believe and am sure that Clemenceau, if he were alive, would take his stand beside Gide to defend with him:

The common basis of our native morality: the RESTLESS *and radiant spirit of France in quest of an ever loftier ideal!*

As I protest in the name of Clemenceau, brought to the fore and falsely cited for purposes of base demagogy, I merely regret not having access to any newspaper in order to reply more vigorously to such lamentable assertions.

Respectfully,
BERTHE ZUCKERKANDL

Glossary of Persons

MENTIONED IN VOLUME IV OF THE JOURNALS

N.B. Not all the names listed in the Index are to be found in this Glossary. Servants, tradesmen, chance acquaintances, and others sufficiently identified in the text — together with the most famous in all domains — have been omitted here. Other names have simply resisted research.

Originally intended to identify the specifically French names that are presumably known to the author's compatriots, the Glossary has grown in the making to include all the persons about whom English-speaking readers might have questions.

Certain names included in the Glossaries of Volumes I, II, and III are reproduced here because they are mentioned again in this volume.

J. O'B.

ABDALLAH, SI, Frenchman converted to Islam, who lives in the Arab fashion in Fez.

ACHARD, MARCEL (1899–), French dramatist of fantasy and gay burlesque, best known for his *Jean de la lune* (1929).

ALAURANT, CAPTAIN, officer of the Leclerc division, who was much influenced by Gide's *Journals*.

ALBÉNIZ, ISAAC (1860–1909), Spanish composer often inspired by folk themes.

ALIBERT, FRANÇOIS-PAUL (1873–), French poet of Virgilian temper, strongly influenced by Mallarmé.

ALLÉGRET, ÉRIC, fourth son of Élie Allégret, the Protestant missionary and tutor of André Gide.

ALLÉGRET, MME MARC, née Nadine Vogel.

ALLÉGRET, MARC, third son of Élie Allégret; adopted by André Gide, whom he accompanied on trip to the Congo (1925–6). Excellent scenario-writer, author of *Lac aux dames*.

AMADO, JORGE (1912–), Brazilian novelist, known in English for *The Violent Land*.

AMPHOUX, MR., neighbor who lived on the same floor as the Reymonds, avenue Roustan, in Tunis.

AMROUCHE, JEAN (1906–), French poet and editor of Arab stock, born at Ighil-Ali (Kabylie), who edited in 1940–1, with Armand Guibert, *La Tunisie Française Littéraire* and from 1943 to 1947 *L'Arche*, which André Gide founded. At present he conducts literary interviews for Radiodiffusion Française.

APPUHN, CHARLES (1862–1942), French historian and Germanic specialist, head of the German section of the Bibliothèque et Musée de la Guerre.

ARAGON, LOUIS (1897–   ), French poet, novelist, and journalist who abandoned surrealism in favor of militant Communism, became editor of the Communist daily *Ce Soir* before the war, and during the German occupation was one of the most articulate poets.

ARON, ROBERT, French essayist on political, economic, and philosophical subjects.

ASTRE, G.-A., French professor at the Lycée Carnot in Tunis, who had recently arrived when André Gide heard him lecture in May 1942.

AURY, DOMINIQUE, French writer and translator, reader for the Éditions Charlot, then managing editor of *L'Arche*, at present managing editor of *Cahiers de la Pléiade*.

BACHRACH, ALEXANDRE, Lithuanian belonging to the Russian colony of Grasse and intimate friend of Ivan Bunin.

BAINVILLE, JACQUES (1879–1936), French historian and essayist, long a contributor to *Action Française* and founder with Massis of the *Revue Universelle;* elected to the Academy in 1935.

BAKUNIN, MIKHAIL (1814–76), Russian anarchist.

BALLARD, JEAN, French essayist and editor of the Marseille review *Les Cahiers du Sud*.

BARRAULT, JEAN-LOUIS (1911–   ), French actor, and co-director, with his wife, of the Compagnie Madeleine Renaud — Jean-Louis Barrault; collaborated with Gide in adapting Kafka's *The Trial* for the stage.

BARRÈS, MAURICE (1862–1923), French novelist who early won a place of distinction through his youthful "cult of the ego" and then evolved into a traditionalist and advocated "the cult of the earth and the dead"; his novels of Alsace-Lorraine preached a return to regionalism and expressed his ardent nationalism.

BARYE, ANTOINE LOUIS (1796–1875), French sculptor who specialized in representing animals.

BATAILLE, HENRY (1872–1922), French dramatist of popular comedies of the psychology of love, such as *Maman Colibri* and *La Marche nuptiale*.

BECQUE, HENRY (1837–99), French realistic and satirical dramatist of *Les Corbeaux* and *La Parisienne*, models of the naturalistic theater.

BÉNARD, LIEUTENANT JEAN-PIERRE, French officer under the command of General Koenig, who had been Cairo correspondent of the Havas news agency; at present Secretary of Embassy in Washington.

BENDA, JULIEN (1867–), French philosopher and essayist, who has consistently defended intellectualism against Bergson and Sorel. His best-known work is *La Trahison des clercs* (1927).

BENJAMIN, RENÉ (1885–1948), French popular dramatist and polemicist.

BÉRANGER, PIERRE JEAN DE (1780–1857), French writer of popular songs.

BÉRAUD, HENRI (1885–), French journalist and novelist.

BERGSON, HENRI (1859–1941), French philosopher of "creative evolution," who exalted the faculty of intuition over the pure intellect.

BERNARD, CLAUDE (1813–78), French physiologist, known as the founder of experimental medicine.

BERNARD, TRISTAN (1866–1947), French comic dramatist, known especially for *L'Anglais tel qu'on le parle, Le Petit Café, Triplepatte.*

BERNARDIN DE SAINT-PIERRE (1737–1814), French disciple of Rousseau and pre-romantic writer, whose sentimental novel *Paul et Virginie* (1787) sounded a new note in literature.

BERSAUCOURT, ALBERT DE (1883–), French literary critic who has written on the Parnassians and certain symbolist poets.

BIDOU, HENRY (1873–1943), French historian and essayist, best known for his *History of the Great War,* his *Chopin,* and his literary criticism.

BLOY, LÉON (1846–1917), French Catholic novelist and essayist of passionate, iconoclastic vigor, most famous for the eight volumes of his journal (1898–1920).

BLÜCHER, GEBHARD-LEBERECHT VON (1742–1819), Prussian general whose timely aid to Wellington at Waterloo decided the battle.

BLUM, LÉON (1872–1950), French critic, essayist, and political figure. Member of the Council of State (1895); president of the Socialist Party; director of the newspaper *Le Populaire* (1921–40); Prime Minister (1936–7, 1938, and 1946).

BOILEAU, NICOLAS (1636–1711), French poet of the classic age, best known for his *Art of Poetry* and his *Satires,* which established him as the critical arbiter of the reign of Louis XIV.

BOLESLAVSKI, RICHARD (1889–), Polish volunteer in the Russian army in the first World War, who wrote interestingly of his experiences as a Polish lancer.

BORNIER, HENRI DE (1825–1901), French poet, and dramatist in verse of *La Fille de Roland.*

BOSSUET, JACQUES BÉNIGNE (1627–1704), French bishop and famous preacher at the court of Louis XIV.

BOURDET, MME ÉDOUARD, wife of the French dramatist, who wrote a book on her husband.

BOURDIL, ANDRÉ, brother-in-law of Jean Amrouche; painter who made an excellent portrait of Gide, later used as frontispiece to a Swiss edition of *L'Immoraliste*.

BOURGET, PAUL (1852–1935), French novelist, dramatist, and essayist, who with Anatole France and Maurice Barrès dominated the literary scene before the first World War. His most characteristic novels are the psychological study *Le Disciple* (1889) and the sociological thesis *L'Étape* (1902).

BOUSQUET, JOË (1898–1950), French poet and novelist who lived in Carcassonne, condemned to immobility by his wounds received in the first World War.

BOUTELLEAU, GÉRARD (1915–), son of the writer Jacques Chardonne (Jacques Boutelleau) and at present one of the heads of the publishing house of Stock in Paris.

BOUTELLEAU, HOPE, English wife of Gérard Boutelleau.

BREHM, ALFRED-EDMUND (1829–84), German traveler and naturalist, author of an *Illustrated Life of Animals*.

BRETON, ANDRÉ (1896–), French poet, novelist, and critic, who founded and led the surrealist group.

BRISSON, PIERRE (1896–), French journalist, at present editor of the Paris *Figaro*, who is known for his drama criticism.

BROMFIELD, LOUIS (1896–), American novelist of *The Green Bay Tree*, *The Rains Came*, etc., and essayist.

BRUNETIÈRE, FERDINAND (1849–1906), scholarly French critic and historian of literature, who applied theories of evolutionism to literary *genres* such as the novel, poetry, criticism, the theater.

BUCKLE, HENRY THOMAS (1821–62), English historian who applied the theories of Darwin and Comte in his *History of Civilization in England*.

BUFFON, GEORGES LOUIS LECLERC, COMTE DE (1707–88), French naturalist.

BUNIN, IVAN (1870–), Russian novelist and writer of short stories who carried on the tradition of Tolstoy and Chekhov. Since the Revolution he has lived in France; he received the Nobel Prize in 1933.

BURNHAM, JAMES (1905–), American writer on philosophy and political science, best known for *The Managerial Revolution* (1941).

BUSSY, DOROTHY, English translator of André Gide (*The Immoralist, Strait Is the Gate, The Counterfeiters*, etc.), sister of Lytton Strachey and wife of the painter Simon Bussy.

BUSSY, JANIE, daughter of Simon and Dorothy Bussy.

BUSSY, SIMON (1870–), French painter, pupil of Gustave Moreau, in whose studio he worked contemporaneously with Matisse, Rouault, Marquet, and others. His works in oils and pastels consist of landscapes, pictures of animals, and portraits, notably of Valéry and Gide.

BUTLER, SAMUEL (1835–1902), English novelist of *The Way of All Flesh* and vigorous satirist of *Erewhon*, etc.

CACCIOPOLI, PROFESSOR, son-in-law of Bakunin and professor of philosophy at Naples.

CAILLEUX, DR. ROLAND (1908–), French doctor at Chatelguyon and author of several books, among which *Une Lecture* recounts the effect of reading Proust. André Gide's doctor in Nice, who drove him from Vence to Vichy in 1940.

CAMUS, ALBERT (1913–), French novelist of *The Stranger, The Plague*, etc., dramatist, and essayist.

CARCO, FRANCIS (pseud. of François Carcopino-Tusoli, 1886–), French novelist, poet, and art critic, who has given literary existence to the life of the Paris underworld and sordid streets.

CARDAN, GIROLAMO (1501–76), Italian mathematician, physician, and astrologer, whose autobiography, *De Vita propria*, is appreciated for its frankness.

CARDUCCI, GIOSUE (1835–1907), Italian poet and scholar, spokesman of democracy, and vigorous satirist; received the Nobel Prize in 1906.

CARPEAUX, JEAN-BAPTISTE (1827–75), French sculptor.

CATTAN, MAÎTRE, French lawyer in Tunis.

CHACHA, MME DE GENTILE, Martiniquan widow of a Tunis lawyer and mother of Mme Théo Reymond.

CHAMFORT, NICOLAS-SEBASTIEN ROCH, called DE (1741–94), French moralist.

CHAMPAIGNE, PHILIPPE DE (1602–74), French painter of Flemish birth, known for his religious subjects and austere portraits.

CHARDONNE, JACQUES (pseud. of Jacques Boutelleau, 1884–), French novelist and essayist, appreciated for his delicate analyses of spiritual and emotional problems. Under his real name, he is a member of the Stock publishing firm. Elected to the Academy in 1950.

CHARRAS, MLLE, school-teacher at Bourg-lez-Valence.

CHASSÉRIAU, THÉODORE (1819–56), French painter, pupil of Ingres, known for his classical subjects.

CHATEAUBRIAND, FRANÇOIS-RENÉ DE (1768–1848), French poet, novelist, essayist, and political figure, who ushered in the romantic movement and left examples of a noble style for future generations.

CHÂTEAUBRIANT, ALPHONSE DE (1877–), French novelist who has specialized in depicting the country gentry of his native Vendée; already before 1940 he had become an apologist of fascism.

CHENG-HUA, SHENG, Chinese professor of French, formerly at the National University of Fuh-Tan, Shanghai, who has translated many of Gide's works.

CHEVALIER, AUGUSTE (1873–), French naturalist, professor at the National Museum of Natural History.

CLAUDEL, PAUL (1868–), French poet and diplomat (Ambassador to Tokyo and Washington), whose odes and verse dramas (L'Annonce faite à Marie, Le Soulier de satin, etc.) struck a new note of genius. Elected to the Academy in 1946.

CLODION (pseud. of Claude Michel, 1738–1814), French sculptor.

CLOUARD, HENRI (1885–), French critic and essayist of the neoclassic revival, editor of the reactionary Revue critique des idées et des livres from 1908 to 1913.

COCTEAU, JEAN (1889–), French poet, novelist, and dramatist long associated with all advanced artistic movements.

COLETTE, SIDONIE GABRIELLE (1873–), French novelist of subjective and sensual inspiration, one of the great stylists of her time.

COPEAU, JACQUES (1879–1949), French critic and theatrical producer, who, after founding the Nouvelle Revue Française with Gide and others in 1909, revolutionized the French theater in 1913 by creating the Théâtre du Vieux-Colombier, with its new style of simplicity and sincerity.

CORTOT, ALFRED (1877–), French pianist and conductor, director of the École Normale de Musique in Paris.

COUPERIN, FRANÇOIS (1668–1733), French organist and composer at the court of Louis XIV.

COURTELINE, GEORGES (pseud. of Georges Moinaux, 1860–1929), French satirist in drama and fiction, who ridiculed officialdom in civil and military life.

COUSIN, VICTOR (1792–1867), French philosopher of electicism, who became a peer and Minister of Education.

CROCE, BENEDETTO (1866–), Italian philosopher and historian.

CURTIUS, ERNST-ROBERT (1886–), German philologist and critic, who has taught French history and literature at Bonn, Marburg, and Heidelberg.

CURVERS, ALEXIS, Belgian husband of Marie Delcourt.

D'ANNUNZIO, GABRIELE (1863–1938), Italy's greatest literary artist since the mid-nineteenth century, who in his poems (*Laudi*, etc.), his novels (*Il Fuoco, Il Piacere*) and plays (*La Città Morta, La Gioconda*) broke with classicism and introduced the new inspiration of foreign writers such as Hugo, Baudelaire, Whitman, Bourget, Dostoyevsky, Nietzsche. Eventually, abandoning æstheticism, sensualism, and his international reputation, he became the national prophet of Italian imperialism.

DAVET, YVONNE, friend and for many years secretary of André Gide; translator of George Orwell and author of a study of Gide's *Nourritures terrestres*.

DAVID, JACQUES-LOUIS (1748–1825), French classical painter, gifted in draftsmanship, of the Revolution and Empire.

DEBUSSY, CLAUDE ACHILLE (1862–1918), French composer, whose new harmonies and literary associations (as a faithful member of Mallarmé's group he composed lyric poems inspired by Verlaine, Mallarmé, Louÿs, Rossetti, etc.) led to the apotheosis of symbolism in music in his opera *Pelléas et Mélisande* (1902).

DE KRUIF, PAUL (1890–), American writer of popular studies on medical subjects.

DELACROIX, EUGÈNE (1799–1863), French painter of the romantic school, known for his brilliant color.

DELCOURT, MARIE, Belgian classical scholar distinguished for her *Life of Euripides*, studies of Æschylus, the legend of Œdipus, Pericles, Erasmus, etc.

DELILLE, JACQUES (1738–1813), French neoclassical poet of nature and translator of Virgil's *Georgics*.

DELON, GUY, *see* Haddou, Si.

DEMOLINS, EDMOND (1852–1907), French social scientist, editor from 1886 to 1907 of *La Science sociale, suivant la méthode d'observation*.

DENOËL, JEAN (1904–), great friend of such writers as Jacob, Cocteau, Mauriac, Maritain; lived for some time in Casablanca and was associated with Max-Pol Fouchet in editing *Fontaine*.

DÉROULÈDE, PAUL (1846–1914), French popular poet and dramatist of patriotism.

DÉTAILLE, JEAN-BAPTISTE ÉDOUARD (1848–1912), French painter of military subjects.

DIDEROT, DENIS (1713–84), French philosopher, critic, dramatist, etc., who edited the great *Encyclopédie*; a fecund writer and one of the great forces of the age of Enlightenment.

DORCHAIN, AUGUSTE (1857–1930), French literary historian and editor of Ronsard, Corneille, Marceline Desbordes-Valmore.

DOYLE, SIR ARTHUR CONAN (1859–1930), English doctor and novelist, creator of Sherlock Holmes.

DRIEU LA ROCHELLE, PIERRE (1893–1944), French novelist, essayist, and dramatist, whose work reflects the unrest of the twenties and a sincere form of fascism that made him an intellectual collaborationist during the German occupation.

DRIOTON, ABBÉ ÉTIENNE (1889–), French Egyptologist living in Cairo.

DROUIN, DOMINIQUE, (1898–), son of Marcel Drouin; has spent much time in Ethiopia and has long been engaged in the film industry.

DROUIN, JACQUES, son of Marcel Drouin and nephew of André Gide.

DROUIN, JEANNE (1868–), née Rondeaux, sister of Mme André Gide and wife of Marcel Drouin.

DROUIN, MARCEL (1870–1946), French professor of philosophy in Alençon, Bordeaux, and Paris and, under pseudonym of Michel Arnauld, essayist and critic. As a classmate of André Gide and Pierre Louÿs, he founded with them *Potache-Revue* and *La Conque* (1891); in 1909, after a brilliant record at the École Normale Superieure and sojourns in Germany, was instrumental in founding the *Nouvelle Revue Française* with his brother-in-law, André Gide.

DU BOS, CHARLES (1882–1939), French literary critic of great taste and penetration, who devoted much of his interest to foreign literature (notably English); he wrote a book on André Gide at about the same time that he was being reconverted to Catholicism.

DUHAMEL, GEORGES (1884–), French novelist (incidentally poet, essayist, dramatist), who won fame for his depiction of suffering humanity as seen by a military surgeon and proceeded to paint a picture of modern society (*Pasquier Chronicles*). After being a most effective editor of the *Mercure de France*, he was named perpetual secretary of the French Academy.

DUVERNOIS, HENRI (1875–1937), French novelist and dramatist of psychological finesse.

ECKERMANN, JOHANN PETER (1792–1854), German amanuensis of Goethe and author of the famous *Conversations of Goethe with Eckermann*.

EHRENBURG, ILYA (1891–   ), Russian journalist, poet, and novelist, ever a popular reporter for, and spokesman of, the U.S.S.R.

EICHENDORFF, JOSEPH VON (1788–1857), German romantic poet.

EM., *see* Gide, Mme André.

FARGUE, LÉON-PAUL (1878–1947), French poet in verse and prose of the delicate world of imagination and hallucination.

FARRÈRE, CLAUDE (1876–   ), French popular novelist, and member of the Academy.

FAUCONNIER, HENRI, French novelist, whose *Malaisie* won the Goncourt Prize in 1930; left Tunisia in 1939 after staying several years. Gérard Boutelleau planned to take over his beautiful old house and lodge André Gide, but the plan was never realized.

FAUS, KEELER (1910–   ), American foreign-service official who met André Gide in 1941 while serving in the U.S. Embassy in Vichy; in 1945, as Secretary of Embassy in Paris, he had further contacts with Gide.

FÉNELON, FRANÇOIS DE SALIGNAC DE LA MOTHE (1651–1715), French bishop, royal tutor, and exponent of quietism, for which he was condemned by Rome at the instigation of Bossuet; his most famous work is the *Aventures de Télémaque.*

FERNANDEZ, RAMON (1894–1944), French literary critic and novelist.

FLEURET, FERNAND (1884–1945), French poet, novelist, and literary historian, who parodied writers of the sixteenth and seventeenth centuries; his mannerism and taste for the erotic won him the designation of the "last satiric poet."

FLORY, MARCEL, professor at the *Lycée* of Tunis, who became Secretary of the French Embassy in Washington and later occupied the same position in Cairo.

FONTAINAS, ANDRÉ (1865–1948), Belgian-born symbolist poet and disciple of Mallarmé, interpreter of English-language poets such as Shelley and Poe, and sensitive art critic.

FORD, JOHN (*fl.* 1639), English dramatist of *'Tis Pity She's a Whore,* etc.

FORSTER, EDWARD MORGAN (1879–   ), English novelist of *A Passage to India* (1924), *A Room with a View* (1908), etc.

GABORIAU, ÉMILE (1835–73), French writer of detective stories, creator of M. Lecoq and Père Tabaret.

GALLIMARD, GASTON (1881–   ), French publisher, who became administrator of the *Nouvelle Revue Française* when founded in 1908–9 and later of the publishing house of Gallimard — *NRF*; also acted as business manager of Copeau's Théâtre du Vieux-Colombier.

GAUTIER, EMILE FELIX (1864–1940), French professor at the University of Algiers, great authority on North Africa and its civilization.

GAUTIER, THÉOPHILE (1811–72), French poet and novelist, who, heading the school of art for art's sake, acts as a pivot between romanticism and naturalism.

GEORGE, STEFAN (1868–1933), German poet strongly influenced by French symbolism, who renewed German poetic style; besides Shakespeare and Dante, he translated Baudelaire and several more recent French poets.

GÉRALDY, PAUL (pseud. of Paul Le Fèvre, 1885–   ), French poet and light dramatist of love, best known for *Toi et moi* (1913).

GIDE, CATHERINE (1923–   ), daughter of André Gide; now Mme Jean Lambert.

GIDE, MME ANDRÉ (1867–1938), née Madeleine Rondeaux.

GILBERT, G. M. (1911–   ), American psychologist, who was prison psychologist at the Nuremberg trial of the Nazi war criminals.

GILLOUIN, RENÉ (1881–   ), Swiss literary critic and journalist.

GIRAUDOUX, JEAN (1882–1944), French poetic novelist and dramatist of fantasy and preciosity.

GIRODET-TRIOSON (pseud. of Anne Louis Girodet de Roussy, 1767–1824), French painter, pupil of David, best known for his *Entombment of Atala.*

GOBILLARD, PAULE (?–1946), French painter who studied with her aunt, Berthe Morisot, and with Renoir; elder sister of Mme Paul Valéry and close friend of Mallarmé, Redon, Degas, etc.

GOBINEAU, JOSEPH-ARTHUR DE (1812–82), French diplomat and writer responsible for certain modern race theories.

GOGOL, NICOLAI VASILIEVICH (1809–52), Russian novelist of satirical works, such as *Dead Souls.*

GOURMONT, REMY DE (1858–1915), fecund French literary critic and novelist, one of the founders of the *Mercure de France* (1890), for which he wrote assiduously for the next twenty-five years, apologist and spokesman for the symbolist movement.

GRANADOS, ENRIQUE (1867–1916), Spanish composer of piano pieces and of the opera *Goyescas*, made from some of them.

GRASSET, BERNARD (1881–   ), French publisher and journalist, who founded a successful publishing house under his own name.

GREEN, JULIEN (1900–   ), French novelist of American parentage and French education (*The Closed Garden, Avarice House,* etc.).

GRIMM, MELCHIOR (1723–1807), German chronicler of Parisian

intellectual life, whose correspondence records the achievements of the *philosophes*.

GRIMMELSHAUSEN, HANS JACOB CHRISTOFFEL VON (1625–76), German novelist and satirist appreciated for his *Simplicissimus*, a picaresque novel of the Thirty Years' War.

GROETHUYSEN, BERNARD (1880–1946), German-born and naturalized French philosopher, critic, and historian of ideas. Of Dutch and Russian parentage, he had the European spirit. A close associate of many French writers and artists, he was an ardent Communist.

GROS, ANTOINE-JEAN, BARON (1771–1835), French painter of historical scenes, pupil of David.

GUÉNON, RENÉ, French Yogi philosopher and authority on Hinduism.

GUÉRIN, PIERRE-NARCISSE, BARON (1774–1833), French painter of classical subjects and teacher of many of the romantic painters.

GUILLAIN, ALIX, French translator of Georg Simmel and other German writers.

GUILLAUMET, HENRI (1902–40), French commercial aviator.

GUIZOT, FRANÇOIS (1787–1874), French historian and statesman, liberal Protestant, and champion of the middle class.

GUTTIEREZ, dentist in Tunis.

HADDOU, SI, Frenchman named Guy Delon converted to Islam under influence of René Guénon; head of the American fonduk at Fez, an animal hospital. He lodged André Gide in the house of a Swiss named Brown whom the war had prevented from returning to Fez.

HAMMETT, DASHIELL (1894–), American writer of thrilling detective novels, such as *Red Harvest, The Maltese Falcon, The Glass Key*.

HEBBEL, FRIEDRICH (1813–63), German poet and dramatist.

HELL, HENRI (pseud. of José Lasry), Venezuelan naturalized collaborator of Max-Pol Fouchet on the review *Fontaine*; active in UNESCO, where he is concerned with poetry and music.

HENRIOT, ÉMILE (1889–), French poet, novelist, and journalist; member of the French Academy.

HERBART, ÉLISABETH, Mme Pierre Herbart, née Van Rysselberghe.

HERBART, PIERRE (1903–), French novelist and journalist, author of *Le Rodeur, Contre-Ordre, Alcyon*, who accompanied André Gide on his trip to Russia in 1936.

HEREDIA, JOSÉ-MARIA DE (1842–1905), French poet of the Parnassian movement, whose single volume of sonnets, *Les Trophées* (1893), won him election to the French Academy.

HEURGON, JACQUES, French professor of Latin, formerly at the University of Algiers, now at the University of Lille; married Anne Desjardins, the daughter of Paul Desjardins.

HOGG, JAMES (1770–1835), Scottish poet known as the "Ettrick Shepherd" and author of the prose *Confessions of a Justified Sinner* (1824).

HOLBACH, BARON D' (1723–89), German-born philosopher and friend of the Encyclopedists, who appreciated him for his *Système de la nature*.

HÖLDERLIN, JOHANN CHRISTIAN FRIEDRICH (1770–1843), German lyric poet and novelist.

HUEFFER, FORD MADOX (1873–1939), English novelist and critic, also known as Ford Madox Ford, who collaborated with Conrad on *The Inheritors* (1901) and *Romance* (1903).

HUGO, FRANÇOIS-VICTOR (1828–73), son of Victor Hugo, and French translator of Shakespeare.

HUGUES, notary at Vence.

HUME, DAVID (1711–76), Scottish historian and philosopher.

HYTIER, JEAN (1899–), French professor of French literature at Columbia University; penetrating critic of contemporary literature, widely known for his studies of æsthetics and for his *André Gide* (1938).

INGRES, JEAN-AUGUSTE DOMINIQUE (1780–1867), French painter famous for the perfection of his draftsmanship.

INONU, GENERAL ISMET (1884–), President of the Republic of Turkey since 1938.

ISTRATI, PANAÏT (1884–1935), French novelist of Rumanian birth, appreciated for the exoticism of his foreign settings.

JACQUES, LUCIEN, French painter and writer whose recollections of the war of 1914, *Carnets de Moleskine* (1939), were prefaced by Jean Giono in a violently antimilitaristic spirit.

JAMMES, FRANCIS (1868–1938), French intimist poet, who sang of his native Pyrenees with a childlike sensuality and an increasingly orthodox Catholic faith.

JELLICOE, JOHN RUSHWORTH JELLICOE, 1st VISCOUNT (1859–1935), English admiral of the fleet that routed the German navy at Jutland in 1916.

JOUBIN, LOUIS (1861–1935), French marine biologist and editor of the *Annales de l'Institut Océanographique*.

JÜNGER, ERNST (1895–   ), German novelist best known for two novels based on his experiences as an officer on the western front in 1914–18.

KAFKA, FRANZ (1883–1924), Czech novelist and essayist, in German, of man's estrangement and sense of guilt in an incomprehensible universe: *The Trial*, *The Castle*, etc.

KAVAFIS, CONSTANTIN P., Greek poet born in Constantinople and living in Alexandria.

KELLER, GOTTFRIED (1819–90), Swiss novelist of realistic fiction in German.

KLEIST, BERND HEINRICH WILHELM VON (1777–1811), German poet, dramatist, and novelist of the romantic movement.

KOESTLER, ARTHUR (1905–   ), Hungarian-born journalist, essayist, and novelist, now writing in English.

LA BOÉTIE, ÉTIENNE DE (1530–63), French member of the Bordeaux Parliament, author of a treatise against tyranny, and great friend of Montaigne.

LAMARTINE, ALPHONSE DE (1790–1869), French romantic poet and political figure.

LAMBERT, JEAN (1920–   ), French literary critic and translator from the German of Hermann Hesse and others; son-in-law of André Gide.

LAMENNAIS, FÉLICITÉ ROBERT DE (1782–1854), French Catholic apologist and political liberal who fought Gallicanism.

LA METTRIE, JULIEN DE (1709–51), French doctor and materialistic philosopher.

LANDOWSKA, WANDA (1877–   ), Polish pianist and harpsichordist, who by her teaching, playing, and inspiration of composers revived the harpsichord.

LA ROCHEFOUCAULD, FRANÇOIS, DUC DE (1613–80), French writer of the most famous collection of *Maxims*.

LAST, JEF (1898?–   ), Dutch poet and novelist, who has traveled in Spain and Morocco, and accompanied André Gide on his trip to Russia in 1936.

LAURENS, PAUL-ALBERT (1870–?), son of Jean-Paul Laurens; French painter and professor at the École des Beaux-Arts; intimate friend of André Gide, whom he accompanied on his first trip to Africa (1893). His portrait of Gide is in the Luxembourg Museum, Paris.

LAURENS, PIERRE, son of Jean-Paul Laurens, and a painter himself; professor at the École des Beaux-Arts; great friend of Charles Péguy, whose portrait he painted.

LÉAUTAUD, PAUL (1872–), French self-taught novelist and critic, long associated with the *Mercure de France* and appreciated for his outspoken drama criticism and caustic wit.

LECLERC, JEAN (pseud. of Philippe de Hautecloque, 1902–47), French general who led a division of Fighting French forces across the Sahara from the Chad, entered Paris in command of the 2nd armored division, and later took Strasbourg.

LECOMTE DU NOÜY, PIERRE (1883–1947), French medical biologist who long held an important position at the Pasteur Institute in Paris; author of *L'Homme devant la science* (*Human Destiny*).

LECONTE DE LISLE, CHARLES (1818–94), French poet of the Parnassian school, whose work is steeped in classical culture.

LEFÈVRE, RENÉ, French film actor who played the title role in *Jean de la lune*, author of a film on the Salvation Army (*Musiciens du ciel*) and of a book of memoirs (*Le Film de ma vie*).

LEMAÎTRE, JULES (1853–1914), French literary critic and exponent of the impressionist method in criticism.

LESAGE, ALAIN-RENÉ (1668–1747), French realistic novelist of *Gil Blas* and *Le Diable boiteux*.

LESCHI, LOUIS, professor at the University of Algiers, archæologist.

LEVESQUE, ROBERT, French professor in Rome and Athens, who frequently accompanied André Gide on trips in Italy, Greece, and Egypt; author of studies and translations of contemporary Greek literature.

LINNÆUS (Carl von Linné, 1707–78), Swedish naturalist, and founder of modern botany.

LITTRÉ, ÉMILE (1808–81), French positivist philosopher, whose dictionary of the French language is still a standard work.

LOTI, PIERRE (pseud. of Julien Viaud, 1850–1923), French novelist of the sea and of far places, admired for *Pêcheur d'Islande* and *Aziyadé*.

LOUŸS, PIERRE (1870–1925), French poet and novelist of *Chansons de Bilitis* (1894), *Aphrodite* (1896), and *Les Aventures du roi Pausole* (1900).

LUNACHARSKY, ANATOLY VASILIEVICH (1873–), Russian politician, dramatist, and essayist, who played an important role among the Bolsheviks.

LYAUTEY, LOUIS HUBERT (1854–1934), French marshal and colonizer, who organized the French protectorate in Morocco. Member of the Academy, 1912.

MAINTENON, MME DE (1635–1719), née Françoise d'Aubigné, French mistress and secret wife of Louis XIV, over whom she exerted a powerful influence.

MAISTRE, JOSEPH DE (1754–1821), French philosopher and essayist, who, as Ambassador of the King of Sardinia to the Russian
court, wrote his *Considerations on France* and *St. Petersburg
Evenings* to contradict the philosophy of Voltaire, Montesquieu,
and Rousseau in favor of absolute monarchy and papal infalli-
bility.

MALAQUAIS, JEAN (pseud. of Jan Malacki, 1908–   ), Polish-born
French novelist, who in 1939 won the Renaudot Prize for his first
work, *Les Javanais* (*Men from Nowhere*).

MALEBRANCHE, NICOLAS (1638–1715), French Cartesian philosopher, author of *The Search for Truth*, who stressed the dualism
of mind and matter.

MALHERBE, FRANÇOIS DE (1555–1628), French poet, more important for his influence as codifier and purifier of language at
the beginning of the classical period than for his poems.

MALLARMÉ, STÉPHANE (1842–98), French poet, whose intellectual purity and hermetic style influenced a whole generation of
writers despite the limitation of his first *Complete Poems* to forty
copies. His weekly receptions in his Paris apartment (1886–98)
gathered the artistic élite of the Continent in fascinating conversation.

MALRAUX, ANDRÉ (1901–   ), French novelist of *Man's Fate*, *Man's
Hope*, etc., and organizer of a bombing squadron for the Spanish
Republican army in 1936; adviser to General de Gaulle.

MARIVAUX, PIERRE CARLET DE CHAMBLAIN DE (1688–1763),
French dramatist and novelist of great sensibility and psychological penetration, whose name (*marivaudage*) stands for witty
banter about love. His journals were inspired by Addison, and his
novels in turn influenced Richardson.

MARMONTEL, JEAN-FRANÇOIS (1723–99), French editor, critic,
and author of philosophic novels.

MARTIN DU GARD, HÉLÈNE, Mme Roger Martin du Gard.

MARTIN DU GARD, MAURICE (1896–   ), French journalist, critic,
and long chief editor of the *Nouvelles littéraires*.

MARTIN DU GARD, ROGER (1881–   ), French novelist and dramatist, who won the Nobel Prize in 1937, chiefly for the vivid realistic
novel in many volumes, *The World of the Thibaults*.

MASSIS, HENRI (1886–   ), French literary critic and essayist, de-
fender of the Latin inheritance in his *Defense of the West*, who
severely criticized Renan, Gide, Duhamel, France, and Benda in
the nationalist *Revue universelle*.

MAUCLAIR, CAMILLE (pseud. of Camille Faust, 1872–1945),
French poet, novelist, and critic, who revealed and defended
much of the best in modern French art and literature.

MAULNIER, THIERRY (pseud. of Jacques Talagrand, 1905–   ), French political writer and literary critic.

MAURIAC, CLAUDE, French critic of literature and the films, and son of François Mauriac.

MAURIAC, FRANÇOIS (1885–   ), French novelist, dramatist, and essayist, appreciated in English for *Thérèse, Vipers' Tangle*, etc. A Catholic writer of great vigor, he was elected to the French Academy in 1939.

MAUROIS, ANDRÉ (pseud. of Émile Herzog, 1885–   ), French novelist, biographer, and essayist, whose facile clarity made his lives of Shelley, Disraeli, and Byron world-famous and opened the French Academy to him in 1938.

MAUROIS, GÉRALD, elder son of André Maurois; during part of the war he worked in a perfume factory in Grasse.

MAURRAS, CHARLES (1868–   ), French poet, essayist, pamphleteer, and political leader of the Action Française movement; exponent of decentralization and a return to monarchy, who was tried in 1945 as the ideologist of the Vichy government and sentenced to life imprisonment.

MAYRISCH DE SAINT-HUBERT, MME ÉMILE (?–1947), wife of the director of the great Luxembourg metallurgical syndicate named Arbet. A woman of great culture in French, English, and German, she received poets, philosophers, painters, and sculptors in her château of Colpach in Luxembourg, which became a meeting-place of French and German cultures. She traveled in the Orient with the late director of the Musée Guimet and in the Near East with André Gide.

MECKERT, JEAN, French novelist, who reflects the point of view of the masses.

MEREZHKOVSKI, DMITRI (1865–1941), Russian novelist, poet, and essayist, leader of the symbolist movement in Russia and proponent of a neo-Christianity.

MICHAUX, HENRI (1899–   ), Belgian-born French poet and painter, appreciated for his strong personal fantasy and the exoticism resulting from his extensive travels, real and imaginary.

MONDZAIN, painter from central Europe who lives in Algiers; his wife, Dr. Mondzain-Lemaire, treated André Gide.

MONTESQUIEU, CHARLES LOUIS DE SECONDAT DE (1689–1755), French political philosopher, best known for his *Lettres persanes* and his analysis of political constitutions, *De l'esprit des lois*.

MONTHERLANT, HENRY DE (1896–   ), French novelist, essayist, and dramatist, who first epitomized the restless and cynical youth of the twenties and then produced a series of cruel novels of great power and technical skill.

MOPPÈS, DENISE VAN, French translator from German and English.

MORIZE, PHILIPPE, self-styled hero of the French bombing forces attached to the RAF, who under the name of Philippe La Chesnaie wrote his supposed experiences in a volume entitled *Daphné 17*, which was dedicated to André Gide; his pretense was later considered to have been exposed.

MORTIMER, RAYMOND (1895–), English writer and literary editor of the *New Statesman and Nation*.

MOUNIER, EMMANUEL (1905–50), French Catholic writer and founder and editor of the monthly *Esprit*, leader of the personalist group.

MÜHLFELD, LUCIEN (1870–1902), French novelist and literary critic.

MUSSET, ALFRED DE (1810–57), French romantic poet and dramatist of lyric quality, grace, and exquisite humor.

NAVILLE, ARNOLD (1879–), Swiss financier, early interested in the work of André Gide, on which he published bibliographical notes in 1930 and again in 1950; long a close friend of Gide's.

NERVAL, GÉRARD DE (1808–55), French romantic poet in verse and in prose, appreciated especially for his beautiful short novels *Aurélia* and *Les Filles du feu*.

NEUVILLE, ALPHONSE MARIE ADOLPHE DE (1836–85), French painter of military subjects.

NOAILLES, ANNA, COMTESSE DE (1876–1933), French poet and novelist of delicate talent and vibrant sensitivity.

OHANA, MAURICE, young French composer.

OLIVIER, SIR LAURENCE (1907–), English actor, known for his interpretations of Shakespeare and his inspired direction of the Old Vic Theatre Company.

PAGANINI, NICOLÒ (1784–1840), Italian violinist.

PASCOLI, GIOVANNI (1855–1912), Italian poet of the simple, rustic life.

PASSEUR, STÈVE (1899–), French dramatist of psychological melodramas, such as *Les Tricheurs* (1932) and *L'Acheteuse* (1930).

PATRI, AIMÉ, French professor of philosophy in the *lycée* of Tunis who is at present editor-in-chief of the literary monthly *Paru*.

PAULHAN, GERMAINE, Mme Jean Paulhan.

PAULHAN, JEAN (1884–   ), French æsthetician, essayist, and inspirer of modern literature; from 1925 until 1940 he was chief editor of the *Nouvelle Revue Française*.

PÉGUY, CHARLES (1873–1914), French poet and essayist, who exerted a very great influence through such works as his *Jeanne d'Arc*, *Notre Patrie*, *L'Argent*, as well as through the review he founded and edited, *Les Cahiers de la Quinzaine* (1902–14).

PÉREZ, CHARLES, student at the Tunis *lycée*, who served as André Gide's secretary; later he joined the Free French forces and was seriously wounded in Germany.

PIRENNE, HENRI (1862–1935), Belgian historian of Europe and rector of the University of Ghent.

PISTOR, FERNAND (?–1944), former professor at the *lycée* of Algiers, who left teaching to become war correspondent for the French radio and was killed in the fighting at Marseille in August 1944; met André Gide at Sidi-bou-Saïd.

POURTALÈS, GUY DE (1881–   ), Swiss biographer and music critic of French Protestant origin, known for his *Life of Liszt*, *Richard Wagner*, etc.

PROUST, MARCEL (1871–1922), French novelist, whose one great work in sixteen volumes is a masterpiece of psychological penetration and of poetic re-creation of the past through the involuntary memory.

PUGET, PIERRE (1622–94), French sculptor, painter, and architect, appreciated especially for his statues of classical subjects in the Louvre.

RAGU, DR., director of the Centre Antoine Cassar hospital in Tunis and well-known dermatologist.

RANCÉ, ABBÉ ARMAND DE (1626–1700), French reformer of the Trappist Order.

RAUSCHNING, HERMANN (1887–   ), author of German birth, known for *The Revolution of Nihilism* (1939) and *The Voice of Destruction* (1940). President of the Danzig Senate in 1932, he left the Nazi Party in 1935 to become a Liberal Conservative; in 1948 he became a U.S. citizen.

RAVEL, MAURICE (1875–1937), French composer of ballets, orchestral compositions, piano pieces, and songs.

RAYNAUD, PIERRE, Air-France pilot who carried André Gide as a passenger on several occasions; self-made man, remarkable for his sleight-of-hand tricks, and friend of Saint Exupéry.

REBATET, LUCIEN, French journalist of the extreme right wing, who contributed to *Je suis partout*.

RENAN, ERNEST (1823–92), French philologist, historian of religions, and philosopher, most famous for his unorthodox *Life of Jesus*.

RENAUD, MADELEINE, French actress, wife of Jean-Louis Barrault and with him co-director of the repertory company that plays at the Marigny Theater in Paris.

RETZ, PAUL DE GONDI, CARDINAL DE (1613–79), French historian of society, whose racy *Memoirs* depict the courts of Louis XIII and Louis XIV.

REYMOND, SUZY, daughter of Théo Reymond.

REYMOND, THÉO, French architect in Tunis. He and his wife, herself an excellent ophthalmologist, lodged André Gide in Tunisia, first in their house at Sidi-bou-Saïd and later in their apartment in the avenue Roustan, Tunis, where they were obliged to leave him when a tumor forced Mme Reymond to be operated on in Marseille.

REYNAUD, PAUL (1878–   ), French statesman, many times Minister, who resigned as Premier in June 1940 rather than accept capitulation to Germany.

RILKE, RAINER MARIA (1875–1926), German poet, born in Prague, who lived long in Paris in close association with the sculptor Rodin. His elegies and other poems are thoughtful works of great artistry.

RIMBAUD, ARTHUR (1854–91), French poet of great originality, whose two works revolutionized modern poetry. Abandoning literature entirely at the age of nineteen, he ended his life as an adventurer and business representative in Abyssinia.

RIVAROL, ANTOINE (1753–1801), French essayist and pamphleteer, best known for his *Discourse on the Universality of the French Language*.

RIVIÈRE, JACQUES (1886–1925), French critic, and editor of the *Nouvelle Revue Française* from 1919 to 1925 after having been identified with the review from 1909. His vivid correspondence with Alain-Fournier and with Claudel is greatly admired.

RODENBACH, GEORGES (1855–98), Belgian poet and novelist of symbolism, who wrote in Paris.

RŒDERER, PIERRE-LOUIS (1754–1835), French statesman and historian.

ROMILLY, SIR SAMUEL (1757–1818), English legal reformer of Huguenot ancestry, beloved Whig Member of Parliament, and author of lively *Memoirs*.

ROSENBERG, FÉDOR, Russian from Livonia, whom André Gide met in Florence during his wedding trip (1895).

ROSTAND, JEAN (1894–), French biologist of many, often very popular publications.

ROTHERMERE, LADY, née Mary Lilian Share, English wife of Lord Rothermere, proprietor of the *Daily Mail* and other London newspapers; she translated Gide's *Prometheus Ill-Bound.*

ROUGEMONT, DENIS DE (1906–), Swiss essayist of original and penetrating mind, known in English for *The Devil's Share* and *The Last Trump.*

ROUVEYRE, ANDRÉ (1879–), French caricaturist, who contributed to *Le Rire,* etc., and collected his drawings in several volumes.

ROY, JULES (1907–), French poet and novelist, whose writing is inspired by his experience as an aviator.

RUDE, FRANÇOIS (1784–1855), French sculptor, best known for his relief of the *Marseillaise* on the Arc de Triomphe.

SADE, DONATIEN ALPHONSE, MARQUIS DE (1740–1814), French novelist of erotic works, whose name has come to designate a sexual perversion.

SAILLET, MAURICE (1915–), French literary critic of subtle mind and delicate sensitivity, who often writes under the name of Justin Saget; associated with Adrienne Monnier in managing her bookshop in the rue de l'Odéon.

SAINTE-BEUVE, AUGUSTIN (1804–69), French critic belonging to the romantic school, whose *Monday Chats* and *Literary Portraits* have outlived his poems and single novel.

SAINT-ÉVREMOND, CHARLES DE SAINT-DENYS DE (1610–1703), French essayist, known for his voluminous, witty correspondence, written during his forty-year exile in England.

SAINT EXUPÉRY, ANTOINE DE (1900–44), French novelist and aviator, whose *Night Flight* and *Wind, Sand and Stars* brought a new heroism into French fiction.

SAINT-SIMON, LOUIS DE ROUVROY, DUC DE (1675–1755), French historian of society, whose *Memoirs* are the memorial of court society in his age as well as a masterpiece of literature.

SALACROU, ARMAND (1900–), French dramatist of psychological insight and unusual experimental techniques, best known for his *Inconnue d'Arras* (1935).

SAND, GEORGE (pseud. of Aurore Dudevant, 1804–76), French romantic novelist.

SARDOU, VICTORIEN (1831–1908), French dramatist of manners, much appreciated in his time for his consummate but mechanical technique.

SARTRE, JEAN-PAUL (1905–), French philosopher, dramatist,

novelist, critic, and chief exponent of French existentialism, best known for such plays as *The Flies* and *No Exit* and for the long novel *The Roads to Freedom*.

SAUCIER, ROLAND (1899–   ), French director of the bookshop of the Librairie Gallimard, boulevard Raspail, since 1920.

SCARLATTI, DOMENICO (1685–1757), Italian virtuoso at the harpsichord and composer, who revolutionized piano-playing.

SCHIFFRIN, JACQUES (?–1950), Russian-born French publisher, who created the well-known Éditions de la Pléiade, in which he brought out the first complete edition of André Gide's *Journal*; close friend of Gide, whom he accompanied to Russia in 1936; in America for the last several years, he was one of the officers of Pantheon Books.

SCHLUMBERGER, JEAN (1877–   ), French novelist of psychological insight and one of the founders of the *N.R.F.*

SCHWOB, MARCEL (1867–1905), French prose-poet of the symbolist period, whose great erudition, visual imagination, and ironic, flexible style gave him a significant place in modern letters.

SHCHEDRIN, N. (pseud. of M. E. Saltykov, 1826–89), Russian realistic and satiric novelist, whose *Golovlyov Family* and *Bygone Days in Poshekhonie* expose the venality of the ruling class and empty traditions of manorial society in czarist Russia.

SILLER, FRÄULEIN EMMA, for many years the tutor of the Rondeaux girls, of whom the eldest became Mme André Gide; often visited Cuverville and helped André Gide in his study of German; eventually returned to her native Regensburg (Bavaria), where she died recently at a very advanced age.

SIMENON, GEORGES (1903–   ), Belgian-born novelist, best known for his detective novels featuring the Commissaire Maigret.

SOLOGUB, FYODOR (pseud. of Fyodor Teternikov, 1863–1927), Russian poet and novelist of symbolism, as in *The Little Demon*.

SOUPAULT, PHILIPPE (1897–   ), French poet, novelist, and essayist, who abandoned Dadaism and surrealism in favor of adventure novels of a poetic nature, and political analysis.

SPARROW, MME, Polish doctor in Tunis; close friend of the Gérard Boutelleau family.

SPENDER, STEPHEN (1909–   ), English poet and critic, co-editor of *Horizon*, 1939–41.

STROHL, JEAN (1886–   ), Swiss biologist, dean of the Faculty of Sciences, University of Zurich, and author of studies in the history of the natural sciences and in teratology.

SUARÈS, ANDRÉ (1868–1948), French poet and essayist of flamboyant nature and broad views, whose essays on Wagner, Dostoyevsky, and Pascal are penetrating and original.

SUSTERMANS, JUSTUS (1597–1681), Flemish painter, known chiefly for his portraits of the Medici.

THÉRIVE, ANDRÉ (1891–   ), French novelist, literary critic, and grammarian.

THIBAUD, JACQUES (1880–   ), French violinist, who has often played trios with Alfred Cortot and Pablo Casals.

THOMAS, HENRI, French poet and novelist, translator of Goethe's *Tasso*, of Ernst Jünger, and of Melville; during the war he worked in the French section of BBC in London.

TOCQUEVILLE, ALEXIS DE (1805–59), French publicist and statesman, author of *Democracy in America*.

TOMLINSON, HENRY MAJOR (1873–   ), English journalist and novelist.

TOURNEUR, CYRIL (1575?–1626), English poet and dramatist of *The Revenger's Tragedy* and *The Atheist's Tragedy*, somber plays of revenge.

TOURNIER, bookseller in Tunis and friend of André Gide.

TOURNIER, JEAN, son of the Tunis bookseller, who now manages his father's shop.

TRUC, GONZAGUE, French literary critic and journalistic philosopher and theologian.

VALÉRY, JEANNIE, Mme Paul Valéry, née Gobillard.

VALÉRY, PAUL (1871–1945), French poet and essayist, who began his career when as a law student he met Pierre Louÿs and André Gide, then Mallarmé, whose chief disciple he became. After a brilliant start he abandoned literature for twenty years and was persuaded to return in 1917 by Gide. His mature career was crowned by his election to the French Academy in 1925.

VALLOTTON, FÉLIX-ÉDOUARD (1865–1925), Swiss painter of portraits, flowers, and landscapes.

VAN DINE, S. S. (pseud. of Willard Huntington Wright, 1888–1939), American writer of mystery novels.

VAN GOGH, VINCENT (1853–90), Dutch painter of great importance in the French post-impressionist group, known for his crude colors and obvious brush-strokes in portraits and landscapes.

VAN RYSSELBERGHE, MME THÉO (1865–   ), wife of the Belgian painter and, under the pseudonym of M. Saint-Clair, author of a subtle novelette and of delicate literary portraits.

VERLAINE, PAUL (1844–96), French symbolist poet, distinguished for the musical quality of his verse and his rather disreputable life.

VIÉNOT, PIERRE (1897–1944), French statesman, who, after working with Marshal Lyautey in Morocco, became one of the first members of the Free French government in London, where he died; son-in-law of Mme Mayrisch.

VIGNY, ALFRED DE (1797–1863), French romantic poet of philosophic turn, who, like Hugo, also wrote fiction and drama.

VILDRAC, CHARLES (1882–   ), French poet and dramatist, best known for his play *The Steamer Tenacity*.

VIOLLET-LE-DUC, EUGÈNE EMMANUEL (1814–79), French architect and writer, in great part responsible for the Gothic revival through his books and restorations of Carcassonne, Pierrefonds, Notre-Dame Cathedral, etc.

VISAN, TANCRÈDE DE (1878–   ), French literary critic, who contributed regularly to the *Mercure de France*, etc.

VOILIER, MME, Parisian proprietor of the Éditions Domat-Montchrestien, which publishes the series entitled "Au Voilier." Great friend of Paul Valéry, she has written under the pseudonym of Jean Voilier.

WATTEAU, ANTOINE (1684–1721), French painter and engraver.

WEBSTER, JOHN (1580?–1625?), English dramatist of *The White Devil, The Duchess of Malfi*, etc.

WILSON, JOHN DOVER (1881–   ), English scholar in Shakespearean studies; professor at Edinburgh, 1936–45.

WITT-GUIZOT, FRANÇOIS DE (1870–   ), French officer of Foch's staff, banker, and social benefactor, author of articles in *Revue des deux mondes*.

WOLF, THEODOR, German editor of an important Berlin newspaper, who, having taken refuge in Nice, was pursued by the Nazis.

ZABOROWSKI-MOINDRON, SIGISMOND (1851–1928), Polish-French professor of ethnography at the École d'Anthropologie in Paris.

ZOLA, ÉMILE (1840–1902), French novelist of the naturalist school, best known for his vast series of novels *Les Rougon-Macquart*.

ZWEIG, STEFAN (1881–1942), Austrian biographer, novelist, dramatist, and poet of ardent international sympathies.

THE WORKS OF ANDRÉ GIDE

POETRY IN VERSE AND IN PROSE

Les Cahiers d'André Walter (Librairie de l'Art Indépendant, 1891)	The Notebooks of André Walter
Les Poésies d'André Walter (ibid., 1892)	The Poems of André Walter
Le Traité du Narcisse (ibid., 1891)	The Treatise of the Narcissus
La Tentative amoureuse (ibid., 1893)	The Attempt at Love
Le Voyage d'Urien (ibid., 1893)	Urien's Travels
Les Nourritures terrestres (Mercure de France, 1897)	*Fruits of the Earth (New York: Alfred A. Knopf, 1949; London: Martin Secker & Warburg, 1949)
El Hadj (ibid., 1899)	El Hadj
Amyntas (ibid., 1906)	Amyntas
Le Retour de l'enfant prodigue (Vers et Prose, 1907)	The Prodigal's Return
Les Nouvelles Nourritures (Gallimard, 1935)	*New Fruits of the Earth (New York: Alfred A. Knopf, 1949; London: Martin Secker & Warburg, 1949)

TALES

*L'Immoraliste (Mercure de France, 1902)	*The Immoralist (New York: Alfred A. Knopf, 1930; London: Cassell & Co.)

N.B. Since 1935 the author and his French publisher have ceased classifying Gide's works in categories. The translator therefore assumes full responsibility for this pigeonholing.

* The titles preceded by an asterisk have been published in English translation. Unless otherwise indicated, all translations are by Dorothy Bussy.

*La Porte étroite
(ibid., 1909)

*Strait Is the Gate
(New York: ibid., 1924; London: Martin Secker & Warburg)

*Isabelle
(Gallimard, 1911)

*Isabelle
(New York: ibid., 1931; London: Cassell & Co.; in *Two Symphonies*)

*La Symphonie pastorale
(ibid., 1919)

*The Pastoral Symphony
(ibid.)

*L'École des femmes
(ibid., 1929)

*The School for Wives
(New York: ibid., 1929, 1950; London: Cassell & Co.)

*Robert
(ibid., 1929)

*Robert in *The School for Wives*

*Geneviève
(ibid., 1939)

*Geneviève in *The School for Wives*

*Thésée
(ibid., 1946; New York: Pantheon Books, 1946)

*Theseus in *Two Legends: Theseus and Œdipus*
(New York: Alfred A. Knopf, 1950; London: Martin Secker & Warburg; trans. by John Russell)

SATIRICAL FARCES

Paludes   Morasses
(Librairie de l'Art Indépendant, 1895)

*Le Prométhée mal enchaîné
(Mercure de France, 1899)

*Prometheus Ill-Bound
(London: Chatto & Windus, 1919; trans. by Lilian Rothermere)

*Les Caves du Vatican
(Gallimard, 1914)

*The Vatican Swindle
(New York: Alfred A. Knopf, 1925) or *Lafcadio's Adventures* (ibid., 1927; London: Cassell & Co.)

NOVEL

*Les Faux-Monnayeurs
(Gallimard, 1926)

*The Counterfeiters
(New York: Alfred A. Knopf,
1927) or The Coiners (London: Cassell & Co.)

CRITICISM

Prétextes
(Mercure de France, 1903)

Pretexts

Nouveaux Prétextes
(ibid., 1911)

Further Pretexts

*Dostoïevsky
(Plon-Nourrit, 1923)

*Dostoevsky
(London: J. M. Dent, 1925;
Martin Secker & Warburg,
1949; New York: Alfred A.
Knopf, 1926; New Direc-
tions, 1949; trans. anon.)

Incidences
(Gallimard, 1924)

Angles of Incidence

*Journal des Faux-Monnayeurs
(ibid., 1926)

*Journal of "The Counterfeiters"
(New York: Alfred A. Knopf,
1951; trans. by Justin
O'Brien; in The Counter-
feiters)

*Essai sur Montaigne
(Éditions de la Pléiade, 1929)

*Montaigne
(New York: Horace Liveright,
1929; London: Blackmore
Press; trans. by S. H. Guest
and T. E. Blewitt)

*The Living Thoughts of Mon-
taigne
(New York: Longmans, Green
& Co., 1939; London: Cas-
sell & Co.)

Divers
(Gallimard, 1931)

Miscellany

*Interviews imaginaires
(New York: Pantheon Books,
1943)

*Imaginary Interviews
(New York: Alfred A. Knopf,
1944; trans. by Malcolm
Cowley)

Attendu que . . . (Alger: Charlot, 1943)	Considering That . . .
*_L'Enseignement de Poussin_ (Le Divan, 1945)	*_Poussin_ (London: *The Arts*, No. 2, 1947)
Poétique (Neuchâtel: Ides et Calendes, 1947)	A Definition of Poetry
Préfaces (ibid., 1948)	Prefaces
Rencontres (ibid., 1948)	Encounters
Éloges (ibid., 1948)	Praises

DRAMA

Philoctète (Mercure de France, 1899)	Philoctetes
Le Roi Candaule (La Revue Blanche, 1901)	King Candaules
Saül (Mercure de France, 1903)	Saul
Bethsabé (Bibliothèque de l'Occident, 1912)	Bathsheba
*_Œdipe_ (Gallimard, 1931)	*_Œdipus_ in *Two Legends:* *Theseus and Œdipus* (New York: Alfred A. Knopf, 1950; London: Martin Seck- er & Warburg; trans. by John Russell)
Perséphone (ibid., 1934)	Persephone
Le Treizième Arbre (*Mesures*, No. 2, 1935)	The Thirteenth Tree
Robert ou l'intérêt général (Alger: *L'Arche*, 1944–5)	Robert or The Common Weal
Le Retour (Neuchâtel: Ides et Calendes, 1946)	The Return

MISCELLANEOUS

*Souvenirs de la Cour d'Assises
(Gallimard, 1914)

*Recollections of the Assize Court
(London: Hutchinson & Co.,
1941; trans. anon.)

Morceaux choisis
(ibid., 1921)

Selections

*Corydon
(ibid., 1924)

*Corydon
(New York: Farrar Straus &
Co., 1950; trans. by Hugh
Gibb)

*Si le grain ne meurt . . .
(ibid., 1926)

*If It Die . . .
(New York: Random House,
1935; London: Martin Secker & Warburg, 1950; edition
limited to 1,500 copies)

Numquid et tu . . . ?
(Éditions de la Pléiade, 1926)

Numquid et tu . . . ?

Un Esprit non prévenu
(Éditions Kra, 1929)

An Unprejudiced Mind

L'Affaire Redureau
(Gallimard, 1930)

The Redureau Case

La Sequestrée de Poitiers
(ibid., 1930)

The Poitiers Incarceration Case

Jeunesse
(Neuchâtel: Ides et Calendes,
1945)

Youth

*Feuillets d'automne
(Mercure de France, 1949)

*Autumn Leaves
(New York: Philosophical Li-
brary, 1950; trans. by Elsie
Pell)

Littérature engagée
(Gallimard, 1950)

TRAVELS

*Voyage au Congo
(Gallimard, 1927)

*Travels in the Congo
(New York: Alfred A. Knopf,
1929; London: ibid., 1930)

Dindiki   Dindiki
  (Liége: Éditions de la Lampe d'Aladdin, 1927)

*Le Retour du Tchad   *in *Travels in the Congo*
  (Gallimard, 1928)   (New York: Alfred A. Knopf,
                               1929; London: ibid., 1930)

*Retour de l'U.R.S.S.   *Return from the U.S.S.R.*
  (ibid., 1936)   (New York: ibid., 1937; Lon-
                               don: Martin Secker & War-
                               burg, 1937)

*Retouches à mon Retour de   *Afterthoughts on the U.S.S.R.*
  l'U.R.S.S. (ibid., 1937)   (New York: Dial Press, 1938;
                               London: Martin Secker &
                               Warburg, 1938)

JOURNALS

*Journal, 1889–1939   *The Journals of André Gide,*
  (Gallimard, 1939)   *1889–1949*
                               (New York: Alfred A. Knopf,
                               1947–51; London: Martin
                               Secker & Warburg, 1947–9;
                               4 vols., trans. by Justin
                               O'Brien)

*Pages de Journal, 1939–1942   *Extracts from the Journals, 1939–*
  (New York: Pantheon Books,   *1942* (in ibid.)
    1944; Paris: Gallimard, 1946)

*Journal, 1942–1949   *Journal, 1942–1949*
  (Gallimard, 1950)   (in ibid.)

Deux Interviews imaginaires sui- Dialogues on God
  vies de Feuillets
  (Charlot, 1946)

CORRESPONDENCE

Lettres   Letters
  (Liége: A la Lampe d'Aladdin,
    1930)

Correspondance Francis Jammes
  et André Gide, 1893–1938
  (Paris: Gallimard, 1948)

Correspondance Paul Claudel et
  André Gide, 1899–1926
  (ibid., 1949)

COLLECTED EDITIONS

Œuvres complètes (Gallimard, 15 vols., 1932–9)	Complete Works
Théâtre (Gallimard, 1942)	Drama
Théâtre complet (Neuchâtel: Ides et Calendes, 8 vols., 1947–9)	Complete Drama

INDEX

THE WORKS OF ANDRÉ GIDE

Referred to in *The Journals*

A NOTE ON THE TYPE IN WHICH THIS BOOK IS SET

The text of this book is set in Caledonia, a Linotype face which belongs to the family of printing types called "modern face" by printers — a term used to mark the change in style of type-letters that occurred about 1800. Caledonia borders on the general design of Scotch Modern, but is more freely drawn than that letter.

The book was composed, printed, and bound by The Plimpton Press, Norwood, Massachusetts. The typography and binding design are by **W. A. Dwiggins.**

WAD